At Home Across the Country

Celebrating 50 Years at Home Hardware

Published by TC Transcontinental 2014

At Home Across the Country : Celebrating 50 years at Home Hardware

ISBN 978-0-9684172-3-2

Published in Canada by
TC Transcontinental Printing

Concept, research & text: Holly Levine
Art direction & design: Ron Mugford
Transcription: Margot Levine
Fact checking & proofreading: Dianne McTavish
Translation: GAT Intl Inc.

Printed in Canada

Every effort has been made to ensure that the information in this book is accurate and up to date as of press time. We regret any errors or oversights.

Photo Credits:

All photography by Greg Fess,
Greg Fess Photography unless otherwise stated below.

T = Top, M = Middle, B = Bottom, R = Right, L = Left, C = Centre

Home Hardware Archives, Pages: vi, vii, 1, 2, 12, 49, 193, 325.

Steven Hawkins: Pages: vii T, 4 T, 8, 9, 10, 15, 16 - 17, 34, 38, 39, 41, 51, 52, 70, 76, 77, 81, 83, 84, 85, 99, 124, 154-155, 184-185, 274, 275, 280-281, 282, 283, 284, 285, 291, 301, 331, 339, 340, 341, 342, 344, 346, 347, 348, 349, 351, 352, 355.

Dreamstime.com images:

Page 12: © Robstark, Page 40: © Wangkun Jia, Page 55: © Paul Mckinnon, Page 95 T: © Louis Henault, Page 95 B: © Rosemary Buffoni, Page 130-131: © George Kroll, Page 213: © Vismax, Page 265 T: © Kalavati, Page 266: © Alain, Page 276-277: © Louis Henault, Page 293 T: © Chris Austin, Page 326-327: © Fotolotti, Page 333: © Arindam Banerjee.

Trevor Weeks, Page: 15 B.

Doug Gingerich: Pages: 59, 257, 294, 334-335.

Dana Seguin: Page: 82.

© Great Takes Photography / Pam Everett: Pages: 132, 133.

Emilie Martin: Page: 217 ML.

Rick Kurzak: Page: 218.

Karen Flanagan McCarthy: Pages: 268, 269.

© Jason Franson: Page: 298.

Marnie Drost: Page: 329.

© Pirak Studios: Page: 353.

© serendipityvideo.com / Cory Meli: Page: 356.

Table of Contents:

Table of Contents:

Home's mission as a Dealer-owned company

is to supply Home Dealers with quality products

and services, to assist them with the programs

to operate effective and efficient stores

at a profitable level, thereby allowing them

to serve the customer with competitive prices

and superior service.

Preface:

It was my good fortune to be introduced to Home Hardware in 1992 when I produced a corporate video for Transcontinental Printing, (now TC Printing, Canada's largest printer and the fourth largest in North America). Over the course of the production period, I visited TC Transcontinental's Owen Sound plant and Home Hardware's printer of record since 1964 when the first catalogue came off the press. During that time, I was given the opportunity of a lifetime when one of the people I worked with at RBW (then the name of TC Transcontinental's Owen Sound plant), invited me to develop a proposal for an innovative project for Home Hardware, their oldest and most important client. Home Hardware's President Paul Straus wanted to publish a Home Hardware magazine. And who better to partner with on such a project than their printer? I spent a year working with Home Hardware and RBW Graphics to develop the concept. Over the course of that year, I sat around the table with many of Home Hardware's senior people, gathering information, brainstorming ideas, developing models and becoming part of a culture. That is when I fell under the Home Hardware spell - from the start, I was impressed by the access I was given to this group of busy and accomplished people. At the end of the year, when the decision was made to proceed, I became editor of Canada's first retail hardware customer loyalty "magalog", Home at Home.

Over the years, I met many of the dealers from across the country when they gathered in St. Jacobs for the semi-annual seasonal markets. They became enthusiastic supporters of the magazine, and put it to work as another effective marketing tool to help them build their business. It was always like greeting old friends when they showed up at the Home at Home booth. A lot of vendors became loyal supporters of, and advertisers in, the magazine, many of them contributing creative ideas that became editorial content in the publication.

Several years later, I was asked to be editor of the Home Hardware history book, written by retired employee Delores Martin and published by TC Transcontinental in 2001. I had met Walter Hachborn, but it was the history book that allowed me to get to know this unique man whose story is at the heart and soul of Home Hardware. I believe that Walter's people skills, his insight and compassion, are extraordinary gifts. But his ability to give countless people across this country the means by which to realize their full potential, his willingness to believe and trust in people, are expressions of genius.

After 17 years as editor of Home at Home, it was time to move on. One day, en route to a meeting with Ray Gabel, I was overcome by the realization that soon I would not have a reason to make this trip anymore, to

meet with someone for whom I had grown to have such respect and regard. I loved how we would be sitting at his table, reviewing the next issue of the magazine when Ray would suddenly get up and leave the room. Two minutes later he'd return with something. He'd put it on the table and inevitably ask one of two questions: "What do you think this is?" or "What do you think this should cost?" He has always been possessed of an engineer's mind, with an immediate grasp of a product's potential and how to make it even better. As I drove along that late summer's day I thought how much I would miss these exchanges and all the other aspects of Home Hardware I had come to appreciate. I thought about the product managers, each of whom had been instrumental in making Home at Home magazine a success by embracing it and convincing so many of their vendors of its value. The magazine would never have succeeded without their and Ray's support. I thought of how many of them had become friends, of the time Doug Straus had called me when I was very ill and told me that I was part of the Home Hardware family now. And then Doug was gone, too soon. I thought of how, in our semi-annual meetings, Paul Straus remembered everything about the magazine and always made a point of thanking our team for the work we had done over the course of any given year. There were more memories, all of them good. I started to think about the qualities that made Home Hardware such a special place - and suddenly an idea popped into my

head: why not mark Home Hardware's 50th anniversary in 2014 with a book that celebrates the special qualities of Home Hardware? The book would be primarily from the perspective of the dealers across the country, to illustrate, through their histories and community involvement, how they embody and express the values and qualities that have made Home Hardware what it is today.

At my meeting with Ray that day, I took a deep breath and made my pitch. Ray must have liked the idea because he suggested that I come back for a formal presentation to Paul Straus and Terry Davis. Two weeks later, I walked into the meeting room to find that Walter was also seated at the table, which I took to be a good sign. We had a subsequent meeting a few weeks later and, as we were wrapping up, I asked Paul, "When do you think you will make a decision?" There was a small pause and he said, "We've made our decision. We're going to do this." The level of trust and confidence expressed in that answer is as good an illustration as any of the Home Hardware difference.

In the spring of 2011, along with Greg Fess, the talented photographer with whom I had worked for years on the magazine, I embarked on a remarkable journey that took us across the country to visit Home Hardware stores from coast to coast. Although it was impossible

to visit every dealer, those we did are exemplars of the qualities that have made Home Hardware such a success. Without fail, every dealer said how much they owed to Walter Hachborn, how his faith in them, his willingness to give them - or their parents - a chance, often when others would not, had allowed them to achieve the happiness and success they enjoy today.

I too acknowledge the debt of gratitude that I owe to Home Hardware overall. Every person I have encountered over the years I have been involved with this great Canadian company; everyone who helped me to do my job as best I could; the many generous, hardworking people I have met along the way. Most especially, I am grateful to Walter Hachborn, Paul Straus and Ray Gabel, for giving me the opportunity to research and write this book.

Holly Levine,
December 31, 2013.

Tributes

Don Kirck
1956 - 2011

On July 16, 2011 Don Kirck, who had been part of the Home Hardware family since 1976, lost a terribly sudden and brief battle with cancer. He was just 55 years of age.

Don came from Walter Hachborn's hometown of Conestoga, a few miles east of St. Jacobs. Walter knew the entire Kirck family, including Don's grandparents, and when he opened the door to Don, the young man fresh out of high school embarked on a career that took him from the warehouse to Vice-President. "He was totally devoted to Home Hardware," the man who was his mentor remembers. During the eighties, Don oversaw the start up of the Debert and Wetaskiwin warehouses and managed them once they became operational. He also became Walter's unofficial chauffeur and confidante in those days as they travelled together across the Maritimes and western Canada. In 1990, Don returned to St. Jacobs to oversee the expansion and retrofit of that facility. He was promoted to Director, National Distribution in 2000 and appointed Vice-President of Distribution & Manufacturing in 2005.

Don was a people person who was always available to the Home Hardware staff and Dealer-Owners. He had a reputation as an excellent supervisor and, as one of his colleagues remembered, "Don always left me feeling I was in charge but had a subtle way of slipping in some good advice." He was active in his community as well and served on the Region of Waterloo International Airport Business Advisory Committee until his passing and was a member of the Stakeholder Committee for the Woolwich Economic Development Action Plan.

Don also loved to sing, but Walter remembers that he was invariably slightly off tune. "He was such a great guy and I loved him dearly."

Dan Logel
1946 - 2009

On December 3, 2009, Dan Logel passed away at the age of 63. He had been Customs/Excise/Market Manager at Home Hardware for 43 years.

It is in his latter role that most people will remember Dan. His ceaseless attention to detail and organizational abilities ensured the seamless success of countless corporate functions and special events over the years, from the semi-annual markets to the annual golf tournaments. Dan was a true people person. He always had a story or good joke to share and enjoyed telling them as much as hearing new ones. His smiling face and contagious laugh will always be missed.

Lawrence Bingeman had a particularly close relationship with Dan. "Dan was very special to me," he remembers, "He was a small man who walked very, very fast and spoke very, very slowly. He'd say: 'Gooood afternooooon. How are you todaaay?' And to any question I asked, he'd always reply, very deliberately: 'Well, we'll haaaave to seeee about that....Maybeee it will...and maybeeee it won't.'"

Chapter 1:

The Founding of Home Hardware

We are all part of the Home Hardware family. If not it's unlikely that you would be reading this book. Most of us know the back-story, how and why the company came to be. In many ways it is a classic small town story, which is appropriate, given that one of the great strengths of Home Hardware is the small town value system embodied by dealers across the country. An extraordinary creation consisting of many integral parts that formed from a single nucleus, as Walter has described his role.

In a nutshell: in 1893, and on the site of the current downtown St. Jacobs Home Hardware store, Henry Gilles bought what was a tinsmith shop, which he converted to a blacksmith and hardware store. His son Alfred Gilles ran the hardware store until 1933, when Henry Sittler, who had been working for another retailer in the village, took over as manager. In 1934, Henry Gilles passed away and Gordon Hollinger, born and raised in St. Jacobs, bought the business. Two years later he started a wholesale division of the hardware business to supply local merchants. Henry Sittler took over as manager, buyer and traveling salesman for this branch of the operation that had a total of four employees, the owner Gordon Hollinger, Enoch Martin, Ross Wahl and Henry Sittler.

By the early 1940s, a young man named Walter Hachborn, who also lived in town, had already been working part time in the store as janitor (and general about-the-store help) for several years. His salary was $8 a week. (To put that in perspective, in the early 1940s, an average annual salary was $1,900. A new home cost about $7,000.) During the years of World War

Two, Walter served as a Staff Sergeant with the Royal Canadian Ordnance Corps in London, Ontario. As warehouse foreman responsible for stores and vehicles, Walter acquired a great deal of knowledge that he was able to bring with him when he returned to work at Hollinger Hardware after the war. In 1948, Gordon Hollinger passed away and Walter, who had been his assistant, took over his responsibilities. Two years later, Gordon Hollinger's widow also passed away and the business was for sale. It had 10 employees and annual sales of a half million dollars. Walter and Henry Sittler wanted to buy the business, but it took some finagling, a silent partner, Arthur

Zilliax, and a bit more cash in the form of a personal loan from a friend of Walter's to make their dream a reality. It was full speed ahead from there. The business grew and the partners' relationships all around the area, with retail customers and the local farmers and the community at large, consolidated and grew throughout the decade. But big changes lay ahead.

In the late 1950s, big box discount stores arrived in Canada and changed the face of retail. One of the biggest impacts of these kinds of stores was their radically new pricing structure - direct from manufacturer to retailer - making the business more cutthroat than ever. In order to survive, many

ORIGINAL STEERING COMMITTEE
Back row left to right: Don White, Herb Zilliax, John Pratt, Bob Ross, Bob Geggie, Lloyd Wagg
Front row left to right: Ed Norman, Graham Ferguson, Al Waldie

small, independent hardware dealers started pooling their purchases and buying direct as well. Product was shipped to central locations and either picked up or shipped out to the individual stores. Distributors sprang up all over. Each operated independently and each had its own philosophy. Most independents had to deal with a handful of different distributors in order to keep their stores properly stocked.

At Hollinger Hardware, Walter Hachborn watched all this unfold, watched as K-Mart and Woolco invaded Canada, watched as thousands of dealers went out of business, not because they were broke, but because they felt they couldn't compete. He started searching for a system that would give small Canadian independents a fighting chance. Pro Hardware, a US-based franchise organization, approached Hollinger about joining them, but Walter quickly realized that they were already doing things better than Pro. He kept searching. Hearing good things about dealer-owned companies, he spent a week at American Hardware Supply Co. in Pittsburgh. He came away convinced that if anything was going to save the hardware system in Canada it was the co-op structure they had established as their operating system. Buoyed by this conviction, he called together 25 dealers from Windsor to Ottawa whom he had got to know over the years, and suggested they go to the States to see for themselves. They were as impressed as Walter and called for another meeting with more Ontario and Quebec-based dealers. On March 20, 1963 122 dealers met at The Flying Dutchman in

Kitchener, Ontario. At a marathon session lasting 12 hours, they decided to establish a co-op based company, which would allow dealer-members to become successful entrepreneurs in their own right. (In all my travels across the county, meeting with dealers, the message has been the same: it is the power of the co-op structure that has made the dealers and the company such a success. As Morris Saffer, who has been involved with Home's marketing and advertising programs in one form or another since the early 1970's, told me, by controlling their own destinies, with a board elected and run by their peers, Home Hardware has avoided many of the costly mistakes of much of their competition.)

The nine-man steering committee from that night in March 1963 became Home Hardware's first Board of Directors. This new board negotiated with Hollinger Hardware to buy the company, with Walter to manage it. The dealers each put up $1,500, their first payment on the new company. The rest was financed on a 10-year promissory note. There were no guarantees, but Walter had faith that they would come through. Walter's salary, on paper, was one half of one percent of sales, which he never took. "If I had," he recalls almost 50 years later, "I'd likely be the wealthiest person in St. Jacobs anyway!"

On January 1, 1964, Home Hardware Stores Limited was born and for the next ten years Walter's life was a constant meeting. He would work all day, drive all over for meetings late into the night, then be back at work by 8 o'clock the next morning. Along the way, he encountered some opposition, people who did not see the value of the concept. He points out with appropriately understated satisfaction that most of those people aren't in business today. He remembers those days as hard but good times. Hard work times.

Walter's genius is expressed in many ways. His ability to identify the business model that would unite hundreds of independents in one of the country's most successful retail chains stands front and centre. But it is his ability to understand and see the best in people that will probably be his most abiding legacy. This book recounts countless stories that illustrate the special gift possessed by Walter, stories of dealers - and many others associated with Home Hardware - whose lives were transformed by the faith Walter placed in them. And by the opportunities he gave them to live up to their potential. People whose eyes shine with deep affection, pride and loyalty when they tell their own stories about how Home Hardware, and Walter in particular, changed their lives. The stories that follow are just a fraction of the countless stories that no doubt deserve to be told. Individually, I found them to be inspiring, touching, entertaining and illuminating. Each of them is distinctive, but they all share a common theme - these are the stories of decent, hardworking people who have always given as much to the company as the company has given to them.

The stories in this chapter belong to some of the people there at the beginning. Charter members, area managers and others who have not only watched the company evolve but have themselves been part of the journey of transformation from dedicated and hardworking individuals to an entity that has become one of Canada's most enduring retail success stories.

I met Bill Robinson at Ernie Week's one-hundredth birthday bash at Weeks of Waterdown in April 2011. Bill was a bit shy at first, but once he understood my project, his reticence vanished. First and foremost, he could not say enough about the life he and his family had enjoyed thanks to Walter Hachborn and Home Hardware. At that lunchtime occasion and later, Bill regaled me with stories. At the spring market later that month, he loaned me a box full of papers and memorabilia, background for the memoir he had not yet got around to writing. We also spoke on the phone more than once and on every occasion he always had a funny story up his sleeve that he would pull out with a flourish, a soft chuckle and, no doubt, a twinkle in his eye.

Bill Robinson was born and raised in Hamilton, at the western end of Lake Ontario. He started working at 16, and joined the army at 18, serving during the war as an infantry instructor and NCO. In 1946, he was discharged, met Audrey and got married. He returned to his job in Hamilton working for Walter Woods, and worked on the dealer service desk for three years. Then in 1950 Bill went on the road, his territory spanning the Niagara region to Stratford. On a cold February morning in 1961, Walter Woods Limited informed all the Hamilton employees that they were closing and everyone there was terminated. He was 34 years old, had a wife and two boys who depended on him and he didn't have a job. On that same cold and blustery day, with nothing else to do, he headed into Toronto to the Hardware Show. He introduced himself to Walter Hachborn at the Hollinger Hardware booth. Bill told Walter his story and said that he was looking for

a job. Walter said he'd call him Wednesday night. The following Saturday morning, Bill headed up to St. Jacobs for an interview with Walter and Henry Sittler. At the end, Walter said they wanted to offer him a job, so when could he start? Bill said "Monday." And that was that. Until he retired in 1992, Bill spent his life "on the road" first with Hollinger as a salesman, then with Home Hardware as a District Manager.

Bill remembers the day in 1963 when Walter called a special sales meeting to explain the concept of dealer-owned wholesale. Everyone was expecting the worst: with so many Canadian hardware dealers closing, it was the end of Hollinger Hardware. But Walter explained that if they were successful in this new program, Hollinger would be in business for years to come. The salesmen were all instructed to bring their best customers to that pivotal meeting at The Flying Dutchman.

In the early days, it was as much about bringing new members on board as it was supporting those already part of the family. Bill still remembers how thrilled he was when Weeks of Waterdown, one of the oldest full-line hardware stores in his area, applied to join Home Hardware.

Weeks of Waterdown

By the time Weeks joined Home Hardware, Ernie and his wife Pauline had taken over the business from his parents who were still helping out in the store they had established years before. Nevertheless, when winter arrived, George Weeks got into his car and headed south to Florida, a trip he made every year until he reached 90 years of age.

school in Sudbury and then spent two years during the war as a civilian instructor for the RCAF at Mt. Hope airport in Hamilton. He even flew secret missions in the far north. He married his first wife Pauline during the war, and took over the store with his brother Irving after the war. Over the years Weeks of Waterdown grew from a small general store into a unique hardware business.

Ernie started helping in the store as a young boy. On Wednesdays, George would close early and he and Ernie would often head up to Hollinger Hardware in St. Jacobs. They would arrive at about 2 o'clock and when the staff went home at 5 o'clock, Walter Hachborn would stay on to get together their order.

Longevity (along with independence) runs in the family. In April 2011, Ernie Weeks celebrated his 100th birthday. He drove himself and his wife Dot, who turned 99 in December, to the store for a party that Dave Smith, whose dad bought the business from Ernie in 1972, had put together. It is very obvious that Ernie and Dave have a close bond, akin to father and son.

Ernie Weeks was born April 5, 1911 in the Acadian village of Bouctouche, NB, where his father George ran a grist mill for the K.C. Irving family, good family friends. Bouctouche was a French settlement and Ernie grew up completely bilingual. The family moved to Ontario in 1917 and settled in Waterdown in 1924 where father George bought the old stone store at the corner of Mill Street and Highway 5. A star athlete in high school, Ernie pursued a number of callings after that, from U of T to St. Peters Seminary in London, Ontario. But his true love was flying. He became a barnstormer, operated a flying

Ernie Weeks spent his entire life in the service of others, making a difference in the lives of many people in the community. His role model was his father George who kept many families afloat during the Great Depression by establishing a "credit system" that allowed people in what was in those days a dairy heartland to trade eggs and butter for badly needed merchandise. When Ernie took over the store, this same philosophy prevailed, and his son Vince can remember many occasions when farmers and town-folk alike would call the house at all hours of the day looking for help. Ernie would always stop whatever he was doing and open the store for them. Ernie was also responsible for many community-based initiatives, including Waterdown's Victoria Day Weekend fireworks displays. He was a founding member of the Waterdown Rotary Club and was instrumental in the building of Rotary Gardens, the senior citizens residence across the road from the family home of many years.

In the early 1970s, Dave Smith's dad, George Smith was working as a sales rep for Niagara Chemicals. One of his customers was Weeks Hardware. He'd come into the store to check the stock. Over the years George and Ernie became friends. One day, George decided he'd had enough of just making ends meet. It was hard on him, hard on his wife June and hard on their four children. There was a gun shop for sale in Hamilton and George told Ernie that he wanted to buy it. But Ernie had other ideas: George would buy Weeks Hardware. According to his son Dave, George Smith had always wanted to own a hardware store, but never thought it could happen. "We'll make it happen," Ernie told him. George bought the store in 1972 when he was 49 years old. He sold their Burlington home to help finance the purchase and the family moved in above the Waterdown store. His wife June quit her job to work in the new business. Young Dave was eight years old and by the time he was 10, he was working on the cash.

Dave remembers that Ernie and his wife Pauline helped his parents out a great deal, including with the financing of the business as the Smiths worked to get their new enterprise off the ground. The Smiths stayed in the old location for another 16 years, and in 1987 Dave and his sister Sandy and her husband Steve Gray bought the business from them. In August 1988, Dave's parents were lost in a tragic automobile accident. Their father had retired, but June was still doing books and buying giftware for the store. They were returning home from the gift show in Toronto when the accident happened. Ernie became a father to Dave at that point.

In March 1989, Weeks of Waterdown moved to its present location on Hamilton Street - there wasn't room for any meaningful expansion plans at the original location. At 25,000 square feet, the new Weeks of Waterdown - "My dad was adamant about keeping the Weeks name" in tribute to Ernie and his family - was one of the biggest Home Hardware stores in the family.

Dave, Sandy and Steve Gray ran and continued to build the business together for many years. In late 2011, 24 years after they bought the business from their father George, Dave, Sandy and Steve made the decision to sell. Dave knew exactly who he thought should buy it and called Ron Cicuttini, who already owned University Home Hardware in Dundas, a neighbouring town. After several months of discussion, the store changed hands in December 2011. In February 2012, Sandy received a lifetime achievement award from the Flamborough Chamber of Commerce for the many causes to which she has contributed her boundless energy, most notably those related to helping abused women.

Frank Hammer: Western Area Manager (retired)

Frank Hammer spent most of his career as an Area Manager for Home Hardware and cannot say enough about Walter Hachborn and the company for which he worked.

It was a Sunday in May 1958. Frank had just moved his family to St. Jacobs from Waterloo. Mr. Hachborn, as Frank still calls him over 50 years later, drove him home from church and asked him to come work for him. Frank was 26 years old. His first job was making local deliveries, and from there, he moved to the warehouse and then the order desk. He was there in 1964 when Hollinger became Home Hardware. In 1978, Walter sent Frank out west to teach five BC dealers how to use a new ordering system. After a few weeks, Frank told Walter that if they ever decided to open up the west, he wanted to apply for the job. Two years later, Frank moved his family to Edmonton. The challenge was to sell the benefits of Home Hardware to dealers who knew nothing about the company. But Frank had a good story to tell - an established company in eastern Canada, a large and well-stocked warehouse, good gross margins in

key categories, all the advantages of Home's own Beauti-Tone paint. Frank knew critical mass was essential - they couldn't have trucks coming from Ontario unless they were full. And he started producing results - a recently signed on dealer helped Frank arrange a meeting in Hinton, Alberta and that night, they signed up 14 dealers.

When Home Hardware merged with Link in 1981, and then bought 50 Revelstoke stores in 1987, Home's western business mushroomed. Walter came out and the pair visited every store. They drove 18,000 kilometers in 15 days. In 1980, Home Hardware had $40 million in annual sales in western Canada. When Frank retired on December 31, 1995, they had reached $500 million. Frank is proud of that growth but typically gives all the credit to Walter, saying he would not have accomplished half of what he did without Walter. Frank left Edmonton just a few years ago - "I got sick of winter" - and now lives in Parksville on Vancouver Island. He worked for Bill and Carol Ormiston for two and a half years and then retired for good. But once Home Hardware gets into your blood, it's there to stay.

Mike Stapylton: London

Mike Stapylton opened Plaza Hardware in London's first plaza on January 1, 1956. In those early days, Mike bought most of his merchandise from DH Howden. Times were hard, not helped by his own inexperience. Times got even harder in the 1960s with the arrival of the so-called discount department stores like Towers, Sayvette, Woolco and K-Mart. On top of which, Canadian Tire was growing and expanding fast which did not make it easy for either the small independents dealers or their wholesale suppliers. It was Mike's good fortune to meet Don Tuckey, one of his fellow hardware dealers in the London area. Don was a charter member of Home Hardware and had been a director since its inception in 1964. Don introduced Mike to Bill Robinson, the Area Manager for south-western Ontario, who convinced Mike to become a Home Hardware in March 1969.

Joining Home Hardware was like turning on the light. Mike benefited from the advice and help of Bill and Harry May, another area manager. His sales and expertise grew along with the store - when he opened, his store was 1,600 square feet, which grew to 3,000 square feet, then expanded to 5,500 and finally 10,500 square feet. By the time he retired in 2010, Mike's annual sales had grown from $31,000 to over $2 million.

Success didn't come easily. Expansion required a lot of planning and due diligence. It meant consultations with accountants, bank managers and Home Hardware. Everything he ordered had to be paid for, along with the bank loans. Mike was always grateful to Head Office for all the backup, support and expertise he received along the way.

Bill Lindsay: Selkirk

Bill was born in Hagersville and raised in Selkirk, Ontario, beautiful farm country that borders Lake Erie. United Empire Loyalists settled the area in the 1700s. In the late 1800s, during oil exploration three wells were drilled. The area boomed in the early 1900s when a large natural gas field was discovered that stretched under the lake. Families from nearby Buffalo and Hamilton started building summer homes along the north shore of Lake Erie.

Bill's father Grant was a licensed mechanic. After serving in the Army, he went into business with his brother-in-law Russell Hurst whose banking and office experience made him the ideal partner in the hardware and tin shop they bought that had served the community since the late 1800s. They changed the name from Winger's to L&H Hardware with Grant the resident expert in plumbing, electrical, heating and sheet metal work. In 1958, they bought the building next door, and after some demolition emerged the following year as a modern hardware store. In December 1963 Grant's son Bill bought out Russell Hurst's shares and he and his father joined Home Hardware as charter members in 1964. They changed the store name to Lindsay Hardware in 1965.

The area continued to flourish throughout the 1960s: Ontario Hydro built the Nanticoke coal generating station, at the time the largest in the world, Texaco built a refinery, Stelco opened a plant, and numerous smaller industrial supply businesses sprang up to support all this activity. The complexion of the neighbourhood also changed: new businesses attracted new residents, and many of the summer homes along the lake became year-round residences. Two new parks, Selkirk Provincial and Haldimand Park, were popular recreational destinations. Business, including Lindsay Hardware, boomed. The tin shop moved and the hardware store expanded. Grant retired in the 1980s and Bill and his wife and business partner Anita bought his shares.

The Lindsays bought land for expansion in the early 1990s, but the recession put those plans on hold. In 2009, Bill sold the business to Jason and Jana Nagel (née Winger - remember the original tin shop!) and they built a new store that opened as Selkirk Home Hardware in January 2010. There's a fitting sense of completion that Bill's daughter Renée is the store's manager.

In addition to a flourishing economy, the area around Selkirk has also had a rich cultural life with three first class museums as well as several private museums and collections. Bill Lindsay was intimately involved with two of these initiatives, the Canadian Drilling Rig – Natural Gas museum started in 1995, in no small part due to Bill's idea for the 1996 Plowing Match, and the remarkable private hardware collection started by his father Grant that Bill has been lovingly cataloguing and housing for years.

The Good Old Days, by Bill Lindsay

In 1946, when my father Grant and Uncle Russell started the business, my father was the tradesman and my uncle ran the hardware store.

We did just about everything: plumbing, heating, electrical and sheet metal work. We also worked on new homes, did home renovations, opened and closed summer residences, as well as service work on the water systems at Selkirk Provincial Park, Peacock Point, and Haldimand Conservation Park, and electrical work at Selkirk Provincial Park. We put in septic tanks and cisterns, using a custom set of forms, and mixed concrete by hand. Tile beds were installed, dug by hand. A lot of the tin shop work was done after hours. Trips had to be made into Hamilton or Nelles Corners to pick up supplies.

The old store had a wood stove in the shop. The paint cans all had to be carried upstairs. Truckloads of clay tiles for septic systems were unloaded by hand, boiled and raw oil, kerosene and turpentine in 45-gallon drums that had to be transferred to the smaller bottles in which they were sold. Glass came in wooden crates, nails in 100 lb. wooden kegs; the black metal sheets for stovepipe came from England. The cash register was an unlocked drawer under the counter and the office was a cubby hole at the back of the store.

I started to help my father at an early age, carrying tools and materials as required. There were no idle moments. I was always expected to do what I was told. There was no back talk or arguing and beginners always got the dirty jobs. The tradesmen were proud of their work and that work was often on display for the public to see. In fact, some of this work can still be seen today.

It was a learning and rewarding experience with many life lessons.

Don White: Oshawa

Irrepressible is the word I would use to describe Don White, a lively, lovely imp of a man whose humanity, decency and enthusiasm for life animate his face and entire being. I suspect that his wife Christine is his anchor and it is evident how happily the two have navigated their lives together.

Don's family has deep roots in the area northeast of Toronto. His great grandfather came from northern England in 1845, settling not far from Oshawa where Don and Christine have spent their married life. His grandmother raised seven children on a farm, doing everything the old fashioned way. "Never set the table for less than 10 people," Christine says. "Never heard her complain once," Don says, completing the picture, a comfortable one-two that comes naturally to them. After high school, Don joined the army. Although the world was at war, in September 1939 Don was too young to serve. He spent two years in the local reserves, went to training camp when he turned 18 and in February 1944, was bound for England where he spent five weeks and was then shipped to Italy where he joined The Royal Canadian Dragoons.

In February 1946, Don came home. After a few restless months - it's hard to top liberating Holland - he joined his father's coal and feed business, more office than storefront. They quickly recognized an opportunity and began stocking farm hardware. Every time a farmer mentioned something he needed, Don had it in stock the following week.

Don and Christine met four years after the war. Christine was at a Muskoka lodge with her parents. So was Don. One afternoon, he played a prank on some friends standing on the lawn. He called them over and dumped a pitcher of water out the window…. just as Christine's father walked by. Three weeks later Don and Christine were engaged. They were married the following April (1949) after Don graduated from Guelph Agriculture College.

They built a home next door to the farmhouse where Don had lived since he was five - and where son Stephen now lives. "We could lean out of bed and turn on the stove," Christine says. The house grew along with their family and today it's a comfortable home with a large pool and garden, a favourite spot for family gatherings and weddings.

By the early 1960s, White's Hardware was buying from several wholesalers. The field narrowed radically after George Klein, Hollinger's local Area Manager,

came calling. "He never tried to pressure me," Don remembers, "but he was so nice, I had to break down and buy from the guy!"

The early days of Home Hardware hold a special place in Don's heart, and he played a central role. He vividly remembers events and people he believes were key to the company's success, including the 1963 fact-finding trip to Cotter & Company in Chicago, organized by Walter Hachborn. He rhymes off familiar names: Ed Norman, Al Waldie, Lloyd Wagg and Ray Gabel all of whom were part of that original group. He credits corporate lawyer Gordon Mackay Sr. with helping to make it all possible. "He'd say,' Well, you can't do this because our Ontario laws won't let you; but maybe we could do it this way.'"

He mentions Ed Norman, a dealer from Barrie, who the group persuaded to join. "He was, in my opinion, one of the major contributors to the success of Home Hardware. He was an accountant, and the whole company drew on his knowledge many times." A few days after our initial interview, Don called. He had forgotten to mention "one very important gentleman by the name of Henry Sittler, who in my opinion, had as much to do with Home Hardware as anyone. Everyone knew that if he made a deal, it would be upheld. His legacy continues today with his protégée, Ray Gabel, following in his footsteps."

Don retired in 2011 at the ripe old age of 87. Christine had already retired. On her sixtieth birthday, she closed that door behind her. Their youngest child Holly has

worked at Home Hardware in St. Jacobs for over 30 years. Their other daughter Heather and her husband Paul McVety owned a Home Hardware store in Lindsay, Ontario.Stephen recently sold the family business. In January 2012, after working side by side in the business, Steve's wife Deb died suddenly just as they were getting ready to share another chapter of their lives together. She lives on in her family's memory and in a young woman from western Canada who is alive today because she received Deb's heart. The store moving into other hands caused a bit of a pang for the man who was Charter Member number eight and sat on the Home Hardware board for 37 years. "I'm a realistic person," Don says. "Steve had an opportunity and I said that it wouldn't be right to hang on."

Christine remembers those days too, when Don was helping to build the business, store by store. "The meetings were on Saturday nights and often ran until 3 or 4 o'clock in the morning. I would pack up the kids and we would stay with Jean Hachborn. She always had coffee and sandwiches ready when Don and Walter got through because they would have a little discussion afterwards."

In the beginning, there were some manufacturers who refused to sell to upstart Home Hardware. Christine remembers attending a hardware show with Peg Aylward, wife of Maritime Area Manager Walter Aylward. At one booth of an uppity manufacturer they tied up two salesmen with an order that, as she says now, "we'd still be selling if they'd actually shipped it out."

For many years, Christine managed the books, and often worked on the floor. "Neither one of us figured we were boss," Don says. "We shared everything and Christine worked as hard as I did. And my son's wife Deb was the same. When you're in business, you're not 9 to 5; it's whenever." "He made the decisions," Christine says. "We talked them over, but as far as the staff was concerned, he was the boss."

The story of the regimental badge of the Royal Canadian Dragoons.

The springbok was adopted for the regiment's badge to commemorate an event from the Boer War in South Africa. One night a sentry noticed a lot of nervous springbok, essentially small deer, moving in the long grass around their encampment. He and his commanding officer took a closer look and discovered that Boer soldiers were attempting to use them as cover as they crawled towards the Canadians' camp. Instead, thanks to the agitated springbok, the regiment was forewarned and able to repel the attack. They chose their regimental badge to honour the creatures that saved many Canadian lives that night.

Don White's War

Don saw a lot of action with his regiment of the Royal Canadian Dragoons. By D-Day (June 6, 1944) they had advanced as far as Rome. The Italians had already surrendered, but although they were liberators to most Italians, they were still fighting the Germans. They drove to the port of Leghorn and sailed to Marseilles. From there they drove through liberated France to Belgium. Three weeks later they went into action in still-occupied Holland.

At 10:30 in the morning on April 15 1945, Number One Troop, Charlie Squadron, consisting of 12 guys, including 20 year-old Don White, and four armoured cars, were the first Allied Troops into the Dutch town of Leeuwarden. Don remembers thousands of people flooding the streets to greet them.

The end of the war arrived at different times in different parts of Europe. Don's regiment was in Germany on V-E Day, May 8,1945.

It was a miserable day. "About 4 o'clock we were doing our normal end-of-day routine. The radio operator got BBC London. Suddenly he yelled: 'The war is over!' Well then - we had a few bottles of vino and we were going to celebrate. But the officer said, 'Put it away and get some sleep. We don't know how the Germans are going to take the armistice and our duty is to get up and go on our way next morning.' So that's what we did. But it really was over."

In 1995, fifty years later, Don returned to Holland with his regiment and Christine. They returned in 2000, 2005 and 2010. In Almelo, a town in Holland liberated by Canadians in 1945, three veterans, including Don, laid wreaths at the memorial. In the Canadian war Cemetery in Holten, 12 of his buddies are buried. His daughter Holly researched the names so that her father, along with Master Sergeant Davidson, the current regimental sergeant, could place a poppy on each of their graves. (In the course of her research, Holly discovered an RCD named W.T. Buddell from Kitchener. Holly worked with

someone with the same name who, she learned, was the nephew of the fallen soldier. Upon her return, Holly gave Will photographs of his uncle's grave.) Don's other daughter Heather laid a flag on each grave. Hundreds of school children sang 'Oh Canada.'

The next day, Don made a side trip to Leeuwarden. Unbeknownst to him, the town had a celebration planned. A cavalcade of jeeps lined up in formation for a parade with Don in the first jeep. "I felt like MacArthur," he says. There were 165,000 people there that day. "And everybody wanted to shake his hand," says Christine proudly, who was there along with their two daughters.

On November 11, 2012, Don White was a member of the honour guard that laid the commemorative wreath at their church in Oshawa on Remembrance Day. Don and Christine invited me to join them and four generations of Whites for the service, and lunch at their home. The hospitality, kindness and warmth of this large, happy and enormously generous family touched me deeply.

On a warm June day I drove to Dunnville to visit Jack and Joy Kohler who live in this small Ontario town that borders the Grand River just 40 miles west of Niagara Falls. Their comfortable home is two doors from St. Paul's Anglican Church in whose choir Jack and Joy have sung for a combined total of over 100 years and where he was baptised, confirmed and married. After two heart attacks, the first while still a dealer, and bypass surgery in 1995, Jack is taking it easy these days. The day after we visited to take our photograph, he and his wife were driving to Florida where they have been wintering for the past 16 years.

There is a Norman Rockwell-esque quality to Jack Kohler's story. He was born (in 1929) and raised in Dunnville. He has lived in Dunnville his entire life, other than for the eight months he spent in Toronto in 1951. The Kohlers lived next door to the co-owner of one of the three hardware stores in town. In May 1951, when Jack was 22 years old, his next door neighbour, one of the two sons who owned the business started by their father in the 1880s, told Jack that they were looking for someone to learn and eventually buy the business. "After a short deliberation, I agreed to be that someone," Jack recalls almost exactly 60 years later. "Little did I know that I would spend the next 38 years in that business, in the same building," Jack started working for the Congdon Brothers at the end of May 1951, at a salary of $25 a week. Six years later, he bought the business, keeping the original name, Congdon and Marshall, until 1962 when it changed to Kohler's Hardware.

Robert Craw was a Hollinger Hardware salesman who lived in Dunnville. Naturally, he called on Jack who remembers the station wagon Robert drove when making deliveries to the local dealers. In the fall of 1963, Jack and his fellow Dunnville dealer, Bob Ross, and the Lindsays from nearby Selkirk were invited by Bob Craw to attend the famous meeting at The Flying Dutchman Motel. Bob Ross was appointed a Director at that meeting.

Jack has countless memories of the early Home Hardware days: the first mini-market, held at the new grocery store across from the warehouse in St. Jacobs; the wonderful Mennonite dinner and local entertainment held after at a rural hall; the door prize he won that evening - a wall mounted dinner bell that still hangs outside the Kohlers' Muskoka cottage. Jack remembers the first "regular" show at the Elmira Fair Ground Buildings, with Director Herb Zilliax handing out and explaining how to use the order books for shopping the show. He remembers the show in 1964 held in the gymnasiums of Wilfred Laurier University, where dealers stayed overnight in the dorms and ate their meals in the cafeteria. He remembers the years at Bingemann Park, in particular the spring of 1975 when the Grand River flooded its banks and came close, but never got into, the show area. He remembers the innovative marketing events, including a Toronto traffic reporter landing his helicopter and joining a dealer meeting, after announcing several Home Hardware "spots" on air (and in the air). And the time he met Hank Snow, whose hit record was being promoted that Christmas and available at Home stores. Jack also remembers the march down Main Street in New Hamburg for a television commercial their agency was shooting: all the dealers and management, led by the famous Burlington Teen Tour Band, marched by the cameras to show the company's strength and numbers. He made sure to point himself out to his customers in the shot on the display banner that hung in his store after that march. He remembers the frequent district meetings that took place in dealers' homes, including the Penners in Virgil and the Kalas in St. Catharines. He remembers pitching in on various projects at the St. Jacobs warehouse as the business grew. And he remembers the first illuminated Home Hardware sign that ran the entire width (all 22 feet) of his building.

At the store level, Jack spent long hours updating fixtures, paying invoices and devising "advertising gimmicks" which were all the more essential with Bob Ross Home Hardware five doors down the street. Jack says that in all the years of healthy competition between the two stores (Bob sold his business in the early 1980s), the relationship between them was always excellent. One of the early catalogues advertised rider lawn mowers and Jack had orders for three. When he called Ray Gabel to see if it was possible to add them, Ray thanked him for the nice orders. "Those were the days," Jack says fondly.

Ten years after Jack retired in 1989, the current owners decided to leave downtown. They bought an old co-op building and land on the edge of town. In 2008, they expanded, a process that included building a brand new HHBC. One day, Jack got a phone call from the owner Bert Mulder. "Jack," he said, "you are going to be part of the new store décor." They planned to hang the original old hand painted plywood sign that had hung at the back of the original store, inside the new store. Jack was touched by that recognition. At the official grand opening in May 2010, Jack was there, after 21 years of happy retirement. Serving as Home Hardware's official PR man, Jack greeted customers old and new, proudly wearing his original red Home Hardware jacket, which the new owners had also kept in pristine condition. Once again, Jack was showing his true colours that day.

Harold Ghent: Preston

Jo Ann Brown's father Harold Ghent (pronounced like "gentleman") was number thirty-one of the original thirty-eight dealers who bought shares in the fledgling company of Home Hardware that took over Hollinger Wholesale Hardware in January 1964. He himself had just taken possession of a "rundown hardware store" in Preston the September before - sales in August 1963 were not quite $1,500.

Prior to buying the hardware store, Harold had worked with the UCO (United Co-ops of Ontario). His background and philosophy no doubt made him a valuable resource as Walter developed the dealer-owned model that would transform the lives of so many struggling hardware retailers across Ontario. The early years were hard and for the first few years all the profits went back into buying inventory. Eventually their meagre income attracted the attention of the taxman. Harold's wife Alice did the bookkeeping under the direction of a friend who was also an auditor. The tax inspector grilled Alice mercilessly, at one point demanding to know the value of the garden produce that they ate so it could be added to their taxable income. That was too much for Harold who phoned the Kitchener tax office to lodge a complaint. The office sent someone out to investigate. When he heard who their auditor was, the persecution stopped - obviously, the man's integrity put them above suspicion.

The original store was always old style hardware. Fabulous creaky wooden floors, aisles and aisles of merchandise, and nails by the pound. Here are a few gems from the treasure trove of stories recounted by

Jo Ann Brown when we met in the spring of 2011, with some additional anecdotes culled from a short memoir that her father wrote before he passed away February 28, 2010.

One of Harold's stories: The neighbourhood druggist came in one day for 107 inch and a quarter finishing nails. When Harold told him the nails were sold by the pound, the druggist wanted to know how many nails that would be. Harold said he had no idea and no intention of finding out. The druggist counted out what he wanted, which came to half a pound. On another occasion he needed small screw eyes, which cost two cents each or 15 cents a dozen. He took six and paid 12 cents. That afternoon, he returned for another six and wanted to pay the per dozen price for them.

Ghent's Home Hardware was likely the only hardware store that sold fresh raspberries. Harold, Alice and their eight children lived on a farm in the nearby community of Ayr. Harold was an old farmer at heart and although he was busy with the store, just couldn't bear to see the land doing nothing. So he planted ever-bearing raspberries, which take a few years to produce. But when they did, the children would all get up early to pick raspberries that would be for sale in quart boxes on the sidewalk outside the store later that morning. The younger kids stayed home and kept picking and Jo Ann would often head out midday to go back home to replenish the supply.

Jo Ann met her future husband Martin when they were teenagers. Her dad would see him hanging about the store and put him to work, a really smart move: not only was Mart the best hire Harold ever made, he soon became their son-in-law. On the wedding day, there was a sign in the store window: "This is a family store. Due to a wedding in the family, the store is closed."

Martin Brown and Paul Ghent, one of Harold and Alice Ghent's sons, bought the business in 1975. In a move designed to retain the vitality of the downtown core, a group of local businessmen convinced them to stay in the area. And as Jo Ann recalls, even after they bought

the store from her father, they weren't the new "blister pack" hardware store. They still had the reputation that if you couldn't find it at Ghent's, you likely couldn't find it anywhere. Jo Ann remembers that, because they were so close to St. Jacobs, her father would often send her up to the warehouse on Fridays after she had finished school to pick up items he'd ordered for the weekend. Often she found herself trying to manoeuver the family station wagon between two huge transport trucks already cozied up to the loading dock. The drivers would stand by and watch until eventually one of them would take pity on her and offer to help.

Later, as a young mother, Jo Ann would do the books at home. The handwritten invoices, a challenge to decipher, were all in a huge pile on a table in the laundry room - and then one day a week, Jo Ann would go into the store to post everything on a humungous machine, the size of a small car, as she recalls.

There were lots of children in town who wanted to buy a gift for their mothers at Christmas. The store set up a display wall: everything on the racks cost $1 - maybe a teacup and saucer that had been part of a set that had got broken. Only young children were allowed to shop in the "dollar store" wall, no parents, no teenagers. The store gift wrapped the item and put a note inside that included the child's name to certify that it had been legitimately bought and paid for at the store! They kept this custom going until they sold the store in 1984.

As with so many retired Home Dealers, Jo Ann says they still miss the people contact, the relationships and customs that sprang up spontaneously in the old country hardware store environment.

Denny Winterburn: Kitchener

From a very early age, Dennis (Denny) Winterburn knew exactly what he wanted in life. In the summer of 1955, when he was going into ninth grade, he got his foot in the door. Not far from where he lived, the first plaza in Kitchener was being built on Frederick Street. Just before Labour Day, Denny tracked down the owner of the hardware store going into that plaza, who told Denny to show up for work that Saturday. It was Ray Gabel, who worked at the store every Saturday afternoon, who taught Denny how to flatten empty cartons - Denny had just been pitching them into the basement. One year later, Denny had a key to the store and was trusted with the cash. "That was my first job, " he says, "and I knew the minute I got there I was going to have my own hardware store."

Walter Hachborn recognized a kindred soul when he saw one, and that first year, he, along with Ray, took Denny to his first hardware show at the CNE. Years later, that drive into Toronto is still vivid in Denny's mind: his dad was a "very, very slow driver" and Walter was anything but. They arrived in record time and Walter put the lads to work. It wasn't until 10:30 that night that Walter realized that they might want something to eat. They worked through the next day as well. Sunday

evening Walter put Ray and Denny on the train so Ray could get back to work and Denny could get back to school. For the rest of his high school years, Denny played hooky every February to go to the hardware show and every February he would serve detentions for his truancy. He tried to reason with the principal, arguing it was not fair that students could miss class for football games and other school sports but he couldn't go to the hardware show! Once, in frustration, the principal took down a large book from a high shelf and showed Denny a page listing the events that students were permitted to attend during school hours. "The Hardware Show," he pointed out, "is not on this list."

By 1963, 22 year-old Denny was managing a hardware store in Burlington. After it closed, Denny bought the fixtures and the inventory and fulfilled his long time ambition of opening his own store in Kitchener. Walter made arrangements for the Home Hardware "fleet" (which consisted of a little pick up truck with a canvas cover and what looked like a "farm truck") to move the fixtures to Denny's new store. Three fellows from the St. Jacobs warehouse were there to help with the job. At 2 AM they were finally on the road. It was pouring rain and halfway there, the little pick up truck got a flat

tire. They pulled over onto the side of the road but there was no spare tire, which really exercised Walter who made his irritation clear. One of the fellows from the warehouse leaned over and whispered to Denny, "One little guy, a few weeks ago, said 'Get that tire off the truck so we can get more hardware on - you don't need the spare tire now.'" By the time they found a spare, got back on the road and offloaded everything including the overflow into Denny's parents' garage, it was seven in the morning. Walter announced that he had to get home so he could go into work. And sure enough, he was in his St. Jacobs office by 9 o'clock.

Because he managed but did not own the Burlington store, Denny did not attend the pivotal meeting at the Flying Dutchman Motel in the fall of 1963. But of course he had the inside track. Denny opened his store in November 1963 - the day President Kennedy was assassinated, he recalls. He operated as an independent for two months before he joined Home Hardware in January 1964. In fact, one of the new Home Hardware Directors visited his store just after he had opened. "Am I part of the group?" he asked. The Director laughed and said, "I'll let Walter tell you."

Rodney & Kerri Robinson: Paisley by Kerri Robinson

Kerri's friend and former customer, Wilma Sluys of Chepstow, Ontario made the Beauti-Tone quilt, which Kerri thought was a creative way to display some of the many Beauti-Tone t-shirts they had collected over the years.

In August 2000, Rodney and Kerri Robinson bought their Home Hardware Store in Paisley, Ontario. It was a real career change for Kerri - she had worked in health care for 12 years prior - but she always had a keen interest in home décor and redecorating, and looked forward to helping others achieve their decorating dreams. Rodney had worked for his father who owned Robinson Feeds/ Home Hardware until August 2000 so he understood the world of retail. Rodney also had experience in the agricultural and construction businesses, both of which came in handy when they opened their Home Hardware. They sold their farms and lived above the store for three months until they found a new home, just five minutes outside of town, in the countryside they loved. It was stressful to buy a new business and move twice in three months, but Kerri and Rodney never looked back.

In addition to expanding the product lines and attracting more female customers, customer service was a primary focus. Kerri concentrated on Paint and Housewares, and a new Gourmet Shop was soon nestled into the front corner of the store. They expanded their selection of Beauti-Tone Paints, Home products and accessories. Kerri gave the paint counter a whole new look and to stay up to date on paint and decorating trends, completed the advanced decorative paint training course and attended the annual paint seminars and spring and fall markets. She always felt even more motivated after returning from these events and was eager to share her knowledge with her customers. She acquired many new and loyal customers over ten years and was known as the "Paint Lady". Many customers only wanted to deal with her and would come back later if it was her day off. She had a lot of innovative ideas, including a Beauti-Tone customer appreciation day that she hosted in her home one year. The Robinsons also added a wider selection of seasonal items and a new toy section. Their customers were so thankful they did not have to drive out of town to find great gifts for all occasions.

Rodney and Kerri improved the store's appearance inside and out, in the process making traffic and workflows more efficient. They finished by painting the exterior using historical colours that worked well with the village of Paisley overall.

Meanwhile, Rodney's goals were to build the hardware and agricultural product lines, and master Home's Systems and Services. He enrolled in the Solid Base Training Series, offered by Home Hardware. Rodney enjoyed helping customers with their plumbing and electrical projects. With his knowledge of farming, he also had a loyal base of local farmers who relied on him for the expanded product line he carried. Another unique feature was their annual Chick Day: Day old chicks, ducks and geese were pre-ordered by customers and delivered to the Paisley store. Understanding the needs of their rural community, Rodney and Kerri were able to offer one stop shopping with a wide range of products and services.

In July 2002, Rodney and Kerri added more storage and Kerri was invited to a casting call by Home's advertising agency, Sharpe Blackmore, and was chosen to appear in one of the commercials in the coming year's television campaign. Appropriately enough, the commercial in which she starred, titled "Always", promoted Beauti-Tone products.

Rodney and Kerri always supported the local community. They were proud supporters of the Paisley Fall Fair, donated items to numerous local events for raffle tables and silent auctions and sponsored a junior race car driver, to name a few. A framed print of Roger Neilson was also purchased through Home Hardware Head Office in St. Jacobs, and was donated to Paisley Minor Hockey, to aid in their fundraising efforts. Both their boys were avid hockey players, so they felt this was very fitting.

Rodney and Kerri were fortunate to have long time employees working along side of them for most of their ten years in business. Great employees make a world of difference in the retail world. Over the years, the opportunity to meet so many different people meant that friendships developed. Feedback from customers for their special service was appreciated and visits from Walter Hachborn were always a highlight.

Their two sons had worked with them on weekends and after school, but both chose different career paths and after 10 years in the business, the Robinsons decided to sell and make some changes too. Kerri continued to work with the new owners so the community kept their beloved "Paint Lady" for a few more months, and after remaining for the transition period, Rodney started working for another local company as a Customer Support Manager. A neck injury in early 2011 forced Kerri to make some dramatic lifestyle changes.

Although Rodney and Kerri are no longer Home Hardware Dealer-Owners, they still love to see Home Hardware's new TV commercials and look forward to getting the flyers, annual catalogue and Home at Home magazine. They send heartfelt thanks to the many friendly and helpful people at head office in St. Jacobs and the Burford Paint and Home Products division for all of their product knowledge and support over the years. Rodney and Kerri feel honoured to still receive an invitation to the Home Hardware markets every spring and fall and will always feel they are a part of the Home Hardware family.

On August 9, 2010, Robinson's Home Hardware officially changed ownership. The new owners are Lee and Susan Allen, Quinn Allen and Reid Allen. The new business name is now Paisley Home Hardware.

The Kennedy family's hardware store was in Pointe au Baril on Georgian Bay north of Parry Sound.

Bill's grandparents, John Sr. and Emily Perks, built the Pointe au Baril store in 1923 so that their 19 year-old daughter would have an income. It was a smart move. By the 1960s, what started as a grocery store - and always remained one - had evolved into a 5,000 square foot hardware store with groceries. It was their Sherwin Williams rep, Doug Saunders, who at that time suggested to Bill's parents Crossley and Edna, that they take a good look at joining Home Hardware. They took his advice.

Lauralee became part of it all in the early 1990s after she and Bill were married. (They met at the TD Bank in Parry Sound where she had transferred from Toronto.) In 2000 Bill bought out his brother Art and his wife Barb, along with his nephew Mike and his wife Jane. Mike now works at Geerlinks HHBC in St. Thomas.

The place was hopping all summer long with cottagers boating across the bay to stock up on hardware and groceries. But the winters were quiet - and long and cold, both Lauralee and Bill point out. By now, they had a place in Florida and have since bought a condo in New Brunswick. Bill and Lauralee sold the business in 2010. But not before another big party. In 2007, they celebrated 100 years of the Kennedy family in Pointe au Baril, Bill's 50 years in the hardware industry and 37 years as a member of the Home Hardware family. Walter and Jean Hachborn, along with Bill Ferguson and their Area Manager, were all there for that momentous occasion.

Ontario

· AURORA · KITCHENER · BROCKVILLE · CALEDONIA · COBOURG · DRAYTON · SHELBURNE · GODERICH · VIRGIL · HAGERSVILLE · INGERSOLL ·

· BRADFORD · ST. JACOBS · TORONTO · MANOTICK · MILVERTON · ORILLIA · KANATA · GANANOQUE · PICTON · PORT PERRY · RENFREW ·
· WATERDOWN · SUDBURY · SUNDRIDGE · OTTAWA · LONDON · WINDSOR ·

It's a true family affair at Aurora Home Hardware Building Centre, a pretty town in horse country north of Toronto. With his down-to-earth approach to life, Stuart Barfitt doesn't fit the idea of a typical Aurora resident, but the area was much different when he first arrived from Newfoundland in 1948. He worked for Canada Packers for 18 years then got into the hardware business when he bought a small hardware store in town. He joined Home Hardware in 1969 after a visit from the local Area Manager

The community has changed over the years, from a small town where they knew everyone who came through the door, to an upscale and growing neighbourhood of chic restaurants and smart shops. Like Stuart, the 25,000 square foot store takes a no-frills approach, a bit out of keeping with the genteel feel of the town, but not surprising given that the majority of their business is contractor-based. Stuart never actually worked in the current building, preferring to build a house a year, and occasionally working at

The Barfitt Family:
When they were kids, the boys worked in the store every day after school, learning the business.

Home Hardware Building Centre
Aurora, ON

Jeff Lee and a quick trip to St. Jacobs convinced him it was the right move. Stuart has been retired for 20 years, although he still builds picnic tables, in one of the many garages on his son Randy's property, that are sold in the store. He had just finished 22 of them on the rainy, cool day in June when I first visited him and two of his three sons at the store. Stuart has building in his blood - on which subject, more shortly. His three sons, Russ, Randy and Robert, and their respective wives, now own and run the business, with 70 employees including a plethora of third generation Barfitts - Robbie and Carlie (Randy's two kids), John (Russ) and Calvin (Robert). The business has had three locations over the years: the original 2,000 square foot store on Yonge Street, then a somewhat larger location at Yonge and Wellington that they moved to in 1974 and their current 25,000 square foot store on Wellington Street East which was a farmer's field in 1986 when Stuart and his late wife Doreen bought the property. The family built the store from the ground up - literally. Doing virtually everything themselves with a little help from their friends. They levelled and compacted the ground, using an old back hoe that is a relic from another era, trucking in fill—at one point there were 20 trucks pulling 100 tons of fill up Yonge Street. They installed their own water system. Randy did all the welding and at one point Stuart remembers, even their Home Hardware rep pitched in - he turned up one day when they were working on the asphalt and someone handed him a pair of rubber boots. The entire project took about 10 months, and they worked through "probably the worst fall" ever, Stuart remembers, often having to push the backhoe through the muck. They kept the old store open and running throughout the building process, moving out the inventory in stages. One week they closed the old store on Saturday night and the next week they opened the new store on Monday morning. "Never missed a day," Randy says proudly.

night creating store displays. When they were kids, the boys worked in the store every day after school, learning the business. Today the three sons have divided the responsibilities in a way that works for everyone, keeping all the Barfitts busy and readying the third generation for the day when they take the business over, still a few years down the road.

Stuart and his boys reminisce about the early days in the original store. They still have the first dollar bill the business earned, to remind them of their start. The Barfitts have been part of a process of change that, in relatively few years, has taken them from a small, old fashioned hardware store where every bill was written and added up by hand, where they did not even bother with a cash register, to a large HHBC with a lot of sophisticated systems. They built the business, with their own physical labour and hard work year after year, so the sense of family values is strong even after all the years, all the changes and all the growth. When it comes to the important stuff, some things never change.

Stuart and his wife Doreen went on several of Walter's study trips: Stuart remembers that Doreen and Jean, Walter's wife, got along famously, even getting into trouble together when Jean blew the bus horn in a town that had strict bylaws against doing that very thing. They got on the road in a hurry that day!

Most of the Barfitt family clambered aboard the original backhoe that broke and levelled the land for their current HHBC. (Stuart's son Robert was on vacation.)

It's a tale of two Home stores in Brockville. For Bob Billings, small is beautiful: his downtown store is just 24 feet wide and one hundred feet deep with an awning over the big front window and a natural display area on the wide sidewalk out front. When we visited in early December 2011, the sleds, shovels and bags of de-icer squatting on the sidewalk hinted at a winter that seemed in no hurry to show up. Bob stood there, every inch the proprietor, waving at the slowly passing vehicles, and chatting with the

Bob Billings:

Billings Home Hardware
Brockville, ON

locals who ambled by. Christmas music from classical station NPR spilled out onto the street. It all made for a pretty picture and the overall impression was of a kinder, gentler time. Bob played the part to perfection, an old time, small town hardware dealer.

Bob started working at his uncle's store, Smart's Hardware in 1949 when he was 13. After his uncle passed away, the new owners didn't want original family members around. Bob decided that there was no way he was letting anyone throw him out, so with the help of a backer in nearby Kingston, he opened his own store in 1965. In 1966, he joined Home Hardware and ran a booming business for many years. The economics of the region have changed in the years since—most of the manufacturing plants have closed and a lot of the younger people have had to leave the area to find work—but Bob still loves his job. He works six days a week, from 7:15 in the morning to 6 o'clock at night. He has three employees these days. Every Tuesday, his wife Carol, who was a nurse for 44 years, comes in to help unpack the order from the warehouse in St. Jacobs. The store is obviously an institution - the word is that if Billings doesn't have it, they don't make it. "It's a crowded store," Bob acknowledges, "I get people coming in who tell me that Canadian Tire sent them. People from Toronto come in looking for stuff." But it almost all went by the boards. In 2009, at the age of 73, Bob had a heart attack and decided that it was time to sell the business. Fortunately, he had his retirement party (attended by Paul and Walter) before he sold the store because over the course of the evening, his doctor asked him what he planned to do. He'd never had a hobby and his heart condition now curtailed most physical activity - he had been a member of the rowing club for 15 years. The doctor warned, "If you sit around for the next eight months, you won't be around for the ninth." Bob took his words to heart, and went back to work.

Up the road a bit north of the 401 and another world away, you'll find Brockville Home Hardware Building Centre. If Bob's store is a charming time warp, Paul Blakney's HHBC is completely and absolutely up-to-date, all gleaming 30,000 square feet of it. They are so different from one another that it's immediately obvious that the two stores fill completely separate needs: "We are not at all in competition with Bob," Paul says. Paul and his general manager Stefanie Chauvin are quite the team. Their comfortable rapport and joking camaraderie that ease the long hours of

Paul Blakney:

Home Hardware Building Centre
Brockville, ON

hard work make them seem more like brother and sister than owner and manager. They first met in 2001 when Stefanie showed up as a member of the team of merchandisers sent from St. Jacobs to transform the store from a Beaver Lumber into Brockville Home Hardware Building Centre. "It was my first job as a merchandiser for Home Hardware corporate," Stefanie says, although she officially got her start with Home in 1996 at Tecumseh Home Hardware with Larry and Elaine Seguin and family, to whom, she says, she owes a great deal of credit for her successes to date. She must have made an impression, because a few years later, Paul "snagged her," he says gleefully, and she has been there ever since. Paul earned his stripes (he comes from a military family) working with Ken O'Connor who now owns the HHBC in neighbouring Gananoque and who we would be visiting later that week. Like so many former Beaver dealers, Paul cannot say enough about what Home Hardware has done for his business. He admits that some former Beaver dealers "wore green underwear" for a while, but as soon as they saw the new systems changes and product selection, they realized the opportunity they had been given. "It was a big undertaking, and a lot of work," Paul remembers. "The Beaver stores were essentially gutted and ripped apart and the conversion process itself was very cumbersome but we also knew that there was light at the end of the tunnel. We were all excited by how progressive the company was and how many stores there were across the country. And when we saw the pots and pans and kitchen items start flowing in…." Stefanie remembers a former dealer observing that he made 25 cents on a sheet of drywall, but four dollars on a potato brush! Initially, Paul says, it was a bit scary: he wondered, "How are we going to house all this stuff we've never had before?" Since then they have expanded, adding another 10,000 square feet. Which means that there's even more room for all that great product selection, which is, of course, fabulously merchandised throughout the spacious, bright space. "Home Hardware has allowed me to create my own destiny," Paul says.

The original Toledo scale has weighed a lot of hardware over the years and more than carried its weight when it come to generating revenue.

Brad Swanson is a third generation "lumber man," whose grandfather moved from North Dakota to run Beaver Lumber yards in Saskatchewan. In 1982, after running the Franchising Program for Beaver Lumber, Jim Swanson moved his family to Kitchener, Ontario where he took over the Beaver store on Park Street. When his father passed away in 1998, Brad continued the family tradition. Two years later, Home Hardware bought out the 49.9% of the business not owned by Beaver dealers and sold it back to them.

Brad Swanson:

Swanson's Home Hardware Building Centre
Kitchener, ON

Brad remembers that it was an interesting transition. "We went from being a franchise operation to a wholly owned business, which is a totally different environment," he says. "But we also went from a hostile environment to a very trusting environment." At first, the store, along with all other converted Beaver Lumbers, became a Home Building Centre. But Brad quickly realized that the double HH immediately drew in people looking for hardware-related product. Never one to miss a business building opportunity, Brad became a full Home Hardware Building Centre in 2005, which meant they were selling everything Home Hardware had to offer. That was huge, Brad remembers, and for a "lumber guy", a bit scary. "We started getting into pots and pans and fry pans and all those good things. And it was a new world for us." The right sales staff in all the departments was also central to the success of the new business. There are quite a few retirees among the store's almost 60 employees. Brad recognizes that their well-developed people skills and the fact that they like to be busy are important assets. The day we visited to take our photographs, we met two of them: Rick Russell, who was a truck driver for Beaver Lumber in Huntsville before following his future wife to Kitchener, and Matt Harney, a retired police officer and former customer of the store.

Today Swanson's Home Hardware Building Centre is a very large, very busy store: almost 40,000 square feet of warehouse, including a state-of-the-art drive-through lumberyard geared to the contractors who represent 40% of Brad's business, and just under 30,000 square feet of retail space they added to accommodate everything and everyone else. Not bad for a "lumber man."

Gord Dishke has a distinctive way of speaking. His hands seem to grab words out of the air, his brain waiting impatiently for them to be processed then uttered with a conviction lightly seasoned with an acerbic wit. "My mother was an ambitious woman," he says slowly, "and wanted the best for her children." His parents bought a farm when Gord and his brother Garnet were in their early twenties, but by then they had each acquired a trade: Gord trained as an electrician and after a stint in the US, he came

With his father's blessing, Dave changed direction, this time studying architecture. And after two years, he knew exactly where he was going: into the hardware business. He enrolled in a business management course at Mohawk College, taking over as store manager when he finished the course. It was 1995 when Dave and his sister Sara became the second generation of Dishkes in the business. It wasn't easy to convince Gord and Garnet, but their "new fangled" business plan increased sales and profits significantly.

Gordon and David Dishke:

Grand River Home Hardware
Caledonia, ON

"This is David's company. It's not Walter Hachborn's; it's not Ray Gabel's. They work for the dealer."

back home and got a job at Stelco; Garnet was a tool and die maker at International Harvester. Both companies were mainstays in the industrial heyday of nearby Hamilton. Although he admits that he cannot see 20 minutes ahead, Gord can see the shape of things to come four or five years out. It is clearly a family trait because in the late 1960s as farming started to change, the Dishkes knew they either had to get bigger or get out. So in 1971, they bought a farm implements store. They could see the future and it was hardware. The location had parking in abundance as well as a Shell gas station for all those cars pulling into their lot. Home Hardware Area Manager Bill Robinson would stop by regularly for a fill up. Every now and then Bill would ask Gord, "When are you going to join Home Hardware?" And one day, looking ahead a few years, Gord said "Now." The town already had a lumberyard and two other hardware stores, but their application was accepted and in 1984 the Dishkes joined Home Hardware, incorporating and renaming the business Grand River Home Hardware. In 1988 they moved across the road, where they had more room to expand. Which was good because, as Gord recalls, business "took off like a rocket."

Meanwhile, Dave was growing up a hardware kid. He remembers family vacations spent visiting hardware stores, never a highlight for a youngster. He also distinctly remembers when his father and uncle made the decision to join Home Hardware. It was 1984 - Dave and his bike were recruited to deliver the annual catalogue, its front cover indelibly printed on his memory. "We didn't have enough money to mail them out," Dave remembers, "but they had enough money to not pay me."

Throughout high school, Dave worked at the store. When he graduated, he went to college to study horticulture. But he couldn't see where he was going. One day, he asked his father to tell him exactly what he had done from the time he left high school to this very moment as they sat face to face at the kitchen table. According to Dave that talk was "the first step towards what's going on today."

That same year, Gord "retired," but in fact, he just moved into another office and continued to come to work five days a week. And still does almost 20 years later. His wife Charlotte was also a shareholder and worked at the store for many years. Sara left in 1998 and in 2007 Dave bought out the remaining shareholders - his mother Charlotte, his uncle Garnet and cousin Paul.

The old days across the street with 3,500 square feet of retail space have given way to a faster paced, more competitive environment. "My dad and uncle were pretty sharp in the first place," Dave says. He enjoys being part of a dynamic generation making its mark on a well-established and successful company. Their size, - 20,000 square feet of retail space— their hours - seven days a week, 12 hours a day—and their market, with competition both in and around the town, not to mention an unpleasant community situation several years ago, have all offered their own challenges. With 35 employees and three managers, Dave has structured the company to share both responsibility and success, and confesses to "just stealing" Walter Hachborn's original business model. Dave is an active member and vocal proponent of Home Hardware's Young Leaders Group. In 2004, at the urging of Bill Ferguson, he was a candidate for and won the prestigious Young Retailer of the Year Award from The National Hardware Retail Association. In 2006, he was again honoured to receive The Distinguished Alumni Award from Mohawk College. It's all part of a big picture that he can visualize clearly. These days Dave knows with 100% certainty that he made the right career choice.

As long time members of a small town, the Dishkes have always been involved in their community. The one dearest to the hearts of Dishke father and son is the old Caledonia Railway Station built in 1907 by the Grand Trunk Railway to replace an earlier one that burned to the ground on the same site. CN cancelled passenger service in the region in 1957 and the building languished until 1996 when it was abandoned. Ron Clark, who owns The Clark Companies, one of Canada's largest agri-businesses and a leader in many community initiatives, bought it. The building that once boasted the "finest ticket wicket in the country," was restored by volunteers. Handsome once more, today the building houses Caledonia's Chamber of Commerce, its Visitors' Centre and is a popular place for meetings, special events and a favourite spot for wedding pictures.

"My friend and business partner Joel Curtis grounds me with his business acumen and methodical thinking. But we can also leave the business behind and have a few laughs."

This is a story about family and friendship, entrepreneurialism and enthusiasm, hard work and happiness.

Brad O'Neill grew up in a family of achievers – today brother Jason owns seven McDonald's franchises in Ontario cottage country and his other brother Chris heads up Google Canada. Sister Jillian is Director of Marketing for one of Canada's largest Wealth Management companies.

options with different franchisers. Brad and Alana looked at virtually every organization they could think of owning. Finally, their friend Phil Nettleton (of Canadian Pro Marketing, a Home Hardware vendor) suggested Home Hardware. "They treat their vendors, suppliers and employees… with the utmost respect. Their dealers are the core of their values." Brad went on the road with Home Hardware Area Managers to see for himself. He and Alana were living with his parents and sadly, during this time Brad's mother

Brad O'Neill and Joel Curtis:

Cobourg Home Hardware
Cobourg, ON

"Home Hardware is a powerful, powerful company."

And Brad and his business partner Joel Curtis currently own four Home Hardware stores, a number that seems to keep rising. Joel Curtis is no slouch either when it comes to business – before he turned his hand to hardware, he was responsible for taking the MapArt business national.

Brad exhibits an almost giddy delight with his lot in life. And there certainly is a lot in his life. There's his growing family – he and his wife Alana are raising three young children, and the mandatory dogs, in a house on a beautiful property north of Cobourg. There's his boundless energy that ensures he is having fun at whatever is at hand. And there is the business empire that he and his partner Joel Curtis are diligently expanding. The two met over twenty years ago when Brad was working as General Manager of Canadian Tire in Guelph. Joel was running MapArt Canada. They went golfing to devise a strategy to put maps into all CT stores across Canada. Brad lost his 8 iron in a pond, but found a friend for life.

Like a few Home Hardware Dealers of his generation – Brad was 43 in 2011 – Brad grew up in the business, just not at Home Hardware. His dad Ted worked at the T. Eaton Co Ltd as a sports and leisure buyer, so Brad had the first BMX bike in Canada. With the constant travel and the challenges of raising a family, Ted and his wife Lexie made the decision to join Canadian Tire. They landed in Acton and stayed four years. By the time Brad was in high school, the family was off to Goderich where Brad cut his teeth on retail in part-time and summer jobs at his father's store. Ted recognized Brad's drive and talent for merchandising, but also encouraged his boys to try other things. So for three summers, Brad worked as a tree-planter.

After university Brad went to Europe for six months. On his return, Brad accepted a job as a merchandiser at a CTC store in Guelph where he became Store Manager and stayed for almost five years. Meanwhile, his parents moved to Windsor. In 1999 Brad came on board to help his father with construction of a huge new CTC in Scarborough. At a reunion with university friends, Brad met Alana MacDonald who would soon become his wife. Alana quit her job and in 2000 she and Brad moved to Vernon, British Columbia to renovate a CTC. But the fast track at CTC wasn't fast enough for Brad. He wanted to run his own business. In 2004 family realities brought them back to Ontario and he started exploring his

Lexie lost a very short battle with cancer. With nothing clear on the horizon, Brad accepted a job as General Manager at a CTC store in north Toronto. Two days later, the perfect opportunity appeared. The Butcharts in Cobourg wanted to sell their 12,000 square foot Home Hardware store. In typical Brad fashion, the process was fast-tracked; he turned down the other job offer, they made the deal and a very pregnant Alana and Brad took over Cobourg Home Hardware in February 2004.

They kept all the staff: 14 fulltime employees, some part-time and a "professional cardboard crusher" named Johnny Cable, their "special needs" person and general morale booster about the place. Business was good even with some stiff competition coming to town. Brad can't say enough about the support Home Hardware provides its dealers. It's a "powerful, powerful company," he says.

Two years after becoming a Home Hardware Dealer, Brad started looking for another store and began to bounce ideas off Joel Curtis. By now they were almost-neighbours. Joel was a successful businessman who, in his words, "was undergoing a mid-life crisis." He was also blessed with outstanding people skills. They joined forces and bought the HHBC in Port Hope, renovating and transforming it into a "cutting edge HHBC" that did over $300,000 at its three day grand opening in early April 2011. After the Port Hope success, Brad and Joel turned their sights on Newcastle and built a new store that opened in late summer 2011. In October of that year, they took over the HBC in Cobourg.

Is Home Hardware a good program? You bet it is, says Brad. "Especially if you're driven to succeed and you are blessed with an incredible wife who is an amazing mother and a great accountant. I couldn't be more proud to be a Home Hardware Dealer. Proud to help enrich the lives of those we work with and the communities we live in. Proud to enjoy my big Home Hardware family and my immediate family." At his first Home Hardware show, Brad told Paul Straus he was probably the happiest Home Hardware Dealer there was. "I might be a little more mature now," he says a few years later, "but I don't feel any differently."

Early one hot morning in July I arrive at Mar-Span Home Hardware Building Centre outside of Drayton. Large, prosperous farms, many of them Mennonite, spread across the landscape like richly coloured quilts. Six days a week, Mar-Span is a busy place from the moment it opens at 7 o'clock. The contractors show up early, followed by the farmers. I am enjoying a pleasant conversation with Stephen Horst who has worked at Mar-Span for the past three years, when a solid man with a springing step appears and introduces himself as owner Murray Martin. Over the

to build trusses. In short order he had to hire two more to keep up with demand and soon people were asking Murray if he could sell them lumber. Despite a local lumberyard successfully blacklisting him with wholesalers, Nelson Grant from MacMillan Bloedel decided Murray Martin needed a chance. From there, the business grew slowly but steadily.

In 2000, Mar-Span joined the Home Hardware family after a brief stint under the Castle banner. There are many things about Home Hardware

Murray Martin: "My most valuable assets go home every evening and come in the next morning,"

Mar-Span Home Hardware Building Centre
Drayton, ON

phone Murray had been friendly but remote. In person, he is articulate and engaged, with an aura of clarity and conviction. I realize, shortly into our interview, that a profound faith anchors and animates this man.

Murray grew up on a farm five kilometres from the business he owns and operates today. Like his father, Murray always intended to be a farmer. Murray and his new wife Fern bought a pig farm, had their first son Chester and then, the hog market went "into the tank." One day a farmer a few concessions away called looking for Murray Martin, the barn builder. "You've got the wrong Murray Martin," Murray told him. (There are plenty of Martins in the area.) They started talking and Murray who, like most farm boys had been born with a "hand on a hammer and a foot on a ladder," offered to help out for a few weeks. By the time the project was finished they had lined up their next job. Now Murray was in the construction business with 10 employees. It was 1988 and he was 22 years old.

Business was booming but Murray was having difficulty getting trusses. He built himself a small press and created a manufacturing space upstairs in an old barn between the haymow and the granary. (The pigs stayed downstairs.) In those days, three men needed a full day to build twenty forty-foot trusses. (Today, with new technology and equipment, three people produce that many in a half hour.) Murray designed his own truss fabricating equipment and sold the patent rights to an American manufacturer, the royalties covering the costs of building his next plant. For three years Murray worked long hours.

Then Murray and his wife Fern had their second child. Travis was born with a serious heart defect and was not expected to survive. His grieving parents had to make the wrenching decision whether to take him off life support, knowing his tiny body could not bear reconstruction surgery. As Mennonites of a Christian faith, Murray and his family entrust their lives and their lot to God. Their son Travis not only survived, a few days later he was removed from life support. (He was on his honeymoon when we visited.) Murray knew something had to give. "Sometimes when you're burning the candle at both ends you're really not that bright," he says. He sold the construction business to his brother-in-law and kept one employee

that Murray appreciates: "They understand the rural market, have a lot of product and are very strong on the LBM side." Murray especially likes the fact that Home Hardware values people. "My most valuable assets go home every evening and come in the next morning," he says. After joining Home, Murray bought four acres of land on Wellington Road 8 and started building the complex that now houses 16,000 square feet of retail space. A new 14,000 square foot warehouse is adjacent on the same property. The truss plant sits on an additional 10 acres next door.

The busy fleet of Mar-Span trucks - four small trucks, three tractor-trailers and one tri-axle - delivers materials over much of Ontario. Locally much of their business comes from large farms. Mar-Span has 30 to 35 employees on the retail side and another 30 in the truss plant. Which is good because Murray has a lot on the go. He is planning to harvest wheat that afternoon so hopes the badly needed rain holds off a bit longer. His oldest son Chester runs the overhead door sales and service division, his second son Travis operates the farming division and Murray oversees all the marketing. In addition to the HHBC, truss plant and four farms, Murray started another business, Craftsman Hardwoods, to supply the many small Mennonite furniture shops in the area. The manager, Rob Weber, was injured in an accident and Murray essentially created this job for him. Murray also sits on the Canadian Board of a major international charity affiliated with the Mennonite church. One of their recent initiatives is the preparation of dehydrated soup packs made from produce rejected by Canadian food processing plants (25% of all fresh produce is rejected for its malformed shape). Each serving-sized package contains enough protein to fuel a person for 24 hours.

It seems that everything Murray puts his hand to flourishes. He says that his father, who ran a business all his life, gave Murray the valuable gifts of moral support and encouragement. Holding his youngest daughter Karla in his arms, Murray attributes his many successes to God's goodness. "There is a lot of responsibility to use it wisely," he says quietly.

Murray has an interesting formula for calculating the local population: "This township is 10,000 people –not very much – but five cows equals one person – 10 sows (hogs) equals one person – 1000 chickens equals one person. Now we've got millions of population. In the average household, the man goes to the hardware store or the building centre and buys for the three or four people in that household. That same man is now buying for 20 or 30 or 40 people representing our population. So we have to impress that farmer – because the cow can't come in to buy stuff, can she?"

The camaraderie and respect shared by three of Shelburne's cultural ambassadors are evident when they assembled on the stage of The Grace Tipling Concert Hall. John Telfer, Shelburne's CAO and Town Clerk (and avid trumpet player); Murray Fines, owner of Shelburne's HHBC (and Archangel of the arts) and Al Widbur (former owner, now retired, of Stedman's and member of a Barber Shop Quartet for the past 30 years). Murray's cell phone rang incessantly, John used his to track down answers to my many questions and Al gave me local colour. When I asked if he was a customer of Murray's, he did not miss a beat: "Who isn't?"

For a town with a population of just 6,000 people (2011 statistics), Shelburne, Ontario is a very cultured place. In addition to celebrating, in 2012, its 62nd year as the home of the Canadian Open Old Time Fiddle Championship, the town boasts two theatre companies, The Tipling Stage Company with three productions scheduled for its fifth and current season and LP Stage Productions which produces musicals and children's theatre. I suspect that other artistic endeavours abound, such as the Barber Shop

Building Centre, was a member of the Group of Six, as they were soon dubbed. (The five other members were Ed Crewson, Scott Doney, Bill Hill, Brian Horner and Sam Young.) The resurrection of the Shelburne Theatre was part of a more ambitious Economic Community Development plan, of which they were all members, to put the town of Shelburne back on the map. In fact, the process was a true community effort with service clubs, local organizations, companies and generous individuals contributing to

Murray Fines: There's his boundless energy that ensures he is having fun at whatever is at hand.

Fines Home Hardware Building Centre
Shelburne, ON

Quartet I learned about from one of its tenor members, Al Widbur, whom I met in the lobby of the Town Hall on July12, 2012. (Al also sits on the Shelburne Performing and Visual Arts Board of Management.) Covering the lobby walls and up the stairs to the second floor are the works of many local artists, including Laurie McGaw who has been commissioned by The Royal Canadian Mint among others. Her charming portrayal of a grandfather and his grandson playing their fiddles with Fido at their feet is the grand prize for this year's fiddle winner and hangs in pride of place in the foyer. And to my delight, the pharmacy across the street is called Caravaggio.

Much of this artistic activity is staged in the Grace Tipling Concert Hall, on the second floor of the beautiful Shelburne Town Hall. Architect Frank Grant Dunbar, also responsible for neighbouring Orangeville's Town Hall, designed it in 1882. In the late 19th century, Shelburne was a thriving centre: in 1872 the Toronto, Grey and Bruce Railway Line brought prosperity to the town and from 1869 to 1877, its population grew tenfold. For 50 years, the theatre was the area's cultural and social epicentre. Travelling road shows attracted audiences from the town and surrounding countryside who happily gathered for a convivial evening of music or theatricals. But for the majority of the 20th century, Shelburne's concert hall was run down and neglected.

By the early 1990s, the community, "the town above the City (of Toronto)", as the town's enthusiastic Chief Administration Officer and Town Clerk John Telfer calls it, was once again thriving. The Honda plant in Alliston and Shelburne's own KTH auto parts plant have played important roles in the town's most recent renewal. But it was six local businessmen whose drive and vision turned on the house lights once again in Shelburne's Concert Hall. Murray Fines, then owner of the local Home Hardware

the theatre's restoration. Grace Tipling, who played the organ at the local Anglican Church, gave music lessons to the town's children and belonged to several local music groups. When she passed away, the generous bequest she left permitted the restoration of the theatre, named in her honour and to her memory. Part of a designated heritage building, The Grace Tipling Concert Hall has been painstakingly restored to its original glory, including the delicate stencil pattern looping along the ceiling's circumference. With its excellent acoustics, the hall regularly attracts popular artists like John McDermott, Jason McCoy and Amy Sky in addition to the annual Fiddle Championship every August.

Thanks to Murray Fines, five other local businessmen, a committed town council and administration and community, a powerful sense of past and present resonates throughout Shelburne's Grace Tipling Concert Hall. With a long run ensured for the future.

On November 30, 2012, Murray Fines sold his business to Bill Gillam.

Hockey has always played a central role in Bill Gillam's life from his early childhood in Toronto. Born in Cornerbrook, Newfoundland, he inherited a good work ethic from his grandparents, father and mother and with his talent and drive he was able to take his game to a pretty serious level. He earned a hockey scholarship and played for Geneseo State University, a top athletic and academic school in New York State. After university he attended the Philadelphia Flyers rookie camp and played a

In February 2012, Bill was considering five stores, three in Ontario, one in the Maritimes and another in BC. One of the Ontario stores was Fines Home Hardware Building Centre, in Shelburne, that Murray Fines was planning to sell in the next twelve months. Everything accelerated from there and on December 1st, 2012 Bill Gillam became the proud owner and captain of Fines Home Hardware Building Centre, a family-run business for over 22 years.

Bill Gillam: "Murray Fines will be my consultant for the next 10 years. I think of him as a really good friend and respect him and his wife Andrea greatly,"

Shelburne Home Hardware Building Centre
Shelburne, ON

year of pro in the IHL (International Hockey League) for their farm club. Sidelined with a career ending injury, Bill came back to Canada, married his childhood sweetheart and put his undergraduate accounting degree to work at a local CA firm in Peterborough where his friend and mentor had invited him to work for three months. There he found himself doing everything from "shoe box accounting" to audits. His initial three-month commitment turned into six years. One of Bill's audits was on a building centre that had been established in 1878. When the owner passed away suddenly, Bill was asked to step in as interim CEO to the end of the year. In this case, six months turned into 16 years. Once more, Bill put his all into helping to build and expand the building centre and grow the business. When it became evident that the promised partnership was not going to materialize, Bill took his game and the wealth of experience he had acquired and teamed up with his former accounting friend who had sold his CA practice and now owned four Home Hardware businesses in the Peterborough area. His former mentor wanted Bill's help in all four stores, but Bill really wanted to be a partner. And that's exactly what happened. In 2004, the two of them, along with three other partners, built Chemong HHBC, a new state-of-the-art Home Hardware Building Centre. It was Home's first "big box" HHBC, and set the standard for the others that quickly followed. By now Bill had found a home for his well-rounded, multi-faceted background, people skills and interests; a place where both sides of his brain, the artist and the mathematician, were fulfilled. Propelled by boundless energy, Bill was ready for his break away.

Bill is quick to acknowledge the importance of family - he cares for his 95 year-old grandfather as well as both his parents and mother-in-law and he cannot say enough about the support from his wife Carole and their two strapping sons Josh and Mitch who are fine athletes like their dad. So Murray's family oriented business was the first thing that impressed him. "Murray Fines will be my consultant for the next 10 years. I think of him as a really good friend and respect him and his wife Andrea greatly," he says.

Bill knew he was buying a good business: it is always ranked high in annual volume sales in Ontario and he fully intends to continue that trend. Like any good coach, Bill has his team strategy in place. He has plans to enlarge the retail operation and consolidate the various divisions currently dotted across about seven acres of property. In addition, his keen eye is focused on the many subdivisions going up around Shelburne and his intention is to corner as much of that business as possible. But for all his ambition, Bill never loses sight of family: "I am responsible for 55 employees and all their family members as well as Murray and Home Hardware Stores who have made all this possible." The name on the store and the fleet of trucks has changed from Fines Home Hardware Building Centre to Shelburne Home Hardware Building Centre, but the legacy will always live on in the slogan "The Fines Team." And that's just fine with Bill Gillam.

On the shores of Lake Huron, Goderich is an interesting mix: families that have lived there for generations, retirees, cottagers, manufacturing industries and surrounding prime farmland. It seems a charming, tranquil place, dubbed "the prettiest town in Canada" by Queen Elizabeth. That all changed the afternoon of August 21, 2011, when a class F3 tornado

Business was good and Norm and Richard found themselves looking for new growth opportunities. In 2011, they learned that Steve Machan wanted to sell his Goderich store. Discussions were soon underway. By February 2012, the deal was struck but fate almost dealt a very different hand on August 21, 2011. Fortunately, this particular story has a happy ending.

Norm and Richard Watson:

Watson's Home Hardware
Goderich, ON

"The wallet and the heart work together, but sometime the heart has to be bigger than the wallet."

roared off the lake, wreaking havoc and taking one life. It destroyed indiscriminately, levelling homes and businesses in the downtown core and uprooting thousands of trees. But the town is roaring back in the best possible way: rebuilding and restoring and getting on with life.

Fortunately, the Home Hardware store on Bayfield Street on the edge of the downtown core was left unscathed. It was built and opened in 1985 by Ron and Barb Machan who had previously worked at and owned Home Hardware stores in nearby towns. After three years, they sold the business. By then, their two sons Steve and Kevin, true "Home Hardware" kids, were working for the company at the corporate office in St. Jacobs and as merchandisers. In 1991 Steve bought back the Goderich business. He opened a Home Furniture operation within the hardware store in 2005.

In the village of Gorrie one hour away, another Home Hardware family was thriving. Norm and Richard Watson, uncle and nephew, whose slight age difference makes them more like cousins, were operating a busy HHBC. Their family's Home Hardware connection began with Don, Norm's oldest brother and Richard's dad, starting to work at Carson Home Hardware (which had been in the Carson name since 1912) at the age of 12. In 1975 Don and Donna Watson bought out the original owner Richard Carson. In 1978, they built and opened a Home All lumberyard in a new location on the highway. In 1981 Don amalgamated the two busy stores. Norm, who had worked at the store since he was 12 years old, became a partner in 2001. In 2009, Don's son Richard also joined the business and by 2010, uncle and nephew were sole partners.

The sense of family is still strong in the Goderich store. The Watsons may not be true "locals", but Richard's maternal grandparents were from Goderich and his mom Donna went to high school in the town. Although the name on the marquis has changed, the staff hasn't. The Watsons plan to run the business as the "mini combo" Home Hardware and Home Furniture store for the time being. "The wallet and the heart work together," Richard says, "but sometimes the heart has to be bigger than the wallet." They have already bought four acres of land behind the store and hope to build a true "combo" HHBC and Home Furniture store, pending the green light from the town. "People in town know us so we're building on that," Norm says. "We have good loyal customers - contractors that deal with us so now hopefully we will be able to service them even better."

Richard is uncomfortable taking credit for the success of the business: "Dick Carson had a store that did quite well and with Don's determination and hard work, the business thrived and grew, serving a wide variety of customers. We're working to build it further." He is self-deprecating about his career path, but Richard's reality demonstrates another strength of Home Hardware: Richard says that he didn't really pick Home Hardware. Home Hardware picked him. The fact is that many Home Hardware "kids" always have an option to exercise, and that's what Richard did. Whatever his lack of motivation when he was younger, today Richard is enormously enthusiastic about what lies ahead. Home Hardware has a way of doing that to you.

On May 19th, 2012, The Home Hardware Grove was officially unveiled. A partnership between Home Hardware and Tree Canada, it is the first of many new groves that will, over time, restore a 126-acre old growth forest on the edge of town devastated by the 2011 tornado. Once the home of scenic walking trails and century-old trees, the parkland behind the town cemetery is slowly rejuvenating, a vivid example of the opposing powers of nature.

HOME
HARDWARE

GROV'E
MAY 19 2012

COMMUNITY CENTRE

Although Harry says Niagara-on-the-Lake is a sleepy community, it has a beautiful new community centre with a library. The new arena is not far away. Across the highway in neighbouring St Catharines a new hospital is under construction. Penner Home Hardware Building Centre has contributed thousands of dollars to them all.

Harry, Marlene, Kevin and Marcia Penner.

In the late 1940s, Harry Penner's industrious father Peter, who owned a 10-acre farm and did some building on the side, decided that the town of Virgil needed a lumberyard. So he opened one. Pretty much on a shoestring budget, Harry remembers. Peter subdivided the farm to accommodate the lumberyard. And then, almost imperceptibly, it became a hardware store, saws and hammers, pots and pans appearing on the shelves. The business grew, the inventory disappeared and had to be replaced with increasing regularity and Harry's dad soon learned that it wasn't possible to be in two places at once. Peter Penner gave up farming and devoted himself

Today Penner's Home Hardware Building Centre still sits on the piece of land that housed the family's first store. Over the years it has expanded from the original 2-1/2 acres to a total of 13. The old building was absorbed over the years and the store grew, long and skinny, to its present dimensions of 80 feet by 527 feet. A big drive-through lumberyard sits behind the store. Harry and Marlene's son Kevin and his wife Marcia have taken over the day-to-day running of the business, leaving them more time to indulge their wanderlust. They say it's easy to go when they know the business is in the hands of people they trust.

Harry Penner: Today Penner's Home Hardware Building Centre still sits on the original piece of land that housed the family's first store.

Penner's Home Hardware Building Centre
Virgil, ON

fulltime to the lumber and hardware business. His wife started working in the store at the same time. Harry left school at age 16 and joined his parents and siblings Elden and Miriam full time at the store.

Like many independent hardware stores and lumberyards, Penner's Lumber purchased materials and stock from a variety of wholesalers. Even after they joined Home Hardware in 1964, they still bought building materials from another company, a situation that nobody questioned for several years. Then in the early 1990s, someone challenged this practice and told Harry that either he committed 100% to Home Hardware or Home Hardware might not be committed to him. Harry explained to his Area Manager Bill Robinson that he was not quite ready to make a commitment and asked if he would speak to Walter on his behalf. Walter's reply was straightforward: "Leave Harry alone," he said. "He'll come when he's ready." In 1995, Harry was ready. It was a decision he has never regretted. Walter's rationale, he later explained to Harry was: "We have 1,200 stores and 1,200 dealers. And they're all different." For Harry Penner, that story sums up Walter's wisdom and the company's success.

Like his dad before him, Kevin grew up in Virgil, which was actually incorporated into the town of Niagara-on-the-Lake in 1970, two years before he was born. And while the area is still known for its peaches and other produce that thrive in its soft climate, a flourishing wine industry has also taken root in recent years. The Shaw Festival attracts visitors from all over to the centre of the picture-perfect town just a few kilometers down the road from the store. It is not uncommon for tour buses to stop into the Penners' store. Kevin says all customers are welcome, pointing out the challenges inherent in a location that is surrounded on two sides by water and on the third by the US border. They work hard to attract and keep their loyal customer base. Anna Olson, who lives in nearby Welland, often shops in the store.

Harry has seen it all grow up around him. In the early days, there was a service station across from the store. Every now and then Harry would have to go over for something. "You'd look both ways because that's what your mother taught you to do – right? Twice both ways and then you'd just saunter across. Today you wait a long time and when you go you run."

Humble Beginnings, by Harry Penner

I remember a meeting we had in 1965 to bring us up to date on what was happening at Home Hardware.
It was at a dealer's store in Niagara Falls. The meeting was held in the dealer's glass-cutting room, a tiny room about
10 feet by 10 feet. There were 12 of us crowded into it. The table was just covered with stuff: There were binders spread
out on the cutting table along with some tools that Home Hardware had bought for a special price. After the meeting
adjourned, I passed Walter who was standing by the front door. He said something to me that I didn't grasp at first. He
repeated it and I realized he was speaking German - I didn't know that he spoke German until then. He was saying,
"Home to St. Jacobs." With all the time he spent meeting with the dealers, holding meetings and all the other things he
did in those days, he was always happy to head home to St. Jacobs at the end of the day.

In late July 2012, Harry and Marlene headed west in his 2011 orange Camaro on a 13,000 kilometer journey that
fulfilled several of Harry's main passions - his love for the family business, his love of adventure and his love for his hot new
Camaro. In just over four weeks, they visited 26 Home Hardware stores from northern Ontario to Vancouver Island: "The
biggest and the best," Harry says. It was all in the name of research: The Penners are getting ready for their next major
expansion - the last one was in 1985 - and wanted to see what others had done before they finalize their designs and
start building. The last expansion saw them grow to 20,000 square feet of retail; this one, scheduled to begin in 2015, will
expand the floor space to 42,000 square feet, squaring off the long, thin retail space that grew out of the original two story
store on the corner of Penner and Highway 55 leading into Niagara-on-the-Lake. Some of the old warehouses filled with
treasure from a bygone era will have to be demolished, but the big drive - through lumberyard will be that much closer
to the store. Harry remembers his father's cautious frugality as he built his business, and that admirable quality is evident in
Harry's approach as well. But the tales he told of the trip and the way he rewed his motor and booted across the parking
lot suggest that there are times when Harry throws caution to the winds and enjoys himself to the utmost.

Intriguing nooks and crannies beckon as I make my way to the owners' office at the back of Sayer's Home and Décor Centre in Hagersville. David and Cheryl Sayer, who bought the business from David's parents Oliver and Bernice in 1987, sit across from one another at two large desks pushed together, as comfortable as two peas in a pod. Cheryl constantly and quietly works away as she talks, sorting through papers, making quick efficient phone calls. David leans back and gets lost in his stories, which are virtually nonstop. David is a man who, although he speaks quietly, seems to use a lot of capital letters, which is fitting for someone who lives large in the small town of Hagersville.

And Walter, who had never met us, says, 'Hi David, hi Cheryl – how are you? How are Oliver and Bernice?' AMAZING!"

David's endless enthusiasm for life is also amazing. The Sayers give back as much as they get: their reputation for community involvement is well deserved. Their first major fundraising project, featured in a Home Hardware television commercial still memorable over 10 years later, was for The West Haldimand Hospital and Healthcare Foundation. "The first auction in 2000 had one sponsor," David recalls. "It SHOULD have been called the Home Hardware Auction." Susan Coe, Manager of Development

David Sayer: The Sayers give back as much as they get: their reputation for community involvement is well deserved.

Sayer's Home Hardware
Hagersville, ON

You can't miss Sayer's Home and Décor Centre when you drive into town: just look for the sign painted on the wall that abuts their corner parking lot: "We're Proud to Call Hagersville Our Home." The words have always been more than a slogan to the three generations of Sayers who have made this pretty southern Ontario town their home since Oliver Sayer arrived in Canada on a transport ship at the age of 15. An English orphan from The National Children's Home and Orphanage (founded in 1868 by a Methodist minister), Oliver was "hired" by George Risdel, from a line up of seven boys in Hamilton's Gore Park. (When Oliver saw the movie Titanic years later, the scene in the boiler room moved him to tears.) A few years later, George became Oliver's uncle-in-law when Oliver married Bernice Harvey in September 1937. By now, Oliver was an interior decorator. One day in 1952, he went into Smith's Hardware Store in Hagersville to buy a gallon of paint thinner. By the time he left, he owned the business. The family - his wife Bernice, three kids and a dog, - lived upstairs. In the 1960s they joined Pro Hardware. During one particularly lean period, the bailiff arrived to shut them down. Oliver phoned the company's CEO who interceded on their behalf. The bailiff told Oliver, "You have one mighty nice friend there." A few years later, when Walter Hachborn asked Oliver about changing banners, Oliver told him that story to explain why, even though he knew Home's programs would be better, he needed to remain with Pro. "You're a better man than most," Walter said.

In 1995, the time was right to join the Home Hardware family. Wardell's Home Hardware store across the street from their Pro store was for sale. By now, their youngest son David and his wife Cheryl had bought out his parents, although David wisely kept them on as "two great employees." Gord Dishke, who owned the Home store in neighbouring Caledonia took Dave out to lunch. "Either you buy it or I will," he said. They took the hint and changed banners without ever closing, moving the Home Hardware inventory across the street into their store. The spike in growth was instantaneous, David remembers, with people like Tony Krotz and Paul Deacon, who merchandised the store, making the transition easy. That spring David and Cheryl attended their first market. "I pointed Walter out to Cheryl," David remembers. "All of a sudden there was a tap on my shoulder.

for the hospital and Foundation told me that Dave's commitment to the Foundation and passion for the auction ever since have made it the town's premier annual event. In typical David fashion, he deflects the compliment, passing it along to Ray Gabel who is responsible for the wealth of donations to their organization. What makes the story especially compelling is that the mammography unit likely saved the life of the very first patient screened. Last year, the auction raised $51,000 in one night-"HA," David says. "HOW DO YOU LIKE THAT?" When we visited the small rural hospital, both Susan and David pointed out the donor display in the front lobby. Home Hardware Stores Limited has consistently been listed in the top tier. Sayer's Home Hardware is also part of the Ontario Government Passport for Prosperity Program that places co-op students in retail positions and in 2006 was one of four recipients of the Employer Champion Award.

Over the busy years David and Cheryl have also raised their own four girls, along with a few honorary "adoptees" - "I got a DOG and named him SON," Dave jokes - in their beautiful home with its lovely garden just a few blocks from the store. (Dave's uncle, Linus Gowan, in those days Canada's foremost beekeeper, originally owned the house.) They find time to travel in between all their other activities and commitments. When I made a follow up call to David, he regaled me with the story of their recent weekend - a collective 60th birthday party for everyone of that vintage in their hometown. "There were 220 people in a hall that holds 189," David says. Needless to say, a fabulous time was had by all.

The Sayers have recently turned their combined energy and efforts to the newly established Hagersville Food Bank, with David serving as Chair and Cheryl sitting on the Committee. To say that they have a lot on their plates is an understatement. Thanks to them, you can rest assured that soon the recipients of the Hagersville Food Bank will too.

Cheryl and David Sayer with Susan Coe,
Manager of Development for
West Haldimand Hospital.

43

Over the course of researching this book, I have encountered several traditional hardware stores in small towns across the country. But when I visited E.W. McKim Quality Home Hardware, in July 2012, I felt as though I had walked into a Charles Dickens novel. The name has the right tone, the building dates to 1824, and there has been a store on the premises since the mid 1800s.

Although a fire in the 1940s destroyed much of the original interior of the store, the 19th century still whispers from the wooden floors, the worn countertops, the old fashioned ladder that provides access to overflowing shelves up in the rafters. But pride of place belongs to the ancient wooden wheel to be found up the worn staircase, through the over-painted old

seems to suit her. Each of her four sons has worked in the store over the years and today the youngest, 17 year-old Jordan, is upholding the family tradition. Lyn is also shy, but like her uncle, she becomes animated when speaking of the business they both clearly love. Lyn says that when the time comes and she takes over the business, she intends to keep the store true to her uncle, much as he upheld the tradition, even the name, of Ed McKim, over the years. The customers are not shy to attest to its enduring appeal. Jack McNiven, who barrelled through the back entrance brandishing a rubber belt from a lawn mower and made a bee-line straight to Bob, is 78 years old. He has been a customer since he was old enough to "walk, talk or work." Bob and he are quickly engaged in an animated discussion about belts, but not before Jack informs me that this is the best hardware store

Bob Mott and Lyn Pacheco:

E. W. McKim Quality Home Hardware
Ingersoll, ON

door that opens with a creaking pulley. There it stands in all its silent magnificence, a relic from another era that once hoisted up inventory for storage on the second floor. It is no longer in use only because the original manufacturer could not be tracked down to provide a safety certification. Product is still delivered and carried manually through first and second floor entrances at the back - there are no elevators, just narrow staircases.

When we first spoke over the phone, owner Bob Mott seemed a bit tongue-tied. But when I visited his store, his shyness dissipated in the face of my enthusiasm. He should be used to it by now - people have been exclaiming over the store's character and charm since Bob was hired by then-owner Ed McKim in 1955. Originally an independent hardware store that purchased its inventory from a variety of wholesalers including Hollinger Hardware, E.W. McKim joined Home Hardware in December 1964. So while technically not a Charter Member, E.W. McKim has been part of the Home Hardware family since its first momentous year. Bob bought shares from Ed, and became the owner outright in 1977 when Ed retired.

Today the store still consists of three storefronts along the town's high street, each one a mere 22 feet wide by 100 feet long. The original store occupied two of those storefronts, with the second one selling appliances. In 2000 Bob bought the third store, formerly Sears, and amalgamated all three. The original arches, doorways, old windows and other architectural details still remain, although obscured by shelves, bins and boxes of product.

It is somehow in keeping with the Dickensian quality of the place that Bob's niece Lyn Pacheco will be taking over the business when Bob retires. (Bob never married and lives in an apartment over the third "store".) Having grown up with a military father, Lyn says Ingersoll was "home as much as home could be" in those days of cross Canada postings. She has lived in Ingersoll since 1988, and has worked at the store since 1990. Before joining the family business, Lyn worked as a bricklayer, a welder, a plant manager, broadcast engineer, lifeguard, swimming coach. Owning a hardware store

around. Lyn tells me later that although Jack calls himself a hobby farmer, the McNiven family are well-known horse breeders. Jack's farm Killean Acres was home to Canadian Horse Racing Hall of Fame standard bred inductee (2006) Running the Table, a winner in his own right during his three-year career in the 1960s and sire and grandsire of world champions.

As we leave a store that has successfully kept one foot firmly planted in tradition and the other marching steadily into the future, a colourful montage on the hoardings above catches my eye. The work of local artists Cathy Groulx and Rita Milton, and the initiative of the Ingersoll BIA, the murals, depicting household products from a bygone era, were officially unveiled at a ribbon cutting ceremony on May 7th, 2011. (Thanks to Mary Vanderhoeff who has worked at E.W. McKim since 1986 and who quickly thrust the information pamphlet into my hand before I had a chance to open my mouth.)

Ingersoll itself has an interesting history. It was founded in 1793 by Thomas Ingersoll who came to Canada from Massachusetts after the American Revolution. He was granted 66,000 acres of land and founded a town that he called Oxford-on-the-Thames. His son renamed it Ingersoll in his honour in 1852. His oldest daughter Laura (Ingersoll) Secord gained immortality for warning the British of an impending American attack during the War of 1812. Not to mention those delicious chocolates. The surrounding farmland was home to flourishing dairy farms and for years the town of Ingersoll produced internationally acclaimed cheese. In 1866 a locally made "Big Cheese" weighing 7,300 pounds, was exhibited at the Saratoga State Fair in New York and travelled to shows across England. A mere 300 pounds of cheese made the return trip home to be consumed by worthy locals. Today several manufacturing facilities in the area provide employment and, located just off the 401 and only 10 minutes from London, the town of Ingersoll is a pretty bedroom community not far from anywhere. I am disappointed to have to conclude that although he made it to Montreal on his 1842 reading tour, Charles Dickens never visited Ingersoll. If he had, he would have loved it, I am sure. Particularly E.W. McKim Quality Home Hardware.

I experience a momentary trepidation en route to Bradford Home Hardware in Bradford, Ontario as I realize I am about to officially meet the company's then Chairman of the Board for the first time. But my concerns are immediately dispelled by Jim Schaefer's warm welcome.

As he ushers me into his office, with a strategic bird's eye view of the store's busy aisles and checkout counter, Jim gestures to an oversized binder on the credenza that, he informs me, details the responsibilities of the Chairman. "It's an amazing thing to find yourself in the position where all your colleagues want you to represent them as the Chairman and the price. It's a simple but effective approach that has been responsible for the loyal, long-term clientele that keeps coming through the doors of the 12,000 square foot store that the Schaefers finally built in 1987, ten years after moving to Bradford. This customer loyalty is in evidence when we visited in December 2011, in the midst of a year of roadwork that played havoc with access to the store's parking lot and caused a lot of general inconvenience. It's the same philosophy at the heart of their community involvement: they keep it simple and support kids' sports, boys and girls, summer and winter, church groups, The Cancer Society, Heart and Stroke and other good causes across the board and throughout their community.

Jim Schaefer: Jim has always believed in the power of hard work and the importance of participating and making a contribution.

Bradford Home Hardware
Bradford, ON

ultimate authority in the company," he says. "Home Hardware is a big company – I think there are 22,000 employees across the country including retail and the decisions made by the Board affect everyone. It's a big responsibility and a real honour to have their trust."

Jim's road to becoming Chairman in 2009, acclaimed every year since, is a good illustration of Home Hardware's management style and philosophy. The fourth generation of a hardware family in Bolton, Ontario, Jim grew up in the business. He and his wife Elsa worked in and then bought the business from his father Bert in 1971.

When Jim bought the business from his dad their primary supplier was Dominion Hardware. Jim served on their dealer steering committee and quickly realized that it wasn't the right organization for them. "They were focused on their own interests—it wasn't for the dealers," he remembers. Over the years, because the Schaefers had also bought merchandise from Hollinger Hardware, they received an invitation to one of Home's markets. Their first Home Hardware experience was not auspicious: when they showed up, they were refused admission because they were not members. But shortly thereafter, Frank Hammer, the district's Area Manager who Jim remembers as "a prince of a man", made a cold call to their store. Jim was more than ready to listen and they joined very soon afterwards. The Schaefers were Frank's first conversion to Home Hardware, a memory that both Frank and Jim hold dear.

In 1978, just a few years after joining Home, the Schaefers moved the business from Bolton to Bradford. They stuck to their plan, built a good business and three years later, in the midst of a recession and sky-high interest rates, they had the money to buy the property next door. With foresight and good planning, they kept their overheads low and weathered the difficult economic times that saw all three of their competitors close their doors within a month of one another. For the next 25 years, Schaefer's Home Hardware was the only game in town. Despite this monopoly, they prided themselves on offering their customers good service, selection and

Jim's credo is simple. He came up through the ranks. His "business degree" was acquired on the floor of their store. "With Home Hardware, there are a lot of tools available to dealers and we were able to make that work for us. It was so much better than trying to figure it out ourselves. The fact that Home Hardware is a Dealer-Owned company is what makes it really work. Everybody has a vested interest and we all work to help each other. It's a great system. All those people in the aisles of the store aren't here because I'm a great guy, they're here because Home Hardware has merchandising and marketing programs that work, and we use them."

Jim has always believed in the power of hard work and the importance of participating and making a contribution. All that hard work has paid off in so many ways. In 1999 Jim was first elected to the Board of Directors, the year that Home acquired Beaver Lumber, representing the more than 75 stores in District Five. In the year 2000, the Schaefers won the Walter J. Hachborn Store of the Year Award. In 2009 he was elected Chairman of the Board, acclaimed every year until he retired from that position in April 2012. He was on the special committee that drafted Home's five-year plan and is proud to have been part of that process, even prouder that much of it has already been executed. But he is perhaps most proud of the fact that, during his tenure as Chairman, Walter Hachborn was named President Emeritus, in enduring recognition of his role as founder of the company, and Paul Straus became President and CEO of Home.

> "When we joined Home Hardware, we changed over to Home's computer system. Frank Hammer, who lived in St Jacobs, came to the store several nights in a row and we worked together into the wee hours of the morning to get it done. That philosophy has made Home Hardware."
>
> Jim and Elsa's son, Jim Jr., and daughter, Holly, the fifth generation of Schaefers in the business, are actively involved in Bradford Home Hardware's present and future operations. The future looks bright!

Jim seems like too nice a guy to brandish a baseball bat at anyone but on a couple of occasions in the early days, he did carry one around, just in case. The first time was in 1978 when the Schaefers built their store in Bradford. They were in such a hurry to get it up and running that the first delivery of merchandise arrived before the door locks had been installed or the electricity turned on. Jim spent a night in the store along with his trusty bat, protecting the product. He prefers not talk about the other occasions he could have used that bat. Simply put, he'd rather concentrate on the many "Home" runs he and his family have had as Home Hardware Dealers.

While Ivan recalls Walter saying that Henry Sittler wasn't afraid to offer a nickel if something was worth a dollar, Walter could run rings around him in sales.

Kraemer Woodcraft on Henry Street in St. Jacobs enjoys the distinction of being the only Charter member of Home Hardware that is not an actual retail hardware store. As a manufacturer and distributor of store fixtures and custom millwork, it is also in the unique position of being a vendor as well as a dealer, buying product from the warehouse then selling it back to Home in a modified form.

It all came about in the natural way of good neighbours: Daniel Kraemer, who bought the original business, NE Martin Woodworking (est. 1936) in 1951, was quite a people person, his son Ivan remembers, and Walter Hachborn, who was no slouch himself in that department, would often

Walter talked quietly, but when he spoke, you listened. On one occasion, Kraemer was backed up with orders and Home Hardware called about a rush job. Ivan said he couldn't promise the job within the time frame required. Moments later, the phone rang. Walter said, "I hear you can't handle our business anymore." Kraemer got the job done. On time.

Like everyone else, Ivan has always been in awe of Walter, attributing Kraemer's success, and the success of several other businesses in the community, to the fact that Walter believed in them and gave them the chance to flourish and grow. He loves the fact that Walter always remained loyal to his community, refusing to consider relocating to Toronto. He

Ivan and Terry Kraemer: Kraemer Woodcraft is still the preferred millwork vendor for Home Hardware stores across the country.

Kraemer Woodcraft
St. Jacobs, ON

drop in for a visit. By the early 1950s, Kraemer was supplying fixtures to both Hollinger and its dealer-customers. With their habit of thinking big, before too long, Walter and Henry Sittler got it into their minds that Kraemer Woodcraft should become a national supplier of hardware fixtures. One day they set up a meeting for Daniel at the Canadian Retail Hardware Association in Toronto. When he realized the scope of the undertaking, Daniel demurred, but on the drive back to St Jacobs, Walter, Henry and Daniel decided that Kraemer could handle the business for the stores with whom Hollinger was already associated.

When Home Hardware came into being in 1964, Daniel, in his own way of "thinking big", wanted to be part of the innovative venture and approached Walter about becoming a member. Given that Kraemer was not and would never be a retailer, it took some persuading, but the Board accepted Kraemer Woodcraft as a Charter Member.

Daniel's son Ivan may have retired in 2002, but when he walks through the workshop at Kraemer Woodcraft, he greets everyone by name. He has a ready laugh and a soft pleasing accent, remnants of his upbringing on an Old Order Mennonite farm in the St. Jacobs countryside. In those early days, he remembers, Walter had a drafting board set up in his office in the retail store downtown. After school, and on weekends, Ivan would go in and the two of them would work on store planning. "Walter taught me store design," he says. After he finished school, Ivan started working in his father's shop, becoming part owner and foreman in 1960, the year he got married. He bought the business from his father in two stages, owning it outright by 1964. In the early years of Home Hardware, Ivan remembers, both Walter and Ray Gabel would often be part of the merchandising crews that set up stores across Ontario and the East Coast. Ivan remembers impromptu fishing expeditions and spontaneous sightseeing trips that would unfold if the work got done early.

always had a terrific people sense, and almost always knew if a dealer would make it or not. "He could spot it," Ivan remembers. "And I think a bit of it rubbed off on me. It got to the point that when a potential customer walked in the door, I knew within 10 minutes if he was our cup of tea or not." Ivan and his wife now spend most of the winter in Florida. His son Terry, the current President of the company, and another partner, Michael MacLean, now operate the business that still stands on its original location across the street from the corporate offices of Home Hardware. (Ivan had at one point figured out the company has experienced 16 additions to the original buildings.) Some of the company's employees are second and third generation as well. Looking back over the years, Ivan marvels again at the wonderful relationship that has weathered the economic vicissitudes of five decades. They may have stopped making wooden ladders and Crokinole boards due to lack of demand, but working with Home Hardware's store planning department, Kraemer Woodcraft is still the preferred millwork vendor for Home Hardware stores across the country.

With three busy Toronto stores, one in the affluent Leaside-Lawrence Park neighbourhood, another in the popular Beach, and the third, Toronto East Home Hardware, on the urban Danforth strip in between, no one can call Malcolm Firkser a shirker. But he confesses that he may have been one when he arrived from South Africa with his parents Bernie and Zelda and two older brothers Richard and Jeff in 1979.

After almost three years studying at Seneca College and working part time in the store, Malcolm acquired some gravitas and went into the Home Hardware business full time. That allowed Bernie to slow down a bit. Then in 1988, Jeff and Malcolm opened their own store, Sunnybrook Home Hardware. Bernie supplied guidance and collateral for the loan, and kept a close eye on the finances of the new business. In fact, it was Bernie who

Malcolm Firkser:

Toronto Beaches Home Hardware
Toronto, ON

City hardware stores have a special quality, tending toward the small and intimate. With their narrow aisles and crowded shelves, they are reminiscent of the old-style hardware stores we remember from childhood.

The Firksers were part of a major exodus from South Africa at that time. When their original business plan fizzled, a fellow South African, Ray Gork, who owned a Home Hardware store on Bayview Avenue in north Toronto, told Bernie about a Toronto store that was available and set up an introduction with Home Hardware corporate. Malcolm remembers the family's first visit to St Jacobs. Walter Hachborn had taken off the day to spend with them. While Bernie and his wife Zelda were busy with Paul Straus, Walter took the boys on a tour of the warehouse and corporate offices, and then drove them around the Kitchener-Waterloo area. As they passed the University of Waterloo, Walter told Malcolm that he should study business there. Malcolm, who had just finished high school and mandatory army service, wasn't keen for more training. Plus, he admits, at the time, he was "too scared to even think of venturing beyond Toronto." He says he regrets not taking that advice.

Meanwhile, everything was progressing at a rapid pace and in late January 1980, the Firksers opened their first store: Morningside Home Hardware in Scarborough. But Malcolm did not much impress Bill Ferguson, who helped with the transfer of the store. "I don't think Bill liked me much back then," Malcolm admits. "We were both kids, but I was more interested in the girls than hard work. " A South African accent was a novelty in those days, and Malcolm says that his social life "increased ten-fold." While Malcolm was playing, Bill was working extremely hard. It was Bill who taught the Firksers Canadian terminology, trained them on the unfamiliar systems, and helped the family move into their new home after a few months of living at a motel. All these years later, Bill still teases Malcolm. But if Malcolm lacked focus in those first few years, his father did not, quickly realizing the potential offered by Home Hardware.

taught Malcolm that most valuable of retail lessons: "He always watched the bank loan and every six months we'd get a lecture about cash-flow. We always knew when it was coming: his shoulders would droop more and more and more and when his head hit the desk we knew it was lecture time."

In 1996, the two brothers bought a third store in north Toronto, Newtonbrook Home Hardware. They kept it for five years. In 2001, Malcolm bought out his brother, closed the north Toronto store keeping just the Sunnybrook location - they had sold Morningside in 1991. He waited until 2009 to expand again, opening Toronto East Home Hardware on the Danforth that year and The Beaches Home Hardware in 2011.

City hardware stores have a special quality, tending toward the small and intimate. With their narrow aisles and crowded shelves, they are reminiscent of the old-style hardware stores we remember from childhood or summers at the cottage. There's that hardware smell and the sense that somewhere you will find precisely the wing nut or widget you need to finish the project you started. It's a store size that works well for Malcolm.

This has always been a family business and despite the fact that Malcolm is now sole owner of three busy stores, he honours the memory and roles played by his parents Bernie and Zelda. When he opened the store in the Beaches, he gave it the business name of Zellie Investments, in memory of his mother Zelda, who passed away October 30, 2009, one week after he opened his second store, Toronto East Home Hardware on the Danforth near Woodbine. Two years later, he pushed up the opening date of The Beaches Home Hardware to March 19, his father's birthday. "The store has both their imprints on it," Malcolm says.

Zelda Firkser: June 13, 1926 - October 30, 2009
Bernie Firkser: March 19, 1925 - October 12, 2012

One summer Saturday morning, a customer came in at a 10 o'clock and bought a lawn mower. A staff member checked it, as usual, to ensure that it was operating. The customer said thank you and went home. About two hours later, he was back, the veins in his neck and forehead pulsing. "He was wild," Michael recalls and informed him he'd sold him a piece of crap. He was yelling "up and down and sideways" in front of all the other customers, of course. Michael said, "Let's take a look." He took the lawn mower out of the trunk of the fellow's car, unscrewed the gas cap and peered inside - it was empty. So he topped it up, and started the mower with one pull. "It's running perfectly," Michael said. The guy, who was still livid, asked, "What did you do?" When Michael told him, the red ran out of the man's face. Mike says he has never seen anyone beat such a hasty retreat.

I would always see Michael Mirsky, owner of Manotick Home Hardware on the Rideau River, at the Home Hardware markets: whenever he loped by he always had a happy wave, a big hello and a funny story to tell. So perhaps the best way to tell his story is through a few of the many anecdotes he shared with me during our interview for this book.

Michael Mirsky: "I would say that there are two sides to Walter: He's in love with life and he's in love with people."

Manotick Home Hardware
Manotick, ON

In the late seventies, the town of Manotick was largely undeveloped: Michael remembers that west of main street "was one row of houses and a fairground. On the east side of Manotick there was residential area between the Rideau River and main street, which was no more than six or seven blocks. Two gas stations, one restaurant and hardware store a small grocery store tucked around the corner, a small hotel that was sitting there, a couple of hairdressers and feed stores and that was about it." But Michael's father was a visionary and saw this small town as a big opportunity. He started buying up property and became a player in town development. Herb Freitag, who already owned the town's hardware store, bought land from Michael's dad and built a new store. Shortly thereafter, he was diagnosed with MS and knew that sooner rather than later, he would have to sell the business. By now, Michael was ready to exit the soft drinks business that his father had sold to Crush that had in turn sold to Proctor and Gamble. He wanted to get into retail and knew that there were only three possibilities for him: a grocery store, a drug store or a hardware store. No matter what the economy, these are three things no community can be without. Herb won and Michael bought him out "Lock, stock and barrel."

A month after he bought the business in 1987, Michael went to the Home Hardware spring market "all decked out in his red coat." The Freitags were there to show him the ropes. In those days, dealers still pushed around huge order books piled on top-heavy vertical metal carts. "I started going booth by booth," Michael remembers, "checking every item off dutifully. Almost halfway through the second day, Herb's wife Marilyn said, 'You'd better get moving or you won't get finished.' She said that Herb always took one side and she took the other. I said, 'You didn't tell me that when I started. I could have brought my wife down with me and I would have had it done.' That was my first market – I never really did get it finished."

Michael and his dad were invited to Herb's farewell party at the local arena. There were speeches. Afterwards people were milling about and "a little guy, 5'6" - Ottawa Valley to the core - straw hat on, green and green combination, and a twinkle in his eye, Irish," walked up to Michael. "He squinted up at me and said, 'I don't like you.' 'I beg your pardon?' I said. 'I don't like you,' he repeated. 'I'm not shopping at your store.' I shook my head and thought, that's a neat introduction to Manotick! Three weeks later, I took over the store and the first day, in walked this guy. He said 'I'll give

you a try, but don't screw up. 'I said 'Okay - what's your name by the way?' 'Gord Scott,' he said, 'And don't you forget it.' He was in that store at least four times a week for years, always raising Cain. I'd say, 'Gord, go away.' And he'd say, 'I'm not shopping in here again.' But the next day he'd be back. Gordon became more and more of a family pest. If I saw him in the store, I'd know exactly what he was going to do. One year, in the early 90s the Home Hardware Board of Directors held its annual meeting in Ottawa. Mine was one of the stores they would be visiting. I had done the spit and polish thing. They were supposed to arrive in 10:30. At 10 o'clock in walks Gord and I thought, 'Oh God, if Walter sees this…' I remember the bus pulling up and I said 'Gord, you've got to go now. You're going to make me lose my store – get out!' And, he timed it perfectly - as everybody was walking in, he was walking out saying, 'I'll never shop in here again!' He came back in two minutes later and said, 'Until tomorrow.' And then, off he went. I was shaking my head. That was Gordie Scott. A heart as big as all outdoors."

During the Ice Storm of 1998, the power at the store was out for a week. The store remained open, receiving shipments of batteries and kerosene and other supplies. They ran out of essentials very quickly. On delivery day, people were already waiting patiently in the cold for the truck to arrive. Michael still marvels at how the drivers made it through to his and other stores in the area: the power was out; there were trees down all over. They never bothered to stock the shelves, just setting the product out on tables. There was no operating cash register, but the staff kept a record of every sale, writing it all down, and using a solar calculator to add up the tax. If it was a charge account, people signed for it, the old fashioned way. A staff member took a terminal home to process the charges. And so they kept the store going. At home, the Mirskys had power until the first Wednesday after the storm. His wife had the fireplace blazing and everyone, including the dog, was huddled around it. There was an air of adventure in the room. By Friday night, his wife was shivering, the kids were shivering, even the dog was shivering. The fire was going full tilt. Michael said, "Guys, we're out of here." They spent the night at a hotel and Michael went to work the next day. That afternoon his wife called to say the power was back on at the house. Four days later it came back on in the store. The temperature had gone from 70 to 38 degrees. It took a day for the temperature to return to normal. But the community was grateful that the store had remained open and after life returned to normal, there were thank you letters and plenty of homemade pies dropped by the store as gestures of gratitude.

Herb Freitag is in a wheelchair these days, having lost his legs to the Multiple Sclerosis that resulted in him selling his business to Michael Mirsky in 1987. He grew up in the hardware business, working at his uncle's store in Eganville, and became a buyer in Ottawa for another firm. In 1959, he and his wife Marilyn, who was a nurse, moved from Pembroke and bought a small hardware store in downtown Manotick. He bought merchandise from independent wholesalers, including Hollinger and was invited by Wes Garvin to attend the meeting at the Flying Dutchman and be part of the study group that went to the US to research the best business model. He became a Charter Member of the fledgling Home Hardware organization in 1964 and has nothing but good memories of the early days with Walter, Paul Straus and Ray Gabel - all so young then, he recalls. He sat on the Board of Directors briefly, only resigning because, with just two people running the store, it was too difficult for him to get to the monthly meetings in St. Jacobs.

He had been in the business for 30 years when he contracted Multiple Sclerosis and had to sell. One day he was walking up the street when he ran into Michael Mirsky's father who owned the plaza that by then housed Herb's store. After Herb told him why he was selling, Michael's dad suggested to his son that they buy out Herb. There's a family feeling that still prevails - Herb and Marilyn's son remains one of the 33 employees at the 14,000 square foot store (including the seasonal garden centre) and their daughter has recently returned, after a hiatus of several years. Marilyn stops by the store regularly and Michael is always ready and willing to offer a hand if she needs any help with Herb. Michael says that some people see business as cold-hearted. But it has never been that way with Home Hardware. How many ordinary people with small stores, he asks, could walk into the CEO's office and feel comfortable and welcome?

At Home Hardware, the door is always open. Unless someone has locked themself out in which case, it's Home Hardware to the rescue:
One day in the early 90s, when Michael was much younger and more agile, a frantic mother showed up at the store. She had locked herself out of the house with her year and a half old baby locked inside. She and Michael headed back to her house. When they got there, they could hear him on the other side, wailing his little head off. Michael checked out the perimeter, but couldn't find any windows on the ground floor to jimmy. He looked up and saw that the window to the second story bathroom was wide open. Michael was not a fan of heights - "didn't like ladders at the best of times" - but he leaned the ladder against the wall, climbed up, cranked open the window, tearing out the screws in the process, and clambered carefully over the toilet.

He was in. He tiptoed downstairs and as he came around the corner, started murmuring soothing words to the hysterical child. As soon as he saw him, the child stopped crying in mid-wail and looked at him as if to say, 'What are you doing in my house?' He was so indignant, Michael remembers, that he walked toward the door and looked like he was about to start the water works again, but Michael beat him to it, tore open the door, the distraught mother rushed in and swooped the baby up into her arms, smothering him in hugs and kisses. And the kid was still peering over her shoulder at Michael as if to say, 'Who is this weird guy?' Over the years customers would reminisce about Michael rescuing the trapped baby and several years ago, the mother walked in one day and said to Michael, "Good to see you again. This is the guy you liberated all those years ago." A great big, tall guy looked at him and kind of growled. "I said, 'You've heard the story a few too many times, have you?' 'Oh yeah,' he said."

In the 1920s Jim Schneuker's grandfather Alf got a job in the drygoods store on the main street of Milverton, Ontario when his father died. The local hardware dealer liked what he saw in young Alf and soon lured him away with the promise that Alf could buy him out when the time was right. It all came to pass as planned and a few years later, Alf was married

(despite the fact that the store did not even have a computer when Jim and Rita arrived in 1986). Schneuker Home Centre is still often a test store for pilot projects and new applications: "Our staff members are very familiar with the testing process, and I've been told they're pretty particular," Rita says with pride, "so they will often find things that others don't."

Jim and Rita Schneuker:

Jim understands the importance of the local service clubs to the life of a small town.

Schneukers Home Hardware
Milverton, ON

with a son and daughter of his own. Naturally, when the time came, that son Murray starting working part time at the store. By now, the Schneukers were customers of Hollinger Hardware's wholesale division and Jim's father and grandfather attended the pivotal meeting at The Flying Dutchman on March 20, 1963. Schneuker Hardware became Charter Member 87 when Home Hardware came into being on January 1, 1964.

Jim was too young to remember those early days but his initiation into the business followed the same course as his father's. When he graduated from high school, Jim travelled down the road to Wilfrid Laurier University in Waterloo where he met a young woman named Rita Muller. With her cosmopolitan background - her father was an executive whose job took the family to major cities in the US and Canada - Rita urged Jim to step out of his comfort zone and try something new. Thanks to the Home Hardware grapevine, Jim got a summer job at a store in Leduc, outside of Edmonton. Upon graduation with business degrees their independence continued. After a few busy and happy years in Alberta, the call came: there was an opening at the store back home in Milverton. If Jim chose, he could fill the position. The implications were clear. Jim and Rita made their decision and moved to Milverton in 1986.

For Jim it was coming home. For Rita, it was a whole other experience. The first few years, she says, she was "Jim's wife," the out-of-towner who had married the local boy. That changed soon enough when Rita and Jim started their family. Before long Rita was involved in the Milverton community in her own right - from Girl Guides and Cub Scouts to treasurer of the local soccer organization. "A small town is an amazing place to raise a child," she says.

When the children got older, Rita came back into the business fulltime. The store had converted to a Home Hardware Building Centre while Jim and Rita were still out west. Over the years, while it retained the character and charm of a small town store on Main Street, one block away a bustling lumberyard and busy LBM operation were in full swing.

On the surface, Rita has the brisk no nonsense quality of a successful entrepreneur. She and Jim are the perfect combo, his big, easy-going style and ready smile, her bristling energy and heart of gold that make things happen. Milverton is not far from St Jacobs - many St. Jacobs employees call it home - and with that proximity and her business background, it makes sense that Rita was on the Home Team that developed HomeInfo and Prism

To this day, despite her fulltime responsibilities at the store, Rita still loves the volunteer spirit that helped her become a member of her adopted hometown over 30 years ago. When we visited in July 2012 the surrounding countryside was a stunning landscape of green and gold although the farmers were desperate for rain and the entire area was on the edge of a serious drought. Still, the light stands throughout town were festooned with gorgeous hanging baskets, each one a healthy riot of brilliant blooms. The 54 baskets were watered and tended to daily by volunteers, a project that has been growing since 2001.

There's another community-based initiative close to the Schneukers' heart: the Milverton Rodeo Weekend, part of the RAM Rodeo Tour that comes to town for three days every June. The province's agricultural heartland seems an unlikely location for what has become Ontario's longest consecutively running rodeo. In fact, it is a textbook example of the power of small town initiative. Not surprisingly, Rita and Jim Schneuker have been involved from the start. An active member of the Milverton Lion's Club, as were his father and grandfather before him, Jim understands the importance of the local service clubs to the life of a small town. Almost 25 years ago, a group of local businessmen started looking for a way to put the town on the map. The seemingly unlikely idea of a rodeo was born. Initially, the group underwrote the expenses but once the rodeo was viable, they turned its operation over to the three main service clubs in town, The Agricultural Society, The Optimists' Club and The Lion's Club.

When the Milverton Agricultural Society celebrated its 150th anniversary in 2010, the same community spirit funded a large board and batten building alongside the rodeo corral, the town arena and its playing fields. The building sees a lot of action during the annual June rodeo and is a welcome addition to the other facilities on the site: rodeo grounds, community centre/arena and playing fields.

As for the next generation, it's up in the air these days: Jim and Rita's three children, who worked at the store through their high school years, and occasionally at other local businesses as well, are pursuing their own careers. Like all good parents Jim and Rita just want them to be happy. However it works out, there is one thing Rita and Jim know for certain: from big city and big business to small town with all the challenges and rewards inherent in running a successful family business, they are proof that it is possible to have the best of all worlds wherever you live.

"Home allows you to be whatever you want to be within your community and that's the beautiful part —we can still support Home 100% but– if there is an opening for a new product or a new line, we can step right into it. And Home's buyers are always there, to give their thoughts and suggestions on what we're doing."

Christmas is in the air and snow is on the ground on a brilliantly cold and sunny mid-December day as I drive the back roads to John Locke's Orillia store. I have been hearing great things about this store for years from Ray Gabel, who would often suggest that I stop in for a visit. I am glad that I waited - a store all decked out for Christmas is, after all, a store seen at its sparkly best.

that introduces members to local businesses in an evening of networking. Inevitably these people become friends and customers and when they come into the store, they are already comfortable. In other words, John seizes every opportunity to build his business: "Every day it's building and building." He doesn't miss a thing, and seems to have eyes in the back of his head.

John Locke:

John's focus is on making his store look fabulous." I spend my whole life on the sales floor and walk the floor first thing every morning. If we need to change things up, we can do it immediately."

Orillia Home Hardware Building Centre
Orillia, ON

John was a Beaver Lumber dealer for 36 years. After Home bought Beaver in 2001, it only took him a few years as a member of the Home Hardware family to come up with a new strategy for his newly expanded business. He saw an opportunity: none of his competition was advertising to the female market. In 2008, he amalgamated his two Orillia stores into one new 30,000 square foot HHBC, with Home Hardware buying the land for the new building (Home Hardware owns the real estate of more than 150 Home stores across the country). He knew with a store that size he couldn't rely on the lumberyard alone. So he set about transforming his downtown Orillia store from a lumberyard into a destination showpiece. His objective was to attract the lion's share of the community's female shoppers while still accommodating his contractor base -10 acres of land to develop the physical plant and an innate talent for building his business let him do both. The moves he made quickly took his business from 80% contractor and 20% retail sales to a 50/50 split with the majority of that shift attributable to female customers.

There is nothing that John likes more than to see women pushing their shopping carts piled high with product he has selected with them in mind. "You've got to think outside the box," John says. "The key to getting people into the store is to make it a shopping experience. Years ago, women would stay in the car when their husbands came to the lumber store." Not anymore. At Ladies' Nights, over 500 ladies show up, and in the spring, that number climbs even higher.

John's focus is on making his store look fabulous." I spend my whole life on the sales floor and walk the floor first thing every morning. If we need to change things up, we can do it immediately." He knows it's important to listen to his customers and Ladies' Nights are ideal opportunities to circulate questionnaires, hold focus groups and employ other methods to encourage their input. John knows they are his best critics and he takes full advantage of that.

John's store offers support to many worthy community organizations: with each event supporting a different community charity. Last fall a local church set up a yard sale in the store's parking lot to fund raise for a new church organ (the store donated $2,500); in addition, in 2011, the staff helped the local Rotary Club with their annual Festival of Trees event. They are also part of a Chamber of Commerce initiative, "Business After Five"

Home Hardware is clearly number one in John's mind in the relatively short time that he has been part of the family. He wishes he was 40 and admits that sometimes he thinks he behaves like a 20 year old. But no matter how old he is (65 in 2012), John is obviously having a blast. His favourite time of year is the 10 months from March to the end of December. But it's no surprise that he has a plan to perk up the New Year doldrums: how about a month-long Hawaiian Luau with sand and music and lots of warm light? Sounds brilliant to me!

" Walter Hachborn is a legend. When Walter comes into my store it gives me a chance to show him what I can give back to the company that he built. The night the Orillia team won the Walter Hachborn Award (in 2010) it was just crazy. There was so much noise, and me being hard of hearing, I was not aware of what was going on. My store manager announced, "We won store of the year!" Walter offered me his hand in congratulations, but instead I reached out and hugged him and said, "This company has fulfilled my dreams." John and his partner Bill Ecklund accept the award from Walter. Store manager John Green stands to Walter's left.

How do you deal with the pain of a terminally ill child? Why do bad things happen to good people? For some questions, there are no answers. For others, there are good people who help to make the unbearable even one small amount more manageable. In eastern Ontario, a group of Home Hardware Dealers, led by Chuck Hillock, partnered with the Ottawa

get the project off the ground. Home Hardware responded by commissioning a portrait of Roger Neilson by renowned artist Tony Harris and selling 2003 prints at a price of $300 a print. Suppliers to Home's LBM division agreed to donate or supply materials at a reduced cost thanks to Jim Ireton, the dealer in Smith's Falls. The building is designed by Robert Matthews of

Chuck Hillock:

Bridlewood Home Hardware
Kanata, ON

According to Chuck, the two strongest words he associates with being a Home Hardware dealer are flexibility and freedom: the freedom to listen to their customers and the flexibility to respond to their needs.

Senators Foundation to do just that by helping to raise funds to build Roger's House, the pediatric palliative care facility on the grounds of CHEO (the Children's Hospital of Eastern Ontario) in Ottawa. Roger's House is named in memory of Roger Neilson, the assistant coach of the Ottawa Senators who passed away in 2003 after a long-term battle with cancer. He was inducted into the Hockey Hall of Fame in 2002, but his true legacy as an extraordinarily compassionate and caring man permeates the facility that bears his name.

Perhaps because he experienced that parental helplessness himself with his infant son - the happy ending is that today William is a healthy young man who is now a successful Chartered Accountant - Chuck Hillock feels a special connection to Roger's House. Chuck owns two Home Hardware stores in the Ottawa area, the aptly named Capital in Ottawa's Glebe, which he bought from his parents in 1985, and Bridlewood Home Hardware in Kanata that he opened in October 2009. An affluent community west of Ottawa, Kanata is also home ice for the Ottawa Senators. Chuck is a hockey aficionado - he has sat in the same seats since the Senator's first season in the old arena. In the late 1990s, he and a number of his fellow Home Hardware Dealers in the area originated the popular "Stick Kids" promotion, developed with the Ottawa Senators. Every home game one lucky kid, who entered the promotion at their local Home store, spent that game with their favourite team. They watched the pre-game warm-up, played water boy (or girl), met the players, toured the dressing room, got the autographs and garnered a lifetime of memories. The program was a huge success and brought a lot of smiles to a lot of people Chuck acknowledges. A few years after Stick Kids had run its course, the Sens and Home Hardware did it again: in 2003, the Senators Foundation announced plans to build a paediatric palliative care facility to be named in honour of Roger Neilson. As soon as Chuck heard the news, he realized that it "had our name all over it," and asked area manager Bill McCreight to set up a meeting. According to Lloyd Cowin, who has been the Executive Director of Roger's House since it opened in 2006, and who is still responsible for the pediatric care unit at CHEO, Roger's House is a classic story of community involvement making a dream a reality. "It's people like Chuck," he says, "who stepped up and made this happen. We have Roger's House today because the community wanted it." The Sens needed an upfront financial commitment to

EMA Market Architects. The firm also donated a portion of their time to the project and when we visited in late 2011 were working on another project at the facility.

The building is a revelation, high ceilings, a flow of space full of light and peace. Its design was based on extensive consultation with families, staff and patients as to how they wanted the building to look, feel and function. Lloyd says that initially many families had difficulty, thinking that by coming in they were giving up. But there is no sense of despair here whatsoever. The Play Room is airy, high ceilinged and bright even on a drab December day. This is where we did the interviews and we took pictures against the room's "Wall of Stars", each star commemorating a child who passed through this peaceful place on their journey to a place of even greater safety. Roger Neilsen's star shines at the top of the galaxy.

Family History: In the late 1960s, Egan Hillock was a Toronto pressman looking for a career change. For several years, his son Chuck remembers, the family spent their summer vacations driving around Ontario in search of an affordable hardware store. In 1970, they found it. Egan and his wife Amelia poured their life savings into the purchase of the new store on Bank Street in Ottawa's Glebe neighbourhood. They worked side by side growing their new business. Chuck, who grew up in the business, took it over from his parents 15 years later. A "Christmas graduate," Chuck left college after six months, having learned that that his true vocation was hardware. He may not have earned a degree, but he credits the experience for allowing him to find the love of his life, his wife Juliette.

There's a dealer network that taps talent as it comes up the ranks: Laura Ware, who started working with Ken O'Connor in Gananoque in 1998 and has been the store manager there since 2005, is a case in point. Laura grew up in the Thousands Islands and, after high school, came to Ottawa to go to school. She got her first part time Home Hardware job at Chuck's Ottawa store. A few years later, she went back to Gananoque to finish her schooling and applied to the store there for a part time job. One day the Area Manager called Chuck. He was looking at her résumée and Chuck said, "If you don't hire her, you'll be making a huge mistake." The Area Manager took his advice, and today Laura is running one of the largest stores in the country. Chuck would like to see her with her own store one day.

Chuck Hillock and Lloyd Cowin in the Play Room of Roger's House.

We are one, but we are many.

In April 2012 Capital Home Hardware on Bank Street in the Glebe changed hands. Mark Clement, whose Beechwood store burned to the ground in March 2011, assumed ownership. His wife, Isabelle Lamarche, comes from a Home family, and worked in the family business when she was a youngster. Her brother, Jocelyn, owns the store in Casselman, east of Ottawa. For Chuck, the fact that it was the right people at the right time for the right reasons makes it a bit easier to leave the original family business.

Gananoque is undoubtedly the heart of the Thousand Islands, the storied summer playground along the St Lawrence River just east of Kingston. But behind the recreational façade, the tour boats and the history, day-to-day reality can have a rough edge. The recent recession has taken its toll in the area and more families than may immediately be apparent are struggling to make ends meet.

Tantalizing breakfast aromas emanate from the breakfast room and hungry kids crowd around the table to load up their plates. They don't see the triple sink, the commercial grade dishwasher, the fridge and stove, all of which were purchased specifically for the Breakfast Club. They don't know that a nutritionist has helped to develop the menu. All they see, on this cold November morning, is a full plate of warm and delicious food. The trick is

Ken O'Connor:

Gananoque Home Hardware Building Centre, Home Furniture
Gananoque, ON

What Ken likes most about the program is that it doesn't discriminate - if you're hungry on any given morning, you can eat at The Breakfast Club.

Ken and Linda O'Connor, who own the 42,000 square foot HHBC/Home Furniture just south of the highway, are making a quiet but significant difference in alleviating some of the hardship for many of these families: Gananoque Home Hardware Building Centre is one of the major corporate sponsors of The Breakfast Club at Linklater Public School.

The school approached the O'Connors in 2010 - Ken's capable and highly efficient general manager Laura Ware fielded the request and passed it along to Ken. Having been in the community for 10 years, the company was already involved with different local charities - they give to the Food Bank religiously - so it was an obvious fit. What Ken likes most about the program is that it doesn't discriminate - if you're hungry on any given morning, you can eat at The Breakfast Club.

Ken is no stranger to good works: several years ago, his friend, former employee and fellow converted Beaver dealer Rick Kurzac in Kamloops, BC, got him involved in Developing World Connections and Ken had just returned from building a safe house for a group of women in the Philippines when we visited in November 2011.

Ken started working at Saveway Lumber, in 1973, in those days affiliated with Beaver Lumber, in his hometown of Sudbury. He moved south to Scarborough where he worked at the local Saveway Lumber, then for the next ten years held a variety of positions, some at their head office in Toronto. In 1987, he purchased the Beaver Lumber in Kingston, which he closed in 2000 when the company was bought by Home Hardware. They moved to Brockville (now owned by Paul Blakney) and then in 2001, bought an 8,000 square foot corporate store in Gananoque. Ken knew that a major expansion was in his future and one day, driving over the highway he saw a For Sale sign on a building. A bit worried it was too much space, Ken called in the experts from St. Jacobs and "before we knew it, it was a dream come true," he says. He says the transition to Home Hardware was the best thing that ever happened to them. These days there's a lot of activity with the Home Packages, which is essentially a turnkey service that they can offer their customers, from the ground up to the pots and pans and furniture, thanks to the Home Furniture store that is part of their new location.

When the O'Connors went into the furniture business in 2009, they indulged in an ongoing spree of redecorating of their own and have just refurnished their basement after 25 years - it's nice to see that even dealers get excited about all the wonderful product they sell.

to get the kids in and out in time for classroom activity, which leaves about 15 minutes for breakfast on the best of days. The presence of a camera crew only adds to the controlled mayhem on this morning.

A retired high school teacher since 2001 and President of the Linklater Breakfast Club's Board of Directors since 2005, Bruce McLeod knows too well that there are kids who arrive in the morning hungry. And if children aren't properly nourished, that has an impact on everything from learning to behaviour, attention span and attendance. Bruce McLeod stresses that he took over an already successful program and cannot say enough about all the people and organizations who make the Breakfast Club possible. The Linklater Breakfast Club owes its existence to the tenacity of founder Debra Patterson. Her central idea, in no small part responsible for the program's longevity, was to design and run it as a business. Too often programs of this type are started by a well meaning individual and run by teachers "who really have enough to do already," Bruce points out. Operating it like a business bypasses many of the problems that can plague well meaning volunteer organizations and ensures that the primary objective - to nourish hungry children so they can make the most of their school day - is never compromised. The school's principal, Harold Hess, sits on the Board and a core group of 50 very dedicated volunteers not only run the program, they also raise the funds needed to keep it going. Their efforts have resulted in major corporate donors the calibre of Gananoque HHBC. Both the school and the school board have also been very generous: the school provides the breakfast room and the school board donates the custodial care and insurance coverage. Coordinator Diana Ouellet is the organization's only paid employee, a part time position she has held since 2007. It is her responsibility to buy and prepare all the meals and supervise the volunteers. Today Bev MacDonald, a seven-year volunteer, is on duty. Diane also prepares some brown bag lunches with a "good range of nutritious things" that are kept in the refrigerator. Teachers can exercise their judgment in sending kids to the fridge for a calorie boost.

Family is a major theme of the Home Hardware story and it has been my privilege to meet many Home Hardware families as I have traveled across the country researching this book. In addition to their remarkable hospitality, all these families share the qualities of success - commitment, loyalty, experience and most of all hard work. Very hard work. For all the rewards, every one of them richly deserved, it is impossible to overlook the fact that fundamental nose-to-the-grindstone hard work is the foundation of every business I have profiled.

Both Adam and Mark spent "many, many days, hours and weeks working in the store, including the summer months," Adam remembers. "Some of my earliest memories are of working at night with my father at the other store." After high school, Adam studied Music Industry Arts at Fanshawe College but soon realized a brighter future beckoned from home. In 1992, he joined the business. "I told him, if you want to work all the time, you just come right along," Hank jokes all these years later.

The Busscher Family:

Picton Home Hardware Building Centre
Picton, ON

Today the area attracts artists and retirees. Traditional farms have transformed into vineyards.

The majority of the "family patriarchs", now all in some stage of retirement, were hardworking, independent hardware retailers in their early days. I had not encountered a dealer who came from the supplier side of the business until I met Hank Busscher, of Picton, Ontario. His memories provided an interesting perspective on the early days of Home Hardware. As he reminisced about Walter Hachborn and the company it was soon to become, the topic of hard work was top of mind.

In 1963, Hank Busscher, an electrician by trade, got a job with Markel Electric. Home base was Fort Erie, Ontario, near head office in Buffalo, New York. Hank's first task was to read all previous correspondence between his employer and the wholesalers they supplied. Home Hardware is a multi-billion dollar corporation today, so most people may not realize just how small it was in the early 1960s. There were hundreds of wholesalers at the time, Hank recalls, and as a result, it was a lot of work when Hollinger wanted Markel to become a supplier, especially when Walter insisted that their small company receive exactly the same treatment as any other wholesaler. Hank still marvels at the imagination and insight displayed by Walter Hachborn and Henry Sittler, who foresaw that the survival of the independent retailers depended on their ability to band together. And he has nothing but admiration for the dealers who took a leap of faith by joining the fledgling Home Hardware: how hard they worked to ensure its survival and success.

Before long, Walter put Hank to work, conducting product seminars at district meetings across Ontario. On the long drives back home, Walter would detour to visit Home Hardware stores, especially those he thought might entice Hank into becoming a Home Hardware Dealer himself. In 1976, Walter toured Hank down the main street of Picton. When he got home, Hank told his wife Pat that she should start thinking about moving. With Adam and Mark, their two small sons, Hank and Pat moved into the apartment above the Picton store and embarked upon their lives as Home Hardware Dealers.

In 1992, with Walter's encouragement, Hank sold the traditional hardware store that dated to the mid 1800s and moved into 10,000 square feet of retail space up the street. They took the advice of Wally Dankwardt, Area Manager of the paint division, and switched to Beauti-Tone, which Hank says contributed significantly to their subsequent growth spiral. Soon their overall sales per square foot were well above average. "We did a good job," Hank says with modest pride. Pat's talents as a graphics artist were put to highly effective work building and promoting the housewares department (Pat, who still has a distinctive British accent, went to Ealing Art College during the cultural explosion of the early 1960s).

Despite the warnings, Adam relished the work, joining at an interesting time when the company was becoming computerized. The new technology offered both challenges and opportunity to an ambitious young man. Adam assumed the reins as President in 1996 (Hank has never officially retired and still works Sundays). Today both second and third generations are well represented. In addition to Adam and Mark, Adam's wife Chrissy (who coincidentally started working at the store the same year as Adam) works in the office and three of Hank and Pat's grandchildren, Nathan, Mira and Brooke, are gainfully employed over the summer. Mark's wife Ruth-Ann is a teacher, so she takes summers off, although is always available to pitch in if needed.

The population of Picton, around 4,000, has not changed since the early 1900s. But the people who live there have. One hundred years ago Prince Edward County was farmland, with canning and cheese-making predominating in the town. Today the area attracts artists and retirees. Traditional farms have transformed into vineyards. Prince Edward County has become a summer tourist destination with some of the best beaches in Ontario. Restaurants, galleries and specialty shops have sprung up to cater to the tourists. As a result, the Busschers started to consider expansion options to take advantage of the changing demographics of the area. Brother Mark came on board fulltime at this point: a former electrical engineer with Ford, Mark became the lumber business expert - Adam and Hank are unabashed hardware guys. Soon they were ready to embark on the arduous process of building a big beautiful HHBC on the outskirts of town. It was a protracted undertaking, including countless meetings with town council, citizens' committees (some for, some against) and the ongoing partnership with Home Hardware corporate. "We were stretching the retail boundaries," Adam says. "We looked at every available property and chose probably the most difficult one to build on because of the zoning requirements. But it was also the most effective because it is truly the centre of the County." The happy outcome is a 30,000 square foot store with 16,000 square feet of lumberyard on 14 acres of land (real estate owned by Home Hardware). Despite its gleaming modernity, its location on the outskirts of town is not at odds with the historic and picturesque town.

It is a big, boisterous and happy family that I encounter on my visit to Picton. But like so much about the success of the Busscher family, this is no accident. Working so closely together requires forethought and effort to ensure clarity, an effective structure and success. It is a lot of work. Very hard work. But there is no question that it all works.

In 2007, Adam won the NRHA's Young Retailer of the Year award. In 2009 he was appointed to its Board and in 2011 voted to Executive Vice Chair for the Association - representing Canada. With 36,000 independent hardware retailer-members across North America, the organization's mandate is to help them become more successful and more profitable regardless of the banner under which they may operate. Adam and Mark are also both active members of Home Hardware's Young Leaders program.

Port Perry has its own resident celebrity. Bill Lishman is the author of "Father Goose" that tells the story of how he became the surrogate father to a flock of eighteen Canada geese, eventually building a micro light aircraft of his own design that led the flock in a V-formation to their winter haven in Virginia. They returned to his fields the following spring. Three years later, his story was fictionalized and made into a film, "Fly Away Home". Bill and his wife moved to a farm outside of Port Perry in 1996. They love the small town charm of the town and are loyal Home Hardware customers.

Welcome to Port Perry on the shores of Lake Scugog, home to lovingly restored historic homes, a charity casino, lively summer festivals on its downtown streets, picturesque ice-fishing huts on its shallow lake (weather permitting, of course) and a Home Hardware store on Main Street that still boasts the look and feel of an old-style hardware store - wood floors, tin ceiling. Inevitably, with so much charm in such abundance, in 2003 Hollywood came calling, looking for a location to shoot a political comedy called "Welcome to Mooseport", starring Gene Hackman, Ray Romano and Marcia Gay Harden.

Raj Bhatia:

Port Perry Home Hardware
Port Perry, ON

Owner Raj Bhatia has a history of taking on new challenges - he studied engineering in Scotland and England, then in 1973, moved to Canada where he worked as a mechanical engineer for almost 20 years in Montreal, Ottawa, Peterborough and Toronto. It was on a whim that he became a hardware retailer in 1990 when he bought the business in Port Perry. So he was game for the "Mooseport" experience, as long as it didn't interfere with his day-to-day business. The film company transformed the store into Handy Harrison's Hardware (owned by Ray Romano) for the cameras, while it continued to operate as Port Perry Home Hardware in the real world. According to Raj, it was a thoroughly enjoyable experience, happily with no ego on display on the part of the big name stars. A few years later, in 2011, the store became a set for an episode of the Canadian TV show Nikita. The shoot took place over a Friday night and included a stunt driver going through a specially installed plate glass window. The mess was cleaned up and the store was back in working order by 10 AM the next morning. The locals were thrilled to have stars in their town, and Raj was happy with all the free publicity.

When I started this project, Walter reminded me that although there are a thousand stores, there are thousands of stories. And, as usual, Walter was right. The challenge with this book has been to limit the number of profiled stores and the number of stories for each store. Steve and Karen Maxwell, owners of Renfrew Home Hardware Building Centre, have been one such struggle: they provide countless illustrations to support the main thesis of this book - the Home Hardware difference. As I listened to Karen give the How it Works in My Store presentation at the Spring 2011 market,

to practice in a smaller community. From the moment he arrived, one of Steve's goals was to bring new doctor recruits to the community. Renfrew already had a recruitment committee, but Steve quickly realized that it "was doing its thing and the hospital was doing its thing and the community itself wasn't really involved aside from a few members of that recruitment committee," Karen being one of them. They were able to recruit a few doctors but after that, things dried up. In addition, not only were they faced with two imminent retirements, their forecasts showed about two thirds of

Karen and Steve Maxwell:

Renfrew Home Hardware Building Centre
Renfrew, ON

I was struck by two things: her passion and the level of commitment to their community. In many ways, this is not unusual - I have encountered the same qualities across the country. As Karen said in her opening remarks, "You're the people I've learned the most from over the course of my career in retail and with Home Hardware."

Karen is another "hardware" baby: her parents Larry and Marilyn MacNeill bought the business in 1987 and immediately set about making it the dominant building centre in the area. Karen and her husband Steve joined the business as partners in 1994. In 2005 the business had outgrown the original location and they built a new store: 25,000 square feet of retail, an 18,000 square foot drive-through warehouse and a rental shop. There are 51 employees. There's a lot of competition, both in town and throughout the surrounding area. Ottawa is just 45 minutes away. Karen and Steve officially took over the business in 2006 shortly after they moved into the new store. Running the business is a handful by itself. Then factor in Karen and Steve's belief that community involvement defines them and you begin to get an understanding of the depth of commitment. And the amount of work. Their reputation for charitable giving means that the store receives a lot of requests. They developed a form that defines their parameters for giving, but all requests receive the courtesy of a reply. As Karen said, if someone has given his or her time to collect for a cause, then it likely has merit.

Among the numerous activities supported by Renfrew HHBC, one stands out for its ambition and scope: their commitment to community health. In 2007, Renfrew HHBC got very involved with Hospice Renfrew, the first such facility to be built to provincial standards in a rural setting. Over the years, various fundraisers have funnelled money to different departments within Victoria Hospital Renfrew, the local community hospital as well. But, as with so many rural communities across the country, Renfrew was suffering from a dearth of doctors, which is not good for the health of the overall community: families don't want to move to a place without enough doctors; the local economy overall cannot thrive.

Fortunately, in the summer of 2005, a young doctor named Steve Radke moved with his wife and their young family to Renfrew, immediately after he graduated from medical school. Given the need for family doctors in virtually every community across the country, Steve could have gone just about anywhere. But they liked the Ottawa area and Steve knew he wanted

the local physicians would retire in the next five years. Renfrew and the surrounding area have a population of about 20,000 people (which balloons during the summer). All it takes is a calculator to realize there was a problem brewing.

One of the more remarkable aspects of Renfrew's doctor recruitment story is how quickly everything came together: the hospital, medical providers, business community and the local municipalities all found themselves at the table at one time, thanks to the driving force and advocacy of people like Karen Maxwell. They came up with a new recruitment strategy that Steve says is "spectacular" because it never allowed politics and other issues to get in the way of the main goal. Framed within the context of community economic development, it quickly went beyond being the hospital's responsibility and a process that can often take years was completed within a matter of months.

Steve Radke marvels at Karen's community involvement: "She's very committed from many perspectives. She's been a strong supporter of our charity - The Renfrew Victoria Hospital charity golf tournament - in terms of financial sponsorship and attendance and involvement and she's taking it a step further by being involved in the recruitment committee. Karen is ready to be the business leader who says to other businesses - here's the issue our community is faced with. We're looking for your support."

The commitment within the business community is not insignificant: the recruitment program will cost $2.1 million. At the time of writing, the committee had secured $1,446,000, the majority coming from the Renfrew Industrial Commission and $140,000 - $10,000 per doctor - from Renfrew Home Hardware Building Centre. Karen acknowledged in her presentation that this was a large commitment, "but we consider it to be an investment in the economic health of our area. Steve and I feel that our staff and the growth of our business will benefit."

The goal to replace the doctors planning to retire over the coming five years is being realized. The incentive is a signing bonus for a five-year commitment. After that, Steve is confident that the community will have worked its magic, the new doctors will be settled in, their practice established and they'll be happy to call Renfrew home.

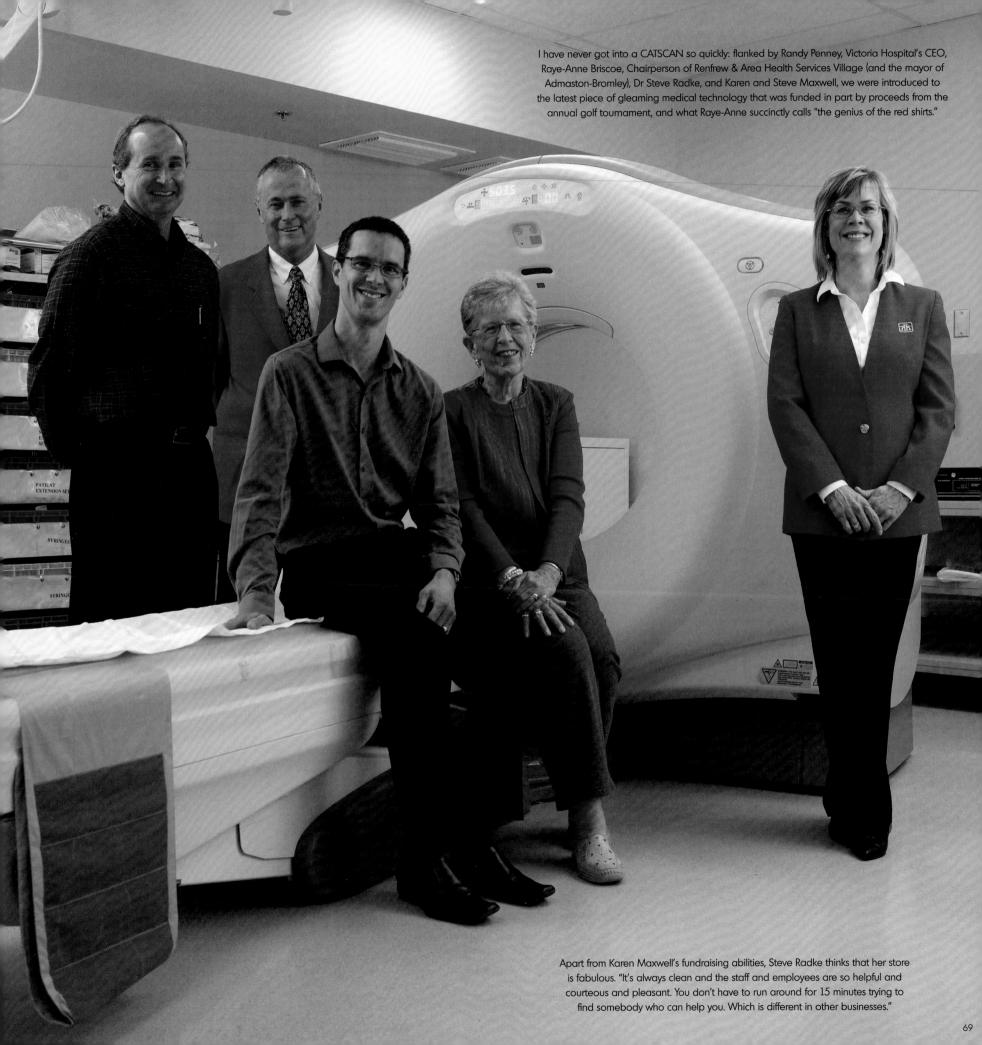

I have never got into a CATSCAN so quickly: flanked by Randy Penney, Victoria Hospital's CEO, Raye-Anne Briscoe, Chairperson of Renfrew & Area Health Services Village (and the mayor of Admaston-Bromley), Dr Steve Radke, and Karen and Steve Maxwell, we were introduced to the latest piece of gleaming medical technology that was funded in part by proceeds from the annual golf tournament, and what Raye-Anne succinctly calls "the genius of the red shirts."

Apart from Karen Maxwell's fundraising abilities, Steve Radke thinks that her store is fabulous. "It's always clean and the staff and employees are so helpful and courteous and pleasant. You don't have to run around for 15 minutes trying to find somebody who can help you. Which is different in other businesses."

Ron's partner in the Brantford store is Dave Liesemer, whose brother now owns the store in Mildmay originally owned by their parents, who were Charter Members. For some unknown reason, the father was always called "Jiggs". They were known for their fabulous Christmas displays. People would drive from miles around to visit during the holiday season.

On a sunny morning in April 2011, Home Hardware Dealer Ron Cicuttini was on the chair lift heading up Blue Mountain. The conditions were perfect - lots of snow, lots of sun, blue sky forever, mild-and Ron was looking out over Georgian Bay thinking, "This is the life." Maybe, after almost 40 years, it was time to sell his two successful stores (one in Brantford, the other in Dundas, Ontario) and relax. And then the phone rang.

It took time. In 1979, Ron was 23 and was attending McMaster University. He had also been managing the store since he was 21. One evening his father informed the family that he had a buyer for the original store in East Hamilton. The deal was done. Ron knew it was now or never. He took a deep breath and asked his father if he would sell it to him instead. So Ron quit school and took over the family business. Seven years later, in 1986, he

Ron Cicuttini: "Even when I was a kid, Weeks was a big deal."

Weeks Home Hardware
Waterdown, ON

It was Dave Smith, who along with his sister Sandy and brother-in-law Steve Gray, owned Weeks of Waterdown. He wanted to know if Ron was interested in buying the business. It took a while to sink in - after all, Sandy and Dave's dad had bought Weeks from Ernie Weeks in the 1970s and it was an institution in the pretty Victorian town next door to Dundas. But Ron and Dave had "been friends forever", so Ron knew the offer was serious. Six months later, on October 18, 2011, the Cicuttinis added Weeks to their family enterprise.

Ron's story is an excellent illustration of the generation that bridges Home Hardware's founding culture to that of the future. His father Mario, an Italian immigrant who worked at Dofasco, decided that he wanted to own his own business. So in 1970, he did just that, mortgaging the house again, much to his wife Marie's consternation, and starting down a completely different track. For a long time, young Ron was one of his few employees. Ron still hasn't forgotten the long hours and hard work he put in every day after school and all day Saturday starting at age 13.

There were moments of illumination as well, notably when he saw Walter in action for the first time: "I'll never forget it," Ron says. "It was at a hotel on the Hamilton mountain, in a dingy basement meeting room with wood paneling. There was this little man with a bow tie up at the front telling us what the future was going to be in retail and the hardware industry. He told us to expect this, and what we were going to do and what we were going to change. And everything kept coming true. I was just a youngster when I was going to these meetings, just dying to go so that I could listen to Walter. Because this man could see the future."

Walter helped Ron to see his own future, one he knew would always include Home Hardware. He also knew that he wanted to sit on the Board of Directors with Walter. But, he didn't want to just sit there and not contribute. So he set out to make it a reality.

and his dad bought the store in Dundas. When Ron brought in computers, his dad decided it was time to retire. The new store was in the University Plaza where Hamilton meets Dundas not far from the McMaster campus. Which was a good thing because over the next 13 years, Ron went to night school on that campus, summer and winter, to finish his undergrad degree and earn his MBA. All while running a business fulltime and helping his wife Linda raise their four children.

Ron says that he and Linda bought the business in Waterdown with them in mind. They have all expressed an interest in perpetuating the family business. Their oldest son Michael is helping Ron run the Waterdown store. Like his father before him, he is learning the business from the floor up.

And the dream Ron had as a 14 year-old boy, of serving, on the Home Hardware Board? It also came true. In 1995, Bill Robinson, the local Area Manager and the man whom Ron cites as having been the major influence on his career, dropped in as usual and asked if he was planning to run for the Board. "I'm not ready," Ron replied. "You won't have another chance," Bill told him. Ron ran. He retired in April of 2012 after serving for 17 years, one of the longest sitting members of Home Hardware's Board. Linda remembers their first Board meeting: their youngest child Julia was five months old. "All these grandmother types" kept asking to hold the baby.

Brigitte's first job in the 1960s was to peel potatoes in the basement of her father's restaurant. A self-confessed drama queen, she used to cry and milked it for all it was worth. She says their restaurant had the best potatoes because they were flavoured by the salt from her tears.

Brigitte Michel emanates enthusiasm. Her passion for the business, for Home Hardware, for life, came pulsing through the phone lines during our first interview over a year before we actually got to Sudbury for the photo session. With her words tumbling out in a profusion of interesting, often amusing information -- this woman is as funny as she is smart—Brigitte gave me a quick outline of A&J Home Hardware, the business started by her father Arnel (the A) and Jim Latreille (the J) in 1973. Her father was a

at Shoppers Drug Mart—but they decided to give it a shot.

The store is a conglomeration that has grown over the years. As space became available in the mall, the original 4,000 square foot store expanded. On two levels - even though everyone, including some of Home's management, said it would never work. But Arnel made sure it not only survived but prospered. Today the business, still on two floors, is 18,000 square feet, and every inch has been put to work. The plumbing and paint

Brigitte Michel: Her tiny office is tucked into an old elevator shaft in a corner.

A & J Home Hardware
Sudbury, ON

Sudbury entrepreneur who got into the business originally as an investment. When his partner decided it wasn't for him, Arnel bought him out. Every morning before the store opens, he still arrives to set up the seasonal merchandise on the sidewalk of the plaza that the Michel family owns as well. Then he goes around the corner and has breakfast at Gloria's, the restaurant named after his sister and now run by his son Bruno, a philosophy and French Literature major who went back to school to become a chef. This is an interesting family, to say the least.

Like a lot of Home Hardware "kids", Brigitte swore she'd never take over the family business. "When you grow up in a family like mine, everything is about work. You go home and if it's busy at the store – oh you have to go help at the store. I think our parents breathed and ate everything Home Hardware. " When she was old enough, Brigitte got her Bronze Medallion to be a lifeguard. It took her three attempts - did I mention she's tenacious? - after which she got a summer job at a camp on an island in Lake Nippissing "because I knew my dad couldn't get me home to do anything." But if Home Hardware is in your blood, there's not much you can do about it: when Brigitte was studying at Ottawa University, she was inexorably drawn to the Trudels' Home Hardware store on Rideau Street. Her first job after school was in Barrie and she found herself living above the local Home Hardware store.

She finally succumbed to her fate in 1991. Her mother Laurette called and told her she needed her to come home to run the store - her brother Bruno was taking over the family restaurant and planning to go back to school. Her parents were running the business again and finding it very difficult. Brigitte and her then-husband were living in Toronto at the time -- she was working

departments are in the basement, despite Walter's rejoinders to move their biggest departments upstairs: Brigitte's response is that this design ensures that customers see everything in the store. Her tiny office is tucked into an old elevator shaft in a corner. Papers are piled four deep on her desk - that way, Brigitte says, she always knows where everything is. Their 47 employees, some of whom have worked there for close to 40 years, have played a big role in the business' success.

Today Brigitte and Marc, one of her four brothers, and her sister Valerie run the Home Hardware business. Brigitte has been a member of the Home Hardware Board of Directors since 2003. It's not difficult to see why. When we talked about this project, she instantly suggested that the ten area Home Dealers come together for our "photo opp" which we planned to take at The Big Nickel, Sudbury's famous landmark. True to the cooperative roots of the corporate structure, the ten stores in the Greater Sudbury area function as a loose collective. It is a system that has worked well for years as an effective bulwark against the competition - there may be Wal-Mart, Lowes, Canadian Tire and Home Depot in the area, but there's only one of each. There are ten of them. Not only do they have each others' backs, they also band together on many community initiatives from Cancer Research fundraising to a Seniors' Curling Bonspiel. The common cause can often go even further: when 2nd Avenue Home Hardware owner Steven Stefanuto's mother Paula passed away several years ago, people from the other area Home Hardware stores, plus Area Manager Brian Cook, took over so that the store's staff members could attend the funeral. Brigitte attributes this rich culture of cooperation to the people at the helm of the Home Hardware organization: "These cultures don't just happen," Brigitte says. "It comes from the people who established the company."

The people in the photo from left to right:
Harry Sheppard and Lonie Doherty
(Walden HH); Valerie, Arnel, Brigitte,
Marc and Laurette Michel (A & J HH);
Michelle, Nick, Mike and Claudette
Skakoon (Skakoon HH); Claude and Eric
Bouffard (Jean's HH); Judi Fex (Evans HBC);
Mike Lemieux (Hanmer HH); Steven, Peter
and Heather Stefanuto (2nd Avenue HH);
Louise and Ben Soucy (Val Caron HBC);
John Gouchie (Levack HH);
Graham Pitman (Garson HH).

Harold Hill was 88 years old when we visited his home in late June 2012. His knees aren't so good anymore but everything else about him seems pretty fine, including his memories and sense of humour. He still lives in the comfortable house he built in 1959, up behind Peter's Home Hardware Building Centre. The day before our visit, Harold and his tractor had mowed the large back lawn. In the warm weather he often rides down on his motorized scooter to have lunch with his grandson Drew who has worked for Peter for the past 15 years.

Sundridge is a sleepy village tucked beside Highway 11 not far from Algonquin Park, a year-round destination for nature lovers and outdoor enthusiasts. The village sits placidly on the northern shore of Lake Bernard, which boldly stakes its claim in the pantheon of firsts as the world's largest freshwater lake without an island. If that seems a touch far fetched, the town's propensity for producing first class hockey players is not.

For many years, Harold Hill, one of those Sundridge hockey players, worked at the Kidds' original hardware store. After he returned from the war, Harold served as a ranger in Algonquin Park, often snowshoeing the eight-mile trek to the main road into town to play hockey. He remembers one morning spying someone crossing the ice on Round Lake. Eventually the speck transformed itself into Peter's father coming to round him up for a game. But spending weeks on end in a lonely cabin in Algonquin Park

Peter Kidd: If you grew up in Sundridge as Peter did, it was pretty much de rigeur to play hockey.

Kidd's Home Hardware Building Centre
Sundridge, ON

Sundridge does possess a good-sized Home Hardware Building Centre, down the road from where the grandfather of current owner Peter Kidd opened his original 2,400 square foot hardware store in 1928. In 1945, Peter's father Keith and his brother Harold returned from the war (Keith piloted Lancaster bombers, earning the Distinguished Flying Cross; Harold was a navigator) and took over their father's business. Although they attended the famous meeting at The Flying Dutchman in 1963 they did not join Home Hardware until 1980. In 1985, Peter and his brother-in-law Dan Hall bought out the brothers and five years after that moved the business to its current location. Today Sundridge Home Hardware Building Centre has 19,000 square feet of retail space with its lumberyards covering several acres bringing the total to 33,000 square feet.

The original store was classic small town hardware, pride of place held by the woodstove that was the building's only heat source. Late into the evening a crowd of regulars, known as the Hot Stove League, gathered to discuss the business of the day - inevitably more about the town's hockey team, The Sundridge Beavers, than actual store business. In those days - the late 1940s and throughout the 1950s - the team won a lot of games, often becoming the Intermediate A Champions. For several years their coach was "Bucko" McDonald, a former defenseman with the Toronto Maple Leafs and Detroit Red Wings and winner of two Stanley Cups. (According to the official Site of the Hockey Hall of Fame, "Bucko" is best remembered for coaching Bobby Orr, insisting against his father's wishes that he was "born to play defence"). For a midget-sized town, Sundridge has produced a disproportionate number of world-class hockey players, including Peter's best friend Bob Attwell, left-wingers Keith and Bill McCreary who played for Pittsburgh and Atlanta in the 1970s and Greg DeVries who won the Stanley Cup with the Colorado Avalanche in 2001. The town's reputation as the unofficial NHL of the North even garnered it a Hockey Night in Canada feature one season in the early 1970s.

was not a life for a married man, although he has fond - and in some cases, hair-raising - memories of his days as a park ranger. Including the time he was surrounded by a pack of curious timber wolves and the summer night five bears stopped by his cabin at Tea Lake. On another occasion he inadvertently cut through his boot with an axe, badly slicing a toe. He never went to a doctor and played hockey the following day. After five years as a park ranger, Harold moved into town where he worked for Peter's dad for the next thirty years. He says he was "just a clerk," but Peter clarifies: "He did everything." He retired from the store in 1983. By then he had already "hung up his skates" but he still keeps the mementoes nearby and has a treasure trove of medals and memories.

If you grew up in Sundridge as Peter did, it was pretty much de rigeur to play hockey. But Peter admits that the only reason his knees are bad is from driving his kids to their hockey games when they were young, although his wife did most of that, he acknowledges. His talents may have been modest, but his son Josh was drafted by the LA Kings in 2007 and played a year in the AHL. His daughter, who plays hockey at Western, and whose name is Sydney, once sent a letter to Sydney Crosby trying to "draft" his sister to attend Trinity College where Sydney Kidd played on the school hockey team. During her school years, Peter's other daughter, Maddison, played every sport BUT hockey.

Peter remembers his father Keith saying: "Spend your time as well as your money." Judging from the quiet care he put into our morning in Sundridge and how generous he was with his time and his own memories, Peter is doing a good job of following his advice.

The Trudels have been Ottawa's go-to downtown hardware store for generations, ever since the founder Napoleon Trudel opened the original store on Rideau Street in 1925, not far from the Houses of Parliament. Today, after a move to Besserer Street in the eighties, the store is conveniently located on George Street in the heart of the Byward Market, about two streets away from its original home. Elaine Trudel-Reeves says that the initial move was a horrendous job and laughs as she recalls that her father John hired a baseball team to help speed up the move.

with each passing decade. Old buildings have given way to exclusive condominiums and new restaurants and boutiques are opening regularly. Ottawa being a government town, and Trudel being the only hardware store in the area, they have a broad range of customers which makes it imperative that they carry a large assortment of goods to meet their clients' needs. Jonathan says they're always busy "on the floor" which he loves. Jonathan studied music but the business "is in my blood," he says fondly. He does not have an official ownership stake in the business, but that will come when

Elaine Trudel-Reeves: The Trudels have been Ottawa's go-to downtown hardware store for generations.

Trudel Home Hardware
Ottawa, ON

It's not hard to imagine what it was like all those years ago, although these days there is a contemporary urban bustle on the streets and sidewalks. Elaine's son Jonathan worked in the family business growing up, although not in the original Rideau Street building. The photos of the original store on the wall substantiate his claim that the old business was small and so crowded that there was merchandise stacked to the ceiling. Indeed, Napoleon was known to say ,"If we don't have it, you don't need it."

Until 2007 Jonathan's uncle Marc worked in the downtown location with his sister and co-owner Elaine. They decided to expand and opened a second location in Kanata where Marc lives. Currently, Elaine owns the downtown store and Marc the Kanata store. Their families assist them in running their respective businesses.

Everyone over the age of 40 knows their store and even younger people in the neighbourhood quickly become regulars. Elaine's father John knew many politicians who frequented his store in the sixties, seventies and eighties. In fact, John worked until well into his seventies and even later, often popping in to see what was going on in the store he called his second home. The clientele downtown is eclectic as the core of the city changes

the time is right. And with the memory of his grandmother and grandfather, Charter Home Hardware members who both passed away within five months of each other in 2011, the generational imperative is likely a bit more top of mind these days.

There are challenges and rewards inherent in being part of a family business but my sense is that they are one and the same: the expectation that he would automatically come into the business may initially have been a bit of a challenge when he was younger. But while Jonathan took the route of many "Home Hardware kids", going elsewhere initially, he did come back into the family fold and is now dealing with the business that he obviously finds enormously rewarding.

Jonathan's great grandfather Napoleon, who founded the business, died before he was born, but Jonathan says that his grandfather John instilled in him a love of retail. "He used to bring me around to the store when I was about eight years old. He'd take me out to lunch to different places and introduce me to some of the people around here." He remembers attending his first Home Hardware market when he was about 12 years old. "But I never got stuck in a bassinette behind the counter," he says with a grin.

We were invited into Don's magic emporium in the basement of his and Eleanor's comfortable home. He decided to perform a complicated trick called Super X Levitation, with his son Dave his willing and trusting subject. The trick was performed flawlessly.

When Paul Straus first saw one of Don's more popular tricks—magically turning plain paper into $5 bills—he wanted to know if he could borrow it for the sales force!

After more than 50 years as a hardware dealer in his leafy hometown of London, Ontario, 87 year old Don Tuckey has earned the right to sit back and enjoy himself. His youngest son David, third generation owner (second generation as a Home Hardware Dealer), took over the business in 1994, but for several years afterwards, Don would still work at the store, often staying late into the night. "Ten o'clock was usually the magic hour to stop," he says with a twinkle.

Don remembers rolling back in at 3 or 4 o'clock in the morning, wondering what the tired fellow at the reception desk must have thought they were up to. In the early days, Tuckey's was the only Home Hardware store in the area so Don and Eleanor's basement became command central for southwestern Ontario. Don would borrow chairs from the funeral home where he had once worked and independent dealers from Tillsonburg, Strathroy, Lambeth and other towns in the area would come to learn what Home Hardware could

Dave Tuckey:

Tuckey Home Hardware
London, ON

Don was one of a dedicated group of independent hardware dealers in southern Ontario recruited by Walter Hachborn to help him research and develop what would soon become Home Hardware Stores Limited.

Magic has played a major part in Don's life: he fell under its spell while serving in the Navy during the Second World War. From thereon in, it served as an intriguing counterpoint to his "day-to-day life," which in many ways was far from ordinary.

"I've had three careers in my life," Don says. "The first was when I graduated as a licensed embalmer at the funeral home two doors down. The second was when I served in the Navy for three years during the war." The third was when he and his father Elmore, who opened the original Tuckey Hardware in 1946, became the ninth store to sign on as a Home Hardware Charter Member.

Don was one of a dedicated group of independent hardware dealers in southern Ontario recruited by Walter Hachborn to help him research and develop what would soon become Home Hardware Stores Limited. "We wanted everyone to be on an equal basis," Don remembers. "So no matter if one was buying $1 million a year and another was buying $50,000 there was no difference between the biggest and the smallest."

Almost 50 years later, I am keenly aware of Don's enormous pride and satisfaction in how that core group structured the company to stand the test of time, allowing it to grow and prosper in the good years, ensuring that it remains viable and solid during the lean.

Don served on the Home Hardware Board of Directors for ten years, from September 1964 to April 1974. He remembers those Board meetings with great affection. Everyone would convene at eight at night, after their workday, and continue until all business had been addressed. Dealers who lived too far to drive home were booked into The Flying Dutchman Motel.

offer them. "Most of them came on board," Don says simply. "And that's how Home Hardware started in southwestern Ontario."

Don and Eleanor had three children, two sons and a daughter. Their older son Ken has had a successful career in the automotive industry. Their daughter Barb raised her family and has now returned to her career. After he graduated from university, their youngest child Dave returned to the store fulltime, where he had worked since he was 14 years old. Somehow he always knew he would. And although the decision pleased his parents enormously, they never exerted pressure on him to do so. In 1990, the building was expanded to five times its original size. The old building was demolished, the new building rebuilt on the same location, merchandised and opened without Tuckey Home Hardware closing for a single business day.

Dave became the official owner, with his parents still retaining a small percentage of the shares, when Don retired in 1994. "I told him - 'Now you're going to be the boss," Don says. "If you want help, I'm available but I'm not going to tell you to do this or do the other thing." He said his father did the same for him, not forcing him to take over the business and getting out of the way when he did.

When the Tuckeys joined Home Hardware in 1964, there were 35 hardware stores in the London area. Today London has gone completely red: every one of the remaining six hardware stores is either an HH or an HHBC. These days Wortley Village is a charming enclave that has been voted "one of Canada's coolest neighbourhoods." A mix of residential and commercial, it boasts a creative mélange of cafes, good restaurants, galleries and shops. The façade of Tuckey Home Hardware fits right in.

One of the challenges of subsequent generations is to make their own contribution. In the years since he took over from his dad, Dave has put his own mark on the business. He purchased the adjacent building to create an expanded paint department, doubled the size of the parking lot and opened a garden centre. Further expansion plans are in the air. Dave is proud that there has been a sales increase every year but one. Under his ownership the store is open seven days a week, with a staff of 20 full and part time employees. In whatever spare time remains, Dave is an avid runner and in 2010 completed the Boston Marathon. Like his father before him, when it comes to running a successful business and living a charmed life, Dave clearly has the magic touch.

Don's fascination with magic began in the Navy and has lasted more than 50 years. The big stage tricks, like levitating, sawing people in half, and making rabbits disappear are his speciality. They require a lot of preparation, props and a good assistant—that role filled by his wife Eleanor who bears a remarkable resemblance to Queen Elizabeth—and the gift of the gab, his son points out. Over the years, Don put on shows for church groups and at the Community Centre in their summer hometown of Bayfield and at their own Christmas parties. In the early Home Hardware days when budgets were smaller Don was often the entertainment at the Markets at Bingemans and even provided the entertainment at one early staff Christmas party. In recent years, he and Eleanor staged a few shows at Retirement Homes and were often asked by the residents if they were moving in!

The Seguin Family:

Belle River Home Hardware, Countryside Home Hardware
Windsor, ON

Family is a recurring theme in the stories I have written for this book. The story of the Seguin family in Windsor, Ontario, is a slight departure from the typical multi-generational family tale. What started as a family feed store almost 70 years ago eventually became three separate and successful Home Hardware stores run by three different lines of the Seguin family.

Arthur Seguin started working in the family feed store in the mid 1940s. According to Arthur, it was a tough business and tough times. He quickly realized that in order to survive, they needed to diversify. By the time Arthur officially took over from his mother Corinne in 1955, Seguin's Feed Store on Girardot Street had become Seguin's Hardware Store. In 1967 Arthur made the decision to join Home Hardware. By now Arthur had four children, three sons, Larry, Dennis and Bernard and a daughter, Carol, all of whom grew up as "Home Hardware kids", working at the store after school and over the summers. In 1974, Arthur built a second store, Countryside Home Hardware on Malden Drive in LaSalle, about 15 minutes from the original store. His two older sons, Larry and Dennis, managed it for him. In 1982 his youngest son Bernard, Carol and her new husband Frank bought the original store from Arthur. Arthur retired at age 55, having taken care of each of his children. In 1988, Larry built a new store in Tecumseh on the other side of town and went into the LBM business. Dennis bought his share of the store in LaSalle. At the original store, Carol and Frank bought out Bernard who left the business for other endeavours. Now everyone who wanted one had a Home Hardware store. And Arthur, who took off his red shirt and told his children not to call, had three stores across town he could visit whenever the mood took him.

By now the second generation (or third, depending on how you track it) was building young families of their own: Larry and his wife Elaine had two children, Brent and Kimberly; Dennis and his wife Janis had four - sons Shane, Ryan and Chad and daughter Dana; Frank and Carol Skuhala had two daughters, Erica and Vanessa. The Seguin dynasty was expanding. While Arthur never had the luxury or benefit of a formal business education - he left school when he was 14 - he has a natural talent for retail marketing.

He was the first Home Hardware Dealer to order a carload of peat moss. He was also the first dealer to understand the power of flyer advertising, and is understandably proud of that fact. When he first suggested it to the group of Windsor-area Home Dealers who met at his store once a month, there was some initial scepticism. Before long flyers had become a central component of Home Hardware's National Advertising program. These days he derives much pleasure from watching his family expand the business he took over from his mother all those years ago.

Life has a way of taking us by surprise. And families have a way of rising to the occasion when those surprises aren't good. In 2001, Dennis Seguin passed away, leaving his wife Janis with four children who were just entering early adulthood. As Shane describes it, with the gravitas of the oldest brother, "One day we went from working part time at the store to owning a business." He credits Uncle Frank and Aunt Carol with helping them to weather the first few difficult years. By 2003, Shane, Ryan and Chad had hit their stride. They bought out their mother Janis, who still works in the business, and in 2010 were ready to start expanding, buying an existing Home Hardware store in Belle River, a half hour from Countryside. The three boys—Dana is part of the business but is in the midst of completing an MA in psychology—have melded into a successful team: they appreciate the support and backing provided by the Home Hardware family of which they are a part and count on each other day-to-day. They have plans to keep growing.

Three generations of Seguins stand before the municipal building down the street from Countryside Home Hardware: Family patriarch Arthur Seguin with his daughter-in-law Janis and her four children, Shane, Ryan, Chad and Dana.

Frank and Carol Skuhala, their two daughters Vanessa and Erica and Erica's fiancé David Iverson. Both sisters grew up in the business - Erica was a year old when her parents purchased the store in 1985. Vanessa is a French teacher with the Windsor Public School Board but continues to do office work part time at the store.

The Skuhala Family:

Yorktown Home Hardware
Windsor, ON

The Skuhalas' store in the Yorktown Plaza is 8,000 square feet of frenetic activity the morning we visit. Owners Frank and Carol Skuhala have a true family business: their older daughter Erica is a registered nurse, but fell under the Home Hardware spell and came into the business full time a few years ago. Her younger sister Vanessa works there part time. After Erica and David Iverson became a couple in 2002, he also started working in the family business. For the foreseeable future, the Skuhalas plan to keep working - they have a winter home in Florida - but are also making plans to formally pass the business along to the next generation.

The Seguin Family:

Tecumseh Home Hardware Building Centre
Windsor, ON

Until recently, Tecumseh Home Hardware Building Centre was the largest Seguin store, two and a half acres of property housing 20,000 square feet of retail space and a 5,000 square foot lumber yard with over 50 employees. That pride of place was assumed by the Essex HHBC when the family of Larry and Elaine took over in March 2013.

Like many other dealers, Larry says that the decision to join Home Hardware was the best move their family made. He remembers talking to his dad about it back in the mid 1960s. There were other banners on either side of them, but they are long gone. "If it hadn't been for Home Hardware, we would not be here today either," he says.

Larry and Elaine Seguin have already started the process of transferring shares to their two children, Brent and Kimberly. That way, he explains, they can do other things, like spend two months in Florida every winter and go on Walter's latest Study Tour in November 2012, the fourth trip they will have taken with him over the years.

Brent studied accounting, never intending to become a hardware dealer, but one day discovered that he was working at the store fulltime and realized it was where he belonged. Kimberly graduated from university but today is part owner with Brent and Larry. Like their cousins, Brent and Kimberly understand that having a successful family business requires a clear structuring of responsibilities. "We've had a plan from day one. When our Dad is here, he holds the reins. When he's not around, I take it over to a degree. We make sure we both have a say." "I couldn't imagine not working with Brent or my dad," Kimberly says. "We see each other every day and I couldn't imagine it any other way."

A few blocks from Tecumseh Home Hardware Building Centre stands a beautiful church that has been part of the community since 1873. Several years ago, however, its steeple was deemed architecturally unsound and removed to allow structural repairs to be made to the church roof. Tecumseh HHBC is supplying materials for the restoration. In the meantime, the clock and the church bells are back in working order so the community can once again enjoy the stirring sound as they peel out across the neighbourhood.

the Maritimes

In his many years in the hardware business, Walter Hachborn has made a lot of friends across the country. One of those friends was Walter Aylward. Shortly after Home Hardware became a reality in 1964, Walter A, in those days an independent hardware dealer, approached Walter H about joining Home. Walter told him that he was afraid it would be too expensive to ship product to Nova Scotia. Fortunately, the Nova Scotia Walter knew an independent trucker in the Maritimes who hauled fish to Ontario. The Ontario Walter made a deal to hire the empty trucks to ship hardware back to Nova Scotia. There was only one problem: Home Hardware didn't have any dealers in Nova Scotia. So Walter A hit the road, visiting independents across the province to convert them from their existing wholesale alliance to become members of Home. More and more dealers were coming on board, thanks to his tireless efforts, and in 1967 he sold his store to become Maritime Area Manager full time. He was successful in bringing independent dealers from the other Maritime provinces into the Home Hardware family fold. Walter Hachborn remembers that Walter Aylward nevertheless always insisted that he come down from St. Jacobs for the official signing up of a new Home Dealer. "I got to know the Atlantic provinces better than Ontario," Walter says. "I got into every corner because of Walter."

· ANNAPOLIS ROYAL · BARRINGTON PASSAGE ·

Nova Scotia

Despite the challenges and responsibilities of running businesses in towns an hour apart, the Lawries are involved in every aspect of their community, including The Historic Gardens in the centre of town. Both Rob and Joanne recently helped fund a five-year business plan for the gardens, a jewel in the crown of this tiny community that attracts visitors from around the world.

Annapolis Royal is one of the prettiest and most historic towns in North America, strategically situated at the mouth of the Annapolis basin. It is also the continent's oldest European settlement, founded and named Port Royal by a French expedition in 1604 that included Samuel de Champlain. For the next century, it was hotly contested ground, changing hands between the English and French seven times over the course of 17 battles. In 1710, along with the rest of Nova Scotia, it became British and was renamed Annapolis Royal in honour of then British monarch Anne. Today it still retains a strong Acadian flavour alongside its Mi'kmaq heritage.

Rob & Joanne Lawrie:

Annapolis Home Hardware Building Centre
Annapolis Royal, NS

Rob Lawrie spent many childhood hours in the back seat of the family car with his brother and sister as his parents, Robin and Beth Lawrie, drove around Nova Scotia looking for a Home Hardware store to buy. In 1981, they found the perfect spot and in 1982 built and opened a greenfield store in Annapolis Royal, an idyllically beautiful heritage town at the mouth of the Annapolis basin. With their parents working long hours in the store, Rob and his sibs grew up "hardware kids", spending their summers playing sports and splashing around in the outdoor community pool – when he wasn't helping out at the store.

Rob came home after university to work in the business, as he knew he always would. He met his future wife Joanne in 1994. With a business degree from St Mary's and years of part time work at Canadian Tire, Joanne has her own retail credentials. In '96 they married and three years later bought the hardware store from Rob's parents. The Annapolis store is now an HHBC, a conversion that took place in 2008. Just as they were getting into the swing of things, an opportunity came along to purchase the existing HHBC in Meteghan, an hour away. So life got hectic all over again.

"Your staff are your store. I am just the orchestrator," says Rob. "You have to give them tools and training, but then the freedom to go and do it. We're proud of our seasoned staff that has made our business a success. One of them just celebrated 25 years of continued service. Many have been with us for 10, 12 or 15 years. Some have left and then come back, so something must feel right to them."

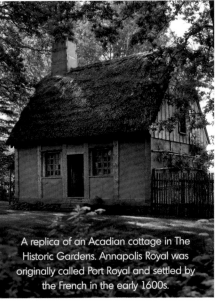

A replica of an Acadian cottage in The Historic Gardens. Annapolis Royal was originally called Port Royal and settled by the French in the early 1600s.

About 10 years ago, Rob's beloved community pool fell into disrepair and had to be filled in. So in 2007/2008 when the community started fundraising for a new one, Rob dove right in, and volunteered to sit on the committee. The pool up and running, Rob is responsible for the operations and maintenance of the mechanics and facilities. This includes on-going maintenance and the annual start-up and shutdown. This is where we found the Lawries one lovely evening in late June 2011, watching their own "hardware kid", five-year old Gabrielle, at her swimming class. She has already told her parents that she wants to be a Home Hardware Dealer when she grows up.

The Wilson Family: The Wilson family has been in Barrington Passage since 1760.

Wilson's Home Hardware Building Centre, Wilson's Home Furniture
Barrington Passage, NS

It's a gorgeous sunny day in June 2011 at Buzz and Ruth Wilson's beautiful home overlooking Barrington Passage and Cape Sable Island, on the southern tip of Nova Scotia. Some days, seals sun themselves on the rocks below. Wilson's Home Hardware Building Centre - all 40,000 square feet—gleams in the distance. The store is situated on the same piece of land as the original Wilson's General Store, which Buzz' father Fred bought in 1924. The Wilson family has been in Barrington Passage since 1760. A flourishing family business was already in place by the early1800s. Walter "Buzz" Wilson and his sister Dorothy took over the family business in 1945 after their mother died. "Buzz" was all of 19 and his sister just 20.

But our story begins in the 1960s when "the two Walters" first came calling. Wilson's General Store had been a fixture in the community since the 1920s, but by the mid to late 1960s, the big chain department stores were getting into hardware more and more, making it very rough for the small independents. It was a natural evolution that in 1967 they became part of the Home Hardware family, one of the first Maritime independent stores to do so.

In fact, Buzz insists that half the hardware stores in Canada owe their existence today to Walter Hachborn. For David Wilson, Buzz' son who took over the business from his father in1987, it's the Dealer-Owner model that makes it work: "We've had many types of stores and we always use Home Hardware as THE model. It's too bad there isn't a Home Hardware in all areas of business." David's son Michael has recently become the fourth generation to join the family business.

In 1981, Walter was guest speaker at an anniversary dinner the store held in a hall on Cape Sable Island. Bruce Christie, then the store's general manager, presented a painting by his wife Bertha to Walter. Twenty-five years later, Walter was back to present Wilson's with the Store of the Year award. Bruce, since retired, was there and Walter mentioned that he still had the painting hanging in his living room.

Wilson's Home Hardware Building Centre continues to play a central role in the day-to-day life of a community that has changed in many ways since the 18th century but in terms of its values remains the same. Serving the community is still key. In 2010, Wilson's Home Hardware Building Centre won the Nova Scotia Corporate Volunteers of the Year award. Over the years, they have been involved in countless fundraising initiatives for different worthy causes. Currently their biggest event is a Ladies' Gala spa night in mid-October. They clean out the power aisles and invite different organizations to set up tables, charge $10 a ticket with proceeds split between the different local volunteer groups. For the first three years of the fundraiser, all proceeds went to the Canadian Cancer Society's Relay for Life. In 2010, they raised about $17,000, with proceeds going to IWK (Izaac Walton Killam) the Maritimes' children's hospital in Halifax that they chose as their beneficiary because so many people in the area use the facility. The staff has organized a group called For Kids' Sake, which provides funds for kids with various special needs.

With the help of his son David, "Buzz" was game to clamber out to the distinctive shore rocks at the foot of his property. Barrington Passage and Cape Sable Island are in the background.

Murray Marshall feels privileged to have travelled with Walter on three Home Hardware trips. When it came time to unload the luggage, he remembers, Walter would often climb into the luggage department and start throwing off the bags. "But that's Walter. He's a hands-on fellow and he was willing to do anything. Of course with Walter being the Godfather of everybody, we try to follow his example and it's been just a great learning experience. He has taught me many, many things down through the years."

Murray Marshall and Tim Sabean show off the Zamboni, their current promotional vehicle, at the local arena. The Wilson's Home Hardware Building Centre name and logos are "all over it," Murray says proudly. In 2010, a group of local people built a community playground next door to the arena. Wilson's contributed most of the materials, either at cost or as a donation. "We very rarely refuse anyone and have had that attitude down through the years," says Tim.

Over the years, a number of the employees who had played a role in the success of the Barrington Passage store were eager to buy into the business, but Buzz wanted to keep it in the family. At the same time, he wanted to help out the loyal employees looking for the business opportunities with Home Hardware that he had enjoyed. In 1968, he found

Tim Sabean and Murray Marshall:

Wilson's Home Hardware Building Centre
Digby, NS

the solution and bought Turnbulls, an independent hardware store in Digby, which allowed interested employees to buy in to that store. One of those employees was Gary Sabean, who was still the company controller when we visited in June 2011. The Digby store soon took on its own family complexion. In 1973, Murray Marshall joined, and according to Buzz, kept the business going for the next 35 years. "Young" Tim Sabean, Gary's son, joined in 1987 and married Murray's daughter, Andrea, just to keep it all in the family. Andrea has been with the business since 1986. But the family ties don't stop there. Murray's brother Larry started as a delivery truck driver in 1972 and currently runs the building supply end of the business. Murray's sister Phyllis Vree, who joined the business just three weeks after Tim, looks after the accounts receivable. And all of Murray's five kids, Tim and Andrea's children, Jessica and Drew, as well as assorted cousins and other relatives, have at one time or another worked full or part time in the business.

In 2004, Buzz sold his share in the Digby operation and Murray Marshall retired from active duty. "I was here for 35 years and operated the company for many of those years, in a secondary capacity and eventually in the top spot. I enjoyed every minute of it and could have kept going but Tim and my oldest daughter wanted my job!"

Today Tim and Andrea carry on the Marshall–Sabean family business after purchasing the remaining shares from Murray Marshall in December, 2012. They have kept the Wilson name in recognition of Buzz' role and its history in the community.

The company has a long history of fund raising for the Atlantic Chapter of the Breast Cancer foundation. It has always been a staff initiative and originally took place at the store. The first year they expected 40 people and 75 showed up. They raised $1,100 that evening. By the second year, they had to limit attendance to 350, selling tickets at the door for $10 a piece. They sold out in less than an hour. There were waiting lists to attend. The company finally handed the project over to another group, but in their years of involvement raised about $70,000. Staff organizers were recognized for their efforts by the Breast Cancer Foundation.

Bruce Elliott: Bruce decided to call 'the other Walter'.
"It was like speaking to the messiah."

Chester Home Hardware
Chester, NS

This is a story of true grit. Bruce Elliott grew up in the family business, a general and grocery store in New Ross, one of the third generation Elliotts in town. In the early 1800s, New Ross had been settled by ex soldiers given land grants by the British army. True to his roots, Bruce joined the navy but came back home in 1964 to run the family business. In 1976, he was getting bored with grocery – "everything's the same from week to week," he says. Looking for a challenge, and encouraged by the dealer in Hantsport, Bruce decided to open a Home Hardware store. He contacted Walter Aylward, then the District Manager, who gave him the green light to proceed.

He had the hole dug (building onto the existing grocery store in New Ross) when Walter suddenly told him that he didn't know for sure that he had the business after all. Bruce decided to call 'the other Walter.' "It was like speaking to the messiah," Bruce recalls almost 40 years later. "He said, 'Bruce, I'm coming to Halifax in two weeks. Come in and we'll sign the papers.' That was it, so I knew I was on my way to becoming a Home Hardware Dealer."

But that wasn't the end of his troubles. Just after he got the hole dug, a fire wiped him out. It was April 11, 1977. Under insured, he lost everything. "I had been planning to go to the spring market, but I made a snap decision to get out of it, just walk away. I figured I'd build a house and go work for someone else." His CA told him in no uncertain terms that he couldn't work for anyone else. So, Bruce went to the spring market after all. "I came home, started rebuilding, and was open and ready in August."

Bruce built on his success slowly and steadily and today owns four stores: Chester, as sole owner, and Greenwood, Middleton (with a Home Furniture) and Bridgetown, an HHBC which he co-owns with his original partner Don Marshall. He works a lot from home these days, thanks to computers and the fact that he has good managers in place, including his step-son Darin Baker who runs the Chester operation, located in one of the most beautiful and picturesque towns in Canada. In fact Walter Hachborn confessed that if he weren't already living in St. Jacobs, he would want to live right here, in Chester, Nova Scotia.

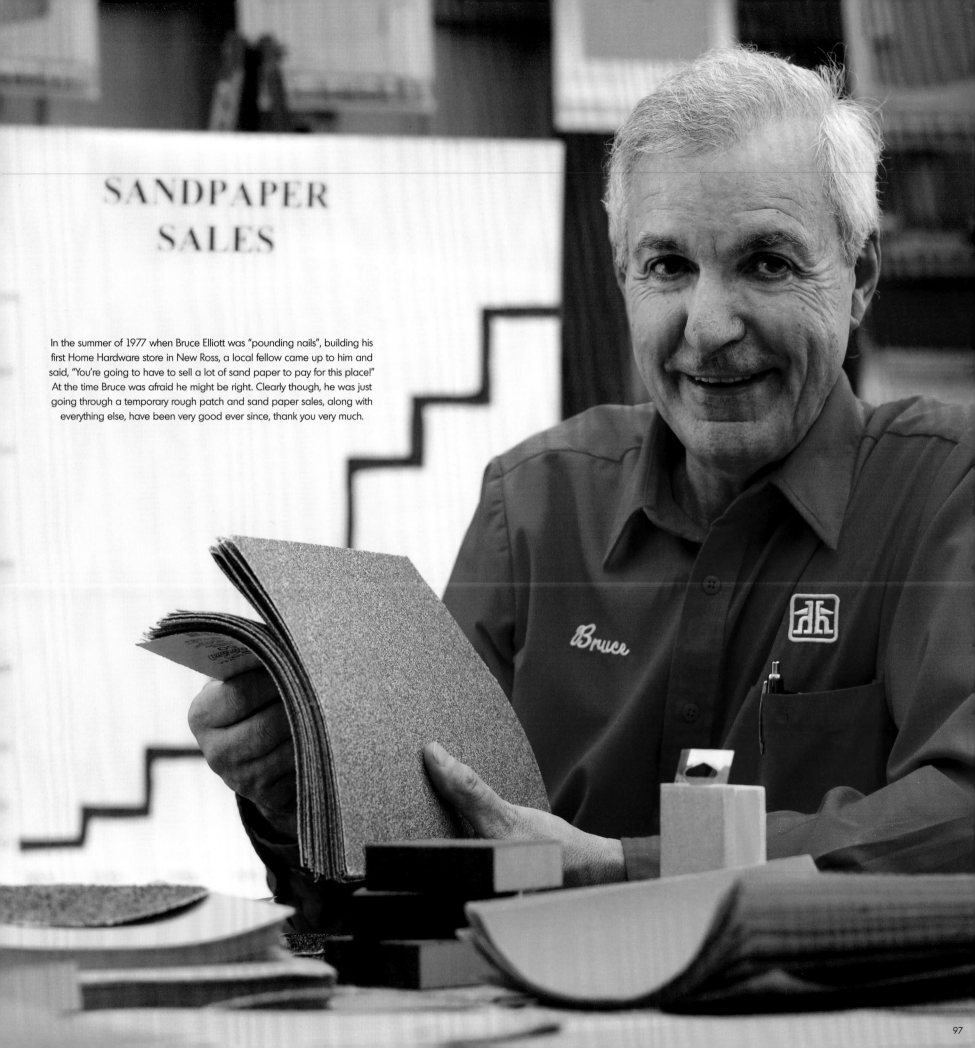

SANDPAPER SALES

In the summer of 1977 when Bruce Elliott was "pounding nails", building his first Home Hardware store in New Ross, a local fellow came up to him and said, "You're going to have to sell a lot of sand paper to pay for this place!" At the time Bruce was afraid he might be right. Clearly though, he was just going through a temporary rough patch and sand paper sales, along with everything else, have been very good ever since, thank you very much.

Proud members of Gow's Home Hardware and volunteer firefighters: Peter Gow (Honorary Captain - Bridgewater), Kerry Ritcey (Honorary - Bridgewater), Tony Allen (Chief – Pleasantville and District), Arthur Morse (Lieutenant ~ Hebbville), Mike Kendal (Firefighter - Pleasantville), Ryan Martin (Black hat – Oak Hill), Scott Bustin (Firefighter – Bridgewater), Reid Whynot (Honorary Chief/Captain – Bridgewater), John Fraser (Honorary – Oak Hill), Kevin Dolliver (Honorary – Bridgewater)

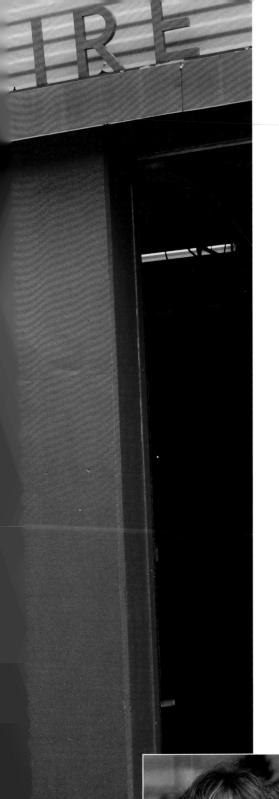

Peter Gow: Peter's grandfather Walter was chief of the Bridgewater Fire Department for over 30 years.

Gow's Home Hardware
Bridgewater, NS

Gow's Home Hardware has a venerable history in the community in more ways than one. Founded in 1848 by Robert Dawson, the business was bought in 1929 by Peter's grandfather, Walter – a good Home Hardware name, Peter points out. Peter's dad Frank, his uncle Ken and his aunt Jean were the driving force through the 1960s and 1970s. In 1966, Gow's Hardware joined Home Hardware, making them one of the first Charter Maritime members. Frank was on the Home Hardware Board of Directors from April 18, 1978 to April 24, 1989. He retired in 1993. Peter joined in 1970 and the business moved to its current location in the Eastside Plaza in 1989.

With three stores, Home is a big employer in town. There is Gow's Home Hardware, Buck's Home Building Centre, a former Beaver location, and Gow's Home Furniture. These three businesses all have different owners. Gow's has 60 employees, and a surprising number of them, including Peter, are volunteer fire fighters for different fire departments in the area. Altogether, they have almost 165 years of service (at four of the 30 fire departments in the trading area). Peter's grandfather Walter was chief of the Bridgewater Fire Department for over 30 years, his father Frank served as chief for almost ten years, and a total of 43 years in the department as a member. Peter, now retired from active duty, served for 25 years. These fine men in uniform are all part of a proud family and community tradition.

"I was what was called a Christmas graduate," says Peter. "I didn't like university, so I lasted from September to December. I came back home and started to work in the store, which at the time was 2,400 square feet. My father heard a rumour that the big department store down the street might be for sale. So he said, 'Why don't you go over and talk to the manager?' I walked over and the store manager basically chased me out of there with a broom! But a week or two later, my father had a call from their Head Office in Montreal and it was for sale. We needed a substantial loan and the Royal Bank manager said, 'Well now we can't loan you that kind of money at all.' So Walter Hachborn flew into Halifax. And my father, Walter and I met on the top floor of the Royal Bank in Halifax. We went into the big boardroom with the oak table and the bankers with their pinstripe suits and I remember my dad and me sitting in the corner, more or less. Walter sat with the bankers and did the talking for us. Every now and then, he'd say, 'Isn't that right Frank?' And dad would answer. In other words, Walter arranged the loan for us. The bank forwarded the money so that we could buy the building. We probably wouldn't be where we are right now without Walter."

Amanda Fancy: "Home Hardware is a great Canadian company,"

Thirty -four is a pretty tender age to become sole owner of a 34,000 square foot Home Hardware store. But Amanda Fancy has worked at Gow's Home Hardware for more than half her life: first as a part-time summer student and then fulltime, after a four year hiatus in Halifax for business college and a brief stint working in another industry. She was looking for a chance to come back home to Bridgewater when there was an opening in the accounting department. Her next move was to Systems Manager. By now Amanda was working closely with then-owner Peter Gow, attending markets and making purchasing decisions. By the time Peter made the decision to retire, Amanda knew the business thoroughly and was the obvious choice to take it over. After a year of talk and a year of due process, Amanda Fancy took over Gow's Home Hardware in January 2012. As the new owner of the oldest business in Bridgewater, Amanda intends to pursue the philosophy her predecessor learned from Walter Hachborn: Treat people the way you want to be treated. "Home Hardware is a great Canadian company," she says. "I wouldn't want to work anywhere else."

The winning Home Hardware team gathered outside Justin and Roxanne's home: from left to right: front row: George McLean (flooring contractor) and Jamie Currie (contractor who installed the cabinets). Back row: Jenny Proudfoot, Marion McLean (George's wife and a Home Hardware employee), Delbert Brown (paint contractor), Karri Tibbel (employee), Kendall Proudfoot, Al Rumley, (electrician) and Jim Proudfoot.

The Proudfoot Family: Team Proudfoot took to the ice with Kendall's wife Jenny stick handling the initiative.

Proudfoots Home Hardware Building Centre
Stellarton, NS

Justin Robar told his mom, "I'm a very lucky boy." And indeed he was, especially on the day in 2009 when The Sunshine Foundation contacted Proudfoots Home Hardware in Justin's hometown of New Glasgow. That's when the Proudfoots learned that a young local boy had submitted a request to The Sunshine Foundation for a makeover, much like he'd seen on some of the TV shows he enjoyed watching. His name was Justin Robar and he was wheel chair bound. He also happened to be an avid Toronto Maple Leafs fan, so it was no surprise that he wanted a bedroom makeover in a Maple Leaf theme.

Team Proudfoot took to the ice with Kendall's wife Jenny stick handling the initiative. A formidably efficient organizer with a beautiful and perpetual smile, Jenny drafted two energetic staff members, Marion McLean and Karri Tibbel, to help make it happen.

The Burford paint department signed on, as well as several contractors in New Glasgow. The room was rewired for the new TV and computer that were part of Justin's request, the walls were painted the team colours, a new

floor was laid, adorned with the Maple Leafs logo, curtains were made in the same pattern, a score clock was installed and Justin's headboard was transformed into a goalie's net.

In addition, after everything was in place, the Proudfoots arranged for Wendell Clark, attending a celebrity golf tournament in the neighbourhood, to stop by for a photo and autograph session. Everyone donated their time and two years later, when we visited to take our pictures, the room was just as awesome and Justin just as proud as on the day he first saw it.

"You know – there's us down here in the Maritimes and they're people out west and there's the Head Office in Ontario but there's no real difference between us. With some big companies, they think they are up on a pedestal. We don't see that with Home though. Everybody's treated pretty well equally. Everybody who works for Home Hardware knows that they are really employees of all the storeowners. They work to make sure all our questions are answered, and our problems are solved." Kendall Proudfoot

"Justin was speechless. Home Hardware did more than I ever thought. They are great, great people, more than a hardware store. They really care about their community."
Roxanne Adams, Justin's mother

Justin Robar shows off his room to Kendall Proudfoot. Kendall and his brother Jim, currently a Director of Home Hardware, own stores in Pictou and Stellarton.

"We're really proud of our staff – like I say, they will make or break it." Carl, Shirley and Ron MacRae gather for a group photo with some members of their staff. Getting permission to shoot on government land with tight security was a good demonstration of their community relations: Ron just picked up the phone and called someone who met us five minutes later to open the gate for us. This photograph was taken at Marine Atlantic, gateway to Newfoundland, North Sydney, Cape Breton.

From left to right: Tom Patey, John Duffy, Joe Musgrave, Ron, Shirley and Carl MacRae, Rosalind Guy and Lloyd Fudge.

Carl MacRae is a happy man. And why not? He's exactly where he's always wanted to be. He and his wife Shirley have built a successful Home Hardware store in North Sydney and are in the process of handing over the business to their son Ron and daughter Natalie (the business name is Natron, an amalgamation of their children's names). But the journey was long and the road not always easy.

The MacRae Family:

MacRae Home Hardware
North Sydney, NS

Home Hardware has been terrific. I can't say enough about them – the support we've got from them has been really good from day one.

Here's Carl's story, in his own words:

When I was seventeen, I went to work for a guy in Baddeck in the middle of beautiful Cape Breton Island. He was opening a Handy Andy. He hired me for two weeks. Twenty-nine years later, in 1991, I left and bought this store. All the time I was with him, I wanted my own store.

I became manager (of the Baddeck store) when I was 20. A few years later, we joined Home Hardware. So I became a Home Hardware Dealer, more or less, but I was still just the manager. When the owner sold the store, I didn't have the money to buy it. The new owner offered it to me for $28,000. That was a lot of money. He said, 'Well Carl, you work in it for a year and if you can make a go of it, you can buy it later.' We made a go of it but the price kept going up and I never could afford to buy it. I went all over Cape Breton Island looking for a Home Hardware store. Then one day the guy who owned the North Sydney store asked me if I'd like to buy his. I said, 'I'd like to but I don't really have that much money.' I was just getting a salary and bonus. He said, 'I'll sell it to you for a dollar.'

That scenario didn't work out. The store wasn't even worth a dollar. But a few months later, Paul Straus called with a plan to get us our store. Shirley and I bought our first store in May 1991. It was five thousand square feet and it was going bankrupt, but we felt we could turn things around and we did well. After being in business for four years, we needed more space. On my way home, I used to drive by an old grocery store that had been closed for many years. And every time I'd think to myself, 'Oh my, that's such a good location, it's a better size.' We didn't have any room for growth where we were. I kept thinking how much I'd love to have it. About three years later I went to see the owner. He'd wanted $500,000 but knocked it down to $250,000. He sent a guy to show it to me. There was snow on the floor

where the roof was completely gone. It was just a mess. I said, 'This is perfect, this is just what I want.'

The bank said it was worth $75,000. I knew that wasn't going to fly. I put a plan together and went to the owner. I told him I would give him $250,000 for his building. Well that got him off his chair right away. But I said, 'This is the deal: you give it to me for two years rent-free. I'll take that money and fix it up. This is what I can afford to pay per month,' which I had worked out over 14 years. 'If I go down the tubes, you'll have a building that is all fixed up right. If I don't go down the tubes you get your $250,000.' We shook hands – no lawyers involved. But now I had to get rid of my building. I got on the phone to everybody I could think of. Finally a guy offered me $80,000, about $5,000 less than I still owed. I thought it's either going to happen here or it's not. I told my accountant and my banker that I was buying a building appraised at $75,000 for $250,000. But doing it this way, I wasn't obligated to the bank.

We opened two months later on a Tuesday. No advance advertising. I came to work that morning and Public Works had all the streets blocked off in front of the store. I thought, 'Oh my God - what's this day going to bring?' At 5 o'clock I looked in the till and I think we'd done $3,700, compared to sales over at the other store of $800 a day. So I thought, 'This is going to work.'

"When we bought the store, there wasn't much stock left in it and I remember this guy wanting a gallon of paint. I got the paint and started to mix it and we didn't have the colour. I said, I'm sorry sir, we don't have the colour to put in that. He said, 'That's too bad. I really would have liked to give you the business.' I said, could you wait an hour for it? The customer said he could. So I hopped into my car and ran over to the Sydney store, got some colour and came back and mixed it for him. I had a customer for life."

The three generations of Payzants are showing off the day we arrive to take our photographs for the book. There's a lot of horsing around and good natured joking, especially between the three of the four second generation brothers in attendance, Andrew, the youngest, Jim, the oldest and Jeff. (Fourth brother Larry is at the store in Sackville, NB, so can't join us.) Father John looks on with a smile. He still comes to work every day

supporters of IWK, the only children's hospital in the Maritimes, Lions Club, Kinsmen Club, all of Home Hardware's corporate charities, and the list goes on. But the cause that means the most to them is The James Fund, founded by Syd Birrell in memory of his son James who died of neuroblastoma, a devastating childhood cancer. Although James died in 2001 at the age of eight, the Payzants first got involved through a major fundraiser

The Payzant Family: *"When an opportunity came along, no one sat down and said, do you think we can handle this?"*

Payzant Building Products Limited
Sackville, NB, Lower Sackville, and Dartmouth, NS

(Andrew calls him their "internal auditor"), but has passed on much of the day-to-day business to his four sons. And now the next generation is coming on board. Jeff's son Matthew represents the newest generation of Payzants on this day. We sit in the public gardens below Fultz House Museum, where the family has donated a gazebo in memory of their wife, mother and grandmother, Shirley Payzant. The park, next to a busy artery linking Lower Sackville to nearby Halifax, is just across from the site of Blackburn's original store where John Payzant started in the hardware business in the early 1950s. In the spring of 1964, Blackburn split up his business, and sold the different components, one each to the three young entrepreneurs who had worked for him. Only Payzants has stood the test of time.

While no one will deny that there are challenges inherent in a family business - they all agree it boils down to two key ingredients, respect and patience - the four Payzant brothers have devised a division of labour and built a very successful business that now includes two HHBC stores, one in Lower Sackville, Nova Scotia, the second in Sackville, NB and an HBC in Dartmouth, Nova Scotia.

Like virtually every Home Dealer across the country, the Payzants are deeply involved in their communities. Every cause is worthy, as Andrew points out, but for the past 30 years, their focus has been on kids. They are

in 2006, The Ride For Cancer, supported by Home Hardware corporate. David Visschedyk, who had the same cancer as Terry Fox, rode his bike across Canada to raise awareness and money for The James Fund. The final destination was Sackville, Nova Scotia. The enthusiasm for the event was enormous: staff and customers together donated a total of $31,000, the largest single contribution the store and business has ever made. "The James Fund is a symbol of the hundreds of different things we've done to support the community around kids," Andrew says. "It's such a privilege that we are in a position to be able to do this."

Syd Birrell, father of James and author of "Ya Can't Let Cancer Ruin Your Day" does not consider himself to be a fundraiser. . He's an organist and conducts choirs and sort of "dabbles" in fundraising: "After the event a real fundraiser said to me, 'Do you know how hard it is to raise $25,000?' So I realized that it was a really big deal for those guys to do that. It shows a sense of family, sense of community. This was Andrew's goal: you can make the world a better place. You can turn adversity into triumph. They bought in big time and that feeling is still there five or six years later."

Andrew Payzant on being company CEO:
"I only had one promotion in my life, back in 1978, when my dad told me I should move from the warehouse to customer service. Since then, I change the title on my business card every now and then. For a while I'd keep pace with Paul Straus. When he went from one title to another, I'd think, oh, that sounds good, so I'd change mine to that too!"

European Tour 1989

We left our "home and native land" the 28th of May,
A study tour was due to start, and we had a part to play.
Ambassadors in bright red coats, we represented "Home",
We climbed into a mammoth plane, and jetted off to Rome.

The night was short, the trip was long, we hardly slept a wink,
But the gorgeous sunrise that we saw made up for it (I think). A tour of
ancient ruins was the first thing on our list,
Then it was to the Jolly Midas to catch up on sleep we missed.

The Roman Colosseum was a sight you should behold,
Where gladiators did their thing, it got quite gory I am told.
We saw the homes of emperors, of Caesar and of such,
I found it just incredible, this city has so much.

Before we left this ancient place, we toured St Peter's and the Square,
The works of Michelangelo are displayed in splendour there.
We saw the Pope and took our place with many thousands more,
In fact I never saw such crowds in all my life before.

Now in the City of the Vatican the rules are very tight,
To see the riches of the church, one's dress must be just right.
Poor Bill didn't measure up, his knees were "in the nude",
He had to stand and wait outside in lieu of being rude.

The saying goes that when in Rome, do as the Romans do,
So we sang some great Italian songs, ate lots of pasta, too.
Hotel Columbus had us in and treated us real well,
We met a stately Cardinal, ate lunch and stayed a spell.

Then off we went to Florence, by coach and not by plane,
And it was nice being on the road with such good friends again.
The Alexander and the Fleming were our homes away from home,
We saw the tomb of Michelangelo, who "was retired" here from Rome.

Now I just have to tell you of a side trip that we took
To the leaning Tower of Pisa, just so we could have a look.
A famous wonder of the world, it seems to have a blight,
Because it's leaning to the left -- or is it to the right?

We went into this leaning tower, and round and round we went
On smooth , worn stones of marble, until my breath was spent;
Always circling upward, I was inclined to stop --
Then Walter took me by the hand and led me to the top!

Well, it was worth the effort, and I'm so glad I did,
The satisfaction of that climb made me happy as a kid.
The height gave Don a tingle -- but I can't tell you where,
He just found it so thrilling after climbing way up there.

On June 2nd we left Florence and continued on our way,
The rain had stopped, the sun was out, it was a glorious day!
We travelled through vast vineyards and fields of poppies red,
The beauty of Italia is all that has been said.

The hour had reached past noon -- time when Joe came on the "mike",
And said he had a treat for us, that he was sure we'd like.
So in the village of Cividale, we stopped and had some lunch,
We loved Joe's relatives, they're great -- again, "Joe, thanks a bunch."

Our coach adorned with roses, we continued on our way,
To the old town of Verona, the scene of Shakespeare's play,
Where Romeo wooed Juliette, whose lives were fraught with woe,
True love was theirs, but life was tough, and so they had to go.

We found the Hotel Plaza was a lovely place to stop,
On arriving in Padua -- (and it was among the shops).
The meals were good, the rooms were fine, to us the staff was great,
Tho' we must have tried their patience as we were very late.

We make a trip to Venice where the streets are all awash,
Gondolas are the way to go, no cars or trucks, by gosh!
The Bridge of Sighs, the Grand Canal, the clock at St. Mark's Square,
We saw them all and I was glad for the chance of being there.

We said goodbye to Italy on Sunday, June the 4th,
And made our way to Austria, away up further north,
Today we were presented with an overwhelmming sight,
Our first look at the Alps, both to our left and to our right.

I wish I could describe to you the beauty that we saw,
At towering peaks and lush green valleys, I could only stare in awe.
Such majesty is not by chance, but of a master plan,
Designed for us by God alone, and naught to do with man.

We arrived at Hotel Dorint with lots of time to spare,
In the ancient town of Salzberg -- there is lots of history there.
The Sound of Music, Mozart's home, I can't remember all,
The facts all blend together and my mind is much too small.

We went to hear a concert in the fortress on the hill,
The violins sang softly and the audience was still.
It seemed that we went back in time, and Mozart lived again,
And one could sense the romance of the era way back then.

On June 6th in old Vienna, we helped to celebrate
Dave and Barbara's anniversary, their 25th to date.
There were flowers and "soft" music, and violinists played,
They waltzed, and romance was alive on this, their special day.

Vienna is an ancient town, a wondrous place to be,
In fact the Celts resided here for centuries B.C.
We stayed at the Hungaria, a nice hotel in which to stop,
We heard a concert at the palace, and had lots of time to shop.

Now a word about Graziano, the driver of our bus;
He was a very patient guy and tried to please all of us.
Some people said, "Turn on the air", then some said, "Turn it off",
Some liked the music fairly loud, some people liked it soft.

He turned the music up and down, the air went off and on,
But Graziano always wore a smile, and drove quietly along.
Raphael controlled the other group and kept them all in line,
They followed us (we were number one) and things worked out just fine.

We enjoyed our stay in Munich, though it was, in fact, quite brief,
And the spacious four-star Hungar was to all a great relief.
We enjoyed the buskers in the streets, the excitement and the sun,
To quote Don Myles, we all could say, "Ah, now we're having fun."

I understand that Vic and Sandra kept things lively on bus two,
They entertained with Newfie jokes, their friends, both old and new.
At the festival in Munich, Vic's gallantry took wing,
He wooed the ladies old and young, and gave them all a fling.

Now Victor had a secret wish to be a tourist guide;
And one time on a walking tour he took Don Myles aside.
While Donnie filmed the scenes they passed, Vic played the part with ease,
Describing every detail in delightful "Newfouneze"!

We left Munich on the eleventh and we were Innsbruck bound,
We got up into the mountains, and the road was twisting round.
Snow-capped peaks were thrusting high, and boy, the view was nice,
Walter Aylward liked it all so much he went to see it twice.

And so in Oberammergau we shopped away three hours,
We strolled around and looked, and lunched, and stopped to smell the flowers.
We owe a lot to Walter, and we certainly understand
Just why he left his passport, and we also think he's grand!

As we travelled through the Alps, the scenery held us all in awe,
It was absolute perfection, as God never makes a flaw.
Granite peaks all topped with snow, steep slopes of tall green trees,
Led down to velvet meadows and cool rivers running free.

Our descent down into Innsbruck sure kept us all awake,
As the road plunged sharply downward, we prayed for real good brakes.
The date was June 11th, and we sure were glad to celebrate
Nicole and Harvey's anniversary, and it was their first to date.

We stayed in Innsbruck at the Central and laid down our weary heads,
And it felt so good to snuggle 'neath the duvets on the beds.
Next day would be the last leg of our trip to Switzerland,
When the men would don red coats and be a sharp Home Hardware band.

Monday, we drove into Montreux, and continued right through town
To the shores of Lake Geneva where we would settle down.
At the Hyatt Continental (now this was more our style),
We emptied out our messy bags, and made plans to stay awhile.

On Tuesday morning we hopped a bus and went to Gruyère,
They're famous for their cheese, they also have a castle there.
This day was really special, there were lots of things to see,
But switchbacking round steep mountains was the greatest thrill to me.

On Thursday we went touring through the valley of the Rhone
Where vineyards are competing with the mountains made of stone.
By bus and then by train we journeyed up the mountainside
To the little town of Zermatt -- and it was a long, hot ride.

We wandered through the streets on foot down to the cable cars
Which go right up through the mountains as if heading for the stars.
From the darkness deep within the hill, we came out into the light,
And there we were presented with a most impressive sight.

There stood the famous Matterhorn, its peak all white with snow,
It stands up there so proudly, but I want you all to know,
That I have no wish to climb it, "just looking" is enough,
I know for sure I'd fall right off, and the landing would be rough.

I didn't want to miss a thing, and as we drove along,
I realized that, first of all, these people must be strong.
Their houses perch on ledges, with more steep hills behind,
To climb up there would surely take much stronger legs than mine.

The Congress Ball was held on Thursday night, and I guess that you could say
That all in all it was a fitting way to end the day.
The ballroom was resplendent, and we surely were well fed,
And in a room of sombre black, you can't beat Home Hardware red.

There's just one other couple that I'd like to mention here,
We've travelled many miles with them, and they are very dear.
They've had lots of anniversaries, which now number thirty-eight,
Congratulations to you both, I'm sorry that we're late.

From Montreux to Lugano was the last leg of our tour,
And after three full weeks of European food, I'm sure we all weighed more.
We wrapped things up by going for a cruise around the lake,
The night was warm, the scenery great, and it wasn't hard to take.

Now I can't mention everything in this, my resumé,
Nor everyone who played a part, for it would take all day.
Suffice to say that it was great, a real terrific time,
And now before you all get bored, I'm going to end this rhyme!

Shirley Payzant, June 17/89

Ken's first big Home Hardware meeting was in Dartmouth a month after he joined Proudfoots. He was nervous about meeting the company president for the first time. They were sitting down and someone served them coffee. Ken leaned over to ask Jim when he would meet the president. Jim said, "You just did – he just served you coffee."

Horse sense and hard work: The Wilson family on their horse farm, on Bras d'Or Lake, Cape Breton. Ken and Norma, Aaron and Amber and their children Zoe (6 months) and Maggie and Craig and Brenda and their son Michael and daughter Emma.

"Paul's been to our place and I've been to his barn. Whenever we have a chance to eat lunch together at the Home show we talk about horses. It gives him a good break from the pressures of the business."

It's a cold, misty morning the day we visit Ken and Norma Wilson at their home and horse farm on the shore of the Bras D'Or Lake. He and his wife Norma live here full time these days. Their younger son Aaron, who has converted the garage into a little weekend cottage for him and his young family, now manages the business in town. Their older son Craig runs the kitchen remodelling business, a natural offshoot of the main business. As

He was 41 years old and about to buy his first business. "I came to talk to the owner with nothing but a bunch of dreams. He said 'This place is worth $680,000.' I reached into my pockets and pulled them out. I said 'I'm sorry to even waste your time. So he said – 'Sit down son. There's more ways to skin a cat than one.' Once he said that, I felt, boy there's something here."

The Wilson Family:

Wilson's Home Hardware
Sydney, NS

"Make sure that Walter understands that it's thanks to him that hundreds of Canadian families are able to have good lives."

the family gathers for the photo session, Ken shows me around the perfectly maintained seven-acre property. He says, "Look around you. Isn't this beautiful? You make sure that Walter understands that it's thanks to him that hundreds of Canadian families are able to have good lives like we do. It's thanks to Home Hardware that we are here today."

Ken went to work at the F.W. Woolworth Company in Truro out of high school, starting in the stock room and working his way into management over 15 years. He moved 13 times around the Maritimes, acquiring invaluable retail experience. When he and Norma married, he wanted a better life than seven day a week pressure, just waiting to be fired.

In 1976, Ken and Norma were living in New Glasgow. One night at a Kinsmen meeting, Jim Proudfoot Sr. mentioned that he and his brother John had been thinking of talking to Ken about coming to work with them. During the negotiations, "We never talked salary. I just said – I trust you." They started with a handshake and in Ken's words, "I left hell and joined heaven."

Ken saw enormous potential at Proudfoots Home Hardware, but after seven years helping the Proudfoots build their business, he was ready for his own store. Walter Hachborn suggested that Ken contact the owner of the ailing Sydney store. The owner jumped at the opportunity to sell. It was 1983, the year of the "great recession with super interest rates." Ken recalls.

By the time they hammered out a deal, Ken needed $65,000 up front, which he still didn't have. He and Norma had two young children, a house they'd just bought in New Glasgow…and no money. He sold his house to a well-meaning relative for $65,000, exactly the amount needed. But not nearly enough to buy inventory for a 10,000 square foot store. So they borrowed enough money from a relative in order to get the business started. There was also one other small detail, which he discovered when he phoned St. Jacobs to place his order: according to the person on the end of the line, his store number was no good! Ken said the magic words: "Could you get hold of Walter Hachborn for me?" And in five minutes, everything started rolling again. Only 10 years later did Ken learn that Walter had personally guaranteed payment.

For the next year, they worked seven days a week, taking only grocery money out of the business. They lived with Norma's mother for the first two years, Norma working alongside him in the store. It was an anxious time. One day Ken was in the paint department building a display. He turned around to see a well-dressed man watching him, his arms folded across his chest. Ken asked if there was anything he could do for him and the man said no, but he did have something to tell Ken. He said. "You're going to have a good store here. You're going to do well." Ken thought, that's good news and inquired as to his line of work. The man said, "I own the Canadian Tire Store right across the street." That vote of confidence cleared up Ken's butterflies pretty fast.

Jeff Redden: "My dad always said, give your customers lots of ways to spend their money."

Windsor Home Hardware
Windsor, NS

Clarence's Café is a busy place, especially on Saturday mornings when there's always music, local talent hired by Jeff Redden, owner of Windsor Home Hardware. You're also likely to find more than one politician having coffee at a crowded table, available to listen to the beefs, queries and plaudits of their constituents. It's Jeff's favourite place to brainstorm with other like-minded people in the community, turning dreams into reality to build business and better the small town where he was born and raised.

Clarence's Café serves as a bridge between Jeff's Home Hardware and Home Furniture stores, the latter of which opened in 2010 and is considered one of Home's finest. The café, named in honour of Jeff's dad, is just another example of Jeff's savvy business acumen, which he inherited from his father. "My dad always said, give your customers lots of ways to spend their money," Jeff says, looking around at the people enjoying their morning coffee (and free internet access), customers browsing through the spacious Home Furniture store and lining up at the cash on the hardware side. Today, Windsor Home Hardware and Home Furniture dominate the Fort Edward Plaza on the edge of town. In 1997, Home Hardware was one of the last retailers to leave downtown and "get out on the fringe". The move took the store from 3,000 to 15,000 square feet overnight. Today it is 37,000 square feet.

It was a big decision, and caused some controversy. Jeff remembers that a friend of his dad, and a good customer, was not happy with the decision. "Our plans were well underway and Grant came into the old store when there seemed to be as many customers around as you could imagine. In a loud, obnoxious voice, he said, 'You should stay right where you are. This downtown spot has been here for 100 years. I shopped here, my father shopped here. It will never work in your new location.' He was very adamant, and we just had to sort of ignore him, but it certainly wasn't

what we wanted to hear, especially from good people. A couple of months later we had our grand opening. The store looked beautiful and there was a really positive feeling in the air. People were lined up 30 deep at three cash registers. Grant came up to me in his shirt and tie, his little bowler hat perched on his head. He congratulated me and said that maybe what we were doing wasn't such a bad idea after all."

Clarence Redden died in 2003. "Dad was a very well known person in the community. He was very kind and generous, which we have carried forth to this day, giving back to the community. The visitation was interesting. We had expected to be able to mingle and talk, but what it turned into was just this line of people working their way through the receiving line and out the door. In one door and out the other: the line up was out the door, down the street, around the corner, down the corner and around the corner. The whole community came out. People still had their work clothes on; their tool belts were on and you could see the drywall dust. Everyone stopped to go to Clarence Redden's funeral and then they went back to work."

"Hurricane Juan (2003) came through and it was devastating. The power went out all across our end of Nova Scotia. The store was the first in Windsor to get it back. We had stocked up and were pretty well prepared. We jumped on the radio to let people know our power was back and we were open. We'd never seen so many people waiting outside. So we decided to treat the store like a bar, letting 30 to 40 in at a time and encouraging them to be considerate of others."

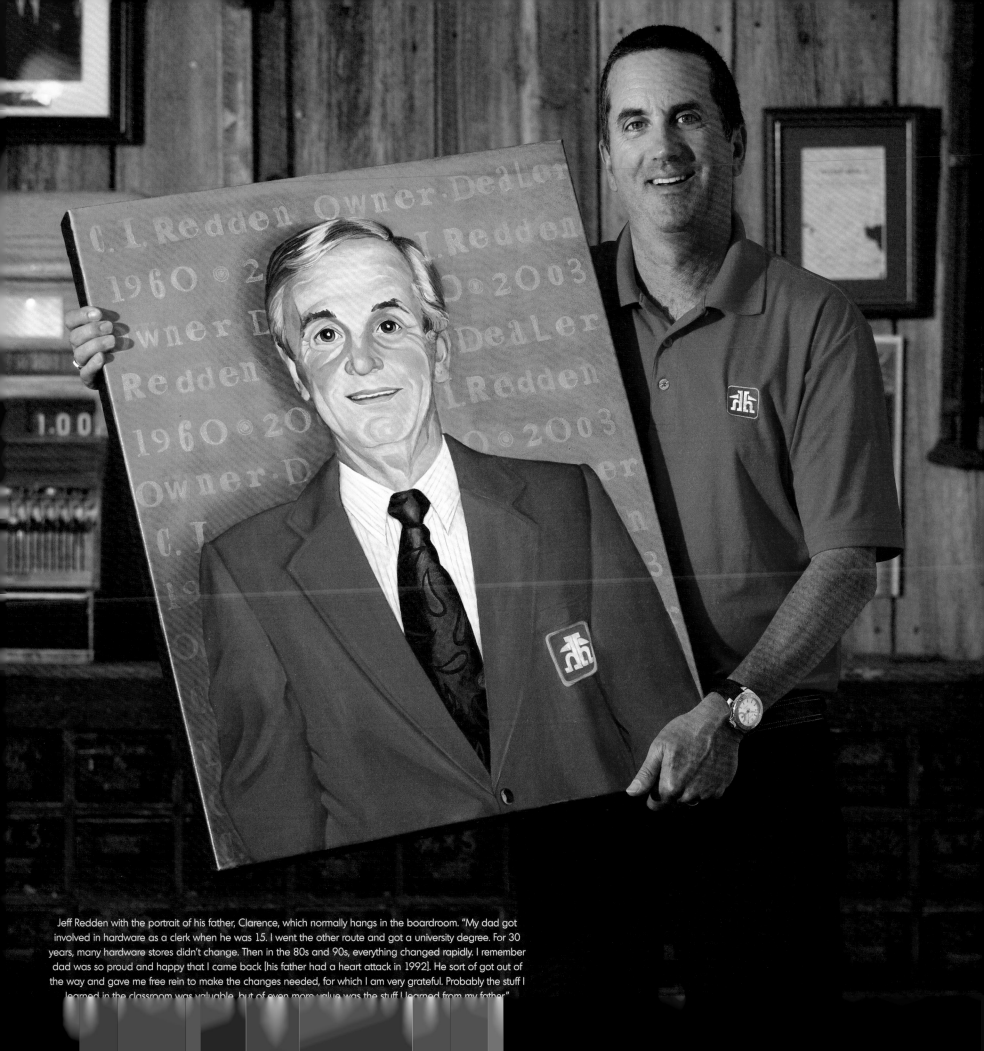

Jeff Redden with the portrait of his father, Clarence, which normally hangs in the boardroom. "My dad got involved in hardware as a clerk when he was 15. I went the other route and got a university degree. For 30 years, many hardware stores didn't change. Then in the 80s and 90s, everything changed rapidly. I remember dad was so proud and happy that I came back [his father had a heart attack in 1992]. He sort of got out of the way and gave me free rein to make the changes needed, for which I am very grateful. Probably the stuff I learned in the classroom was valuable, but of even more value was the stuff I learned from my father."

Newfoundland

· CONCEPTION BAY SOUTH ·

Christine feels honoured to have been able to live, work and raise her family in the community where she was raised. Handyman Home Hardware employs thirty people. Over the years, there have been 250 employees pass through, a lot of them students. "They start in high school, and stay until they're finished university," she says. "We have customers who come in – people whose husbands or wives have passed away, – just to chat. They come in and buy 50 cents worth of nuts and bolts. But they came in to get a hug."

After almost 10 years as one of three women on Home Hardware's Board of Directors, Christine Hand was ready for a new challenge. So in 2012 she decided to run for Chairman. At the time the position became vacant (Jim Schaefer stepped down as Chairman but continues to serve on the Board and operate his Home Hardware store in Bradford, Ontario), Christine was completing an eight-year term as Chair of the Audit and Security Committee, so already had wide exposure to the Home Dealer group. The process is a fast track: Directors are given the opportunity to declare their interest in pursuing candidacy for the position of Chair at the January Board Meeting and have only a few months to campaign: the Chairman is elected by the 16 Board Members following the Spring Annual Shareholders' Meeting.

In April 2012 Christine Hand was elected Home Hardware's ninth Chairman of the Board, becoming the first woman in the company's history to hold that position. Christine speaks eloquently of being a woman in a pivotal role in a company and industry historically dominated by men. "In my 24 years with Home Hardware I have never felt any resistance to participate. I was brought up to believe that you can do whatever you want, so I didn't give that aspect a lot of thought. But since becoming Chair, I realize that it gives other women a sense of pride: you know that there are no ceilings."

The role of Chairman adds to an already busy schedule. Christine's duties generally require that she be away from Home base at least one or two days every month as well as a full week at least twice a year. Not to mention the emails and phone calls when she is home. "I'm at the stage now where I have good solid people at the store. My youngest child is 16 and I've got a really supportive husband who understands that I need and want to be challenged." The last Five-Year Plan ended in December 2012 and a new one was approved at the Board Meeting in January 2013. It's a sure thing that Christine will have a major hand in seeing it through to completion.

Some people are simply radiant. Christine Hand is one of those people. Her voice is girlish and sweet but her words are measured and true. She is also one of the more successful and respected Home Hardware Dealers across the country. A graduate of University of Western Ontario's HBA program, Christine has sat on the Home Hardware Board since 2003. She has been honoured and sought after as a community leader and her store, Handyman Home Hardware in Conception Bay South has been the recipient of industry and Home Hardware awards.

For all that, Christine's initial involvement with Home Hardware was intended to be temporary. In the late 1980s, her parents, Clarence and Betty Morgan, were building the plaza that now houses the store. They approached the Home Hardware Dealer across the street to see if he would be interested in moving. He replied with an offer to sell the store. Clarence and Betty had no retail experience, but wouldn't pass on the opportunity to have an anchor tenant. Meanwhile, Christine had been working as a business

The Manuels River that runs through Conception Bay South is a favourite spot for amateur fossil hunters. In fact, Manuels River is home to one of the largest fossil sites of Trilobites, an extinct class of marine arthropods that inhabited the oceans of the earth for more than 300 million years. They measure from 1 mm up to 60 cm in length. The river is lined with rocks that are between 500 and 600 million years old, remnants of the ancient African continental plate that collided with North American 400 million years ago. As part of her community involvement and just another item on her to-do list, Christine Hand is heading up the fund raising drive that helped build the Manuels River Hibernia Interpretation Centre. In total, the effort raised over 7 million dollars. They couldn't have picked a better person for the job.

Christine Hand:

There's the annual Santa Claus parade - Christine always rides on their float, which often wins top prize, and also makes all the costumes.

Handyman Home Hardware
Conception Bay South, NL

analyst with a computer services company and was on maternity leave with the second of her five children. She offered to help out for a month or so and fell in love with the business. Before her maternity leave was up, she had given her notice and taken on the full time job of running Handyman Home Hardware. Four years later, in 1992, Christine and her husband Tom, who works in his own family business, bought out her parents.

It's pretty obvious that there's nothing about her job and her business that Christine doesn't love. She loves the people – customers and staff. She loves being able to help people solve their problems. She loves being part of the community, the fact that it's a way of life not just a job, not just a career. She loves the fact that everyone knows her – when she drops her kids off at school, people come up to her and say, 'I know you – you work at Home Hardware!' Christine lights up even more than usual when she talks about Handyman Home Hardware's community involvement. There's the annual Santa Claus parade - Christine always rides on their float, which often wins top prize, and also makes all the costumes. She does the breakfast program at the school once a week. She's on the school council. When Communities in Bloom judges were in town recently, she spent the day driving them around. The Zamboni at the local arena is painted up as a yellow Home Hardware truck. Christine says any organization that asks, receives support from Handyman Home Hardware. A few weeks ago there was a Walk-A-Thon for the local Ronald McDonald House. Staff members signed up to walk. Others participate in the Ride for Sight. But the Annual July Pancake Breakfast is vintage Christine. Held at the arena, it's the highlight of the weekend-long festival. The first year, Handyman Home Hardware just sponsored the event. In subsequent years, they branded it their own, taking over the entire operation of the breakfast. Five years ago, Christine introduced the red shirt event – wear a red shirt to breakfast and you win a prize. Last year over 500 people won prizes.

The big question is: where does she find the time? "Well," she explains in her gentle voice, "you fit it in. Our parents told us as kids, you've got the same amount of time as everybody else. It is what you choose to do with the time that makes the difference."

The store's longest-term employee is Darren Kennedy, pictured here with Christine in the Home Expressions department. He joined the staff in 1993 through the Vera Perlin Society, created to encourage the employment of people with special needs. When his year long subsidized program was up, Christine offered him a permanent part-time position at the store. In the beginning, she says, Darren was shy and quiet. Now, he's an outgoing and integral part of the staff.

The story of the Aylwards and Home Hardware begins with the late great Fabian Aylward. His St. Lawrence store was the third Newfoundland independent to join the Home Hardware family, after Ayres and Murray's. The year was 1969, six months after a fortunate chance meeting between Fabian and Walter Aylward on a flight from St. John's. From thereon in, Fabian was instrumental in bringing more independent island hardware dealers under the Home banner. Fabian was also a long-term member of the

phoned Fabian to ask him what was going on. Fabian said, "Well Ray, we thought you'd be glad to get rid of your barrels!" Fabian managed to convince Ray that the demand was innocent, and the barrels kept on coming. Ray probably had visions of half-barrel flower planters festooning every out port in Newfoundland but eventually Fabian fessed up to the real reason and that was that. While it lasted, the barrels fuelled a great party for a lot of people!

Ron Aylward: "Newfoundlanders are a little smarter than mainlanders."

Aylwards Home Centre
Marystown, NL

Home Hardware Board of Directors, serving for over 20 years, from April 18, 1978 to 1996. Fabian's nephew Ron, grew up in the business. He started working fulltime in the St. Lawrence store in 1969, the same year that Fabian joined Home. The following year Fabian opened a second store in Grand Bank, in 1972 the flagship Marystown store opened and in 1974, the store in Placentia. The fifth store in Gander opened in 2003, several years after Fabian had passed away in July 1996.

Home Hardware is a great family story, and Ron's family is no exception. Ron grew up in St. John's but spent his summers as a student working at Fabian's store in St. Lawrence, his family's hometown. He met his wife Dorothy in those early days and there they raised a family of three children. Today, one daughter is a lawyer in Toronto and the other lives in Madrid, Spain. Son Danny joined the business fulltime in 2004 after serving in the Armed Forces for 10 years. These days, Ron is gradually stepping back. Danny is taking on more responsibility and will eventually assume his place as third generation owner.

Newfoundlanders are great story tellers and Ron is no exception. When I asked him for funny stories, they came fast and furious, each one funnier than the one before. But two stand out:

The whiskey barrel planters:
Back in the 1980s, Ray Gabel made a deal with the Ontario LCBO to buy old whiskey barrels. The idea was that customers would cut them in half and turn them into planters. They were sold through the Lawn and Garden department. The first time the Newfoundland contingent saw the barrels at the fall market in St. Jacobs, the light went on. As Ron tells it, Newfoundlanders are a little smarter than mainlanders.

This is what they do with whiskey barrels in Newfoundland: they fill each barrel with five gallons of hot water and then start rolling them, a stay a day. There are about thirty 'stays' or planks in a whisky barrel. After 30 days, there's some pretty potent whiskey in the barrel, called Swish. The canny Newfoundland dealers first ordered a dozen barrels to make sure they were authentic. They were. Word got out and orders from Newfoundland started coming in to the tune of a tractor-trailer full. At that point, Ray Gabel

Walter Hachborn's first Honorary Degree:
One year Walter's study tour included a trip to the Maritimes. On the itinerary was a visit to St John's, with the group then heading down the Burin Peninsula to Saint-Pierre et Miquelon. The plan was to visit three of the Aylwards' stores along the way. On top of everything else involved in such a visit, Ron was determined to host an evening of Newfoundland hospitality at the Marystown store. The centre aisle was cleared out for dancing and skits, and there was abundant music and food. But the highlight of the night was the traditional Newfoundland event known as "screeching in" with Walter Hachborn the honouree. The oilskins and fisherman's hat and rubber boots were all arranged. The trick was to convince Walter to take centre stage. Everyone knows how stubborn he can be, and especially so when he is the centre of attention. After much convincing on the part of Walter Aylward and the dealers, Walter finally agreed that he would participate. Ron remembers that he dressed up in full regalia and said that he loved Newfoundland in the requisite accent, more or less. He even kissed the cod! At this point, in the proceedings, the person being screeched in is traditionally required to down a four ounce glass of Newfoundland Screech, pretty potent stuff. None of the other dealers knew, but Ron and Walter had arrived at a compromise on that one component of the ritual – what looked just like a large glass of rum was in fact a large glass of Coke. Which Walter downed with aplomb. One of the dealers got up and announced: 'Well Walter, you have just received your first honorary degree!'

No one knew that Walter would receive many more honours, including an honorary degree from the University of Waterloo and the Order of Canada. But the first was the night Walter Hachborn was officially screeched in at Aylwards Home Hardware!

Funny stories aside, the Aylwards sponsor many events in their communities throughout the year. The emphasis is always on children. Their main annual fundraiser is a parade to benefit The Children's Wish Foundation. Parades are held all over Newfoundland on the same October weekend. In Marystown, the kids march from the school to the store where the centre aisle has been cleared out. Everyone has hotdogs and pop and a good time. Since the tradition began in 2000, Aylward stores have contributed over $80,000 to The Children's Wish Foundation.

We're on Fogo Island after a windy passage. We arrive to a gorgeous sunny September day that shows the island at its best. The seascapes are sharp and crisp, the colours so bright they hurt, every place we pass is a picture and it's easy to understand why this island of Fogo where they were both born and raised is the only place for Owen and Mabel Combden.

Owen started an independent hardware company in 1972. He and Mabel married that same year. Mabel was a schoolteacher in those days but

These days Fogo Island is flourishing overall, thanks to the extraordinary vision of Zita Cobb, who left the island as a young girl and returned a few years later as a very wealthy and successful woman. The Shorefast Foundation that she has established is committed to ensuring the future viability of the community of Fogo Island. The website outlines its goals and principles, but in a nutshell, the idea is to develop the island as an international culture destination, and to offer artists places to work in a stunning natural environment. To that end, a 30-room luxury hotel opened

Owen & Mabel Combden:

Fogo Island Home Hardware Building Centre
Fogo Island, NL

helped out when she could. Saturdays, Mabel's day off, they'd take their truck off-island to Birchy Bay to pick up lumber. They'd get back home Saturday night and leave the truck to unload Monday night after Mabel got home from school. Some winters they'd come out Monday morning and the truck would have disappeared under the snow that had fallen since Saturday. Most of their other inventory came in on regular truck deliveries, but in the winters, there were times when what Owen calls "that lake of water," meaning the ocean, would freeze up completely and they'd take their skidoos across to meet the freight and haul everything back to Fogo Island. They remember times when nothing could get through for a long week – no food, no hardware.

In 1977, they joined Home Hardware. There was one other applicant for the business. Owen still remembers the expression on Walter Hachborn's face when they met at Hotel Gander: My goodness! I thought you were older! But they were accepted. They began as Home Hardware but became an HHBC in 2006. That same year, they moved all of three or four hundred yards, taking over a building they owned when the lease ended. This part of the island is zoned commercial, but they got special dispensation to build their lovely home next door, hidden behind an oasis of trees that Owen started in the greenhouse attached to the house. The abundant leafiness against grey rock is the perfect metaphor for their flourishing lives and business. Both Owen and Mabel are grateful to everyone – from the island and from Home Hardware – for the support they have received over the years.

in May 2013. Zita Cobb has also bought up many of the older homes, some of them close to 100 years old, which are being renovated and converted into living quarters for visiting artists. Architecturally intriguing studios crop up here and there on the rocks. Owen and Mabel's HHBC is providing some of the materials. Owen sums up the sentiment shared by everyone on Fogo when he says, "It's good for the island."

On an island with a population of under 3000, organizations of all stripes rely on the local businesses for support. Owen and Mabel are no exception. Some of the projects dearest to their hearts include the Iceberg Arena that opened in the late 1990s, and an outdoor classroom at the local school. They have donated Sunflower Growing kits to the children who graduated from kindergarten class. Another favourite was sponsoring Marcus Payne and Darcey Foley to play for the AAA Central Training Academy Ice Park for the 2010-2011 Hockey Season. The Combdens are proud to support these young men and believe that they have great potential as hockey players.

Paul Oram is more than a man around town. He's a man around Newfoundland, with a political career in Danny William's cabinet and an impressive and varied array of businesses. His relationship with the Glovertown HHBC that he now owns began on the other side of the counter back in 1986. His construction business purchased approximately 90% of its supplies from the store, so he got to know the people who worked in the store, many of whom still work here – and now for him — 25 years later. He also owns Greenwood HHBC in Lethbridge, an hour south of Glovertown.

Paul Oram:

Glovertown Home Hardware Building Centre
Glovertown, NL

Paul has a reputation for doing things quietly for people in the community, but one of the projects he's more than happy to make some noise about is the industrial arts program at the Glovertown Academy where he went to school. The IA teacher is a good friend. His old teacher and principal both shop at his store. So Paul really wanted to do something for the school. But beyond that, one of his bugbears is Newfoundland's need to attract young people and skilled trades. He believes that by putting money into school programs such as Industrial Arts, the trend of out-migration to other provinces can be reversed. As a result, his HHBC has committed $25,000 to the Glovertown Academy's Industrial Arts program. Phase One, completed, was to purchase much needed tools. Now they're on to Phase Two, the construction of a separate building to house the Industrial Arts department. The concept is to build a mini-house where students will be able to do the actual plumbing, drywall, flooring etc. In other words, learn by doing. It's a big project and a big idea. Dreamed by someone who has a history of dreaming big and seeing those dreams transformed into realities.

"When you walk in here," Paul explains, "there's a warm feeling. The staff is helpful. Everyone makes you feel welcome – they are true Newfoundlanders and Labradoreans. And everyone is called 'my love.' You wouldn't get away with that on the Mainland. I was a customer here for years and I was drawn to that even then. And I like the fact that today as an owner when I walk in the door I hear my employees continue to do that and continue to connect with people. It's not just selling a product you know. They build a relationship. People come here and they go to Home Hardware in general because they get that personal touch. They get that feeling of 'I own the store.' Everybody feels that they own it."

Amanda Saunders and Kayley Gordon, students in the IA program, volunteered to be our models along with Paul.

Dan McDonald left his native Newfoundland in 1978 when K-Mart, where he worked, transferred him to New Brunswick. In 1982 he found himself in Waterloo. Three years later, he answered an ad in the local newspaper and was hired as a merchandiser for Home Hardware, based out of St. Jacobs. His work took him all over the country. At one time, he and his co-worker Doug McLean who Dan figures has travelled many more miles than he has, tried to make a list of all the stores where they had worked: collectively it came to more than 250. "We traveled from coast to

After seven years as a merchandiser, Dan and his wife Kim, who was from Ontario, sold everything and moved to Newfoundland to take over a rundown store in Goulds outside Dan's hometown of St. John's. He knew he couldn't make the business work without her blessing and involvement: successful stores are about teamwork. So the deal they struck was for five years and if after that, she was not happy, they'd move back to Ontario. Twenty years later they're still in Goulds. But success was not achieved overnight. They started with 4,000 square feet and Dan and two young

Dan McDonald: "Who'd pay $50 for a piece of chocolate?"

McDonald's Home Hardware
Goulds, NL

coast," he remembers. "We'd be in St. John's one day and Vancouver the next." Everywhere he went, he learned something from the local dealers. Most of all he learned to appreciate the great strength of the Home Hardware program: as a dealer, you can pick and choose what you want from it as long as you stick to the core values.

He also learned a lot about the diversity of our country, something new for a boy from Newfoundland in those days. On one occasion, he was working with Azim Virani, owner of Simpson Home Hardware in West Vancouver. The name "Azim" alarmed Dan whose preconceived fears were proven wrong from the start. "Azim was the nicest man you'd ever want to meet," Dan remembers. "West Vancouver is a pretty expensive neighbourhood and there was a Chocolatier store next door. I had never seen one of those stores and every time we'd go out for lunch, we'd laugh and say, 'Who'd pay $50 for a piece of chocolate?' On our last day, Azim took us out for lunch and gave us each a box of those chocolates to take home to our wives." Dealers are responsible for all the out-of-pocket costs for merchandisers who are working on their stores. When Dan and his colleagues got to the airport and dropped off the vehicle they had been using for the past two and a half weeks, the total bill was just $150. Dan said that there had to be a mistake. The counter clerk said, 'You worked for Azim, right? Well, the car's $150.'

employees spent three weeks working every night gutting the place, then filling every nook and cranny with the fixtures he'd brought back with him from St. Jacobs, then filling the fixtures with merchandise. As he says, the store was well merchandised …right up to the ceiling! The challenge was to rebuild the customers' trust that had been eroding until they arrived. Goulds is a small community, which helped, but Dan says that the number one thing that got them integrated into the community was "just staying on the floor seven days a week and talking with the people."

Home service is the philosophy at Gould's Home Hardware. For Dan, it's all about taking care of their customers. Service is their point of difference. Dan hadn't owned the store very long when one day a customer came in with a P trap in his hand. It was Sunday, they were closing and Dan was getting ready to fly to St. Jacobs the following day for the market. When he got home, he was convinced he hadn't done enough to help the P trap person. So back he went to the store, where he gathered up some parts and went to the man's house. By the time he left later that evening, the problem had been solved.

Running a business on Newfoundland has its special challenges, one of the more obvious being that it is an island. This challenge is compounded the moment you have to cross the Strait of Belle Isle to get product from Newfoundland to L'Anse au Clair on the southern coast of Labrador. Just ask Ameneious, known as Mian, and Nancy Turnbull who have owned the HHBC and Home Furniture stores there since 1992. From April to December, the procedure is as follows: product is trucked from the Debert warehouse to North Sydney, ferried over to Port aux Basques, then up the road to Corner Brook. From there, another truck runs it up the northern

In February 2004 Ameneious and Nancy took their first trip south since they had bought the business. They had just got off the plane in Florida when their daughter Susan called: part of the store roof had collapsed under the weight of a huge snowstorm. They panicked, thinking they should get on the next flight home. Instead, they phoned Wilfred Letto, the previous owner, for advice. "Boy," he told Mian, "keep heading as far south as you can!" They weathered that storm, although it took until August for all the repairs to be completed – not too much building and repair happen over the winter at the best of times.

Ameneious & Nancy Turnbull:

Turnbull's Home Hardware Building Centre
L'Anse au Clair, Labrador and Corner Brook, NL

Peninsula to St. Barbe, for another ferry hop, skip and jump across the Strait to Blanc Sablon in Quebec, three miles east of L'Anse au Clair. The Turnbulls pick it up from there. Pretty straight forward - although their "day off" often consists of driving product from their Corner Brook store which they bought in 2009 to the ferry in St. Barbe. But then winter comes. The ferry stops running and for five long months of the year the community is almost entirely shut off from the rest of the world. So if you want to keep your shelves stocked, your winter order needs to be in before that last ferry leaves St. Barbe in mid December. Until recently, the only way to get anything in after mid December was to fly it in. And that was a whole other procedure. Once the product arrived in Corner Brook, it was shipped up the Northern Peninsula to a private airstrip in Sandy Cove, just south of St. Barbe. Small Beaver planes flew between Sandy Cove and Forteau, a small town three miles west of L'Anse au Clair. It was not ideal. It was expensive. It was time consuming - sometimes it took five or six flights to get all the goods across. And it was, of course, dependent on the weather cooperating. Just to put it into perspective, over a normal winter, the region gets between 20 and 35 feet of snow. The Turnbulls remember one winter with over 50 feet of snow. (Walter Hachborn remembers it too, because somebody sent him a picture of one of those Beaver planes parked beside a 50-foot high snow bank.) In 2009, the Newfoundland government introduced a winter ferry pilot project between Corner Brook and Blanc Sablon, which makes getting the weekly shipments throughout the long winter months a whole lot easier. "It has been heaven," Nancy says.

A Home Hardware love story: Ameneious grew up in Charlottetown, Labrador. In 1981, he was working as a mechanic out west. Nancy grew up in L'Anse au Clair, but in 1981, she was working in the financial industry in Deer Lake. One weekend she was home visiting family. Nancy's cousin was Mian's best friend. Mian was visiting him that weekend and came into the house, sat down and didn't say much. "He was pretty shy," Nancy recalls. But a few weeks later, Nancy got a call from a friend who was working out west, asking her whether she was interested in joining her. She didn't go, but she still thinks there might have been a connection between her initial encounter with Mian and the request to come out west. Instead, Mian came back to Labrador and the two were married in 1984. Their two children, Susan and Andy, grew up in the business. They always had recliner chairs in the furniture department. And Nancy says she would settle them into those chairs – Andy was six months and Susan was two _ and "they wore their bum prints into those two chairs," she recalls. They must have absorbed a lot of knowledge over the years because today these two "kids" are the grown up store managers, Andy in Corner Brook and Susan in L'Anse au Clair, clearing the way for their parents to "semi-retire".

Chris Morgan became a Home Dealer in 2007, but hardware and Home were obviously in his blood long before then. His dad managed a building supply store in a community about thirty miles from Springdale where today Chris owns the HHBC. The year after he graduated from high school,

and lighting. "Anything and everything Home Hardware supplies." But his business really took off in his second year. That's when he started building homes as well. "We dabbled a bit the first year," he recalls. "Then our third year we did two homes." The next year they built six and already had a lot

Chris Morgan: "We're not in metro Toronto, "Chris says. "I don't have to put up a sign. Everyone knows I am building the house."

Springdale Home Hardware Building Centre
Springdale, NL

Chris went to Marathon in northern Ontario and worked at the HHBC that is still there. "I almost immediately gained a love for it – a love for everything about it," he remembers 20 years later. He loved having the best of both worlds: being part of a big business in the context of a small town. He worked his way up from the yard to the order desk and could have stayed on and sooner rather than later no doubt be running the place. Instead, he returned to Newfoundland after a year and studied marketing at university.

After he graduated, Chris ended up running the family farm instead. He met his wife-to-be who was born and raised in Springdale. Even in the days before they were married, he would tell her, semi-seriously, how he would love to buy the HHBC in her hometown. Which is precisely what he did in 2007, when he approached the owner and offered to buy it. His accountant said, "Chris, you're a farmer. What are you doing looking at this?" But Chris knew the business was in his blood. Always had been. He was able to take it to another level when he bought the store in Springdale. He's happy that they can be a lot of things to a lot of people in the area. He likes that they can supply everything from flooring and cabinets to bathroom fixtures

of business lined up for the coming year when we met for a quick coffee and photo opp after the Labour Day Weekend in September 2011. He works with a great team of contractors, second to none in his books. And because they are in a small community, everyone knows who's building the new house at the end of the road: "We're not in metro Toronto, "Chris says. "I don't have to put up a sign. Everyone knows I am building the house. So it works well."

I didn't have a chance to tell him what kind of stories we were looking for the day of our interview: he was busy wrapping up some details on a home he and a group of other people from the community had just completed for someone whose home was gutted by fire in April. And he wouldn't name names, and I couldn't take pictures either, but there was another house the same group built for a family that had been going through hard times. "I don't know what the rest of the world does," Chris said, "but us Newfoundlanders, we just kind of pitch together and share the load."

"We leave it up to the customer to supply us with a plan but most everyone around, even when they're shopping online or they go to a bookstore and buy plan books and whatever – a lot of the time they come back to our Home and Cottage designs book. It's a very impressive book with very impressive plans and something for everyone."

The memorial commemorates men from the Trinity shore who fought and lost their lives in the wars of the 20th century, WW1, WW2 and Korea. After the Second World War, The Royal Canadian Legion erected the memorial. Over the years it deteriorated and in 1998 the community undertook to refurbish it through a combination of funding from The Legion, the Lower Trinity Development Association and local businesses including Hindy's Home Hardware Building Centre. Hindy's donated the lights that were installed on the new brick columns that line up in formation around the site and asked Home Hardware supplier MTD to donate lawn care equipment. Unbeknownst to the Hindys, one of the veterans wrote a letter to Home Hardware corporate thanking the organization for its contribution to the war memorial. The story, which epitomizes community at its best, was chosen for an advertising campaign produced in 2001. As Paul says, the war memorial touches so many of the families in the area – "it's deep in people's hearts."

We are on our way to visit the Hindys in Winterton, halfway up the western side of the northern Avalon Peninsula that borders Trinity Bay. We drive through tiny villages with names from another era that speak to the fortitude of the souls who forged new lives out of necessity in a hard and demanding new found land. Names like Heart's Delight, Heart's Desire and Heart's Content which was the landing site of the first Transatlantic telegraphic cable from England.

Nowhere did we experience the famous Newfoundland hospitality and charm to the degree we did when we visited the Hindys in Winterton. We were given an impromptu tour of the town's Boat Museum (the biggest museum in Newfoundland outside of The Rooms in St. John's with a lot of the materials to build it supplied by Hindy's HHBC). Our guide was Howard Cooper, part of a group who helped restore and preserve the art of wooden boat building in rural Newfoundland and Labrador. Ray insisted that we stop

Paul Hindy: Nowhere did we experience the famous Newfoundland hospitality and charm to the degree we did when we visited the Hindys in Winterton.

Hindy's Home Hardware Building Centre
Winterton, NL

Ray Hindy was born and raised in Winterton as were his sons Paul, Lloyd and Charlie. The boys grew up in the business that Ray began in the 1950s. Hindy's Winterton store celebrated its own 50th anniversary in 2009 and in 1989 the Hindy sons took it over and moved the business to its current location on the edge of town. Paul says they would have liked to join the Home Hardware family at that point, but there was already a Home store in their trading area. When it closed in 1996, the Hindys came on board. Brother Charlie left the business and lives and works in St. John's.

In April 2006, the Hindys opened a second store in Carbonear about 30 minutes away on the Conception Bay side of the peninsula. According to Tim Dietrich, Director, Retail Operations, Atlantic Canada, it's Newfoundland's flagship store. Paul is modest about that accolade, attributing it instead to timing and Home's programs and support. But he does say that they are proud of the success they have made of that location. He remembers being at a shareholders' meeting in St John's around the same time that they were getting ready to open the Carbonear store. Walter Hachborn said, 'Carbonear has not been kind to Home Hardware.' And Paul responded, 'We'll change that – you'll see.' It was a great feeling when his competition came to ask if they wanted to buy them out. And now, a few years later, they are the only game in town. In early 2011, they expanded the Carbonear store from 6,000 square feet of retail space to 17,000 square feet and a 60,000 square-foot indoor drive- through lumberyard. Paul's wife Wendy works in the Carbonear store and their 17 year-old son Brandon is planning to join the family business when he graduates from university in a few years.

into the family home where his wife Monica had just taken a batch of tea biscuits out of the oven. Even the normally shy Paul came out of his shell as his mom and dad regaled us with stories from over the years.

There are many things about Home Hardware that Paul finds impressive: "We're part of a company that we own ourselves and we're supporting our own company by buying supplies. The number one thing that stands out in my mind is that Home is always changing, keeping up to date with systems and programs and products. It's phenomenal. You never become stagnant. You're always ahead of the game."As an example, Paul recounts a story he heard from a recent hire that had previously worked with the competition. He was astounded that the HHBC could place a special order on Friday that would arrive the following Monday or Tuesday. At the other business, it could take two to three weeks for special orders to show up. In Paul's opinion, Home Hardware has the best distribution system in Canada, "if not North America." He is also proud of the fact that they employ so many people in the area. "It's good to keep the young people home," he says. "Otherwise they'll end up going to Ontario or Alberta."

New Brunswick

The vibrantly coloured halls of the Crafty Corner Childcare Centre resound with the excited squeals of happy children. Just down the street, the lilac-perfumed summer air is filled with the rustle of prom dresses as nervous high school sweethearts gather around a bubble-filled fountain for photographs. These happy sounds are in stark contrast to the piercing wail of

But that was just one way the Brennans turned tragedy into triumph. To complement the construction of the new store, the founding owners, Raymond and Ann Brennan, created a riverfront park as their way of saying thanks for the support they received during their 30 years in business and for helping the family to rebuild after the flood. Situated at the edge of the store

The Brennan Family: A River Runs Through It – Before and After the Flood. by Rayanne Brennan

Brennan Home Hardware Building Centre
Florenceville-Bristol, NB

sirens that sounded danger, in 2008, when the swollen St. John River spilled over its banks at Florenceville-Bristol and flooded the waterfront properties of this rural New Brunswick town.

Among the property owners affected was Brennan Home Hardware Building Centre, a mainstay of the local economy for over 30 years. The business had only recently become a member of the Home Hardware family of independently owned hardware and building supply stores when disaster struck. At the height of the 2008 spring freshet, over two feet of water lay on the floor of the main floor of the building. Damage was so extensive that the store, converted from a 19th century woodworking factory, had to be torn down and reconstructed from the ground up.

The flood presented the Brennans with both challenges and opportunities. The most significant was the opportunity to build a more spacious and modern retail operation. Temporary quarters were set up at the former Pickle Home Hardware location up the street (today the home of the Craft Corner Childcare Centre) which the Brennans had acquired only months earlier, while blueprints were drawn up for a permanent home for their Home Hardware Building Centre. Within a year, a new 12,000 square foot store was built, attached to the existing 15,000 square foot warehouse.

grounds, Shamrock Garden offers one of the most scenic vistas on the river with a cairn-like stone fountain as its centerpiece.

The green space also honours the memory of the late Marion (Billie) McCain who left a lasting legacy of flower beds, shrubbery and trees in her role as founder and driving force behind Florenceville's beautification committee. It was Mrs. McCain's desire to build a lookout at this site to provide a scenic vantage point to enjoy the natural beauty of the St. John River.

In June 2009, just a little over a year after the floodwaters of the St. John River rushed into their store, the Brennans celebrated the completion of the new store and Shamrock Garden, with three days of grand opening festivities. A few months later, the Brennans held another celebration at this same site, having been chosen to host one of only 16 Maple Leaf Day events across Canada as part of national Forest Week celebrations.

One of the reasons the Brennans became a Home Hardware member was to be part of an environmentally and socially responsible organization. Thanks to Home's support, the family has been able to beautify not only its surroundings but the village as a whole.

One of the local initiatives closest to the Toners' hearts is the community arena, Centre E&P Senechal Center that opened in 2009. Local fundraising contributed almost $4 million to the overall $14.7 million cost of the architecturally award-winning facility that during the day is flooded with natural light. Never much of a hockey player, Timmy hadn't played for over 25 years when someone asked him to join a seniors pick up hockey team to play in the new arena. Although he was 67 years old at the time, and thought it was a crazy idea, Timmy gamely signed on and has been having a wonderful time ever since. Timmy and his youngest grandson Keegan, affectionately known as "Keegs" by the family, suit up in the Home Hardware dressing room for a few turns around the rink.

In a cross-country journey that took us from one wonderful community to another, meeting the nicest people imaginable everywhere we visited, the Toners of Grand Falls stand out even in this illustrious company. They exemplify the qualities often used to describe the Home Hardware difference: family, hard work, community, and decency. The day we spent

improving the product mix and perfecting merchandising techniques. She was instrumental in helping the business transition from a building supply to a hardware store. In the process, Carm helped to make the store a more interesting, welcoming place for all their customers, male and female.

The Toner Family: As Timmy recalls, he and Carm went in wearing guest badges and came out as Home Dealers.

Toner Home Hardware
Grand Falls, NB

with Timmy and Carm was memorable for so many reasons: Timmy's obvious love for the dramatically beautiful landscape of the region, and the cultural heritage of its inhabitants; the deep family ties and pride; their warmth and hospitality.

The Toner family has a long history in this north-western corner of New Brunswick. In fact, Timmy and Carm's home was built on a lot severed from the original family farmstead and Timmy's brother's home is just across the way. Earlier generations had been farmers, but in 1965 Timmy's older brother Brian became a potato broker (Grand Falls is in the heart of McCain country), buying locally and selling to the Montreal market. In the early days, potatoes were shipped by rail but by the mid 1960s, the favoured mode of transportation was trucking. Farmers in the Grand Falls area were doing well, and consequently building storage sheds for their crops. Construction required plenty of cement and plywood, both products that Brian was able to source in Quebec and ship on trucks that would otherwise come down empty to pick up the potato crop. That same summer, Brian started a small construction company. He wasn't planning to open a building supply store – it just evolved. His office was a tiny trailer and his warehouse an old barn. Eventually the demand grew so great that he bought a small building on the corner of Broadway and Main and in 1966 officially established his building supply business. Two years later, Timmy, fresh from university, decided to spend the summer working at the store. He has been there ever since.

Joining Home Hardware was precipitated by the need for a better price for paint. Their CIL rep suggested that they take a look at Home Hardware. The former Home Dealer in the community had died in a plane crash and the family was no longer interested in the business, so there was an opening and a need. In 1973 Walter Aylward invited the Toners to the Spring Market in St. Jacobs. As Timmy recalls, he and Carm went in wearing guest badges and came out as Home Dealers. Several years later, Timmy and Brian bought each other out of their respective businesses – Timmy kept the store and Brian the wood truss plant they had started together a few years prior. By now, Carm was working full time in the store. Drawing on her prior experience with her family's grocery business, Carm focused on

In 2005, Timmy and Carm built a new store across the street from the old location on Broadway and Main, switching banners from HHBC to HH. Although their daughter Nancy initially had no interest in the family business, she and her husband Dave MacDonald came from Halifax to attend the store's grand opening. Afterwards they told Timmy and Carm that they would love to come into the business. For her part, Nancy wanted her young children to have the same opportunity to grow up among family that she had had. Timmy was happy that they satisfied the key piece of advice he had learned at a Succession Planning Seminar at a Home Hardware market: never let your family come into your business until they've worked somewhere else for at least two years. The succession process is almost complete, although Timmy says he's not ready to totally retire: "I've retired from most of the administration tasks. Now I do what I most enjoy, working with customers and assembling things - every barbecue, patio set, swing … So when I'm not selling, I'm assembling. And I love it."

"I have always appreciated that Home Hardware is locally owned. They are the people of our community, working in our community and for our community. I have had many positive dealings with our local store, but it was as a school administer that I most appreciated their community involvement. I would regularly get calls from Timmy asking me to recommend students who might want a part-time job at the store. They wanted good people, not necessarily those with the highest marks, but those who knew the value of a job well done. It always gave me pleasure to see these students working there, sometimes for all their high school and college years, greeting customers with a smile, being helpful and learning lessons that we couldn't teach in school. Happy 50th Anniversary Home Hardware."

Beatrice Long, Grand Falls, NB

Grand Falls
The Bilingual Town

by Timmy Toner

Grand Falls New Brunswick is such a bilingual town that even its official name is posted as Grand Falls in English and Grand-Sault in French in all its official documents and communications. Drive just one or two kilometers west of the town, and you will find yourself in an almost exclusively French speaking area. The same distance east will land you in an English speaking community with an Irish background and heritage. Our town, then, is a community where both cultures tend to meet, mingle, shop, play sports and socialize.

The local school system not only reflects the bilingual nature of Grand Falls, but has also had an enormous influence on our community, culture and overall development. Throughout much of the twentieth century, many of our classes were taught in English with an advanced French class available for the French speaking students. Gradually, over the years, more of the courses were offered to French-speaking students in their mother tongue. In the mid to late nineteen sixties, a new, bilingual high school was built in Grand Falls. It housed all the regional high school students under one roof with a single bilingual administration. Internal upheaval in the late 1980s led to the bilingual school board being replaced with a French board. The English side fell under the jurisdiction of the larger regional entity.

This was a stressful time for both my family and me. Our four kids were all in school and I was a school board member through much of that evolution. We had a Home Hardware store in the middle of the town and did not know what the implications might be for our business. However, things worked out remarkably well. Our kids stayed in the English system, but were able to participate in a very good French immersion program at their school. They all speak both French and English fluently, and three of them have established homes in which their spouses are learning French and their children are fluently bilingual.

We notice in our store that more people are now speaking French than ever before and more of our English population are also able to speak French more fluently. English-French households are part of our everyday lives. Because both school systems offer advanced second language programs and courses to accommodate the needs and abilities of their students, our graduates are now better versed in both English and French.

Socially, the many activities within our town and the larger community surrounding it have created a strong bond among all of our citizens. In fact, recently, a Montreal-based vendor hosted a barbecue in front of our store. He was amazed at the number of people in Grand Falls who knew one another on a first name basis. He told us, unprompted, that he had never experienced anything like it.
Vive la différence!

EDIFICE MUNICIPAL
1999
MUNICIPAL BUILDING

The St. John River forms a horseshoe through the middle of the town. A dam at the top of the falls diverts the water under the town into the powerhouse at the other end of the horseshoe. During the summer very little water comes over the falls, which creates a beautiful gorge over a kilometer long.

Moncton has a population of 125,000 and spreads over a large area, which continues to expand. Like virtually every community across the country, Moncton is passionate about hockey. So in 2007, when the Elmwood community learned that the city was planning to amalgamate the various arenas across town into one central arena, putting their local arena on ice, so to speak, they were not happy. Alvin and Rachelle's son Luc has played hockey there since he was five years old. Their daughter Melanie learned to skate on that rink. For the city, however, it was simple economics – they could not afford to keep five rinks going. So they challenged the local residents to raise half a million dollars if they wanted their own facility. Within 18 months the money had been raised, thanks to the contributions of individuals and businesses such as Elmwood Home Hardware Building Centre, which has its name on one of the dressing rooms – one of eight $25,000 donors to the arena's construction. With additional funding from other levels of government, the arena was built and opened in 2010. It was named the Crossman Community Centre Kay Arena, in honour of Norman Crossman, one of the longest serving city councillors who sided with the community on their fight for their own arena.

You can go home again. Alfred and Marie Leger proved that admirably when they moved back to their native New Brunswick in 1974 after 28 years in Ontario, and opened a Home Hardware store. They met in Toronto, married there in 1960 and began raising their two children but all the time Alfred had a hankering to come back home. He sounded out his brother about opening a hardware store and one day, the call came: I've found a piece of property – are you interested? They were. Marie had retail

there on, all future Leger stores were HHBCs, including Alvin's second store in Dieppe, an area neighbouring Moncton, which he opened in 2001. In 2005, he opened a third HHBC in Magnetic Hill, an area of strong residential growth. He had so much space that in another typical Leger move, he decided to open a combination HHBC and Home Furniture store. While theirs wasn't the first of its kind in the Home Hardware family, they were certainly in the vanguard of this new format.

The Leger Family: Marie Leger became the first woman elected to serve as a Director on Home Hardware's Board in 1988.

Elmwood Home Hardware Building Centre
Moncton, NB

experience (she had worked at Simpsons when they lived in Scarborough), so they made a good team. Four years later, business was good enough that they opened a second store in Richibucto. In 1980 the two brothers amicably split the business. Alfred and Marie kept the Moncton operation and moved from the original location, which they had rented, to the current one which they purchased. That was the era of 21% interest rates, not the best time to assume a mortgage. But property values were down as a result and Alfred's background as a carpenter meant he could oversee renovations and keep an eye on costs. Once the new store was up and running, sales doubled overnight.

By the mid 1980s, their son Alvin was very involved in the business which grew again. They added an additional 8,000 square feet bringing the retail space to 12,000 square feet. Another major achievement: Marie Leger was the first woman elected to the Board of Directors. She served from April 26, 1988 until April 22, 1991. Alfred and Marie decided to retire when her term was up in 1991. Alfred and Marie took another leap of faith in deciding to pass the business on to the next generation: Alfred cites a statistic from the time that indicated a 70% failure rate when a second generation came on board. Nevertheless, in their case, the decision was the right one and the business flourished. Moncton is the heart of the Maritimes, its transportation hub and, with its strong bilingual character, home to a very strong service sector. As a result, the city continues to grow and son Alvin and his wife Rachelle have taken full advantage of the strong economy. In 1997, when he had completed the buyout of the business, Alvin decided to expand into building supplies and converted his stores to HHBCs. He added another 14,000 square feet to the existing retail space in the Elmwood store. From

When I asked Alvin if he still had expansion dreams, his eyes lit up. He and Rachelle are indeed actively considering another store, with immediate plans for a new building for the Elmwood location. Alfred and Marie are so proud of everything accomplished by the next generation, maybe even a tiny bit envious. Alfred sometimes wishes he had got into the business earlier – he was 45 when he moved back to New Brunswick, whereas Alvin was 30 when he took the business over. But then, he thinks about life today – he and Marie are getting organized for the next Walter trip – to Malaysia - and they will be heading back shortly to their Florida home for the winter. When they're in town, they visit the store every day – not to work, they quickly point out, but to shop and visit and pick up their mail. Their store was the first Home Hardware to open a Canada Post Retail outlet. Another first in a long history of accomplishments.

Woman on Board:
   Marie assumed an active management role in the business when the Legers bought a second store in Richibucto. Alfred spent a lot of time over the first three years, getting that business up and running. So when Marie was asked to run for the Board of Directors in 1988, she certainly had the experience. Nevertheless, she was so surprised that she took a few days to consider it before finally accepting. She won election and served for three years, from 1988 to 1991. Marie Leger is proud to have had the privilege to be Home Hardware's first woman Director.

The Acadian colours are reflected in this replica of a traditional lighthouse, many of which dotted the shoreline of New Brunswick's Acadian Peninsula in days gone by.

I know Canadians are crazy about hockey, but when Paul LeBreton told me he had always wanted to be the Wayne Gretsky of hardware, he had to explain before I made the connection. Like so many Home Hardware Dealers I have met in our travels for this book, Paul LeBreton never wanted to leave his hometown. He wanted to bloom where he was planted, in Neguac on the beautiful Acadian Peninsula in New Brunswick. Raise a family, and live a good life. He started implementation of his plan the moment he became an employee at the Home Hardware store in Neguac. Paul remembers being amazed by just how much the store had to sell. He

Neguac Home Hardware Building Centre is a familiar landmark on the Main Street in the town where both Nicole and Paul were born and raised and where they still live. The 18,000 square foot store was built in 1976 to replace the old store that burned down in February of the same year. (There was an office in the new building for Stan, who Nicole remembers, was still in charge of accounts payables until 1979.) Just 30 minutes away from Neguac, the Tracadie Home Hardware is a modern 17,000 square foot store built in 2006 to provide much needed space for the growing business.

Paul & Nicole LeBreton: I understood the Wayne Gretsky allusion: Paul wanted to be the best at what he did.

Neguac Home Hardware Building Centre, Tracadie Home Hardware
Neguac & Tracadie-Sheila, NB

was obsessed with knowing everything about all the products so that if a customer had a question, he had the answer before they asked the question; he wanted to be fast and thorough and … and suddenly I understood the Wayne Gretsky allusion: Paul wanted to be the best at what he did.

Paul and Nicole LeBreton are proud to represent a third generation of Home Hardware store owners; they now operate two stores in Neguac and Tracadie-Sheila with 37 great staff members. It all began on September 21, 1944 when Nicole's grandfather Stan LeGresley bought his first store in Neguac. To this day, customers still associate his name with that store. Nicole's father François, who was the oldest of 11 children, joined his father at the store in the late 1950s. In the early 1960s, it became a true family business with many of François' brothers and sisters also getting involved. In 1968, they joined Home Hardware, with three stores in Neguac and the Miramichi regions. François believed this was one of the best decisions they ever made. He was always proud to represent such a great company. In the early 1980s Paul and Nicole started working at the family owned business with her parents François and Irene LeGresley. In 1984 the second generation "children" each formed their own companies. In 1990, François bought the Home Hardware store in Tracadie-Sheila and Paul became manager of that location in 1995. Nicole became manager of the Neguac store when her father officially retired in 2002. Their two children Martin and Chantal, both university grads, are pursuing careers outside of the hardware business. Today titles seem less important as Paul and Nicole believe in using common strengths and resources to achieve common goals.

Despite the fact that the two communities of Neguac and Tracadie-Sheila are close to one another and the stores are mutually owned and operated, each has its own distinct atmosphere, characteristics and stories. Nevertheless, they have one important element in common: they both sell tickets for the highly successful 50/50 Lottery that has contributed greatly to their two communities. Paul is a founding member of La Fondation Communautaire de la Peninsule Acadienne (one of Canada's community foundations). Paul introduced the foundation to the 50/50 lottery concept, which, he explains is a "win win win" based on philanthropic principles. With this model, money within the fund accumulates, the interest is used for community programs, but the principal is never touched. The LeBretons responded to that key aspect of its structure. Every tickets costs $2. From every ticket sold, one dollar goes to the bi-weekly winner. That's the first "win". The money from investing the remaining dollar is divided equally between the foundation's fund, the second "win", and the other half goes to directly support various local youth organizations in the community, the third "win" of this trifecta. The underlying principle is to always put some aside to let the fund build. Building - now, that's something a Home Hardware Building Centre really understands.

Walter attended the grand opening of the new Tracadie store in 2006. He also planned to attend several other events in New Brunswick over the next few days. Paul was amazed by his razor-sharp memory about the many people in the area he had met over the years. He wanted to know how everyone was doing, including people he hadn't seen for over 10 years. Immediately after the grand opening, Walter and Kevin MacDonald, then the Area Manager, left to drive four and a half hours to Hampton where there was another event the next morning. Walter wanted to detour to Bathurst to visit an HH corporate store. Kevin was busy mapping out different sleep scenarios as they drove, thinking they could spend the night in Bathurst and still get to Hampton in time for the grand opening event at noon the following day. But when he suggested that change of itinerary to Walter, the answer was a firm "No". They stopped in Bathurst and then continued on to Hampton, arriving at 11 that night. And the next day Walter, who was 85 at the time, was up and "full of sparkle."

There are five Youth Centres on the Acadian Peninsula. Through the Fondation, the LeBretons are involved in the two in Neguac and Tracadie-Sheila. We visited the Centre d'animation jeunesse (CAJ) in Tracadie-Sheila, co-founded by Arisma Losier. "We should have more people in the community like Paul and Nicole," he said. "The community needs them." The colourful room was painted by the kids, aged 13 to 18, who use the centre. Its values are vividly displayed on the wall for all to see: Leadership. Love. Opinion. Socialize. Non-intimidation. Respect. Honesty. Friendship.

For the most part, the stories in this book have focused on the positive, the heart warming and inspirational. We are celebrating and sharing success in its many forms. So the story from Sussex, New Brunswick is a bit of a departure, at least on the surface. It came about when I interviewed Mark Cullen. The following day, he sent me a blog he had written recounting the story of a request he had from Rob Wallace, Home Hardware's Manager for Public Relations and Promotional Events. It was November 2008 and the store in Sussex, New Brunswick was hosting a

Of course, I went. They sold over 1,200 tickets and more than 1,000 ladies showed up. There was entertainment, decorators from Beauti-Tone, crafts and more. Much more. Including a photo tribute to Cindy the 39 year-old wife of the dealer, Andrew Hunt. Plus a display of hand hooked rugs that Cindy had made for each of their four young kids.

When I arrived, about two hours before the beginning of the show, Andrew greeted me heartily and gave me a tour. He introduced me to

Andrew Hunt: That night the equivalent of 50% of the whole female population of Sussex turned out.

Sussex Home Hardware Building Centre
Sussex, NB

Ladies' Night with proceeds going to the local branch of the Canadian Cancer Society. But the event was unbearably close to the bone for owner Andrew Hunt: his wife Cindy was in the last stages of breast cancer and sadly did not survive the week. The event was an act of extraordinary love, organized by a circle of Cindy's friends, but shared by over 1,000 women who came out that night. When I read Mark's blog, I knew I wanted to include it in this book. I asked Ray Gabel if it would be all right if I called Andrew for permission to include it. With his blessing, I then called Andrew. He hesitated for a very long moment and I knew he was agonizing over his answer. I understood that his primary concern was the well being of his four young children. I am very grateful that Andrew agreed to let me include Mark's blog in the book and I am especially grateful that this also gave me the privilege of meeting his four wonderful, beautiful children, Isaac, Helen, Sarah and Hannah. The occasion was a good excuse for them to get out of school for the afternoon and they were taking full advantage of it. Personalities were on full display, with 7-year old Isaac giving a hilarious précis of his three sisters, in descending order of age: "She's mean, she's weird and she likes dolls." Seeing them together as a family, on the porch of their grandparent's home, was a testament to the family's strength and endurance. Andrew's quiet pride and happiness made a statement more compelling than any words. The entire experience, Andrew's honesty, thoughtfulness and willingness to participate, as well as his remarkable children, made me realize this too is a positive story, a true celebration of life.

The following is an excerpt from Mark Cullen's Blog, November 19, 2008: (Edited with permission.)

On a Monday morning, I was looking forward to a quiet five days to catch up on my inbox. Then the call came. It was Rob Wallace from the corporate office in St. Jacobs. "How would you like to go to Sussex New Brunswick on Wednesday? Our Home Dealer is doing a fundraiser for the local branch of the Cancer Society. He has sold over 700 tickets already."

"And," Rob added with some hesitation, "his wife has cancer. Advanced cancer. She is receiving palliative care now (pause) and she may not make it to Wednesday."

everyone including his fine garden centre staff and Brian MacArthur of Avon Valley Greenhouses, his #1 plant supplier. Brian would be my 'assistant' for the evening. As we walked through Andrews' extensive gift and tablewares section I remarked that someone very talented must be his buyer… "Who would that be?" I asked innocently enough. He replied, "That is a long story and tonight I am not going to cry."

Andrew made a fine speech before the doors were thrown open. "Tonight your goal," he announced with conviction to his staff and volunteers "is to have fun." He said that Cindy was comfortable but on a morphine pump. That he could get a call in five minutes or three weeks. We all knew the call that he was talking about.

The evening was a great success. We sold over 120 copies of my book, Sandbox of a Different Kind. Much more than that, however, many people reflected on the reason for the evening – to acknowledge the very special person Cindy. I met their four wonderful kids. I met Andrews' mother. Her sister. Heck, the whole family and all of their friends showed up! It is hard to explain here how moving the whole thing was. The celebration was a party, a wake - no, make that a 'pre-wake' - and a reminder that life is short and sweet.

Sussex is a town of about 4,500 people. Only about half of them, I assume, are women. So that night the equivalent of 50% of the whole female population of Sussex turned out. That alone speaks for the strength of friendships and the power of a caring community. Retail is the interaction of people. It is the forming of relationships. The giving of advice and the purchase of goods. At its best it is a level of service that is memorable and meaningful and compelling in a way that moves people to return to a store. The retail experience can be so compelling that a customer will actually bring fresh baking to the store at Christmas, or send a thank you note or invite you to their cottage to go fishing. I've seen this happen many times and it is part of the magic that holds many of us 'career retailers' in the field. But I have never seen anything like this.

Prince Edward Island

· MONTAGUE · CHARLOTTETOWN · SUMMERSIDE · NORTH RUSTICO ·

Two generations of Becks, father George, Melody and Mark flank truck driver Charlie Thomas on delivery day.

If we're lucky, we still have a bit of the kid in us as adults. Which means that Mark Beck is a very lucky guy. On the surface, Mark is Mr. Home Hardware – third generation dealer, who worked at his father George's store during summers; went to university, then worked for Home Hardware corporate, first as a merchandiser out of St. Jacobs then as Area Manager for New Brunswick and PEI; back to work at the store then purchased his own HBC down the road from the original family store. That's the résumé.

Montague is a quiet little town a half hour's drive east of Charlottetown. In 1932, Cecil Beck and Ethan Stewart, Melody and Mark's grandfather and great-uncle opened a general store. Their dad George joined the business in 1964. In those days, the "business" included a general store, a grocery store with a clothing department as well as hardware and seasonal ware all purchased from about a dozen different wholesalers. Walter Aylward visited in 1971 looking to grow the PEI store count from three. On his second visit,

The Becks: To a small boy, the truck drivers were celebrities – they even had their own business cards the size of postcards that became instant collectibles.

Stewart & Beck Home Hardware and Home Building Centre
Montague, PEI

But the little boy isn't far below that successful surface. In fact, all it takes is the arrival of the Home Hardware truck and he's lit up like a top. When Mark was a little guy, one of the highlights of his life was the arrival of the Home Hardware truck. To a small boy, the truck drivers were celebrities – they even had their own business cards the size of postcards that became instant collectibles. (Mark still has a clutch of them that he guards jealously.) The problem for young Mark was that the truck usually came in the evening. So if he wanted to be part of the unloading excitement and stay up past his bedtime, he had to have a nap in the afternoon. It was a small price to pay for the thrill of helping to unload the treasure trove from Home!

This childlike enthusiasm clearly runs in the family. Melody, who is seven years younger than Mark, came back to work at her dad's store in 2010 after leaving nineteen years earlier to go to university. That was followed by a career in conference planning for the federal Government that took her all over the country. She went back to school for her MBA then ran the PEI Business Women's Association in Charlottetown. She came back to work as the company controller because she was looking for a new challenge and her dad convinced her that this was where she would find it. He was definitely right. She is full of enthusiasm for the task at hand – whatever it might be. In the office is a ragged map with stickpins that allowed a proud father to track the many locations across the country that Mark and Melody visited in their professional peregrinations. But those days are over and the whole family is now home. And Home.

he brought along Walter Hachborn. George knew instantly that Walter was a very special person: he was sincere, friendly, knowledgeable and caring. He greeted the staff the same as the owners – everyone was equal. George knew that it was the opportunity of a lifetime to be part of an organization with Walter Hachborn as its leader. He applied immediately and in July 1972 became the fourth Home Hardware store in Prince Edward Island. To this day, he says it was the most important and best business decision he has ever made.

In 2002 George and his brother Barry divided the company, with George keeping the hardware business and Barry moving the furniture business into a warehouse down the hill. This opened up an additional 7,000 square feet of retail space that has become their year-round seasonal department. Like all small town dealers, the Becks play an active role in their community, supporting activities through donations, fundraising BBQs and countless causes supported by their staff members. But one of the biggest community events isn't a fundraiser. It's the Becks' annual Victoria Day clearance sale. In the early 1980s, it was held in the arena then moved to a warehouse on the wharf, but for the past 10 years you will find everything happening in the store parking lot. But better get there early. People drive from all over the island, lining up hours in advance. When she was working in Ottawa, Melody would come home to work at the store that weekend. She remembers one year there was a 48-foot tractor-trailer filled with rolls of wallpaper – 99 cents a roll and 80% sold out by the end of the day. Another year it was lawn mowers at half price. There were 100 customers for 23 mowers. Someone had to break up a fistfight over that!

The Home Hardware store in Charlottetown must be a great place to work. Karen Laverts, whose full time job is Executive Assistant to the Mayor of Charlottetown, puts in two or three shifts a week at the store. That's quite the endorsement of the work place environment, not to mention Karen's energy level and work ethic. "I really love working with people," she explains. "She just has so much energy, she needs to keep busy," owner Paul Johnston offers in an aside.

store but was turned down. Their loss was Home's gain. From the start, competition was fierce, with every retailer in the category offering more or less the same products. AJ couldn't always beat them on price but he knew he could on service. The community clearly agreed: in 2006 Charlottetown Home Hardware received the inaugural "Best Service on the Island" award from the Chamber of Commerce. There is also a Gold Hammer award displayed proudly at the front of the store that opened in 2006.

Paul Johnston & Les Wong:

Home Hardware - Charlottetown
Charlottetown, PEI

In 2006 Charlottetown Home Hardware received the inaugural "Best Service on the Island" award from the Chamber of Commerce.

This comfortable badinage between the two took root in 2002. Karen, in her capacity of Executive Assistant to the Mayor, approached Paul and his co-owner and brother-in-law Les Wong, about becoming a corporate sponsor of the local chapter of Communities in Bloom. Charlottetown had been involved with Communities in Bloom at the national level since CiB was founded in the early 1990s. Paul gives all the credit to Karen for their successful partnership with Communities in Bloom. "Without hesitation we jumped on board and Karen has taken it from its infancy to where it is today." Karen says it is one of the best examples she has seen of good partnerships between local government and business. The synergies are numerous: a plant swap, product demonstrations, environmental tips, the local beautification contest and Charlottetown Home Hardware's co-sponsorship of the local awards night in September every year.

The connection to community is central to Home Hardware - Charlottetown's success. Like so many Home stores across the country, Home Hardware - Charlottetown has always been very involved in their community. The list is long: The Confederation Centre, The Mackenzie Theatre, IWK Children's Hospital, Children's Wish, Boys and Girls Clubs and Tree Canada to name but a few from over the years since 1976 when Paul's dad AJ and his wife Muriel opened their store. In those days, AJ was a manager at a Canadian Tire store in town. He wanted to open his own

Great service begins and ends with great staff, according to AJ's son Paul who, along with his brother-in-law Les Wong, took the business over from AJ on February 1, 1994. It was part of the culture from day one. And it starts on Day One for a new hire: the store operates a buddy system where a trainee stays with a senior employee, sometimes for as long as three weeks, before they graduate to a "red shirt." "We're very lucky," Paul says. "We have forty or fifty men and women - full and part-time - and without them, we couldn't open our doors." Here's another great service story: One of the staff asked a customer if they wanted a carry out. The answer was yes. The customer led the employee out the door, through the parking lot, down the street, around the corner…all the way to the customer's front door. That's service carried to extremes.

"Everywhere I go, somebody taps me on the shoulder and tells me about the good experience they've had in the store," says AJ who has retired from active duty. "And if I go down to the Charlottetown Club on a Friday night, somebody always comes over and he's been at the store that day or the day before. We've set the bar that high. And it's funny, if someone doesn't get that complete service, I hear about that too."

Welcome to Historic Downtown
Bienvenue au centre-ville historique de

CHARLOTTETOWN

This Corner Garden
Adopted by

Home
Charlottetown

Adopt a Corner is one of the many initiatives between the town, CiB and Home Hardware - Charlottetown.
In fact, Home Hardware - Charlottetown adopted two corners in 2011, and we headed over to one of them
for our photograph. The store was short staffed and Les was in the States at his daughter's first volleyball
game of the school year, but AJ and Muriel joined Paul and Karen at the corner of Euston and Queen.

Bill Callbeck, tall, elegant and retired, dropped by to reminisce with Linda McCardle, Garth Wright and Ron. He remembers the days when Walter would stop by to visit; by the time he got to the office, after working his way through the building, Walter knew more about the business than Bill did!

Ron MacDonald had done his homework the day I arrived at Callbecks Home Hardware Building Centre in Summerside, PEI. Or at least, his staff had done their homework, which is not surprising, since Ron originally intended to be a teacher. He handed me a five page, handwritten, single spaced listing, compiled by staff members, of the many community initiatives they have been involved in on an ongoing basis. It's quite the list: free flower seeds for first graders; paint donated for community wall

who works at the store, not simply management. Ron says that the success of the business is directly attributable to the employees, many of whom moved from Bedeque to Summerside and are still there more than 20 years later. Like Garth Wright who started at the Bedeque store in 1971 and who today knows everything – and everyone – there is to know on the building supply side of the business. Others have been there for 10, 15, 20 plus years. Like Karen MacDonald and Aubrey Desroches who both started to

Ron MacDonald:
Ron says the success of the business is directly attributable to the employees.

Callbecks Home Hardware Building Centre
Summerside, PEI

murals and a graffiti wall; the Christmas Toy Collection drive for Social Services; free barbecues for customers, neighbours, and contractors; Ladies' Nights, Fashion Shows, Makeovers, all to raise money for local causes; The Children's Wish on many occasions, all for families of customers; The Prince County Hospital Equipment Fund for which they have raised thousands of dollars; and one of my favourites, a community clean up in front of the competition's store where staff passed out free leaf bags and garbage bags. A few memorable fundraisers were highlighted on a separate page: dialysis equipment at the Prince County Hospital because staff member Albert Gaudet had dialysis there; a Hospice Room in memory of Lori Montgomery, a former staff member who died of cancer; two bursaries for high school grads going into business or retail programs at college or university, in honour of John Callbeck, prior owner Bill Callbeck's son, who died in a tragic accident; $10,000 raised for an Infant Warming Bed for the hospital.

Callbecks has been an island institution since 1899 when it opened for business as a tailor shop in Central Bedeque. Callbecks joined the Home Hardware family in 1972, the second PEI store to do so. Ron started working at the store as a high school student in 1972, and although he graduated from university with his teacher's degree in 1979, he joined the business fulltime in May 1979 and bought the business from Bill Callbeck, along with a partner, in 2002. The Callbeck family moved the business from Central Bedeque to Summerside in 1990. It's a big store - over 20,000 square feet with 16,000 square feet of retail two warehouses, a large LBM yard and more expansion in the works: the Summerside Home Furniture store, also owned by Ron and Donna, will be moving from its current location downtown to its new location across the street from Callbecks HHBC. The ground breaking was just days away when we visited and the store had its opening in January 2012.

Ron and his high school sweetheart wife Donna have owned the business since 2007 when they bought out Ron's original partner. When he talks about the business, Ron says "we" and "us" all the time, meaning everyone

work in the paint department in the early 1990s. Karen is responsible for the beautiful murals that adorn the back walls of the store. Ron points out that from virtually the day Karen and Aubrey arrived, Callbecks HHBC has consistently ranked in the top three stores across the country in paint sales. Then there are Ivan and Mike Gallant with 31 and 21 years in plumbing; David Pearce, Paul Murray, and Bonnie Farrell, 21, 21,and 23 years in building supplies; Hilton Platts with 37 years in the hardware and tool section. The list goes on, 13 employees with over 10 years employment, and another 12 with over 20 years.

Ron also attributes the success of Callbeck's ongoing community involvement to the commitment and effort of employees. In October 2011 when we visited, their most recent fundraising effort was still standing at a funny angle at the curb on the main road that runs in front of the store parking lot: a Little Crooked House in Home Hardware red. The "Red" theme for the 2011 Summerside Lobster Carnival Parade could not have been more perfect for Callbecks HHBC. The staff built the crooked house, someone sewed Little Red Riding Hood costumes, another employee found a wolf costume, the three-ton truck was decked out in a wolf costume. And so a float was created and it was no surprise when Callbecks won best commercial float for the second year in a row. To top it off, Callbecks held a silent auction for the Crooked Little House to raise more money for the hospital equipment fund. Crooked House or any other initiative, team Callbecks is the straight goods in every way when it comes to serving their community.

Lise & Chris Buote:

North Rustico Home Building Centre
North Rustico, PEI

Twenty-six trees were planted on this windswept shore
in November 2010.

Hurricane Ophelia is making her presence felt the morning we arrive in
North Rustico to visit owners Lise Buote and her son Chris (Lise's other
son Patrick, who also works in the family business, is away that day). So
it's a lowering kind of day that's rapidly deteriorating. Our plan is to take
a photograph of the Tree Canada planting on the boardwalk that edges this
sweet little fishing town in the Green Gables Shore region not far from
Cavendish and everyone's favourite redhead. Trish Thorpe, a "CFA" (Come
From Away) originally from England, who has worked at the store since
2005, was the catalyst. In August 2010, a fax came through from Home
Hardware corporate requesting submissions to participate in a national Tree
Canada planting. Trish thought it would be a beautiful way to commemorate
the memory of Lise's husband and Chris and Patrick's father, Wayne
Buote, who had recently and suddenly passed away. The idea was accepted
unanimously by the entire staff as well as by Home Hardware. Twenty-six
trees were planted on this windswept shore in November 2010. Less than
a year later, the trees, still small and frail against the forces of nature, are
taking hold and starting to grow. It's something that could equally be said
about Lise whose eyes mist up as she looks across the shore to the other side
of the peninsula and reminisces about the driving force that was her husband
Wayne. We take the picture and then Chris and Lise head back to the store,
disappearing through the falling rain in the bright red sports car that was
Wayne's last gift to his wife.

The West

Leadership takes many forms, but certain qualities are always in evidence: intelligence, confidence, charisma, a dash of sophistication and more than a soupçon of charm. All of these, plus a talent for story telling and the memories to go with it, were on display when we visited Charlie Reid and his wife Gloria at their Saskatoon home in September 2012.

banner. Charlie's dad retired in 1970 and in 1972, Charlie was elected to serve on Link's Board of Directors on which he sat until 1977. He resigned over a hiring decision of which he strongly disapproved. But the company was in trouble and looking for a buyer so in 1979, Charlie agreed to come back onto the Board to help with the process. Although he didn't know him

Charlie Reid: Charlie was instrumental in bringing the Link Hardware group of dealers into the Home Hardware fold.

Chairman of the Board 1991 - 2002, retired 2002.

Saskatoon, SK

Charlie's distinguished 22-year career with Home Hardware began when, as a member of Link Hardware's management group, he was instrumental in bringing that key group of western dealers into the Home Hardware fold. Charlie served as Chairman of the Board for 11 years, his tenure ending at another turning point for Home Hardware, the acquisition of Beaver Lumber.

Like so many Home Hardware Dealers, Charlie grew up in retail. His father bought a grocery store in Craik, Saskatchewan, halfway between Saskatoon and Regina. A few years later, he bought the local hardware business where it was Charlie's after school job to repair windows. His overseer was an elderly English master tinsmith. Every afternoon, he'd sit on a ledge at the back of the store and read the paper while Charlie repaired windows. After a while, the old gentleman would retrieve a "done" window, and put his putty knife to work. By the time he had finished, he had recovered a large mound of putty that Charlie knew was earmarked for the next round of panes.

After that, Charlie felt that perhaps he wasn't cut out for a hardware career. When he was in Grade 12, his dad bought the local BA Oil Distribution license. Now Charlie got up at 5 o'clock every morning, filled the 45-gallon drums, and loaded them onto the truck. After school he delivered them. He decided that hardware was an easier way to make a living after all.

After high school, Charlie spent a year and a half working at several hardware stores. When his father had a heart attack, Charlie returned to the family business in Craik. Over the next few years, Charlie honed his entrepreneurial chops.

On a trip to the west coast looking for expansion opportunities, Charlie and his father stopped over in Saskatoon. And that's where they found their store: an operation on the edge of the growing town that had a reputation to restore and a world of opportunity to offer. They never looked back.

In 1962, when Charlie was 30, the Reids joined Falcon Hardware, part of Merchants' Consolidated in Winnipeg. In 1967, they switched to the Link

well, Charlie called Walter Hachborn whose response was immediate: "We want to make this happen." It was not the easiest sell to some Link dealers, but the Board knew with certainty that Home Hardware was the right choice. In 1981, with approximately 300 stores spanning northwest Ontario to the Northwest Territories, Link became part of the Home Hardware family, opening the west for Home Hardware. Charlie and two fellow Link Board members, John Blake from High River, Alberta and Harry Blight, from Vancouver, joined the Home Hardware Board at the time of the buyout.

Throughout the 1980s, Home Hardware kept up the pace: the company bought Revelstoke, Walter decided it was time to retire as CEO and the Board embarked on the process of finding a replacement. Charlie was very pleased when Paul Straus was the Board's ultimate choice.

In 1999, just before Charlie's last big coup as Chairman, he had his first heart attack. It was January 3, following a busy Christmas when all the kids and grandkids had come home. Charlie got back into the car after saying goodbye at the airport and said, "I'm having a heart attack." Gloria gave him her famous look, and they switched places. He settled into the passenger seat and passed out. Two weeks later, he was back at work.

Which was probably just as well, because the following year Home Hardware bought Beaver Lumber. For two months Charlie and Gloria lived in Markham, Ontario, so that he would be close to the Beaver head office. Charlie was never around and Gloria did not know a soul. She got a lot of sewing done, she remembers.

After 11 years as Chaiman, Charlie retired from the Board and sold his store in 2002. He has enjoyed a life of remarkable accomplishment. He and Gloria have five children, 12 grandchildren and six great grandchildren. Together they raised a family and ran a successful family business. During his years as a Home Hardware Dealer Charlie also served devotedly on the Board of Directors and was at the heart of pivotal moments of opportunity, major decisions and transformational change that built one of Canada's largest and truly national retailers.

MANITOBA

DAUPHIN · ROBLIN · WINKLER · STONEWALL · MORRIS · NEEPAWA ·

Hardware Merchandising's
2012 Outstanding Retailer Award winner.

At the end of a long day, Owen Connolly likes to unwind by catching a film at his local cinema, the one he owns in his hometown of Dauphin, Manitoba. Owen Connolly, Manitoba Movie Mogul has a certain ring. But the plot line is more prairie pluck than Hollywood hubris. A few years ago the local cinema burned down and when the town approached the major national chains about rebuilding, Dauphin was deemed too small a market. (In fact, although the town's population is 8,000, the overall drawing area

Owen Connolly: Being part of Home Hardware is akin to winning the lottery.

Dauphin Home Hardware
Dauphin, MB

in this rich agricultural region is closer to 30,000.) So the town decided to go it alone. Fortunately, Dauphin already had an established and extremely community-minded organization, Dauphin CountryFest, Canada's longest running country music festival (started in1989) that provides funding to other community-based initiatives. With its backing and the hard work of a determined group of citizens, many of them successful business people like Owen, the community of Dauphin now owns CountryFest Community Cinema, a non-profit organization that itself donates proceeds to other community projects.

Over twenty years ago, Owen and his wife Wanda returned to Dauphin, where Wanda was born and raised and where Owen had moved at the tender age of 15 with the dream of becoming a professional hockey player. Owen was a member of the Dauphin Kings' provincial championship team in 1976-77, and although he did not find a career on the ice, he did find a wife - Wanda Secord was a figure skater at the same rink. By the time they were 18 years old, Owen and Wanda were married and building a future together, so it was fitting that Owen found a job with Revelstoke, working in the LBM world for several years. In the early 1980s, Owen was ready to buy his own business and sensibly, bought what he could afford, which happened to be a Home Hardware store in Grandview, about 30 miles west of Dauphin, transferring his allegiance from lumber to hardware, where it has remained ever since. Grandview (pop. 1000) is a small town, and after several years building and running a successful hardware store, the Connollys were looking to broaden their horizons. On July 2, 1992, they brought Home Hardware to Dauphin, opening a brand new 6,700 square foot store. The years passed, the town grew, the retail landscape posed challenges in the form of competition and economic vicissitudes, but Owen and Wanda persevered and flourished. They grew slowly, acquiring more property in the plaza as it became available. After the final expansion in 2010 that completed the takeover of the entire building, the 22,400 square foot store is a bright and busy and welcoming place that serves a drawing area that extends as much as 50 miles beyond the borders of the town itself.

Today Owen's two daughters Whitney and Brandice work in the business. Whitney (who was on maternity leave with Owen and Wanda's third grandson when we visited) went to law school and her husband Mark Odut played professional hockey in the US before deciding a few years ago to return to Dauphin to work towards taking over the family business. "I didn't think my family would ever get involved with the business," Owen says. "But she knew we'd been thinking about slowing down. The phone rang one day and it was Whitney. She said, 'Don't sell the store until we get home this summer.'" Mark worked part time in the store when he played junior hockey in town and as hardware kids, both Whitney and Brandice grew up "in the back office" and worked in the store as teenagers. Brandice is office manager and wants no part of the business apart from that. Her interest ultimately lies in home care, not Home care. She says to her dad: "Tell me what to do and I'll do it." But any doubts that Owen may have had at the thought of Whitney taking over were quickly dispelled: "Obviously my daughter has some retail blood in her," he says with a proud laugh, "because she took control of things and has done a tremendous job. It was quite humbling to know that your family wants to take over and appreciates what you have done."

For Owen Connolly, being part of Home Hardware is akin to winning the lottery. "I can't imagine what our lives would have been like without Home Hardware," he says. He remembers speaking with Walter when he and Wanda wanted to move up from the small store in Grandview. "I met him at the hardware show," Owen recalls. "I said, 'Here's my situation: we've been there nine years, we don't owe any money, I'm 35 years old - what do I do next?' And Walter said, 'It's time for you to move on. You have a whole life ahead of you yet.'"

In 2012 Home Hardware nominated Dauphin Home Hardware for the Hardware Merchandising Outstanding Retailer of the Year Award, which the store won. Owen is honoured to have won such a prestigious industry-wide award, but for him the real story still remains the fact that he and his family have been able to build a good life in a good town, thanks to Home Hardware.

We pulled into the small Manitoba town of Roblin one early evening in late August 2012 to meet Gerald Stuart who, along with his wife Jody, owns the Home Hardware store on the main street. The streets were empty, the stores had closed for the day and there was no one around. Promptly at 7 o'clock, Gerald unlocked the front door of the store. He had

This isn't the way they used to do it. What's going on?'" But Gerald was undeterred. "I'm stubborn and I don't want to fail, right?" In addition to working 12 hour days for over two years, he and Jody joined committees, sports teams and participated in just about everything and anything. "I just worked hard and spent lots of time playing hockey. We joined the

Gerald Stuart: "I was able to learn from the best," Gerald said. "I picked up traits from Home Dealers across Canada."

Roblin Home Hardware
Roblin, MB

just come back from the golf course, where the majority of the town's adult male population was to be found that Thursday evening, the last Men's Night of a summer that started in mid May. After years of putting in 100-hour weeks at the store he bought in 2001, Gerald is enjoying some well deserved R&R.

Scratch the surface of Gerald's boyish enthusiasm and you will quickly find a driven, ambitious individual whose work ethic and never-say-die determination are grounded in the Alberta farm where he grew up. In fact, he was the perfect candidate for a career with Home Hardware but did not realize it until six months into his first job at the western distribution centre in Wetaskiwin. "I was just packing boxes at first," he said as he remembered those early Home Hardware days. Little by little, his attitude changed. It may have started the first time he met Don Kirck, who shook his hand and beamed and boomed "Welcome Home!" After two years in the distribution centre, Gerald joined the merchandising team, thanks to Brian Reid, traveling to stores across Western Canada. He learned a lot from successful Home Dealers along the way and after another two years in dealer development, he knew that he wanted his own store. He worked as an Area Manager for another few years and credits Larry Kondro, Western Regional Manager at that time, with encouraging and mentoring him in his quest. The experience of working in a number of different capacities at Home Hardware, as well as knowing so many of the people, were real assets. "I was able to learn from the best," Gerald said. "I picked up traits from dealers across Canada."

But realizing his dream did not happen overnight. The store the Stuarts took over had chugged along quietly and successfully for many years but not a lot had changed. Gerald was determined to bring to bear all his knowledge and experience but encountered an uphill battle with every upgrade, update and improvement. When he increased the SKU count by 20%, business fell of instead of growing. "People would say, 'Why are you moving this.

golf course, went to community dances - met lots of people. I have a good personality for that stuff - I would sit down at a table and I got to know about half the table in short order. I can be a bit of a goof ball sometimes so it's sometimes easy for people to laugh at me, right?" After three years, "Bang, things took off," Gerald said.

Gerald epitomizes the best of the Home Hardware ethos. He has bloomed where he lives. The town, due west of Dauphin and close to the Saskatchewan border, has been dubbed the Jewel of the Parkland and is also the Fly Fishing Capital of Manitoba. Surrounded by rich and rolling farmland Roblin is the gateway to two national parks that attract outdoor aficionados of all stripes.

One thing Gerald has already learned with 100% certainty is what an incredible opportunity he stumbled onto when he started working in Wetaskiwin. "At first, it was just a job to me. But slowly it started to dawn on me: Where else do you own your own business, work as hard as you want - be as successful as you want to be - you know - do whatever - it's not too many places in the world where you don't have to answer to anybody but yourself."

Gerald had been Area Manager for all of a week when Walter phoned and announced that he was coming for a visit. "I want you to tour me around," he told Gerald. He and Jody picked up Walter at the airport and they headed out with no clear agenda, visiting stores along the way. Walter sat in the back, refusing to let Jody relinquish her seat and before long the two of them were "bantering back and forth like best friends."

In 1948, a group of Manitoba Mennonites moved to Paraguay. Conscientious objectors who had just lived through the Second World War, they chose a country that would allow them to prosper and raise their families far away from the tumult of the world. One of those families was the Enns whose son Henry was born in 1950.

trade carpenter, are being groomed to take over the business when Henry is ready. But that is down the road. Several Paraguayan-Canadians are on the staff of 50 employees - Henry takes care of his extended family. "I empower my staff, and they make wise decisions," Henry says. "I trust them and together we operate the business."

Henry Enns: *"I cannot imagine another organization worldwide that would surpass Home Hardware. Everybody is pulling for the same double H and I think that's what makes us so strong."*

Parkside Home Building Centre
Winkler, MB

Forty years later, Henry moved "back" to Manitoba - he had never lived there, but had dual citizenship thanks to his parents. Although he was very successful in Paraguay (which Henry pronounces "Parawhay" with a lovely soft Spanish inflection), family circumstances made Canada a better place to raise his family. He and his wife Anna sensibly spent a winter in Manitoba before making a final decision - Paraguay is near the equator with a tropical climate very different from Canada's. They weathered the winter and settled in Winkler, from where his wife's parents originated and where many of their Paraguayan friends had already moved. Henry had no idea how he would make a living, but he had the luxury of being able to take his time. He eventually bought a furniture store on the verge, turned it around and after a year or two was approached by Bruce Hammer about converting to the Home Furniture banner. "We were really enticed by their advertising program and we really like their promotion. Once he showed us the head office and invited us to our first show, we were convinced that this was the way to go." When a local lumberyard became available, Henry bought it and a year later, in 1996, converted it to the HBC banner. He sold the furniture store that has since moved to a larger location in town leaving him to concentrate on lumber, the business that had allowed him to prosper in Paraguay. Since then his Home Building Centre, still known locally as Parkside Lumber, has grown from 1,200 to 16,000 square feet, the last expansion taking place in 2010. His son Jim, who studied business administration at university, and his son-in-law Jonathan Peters, a former

Winkler is a flourishing community that has retained its young people. An aura of quiet prosperity floats over the tree-lined side streets. Rich farmland spreads across the outlying countryside and the commerce, industry and manufacturing that border the town on all sides account for what Henry proudly declares is virtual 100% employment. The vibrant economy is responsible for the high-end electronics shop and excellent cafe (that Henry charmingly calls Yava Yonny's) among other local establishments.

Although they were both born in Paraguay, Henry and Anna clearly have Canadian blood - they love the changing seasons and have a beautiful garden on the large property behind their spacious and comfortable home. Henry also loves to barbecue, Paraguayan style using skewers to rotisserie roast the meat over the coals.

With his South American heritage, Henry is a soccer fan: he started the Winkler Storm and coached the team for 11 years (a semi amateur team, they are now playing at the second highest level in the province) and has coached at the major league level in the province. He has no political aspirations although he is completely committed to the betterment of the community that has more than doubled in size since he and his family moved to Winkler over 20 years ago.

Henry Enns stands in front of an old sod cabin preserved from the early days of Mennonite settlement in the area.

A handwritten sign tacked onto the bulletin board in the staffroom at Stonewall Home Hardware just north of Winnipeg does a good job of summing up owner Katharine Kirk's approach to life. It establishes the parameters of a discount she makes available to store employees: "This perk is for you and for you only. It is not for sisters or brothers, aunts, uncles,

square feet of retail space. "It was either go big or go home," Katharine says with a shrug. Over the years the town has evolved into a pleasant Winnipeg bedroom community with a population of about 4,500. The emphasis is on residential, so Katharine knows she made the right decision to remain a hardware store when she renovated almost 15 years ago.

Katharine Kirk: One day in 1998, her mother told her, "Oh, you just bought the business."

Stonewall Home Hardware
Stonewall, MB

second cousins, third cousins, friends, friends of a friend or anyone else you just feel like giving it to… any abuse of this perk and it will be taken away." Tempered by a broad streak of humour, the message is nonetheless clear and unequivocal.

What you see is what you get with Katharine Kirk, third generation owner of this small town business that became a member of Home Hardware when the company bought Link in 1980. It seems fitting that she lives and works in a town called Stonewall, named after the limestone quarries, now closed, that lie on the outskirts of town. Much of the town's architecture - austere, clean-lined stone buildings that anchor the few but tidy streets - dates back to the town's founding in 1871 when Samuel Jacob Jackson, originally from Ireland, came west from Ontario and encouraged others to join him by offering land tracts to anyone who promised to build their homes to his specifications and plant trees on their properties. Many of the beautiful old trees on the main street date back to the town's founding.

Katharine is clearly related to Jackson, if only in temperament. She started working in the store owned and operated by her parents Robert and Irene Pearson when she was 12. Her father passed away in the 1970s and her mother, Katharine, her brother and sister carried on the business.

Eventually her brother went one way and her sister the other and one day in 1998, her mother told her, "Oh, you just bought the business." After that, Katharine went on a tear, demolishing old buildings, adding at the back for storage and freight, every available square foot being put to work. Today, Stonewall Home Hardware is a compact operation of just under 9,000

Although Katharine's three grown children work at the store - Andrew is 32, Adam is 27 and Crystal is 21 - there is no doubt who runs the business. Despite her reticence, it is obvious that Katharine loves her store and is proud of her accomplishments. And she has every right to be. Not only did she take over when hardware was a male dominated business, she has built it up steadily ever since. These days Winnipeg is spreading ever closer - consumers can get virtually anything they want or need within a twenty-minute radius. Heather Brincheski, the Manitoba and North Western Ontario Area Manager, has dropped in that morning. Like so many Home Hardware Dealers Katharine is extremely modest, so I am grateful for Heather's frequent clarifications, interjections and additions. She tells me what I am already beginning to understand. Katharine is a progressive dealer, always ready to make improvements. In fact, given the value of peer-to-peer interaction, Heather often calls on Katharine to help Retail Operations with larger projects - including store remerchandising, training and store openings. The fact that she can leave her store in the hands of her full and part-time staff, speaks volumes about the business she has built that allows her to be away sometimes for several weeks at a time. "I love it," she says. "I learn something new every day including more of the corporate side which helps me to understand that point of view."

In 2013, Katharine bought a new building and expanded her business. At 14,000 square feet, the new store, slated to open in January 2014, will be double the size of the current location.

Home Hardware - A Lifestyle Choice
by Bud Stupnisky, aided and abetted by Shelley Stupnisky

My addiction to hardware and retailing began at an early age. I grew up in Rossburn, Manitoba in a family business that shifted from groceries to clothing and footwear. My dad's barbershop was in the front corner. I grew

Bud and Shelley Stupnisky:

Morris Home Hardware
Morris, MB

"The business we purchased is best described as historic."

up serving customers, washing floors and cleaning the stock room. We built a new store in 1968, which has since become Dennis Oliver's Rossburn Home Hardware. But my real love was across the street, the Marshall Wells/ Link Hardware Store. As a child I visited regularly, mesmerized by the rows of wrenches and hammers, the fishing rods and baseball gloves, the boxes of bolts, the array of small appliances and dishes and a few pieces of furniture that filled the 3,000 square feet.

I attended the University of Manitoba in the mid-sixties and finally graduated with two valuable results. First, I met Shelley, my wife and love of my life. Second, I learned that in life you should follow your heart. At university I was certain that I never wanted to own a retail business. A government job would be ideal…reasonable hours, weekends free, a good pension plan, security.

We settled in Selkirk, where Shell taught at the Junior High and I drove to my government job in Winnipeg. We loved our small town life, but soon moved to Ottawa. After two years, I was constantly stressed, working long hours and weekends, and travelling a lot, leaving Shell and two small children home alone. One day, after a series of road trips, I told Shell that if I was going to worry this much and work this hard, it might as well be for our own business. I painted a rosy picture of a small town hardware store, a couple of employees, a quiet life with time for kids' activities, volunteer work, golf and curling, not far from Winnipeg and equidistant from my parents in Rossburn and Shell's in Fort Frances. She liked that picture but worried whether she could run a store. I knew that she was perfect for the job - smart, well educated, organized, with great taste and a great personality. We agreed that I should start researching opportunities and financing.

After contacting Home Hardware, Macleod's and Marshall Wells, we picked an affordable Marshall Wells store within a community with all the amenities and the reputation throughout the West for hosting the Manitoba Stampede, the next stop from Calgary for professional rodeo. Every penny we had went into the venture - proceeds from the sale of our Ottawa home, my cashed-in government pension, a loan from the local credit union. The inventory came to a heart-stopping $35,000 over estimates. A quick phone call and my Dad came up with $25,000 and the owner agreed to finance the rest. We had a store!

It's August 25, 1983. We've just passed through Kenora: another two hours to Winnipeg. The northern Ontario landscape gives way to the open fields of harvest-time Manitoba. Combines are rolling, wheat chaff is in the air and the smell is awesome. I am driving a large U-Haul truck with a smaller trailer attached. My companion is my two year-old son Rob. In our car behind me are Shell and four year-old Jennifer. Neither vehicle has air-conditioning or seat belts! It's a hot, dry 30 degrees. We are en route to Morris, Manitoba, population 1,600, 35 miles south of Winnipeg, the heart of the Red River Valley.

One week later we have moved into a farmhouse just north of Morris. It has a cistern for water supply, an old red barn with several families of cats and clouds of grasshoppers that plague our passage from house to vehicle. Today is possession day.

Our First Year – and Home Hardware
The business we purchased is best described as historic: the oldest building in town - 4,000 square feet - a white siding store front with stucco walls; plywood shelving with glass partitions; pink, yellow and blue panels of pegboard. The galvanized plumbing fittings lived in drawer bins 20 feet long and 8 feet high. Duplicates of these are in the Home Hardware museum in St. Jacobs, as is the "cash register" complete with ivory shelf above the cash drawer. We did have a new adding machine and Marshall Wells used a "Telzon" machine to send orders over the phone. There were house wares, paint, plumbing, electrical, automotive, tools, toys, sporting goods, garden supplies, pet supplies and about 1,000 square feet of assorted furniture: mattresses and appliances. Sound familiar?

Fortunately, Nick and Elsie Kohut, the previous owners, helped us out. Elsie became our first and only employee that September. Nick spent several months in the store, training, advising and lending us his truck for deliveries. (Two years later we won our own truck at the Home Hardware market – thank you Sylvania!)

By Christmas I knew we had to make some changes. In spite of the historic magic of the name for me, the reality was that Marshall Wells could not be competitive. By April 1984 our application to become a Home Hardware store was approved and shortly thereafter the new signs were up, and the Spring catalogue was in the mail. The results were dramatic! We experienced 25% sales increases several years in a row, and we started renovating and improving the store. Life was good.

Home Hardware:
A Lifestyle Choice

by Bud Stupnisky, aided and abetted by Shelley Stupnisky

We couldn't have chosen a better fit to our lifestyle than Home Hardware and we are extremely proud to be flying the Home Hardware banner. Economically, Home Hardware's buying power, product selection and advertising program have allowed a small town store to compete with everyone (in Canada) including all the major competitors only 35 miles away in Winnipeg. Training has always been available in everything from merchandising to computers to product knowledge. Home's focus on treating customers with golden rule service is part of our psyche, and gets passed on to our staff. The semi-annual markets have been part holiday (Weber's Charcoal Steak House ribs are a market must), part learning and part buying for 29 years. But what has been most important has been the freedom to focus on what we like to do as a store and the huge opportunities to "follow our heart" and also get the variety, business connections, and merchandising support from Home to help us do our best.

We are not an aggressive "bottom-line", "financial statement" store. We'll leave that to the future owners of Morris Home Hardware. We do many things because we like to do them. We continue to carry a wide variety of merchandise - toys, sporting goods, electronics and home entertainment, major appliances, and a beautiful Home Expressions department because we enjoy it and because it broadens the service we offer to a small community. We try to make our store interesting and exciting for our customers, our staff and ourselves.

Several years ago the local Chamber of Commerce hired a consulting firm to analyse shopping trends in Morris and to identify factors driving shopping elsewhere. We were extremely proud to have been identified by the T-group as the store that set the standard for how a store should treat its customers. We are proud of the compliments we receive weekly from our customers and to be "my favourite store" to so many.

Personally we have had the opportunity to volunteer in many community organizations, watch our children achieve sports and academic excellence and travel to many exotic locations. We have fulfilled a dream to design and build a new home and form many lifelong friendships with our fellow Morris residents. We love our life and still look forward to the challenges and rewards of our "job" everyday.

In addition to running a business and raising two children, the Goldades have served their community as well. Janice is especially proud of the Neepawa Beautiful Plains Community Foundation. She was one of the founding members and served as Finance Chair. As with other foundations of its type, the principal is held in perpetuity and the interest used to fund different organizations and activities across the community. Ron has been a member of the Lions' Club for many years. Lions' Riverbend Park is one of their projects, with the updated playground the most recent addition to the grounds.

Neepawa is home to Ron and Janice Goldade, former Home Hardware Dealers. Ron also served as Home Hardware Chairman of the Board from 2002 until they sold their business in 2008.

Ron Goldade came from Prelate in South Western Saskatchewan. After school he moved to Leader, the next town, where he worked at Macleod's. From there he went to Kindersley with the Co-op. He transferred several times until he landed in Boissevain, which is south of Brandon. That is

He emphasized that he knew they could survive and grow with the Home Hardware program. Walter said, "Leave it with me, I'll get back to you." Later that afternoon, he called back and said, "We'll take you on."

The Goldades were ecstatic. The paperwork was finalized and they were waiting for their first shipment. One morning their Bank Manager, Ron Cowley, came running into the store, yelling: "Your truck's coming down the road!"

Ron and Janice Goldade:

Neepawa Home Hardware
Neepawa, MB   "Home Hardware allowed me to live my dream. And I'm still living it."

where he and Janice met. From there, he was transferred to Dauphin and then to Saskatoon where he was the hardware and floorcovering manager.

The next move was to Lethbridge, where according to Ron, he had the perfect job: lots of money and nothing to do. He rapidly got bored and at that point decided it was time for them to buy their own business. Marshall Wells found them a store in Canora, Saskatchewan.

The early 1980s were difficult years. Interest rates were sky high and Marshall Wells was struggling. The Goldades knew that they were going to be in trouble if they didn't do something. One weekend, while they were at Janice's parents' cabin, her brother mentioned Home Hardware, in those days a relative unknown in the West. The next day Ron and Janice drove to Onanole, the nearest town with a Home Hardware store and introduced themselves to owner Brian Minty. "Brian looked up from his spot at the cash and nodded at someone standing in the aisle," Ron remembers. "'The guy from Home Hardware is right over there,' he said." It was the Area Manager, Tim Oldham, who, according to Ron, was responsible for building Home Hardware in Manitoba and Saskatchewan. The following week Tim was in Canora with the papers. But to their dismay, Home Hardware corporate turned them down.

Ron knew they were "doomed" if they could not join Home. So he called the office in St Jacobs and asked to speak to the person in charge; not knowing the company structure, he didn't know that it was Walter Hachborn. Over the phone, Ron introduced himself, explained who he was, and told Walter how he and Janice had built their business from nothing.

By 1985, the Goldades were ready for another change. After they sold their store in Canora, Home Hardware suggested they visit Portage la Prairie. The trip took them through Neepawa, which they both liked. As they drove down the main street, they saw an empty Beaver building and not much else in the way of competition. They recognized an opportunity and never did go to Portage la Prairie. The next day they made an offer on the property. Twenty-three busy, successful and happy years later, they retired, selling to a young local businessman and current owner of Neepawa Home Hardware, Patrick Guilbert.

Prior to moving to Neepawa from Canora, Ron had been involved in municipal politics. He also sat on the Board of the Canadian Retail Hardware Association at the same time as he first served on Home Hardware's Board. So when Charlie Reid retired and Ron successfully ran to replace him as Home's Chairman of the Board, he had experience with the responsibilities that came with the honour.

Ron and Janice speak of their years as Home Hardware Dealers with the greatest affection and respect. Walter and Paul always said that Home Hardware is a family. And the Goldades lived that reality. As young people going through the difficult times of growing the business, they looked forward to the markets. They weren't just about the merchandise, they were about the people. "We did our work on the floor," they recall, "but at the end of the day we'd head back to our hotel and talk for hours to people who did the same thing we did. We'd laugh and solve each other's problems. We totally understood each other. And those friendships have continued since 1981."

SASKATCHEWAN

· ASSINIBOIA · FORT QU'APPELLE · OUTLOOK · SWIFT CURRENT ·

The Harvey family established roots in Assiniboia in 1920 when their grandfather Lewis, originally from England, moved from Eastend to Assiniboia and opened a farm implements store. From there it was a logical extension into hardware, the business becoming essentially a general store for the community that existed to serve the rich farmland surrounding the town.

By the mid 1980s, the business was changing. It was becoming increasingly important to keep up with the technological advances in point of sale and other key areas of the business. Wilfred started spending more time away, going south for the winter. In his absence, things changed around the store. One afternoon in 1985, Frank Hammer and Larry Kondro dropped in for a visit. The two brothers knew all about Walter Hachborn from their

Graham and Scott Harvey:

Harvey's Home Centre
Assiniboia, SK

"Dad was a tremendous leader," Graham remembers. "He was a lot like Walter Hachborn; they were visionaries."

After serving in WW2 and spending a few years in Toronto, Graham and Scott's father Wilfred returned to Assiniboia in 1949 and started working in the family store. In 1951, the same year that Graham was born, the second generation bought out the first. Four years later Scott came along. The two boys literally grew up in the business: they lived over the store, the original building on Main Street that is now another Harvey family business. When they reached their early teens, each of the three Harvey children, Graham, Scott and their sister Barbara, who today lives in British Columbia, were expected to help out in the store. By now, Harvey's was a member of the Merchants' Consolidated Group, the Saskatchewan, Manitoba and western Ontario equivalent of Hollinger/Home Hardware and other buying groups across the country. Wilf served as its Chairman of the Board for six years. It was during this time that he met and acquired such respect for Walter Hachborn. In fact, at that time, many of Canada's regional hardware wholesale buying groups were members of United Hardware, a consortium that met twice a year to exchange ideas and experience. They sometimes even made major buys together, a highly innovative and unusual situation for competing hardware chains, a cooperative spirit Graham sees as having Walter Hachborn written all over it.

In 1971, after two years at the University of Regina, Graham came into the family business at the request of his father. In addition to their Allied Hardware Store, the retail banner of Merchants' Consolidated, they opened a second store called Harvey's Home Furnishings. Business was so good that in 1975 they built the store that today houses Harvey's Home Centre. The 10,000 square foot store fulfilled Wilfred's dream. Scott, meanwhile, had graduated and moved to Calgary. Like Graham before him, he had no intention of coming back to Assiniboia, let alone the family business. But retail has a way of getting into your blood and that same year, Scott came on board. Three Harveys, two generations. But it worked, each of them growing the business in different ways. "Dad was a tremendous leader," Graham remembers. "He was a lot like Walter Hachborn; they were visionaries. He was a savvy businessman in a methodical common sense way. And he worked with us - if we had an issue, it would be on the table. It might get vocal or it might get pretty intense, but it was dealt with and then it was done. And that made it work as well."

father. They also had old childhood friends whose Link stores had become Home Hardware fairly recently and were great advocates. After Frank and Larry left, Graham and Scott almost immediately made up their minds to proceed with the changeover to Home Hardware despite the fact that their father was a previous Chairman of the Board of Merchants' Consolidated. It was just too good an opportunity to pass up. When Wilf got back from Palm Springs later that month they told him of their decision. "His response was 'Great,'" Graham remembers. "He always understood growth and he knew that we had to go with the people who were moving ahead." Although their father passed away in 1996, the debt they owe him is still very dominant in Graham's mind. "He was my mentor, probably my best friend and my brother's best friend too," Graham says simply.

Over the years the store has enjoyed updates and facelifts. With Moose Jaw just 60 miles north, and the US border 60 miles south, the Harveys work hard to keep the customer loyalty they have earned over the years. Although the town's population has been dropping, a sense of optimism pervades the province and its effects can be seen all over the town of 2,500 that serves the resurging surrounding farming community. The Harveys are proud of their community - their father was on town council for many years and instrumental in the establishment of many important community services. Graham and Scott are very involved in the CIA (Civic Improvement Association), the current umbrella community organization. Across from the original store at 2nd Avenue and Main Street is Central Park, a CIA project and a pleasant spot featured in the 2012 Communities in Bloom calendar. Another CIA project particularly near and dear to their hearts is the Prince of Wales Cultural and Recreation Complex, a few streets away on what I dub Assiniboia's cultural four corners. Not only were the Harveys corporate sponsors, Graham sat on the finance committee. Prince Charles executed the official sod turning in April 2001 and the impressive building, which has been fully operational since 2004, includes the new library, a cinema complex, an auditorium, curling rink and community college. Across the street is the Asaskan Complex (an amalgam of Assiniboia, Saskatchewan, Canada) which houses Town Hall and on the third corner the low rise and architecturally pleasing Shurniak Gallery of Contemporary and Traditional Canadian Art has a delicate bronze horse by notable Canadian sculptor Joe Fafard dancing quietly on the lawn. The fourth corner is laid bare, the future home of the town arena, another project championed by the CIA.

When he was in his 50s, Graham went back to school and earned an MBA. While he clearly has a similar innate talent for retail shared by his father, the experience renewed his respect for the Home Hardware organization. "It's a family - you meet people, you understand people. I'm so respectful of Walter. And Paul Straus is a fabulous leader. I am amazed by the foresight they have to develop a strategic plan and stick with it. And to have a Board elected by the members. These people are working for our well being. It doesn't get any better than that."

When Hanson Hardware joined Home Hardware, it seemed that every day was Christmas. "We had this service, we had this merchandise and it was quite a dilemma because I wanted one of those, and one of those.... our first Home Hardware truck driver would come up from St. Jacobs (before the Wetaskiwin warehouse). He would be carrying product for as many as seven stores. He used to say, 'I can hardly wait until you guys grow your business so I only have to make three stops!' And I'd think, I'll never take a third of a semi trailer. And now we take a third of a B train!"

Our visit to Fort Qu'Appelle, about 40 kilometers northeast of Regina, begins at Hanson Hardware on the town's main street across from the original Hudson Bay building. It doesn't take much imagination to envision what the town was like in its early days because in some ways, not much has changed - the wide main street, the big sky, the battered old signs

When Don took over the family business in 1972, he had loose affiliations with several wholesalers, eventually entering into a more formal relationship with Link, but was glad to join the Home Hardware family when it bought out Link in 1980. "Only Home Hardware seemed to have the internal strength and the internal organization the industry needed. They told us

Don, Elaine and Andrew Hanson:

Hanson Home Hardware Building Centre
Fort Qu'Appelle, SK

"If it wasn't for Home Hardware, I guarantee that we'd all have disappeared from the face of the earth."

hanging in front of local establishments evoke an era that hasn't been too long bygone. Inside the store foyer a sign gives a brief history: the original 1,500 square foot store was built in 1910 by a man called Millen, run briefly by a man called Dillon, then bought in the 1930s by Don's grandfather Arthur who eventually sold it to his two sons, Bud and Don's father Gordon. Don grew up above the store, working sporadically but with no real interest. After school, he moved to Vancouver where he got a job at Woodwards department store and met his future wife Elaine whose family was also in retail.

At first glance Don and Elaine Hanson could not appear more different. Don has a large, comfortable presence and an easy rumbling laugh. Elaine is tiny with the upright posture of a dancer. When Don speaks, he leans forward from the comfortable depths of his chair, closes his eyes to think and carefully shapes his words with his hands. Elaine perches, poised for flight, her body language as much as her expression fiercely intent. But as they speak, it becomes evident that they are very much in sync, linked by shared passions, for their business, their community and their family. Although Don had no intention of returning to the sleepy little town on the shores of Echo Lake, he did just that in 1972 when his father decided to focus on his first love of cattle farming. It was an ideal opportunity for Don to determine whether he wanted to run a family business in a small town and for Elaine to find out whether she could live in one.

"It was the biggest shock of my life," Elaine recalls almost 40 years later. "I had lived and worked in Winnipeg and then moved to Saskatoon. For two years after Don moved back I would visit on the weekends." "She kept moving closer," Don says fondly. By 1975, they were married and the first of their three children was born in 1979. Elaine initially stayed home to raise her family, then worked part time at the store.

Today Elaine focuses mainly on Human Resources, Health and Safety and other "soft" responsibilities, as she calls them. She is very involved with local Chamber of Commerce initiatives to revitalize the downtown core, thanks in no small part to Elaine's vision and tenacity. They have applied to and received grants from Saskatchewan Culture and Elaine is working with a planner to develop a cultural community plan that can be integrated into the official community plan.

they were going to pick us up by our bootstraps and show us how to run a business. Because quite honestly, we didn't really know about business - buy a pair of pliers, sell a pair of pliers… if it wasn't for Home Hardware, I guarantee that we'd all have disappeared from the face of the earth."

The timing certainly was right: Fort Qu'Appelle was undergoing its own transformation in the early 1980s, becoming a retirement and recreational community thanks to its proximity to Regina and the wealth of services it offers. And Hanson Hardware grew with it. For many years, the store co-existed peaceably with the local lumberyard. Eventually, the lumberyard closed and customers started drifting away to the Big Boxes in Regina. Don was losing business as well. They renovated and expanded the original hardware store from 1,500 to 12,000 square feet of retail. They also bought more property around town and began to offer a wider selection of product, rebuilding the customer base in the process. Eventually they made it official and Hanson Hardware became an HHBC in 1995.

Despite his earlier ambitions of becoming a truck driver, a palaeontologist or an engineer, today their youngest child, 27 year-old Andrew, is now also part of the family business. He is completing his accreditation as a carpenter journeyman and manages the auxiliary construction business, a natural offshoot of the banner switch to HHBC and the changing demographic of the area. It's a year round business with a lot of growth potential - Andrew runs a crew of up to a dozen guys. All along Echo Lake, one of four man-made lakes that were originally a long river system, old cabins are giving way to four-seasons homes. A number of Bands own huge swathes of land in the area. They represent almost 50% of the area's population and are an economic force. Andrew and his crew are building houses in all these communities. He loves the work and the lifestyle.

Don remembers the early days. At dealer meetings, Walter would focus on how important it was that they take pride in their work. He would often say that he wished he was young again so that he could re-do the things he knew he should have done better. He'd say, "You boys have such an opportunity - just make sure you make use of it - don't lose it - don't waste it." It seems pretty evident that Don took his advice.

Success is all about attitude. For five generations of Richards, a hardworking prairie work ethic and an unswerving commitment to family, community and Home Hardware have resulted in a well-deserved success in a town that could not be more appropriately named: good things happen when you have the right outlook on life.

and good corporate rates. Bud respected the "lean and mean" approach and knew it was the right way to go. Today Glenn and Wendy's daughter Nicole is continuing the tradition, becoming the fifth generation of Richards to work in the family business (Bud's grandfather, who came from England and originally operated a grain elevator outside of Moose Jaw, became the

Glenn Richards: *"My finest moment has been serving on the Board of Directors with people like Ray and Walter."*

Richards Home Hardware
Outlook, SK

Bud Richard's father Bert moved the family to Outlook when Bud was 12. Those were the "dirty thirties" but even so, their general store on a busy street corner not far from their current location was a major step up from the grocery store they left behind. They sold coal and oil and nails by the barrel, cut glass and even sold food in bulk. Among his many responsibilities, Bud made deliveries, riding his bike or pulling his sled. When he left school Bud naturally went into the family business. He met his wife Ester when she came to town as a telephone operator, working in a building coincidentally on the site that now houses Richards Home Hardware. A fire in 1955 destroyed the original store where the newly married couple lived upstairs. They rebuilt and the business remained in that location until 1968. The following year Bud and his partner Ken Harris bought the Macleods Hardware store in the current spot on Franklin Street. The 1980s were a busy decade: Bert made the decision to retire to Vancouver Island, and Bud and Ester's youngest child Glenn joined the family business, after a few years at university. Bud had never expected any of his three children to take over the business. Glenn arrived at the decision independently, more or less resuming in a much more significant way many of the chores he already knew and loved from working in the business after school and over the summer holidays. The timing was fortuitous because Ken Harris wanted to sell his interest and move on. In 1986, Bud, with Glenn's endorsement, joined Home Hardware. The decision was easy, he recalls. Two reps from competing companies came calling. The first rep offered to fly him to the company's head office in Winnipeg, promising a big night out on the town, a fine hotel, a good meal and a tour of operations. In contrast, Frank Hammer invited Bud to visit Home Hardware's western distribution centre, just a short drive away in Wetaskiwin, Alberta, with reasonably priced hotel rooms

store's bookkeeper when the family moved to Outlook). Nicole came on board after her parents bought their second store in Rosetown, about 45 minutes west of Outlook. In the three years since, they have established responsibilities and rhythms that work: Nicole recently bought her own home - not bad for a 21 year-old.

What makes small towns everywhere tick is the level of community involvement and in Outlook the Richards are prime examples of that commitment. The Richards are especially proud of The Sky Trail, the longest pedestrian bridge in Canada. It started life in 1912 as a CPR bridge soaring 150 feet high and 3,000 feet across the South Saskatchewan River. A good portion of its structure was built in 1885, originally slated for use over the St. Lawrence River outside Montreal. This portion was taken apart, transported and reassembled in Outlook in 1911. After its active life ended in 1987, the bridge was neglected for many years, and eventually donated to the community. It now enjoys a new lease on life as a part of the Trans Canada Trail and a prime vantage point from which to watch migratory birds - Outlook is situated on the North American Central Flyway. Funding came in part from government and corporate sources with the citizens of Outlook playing a major role in making it a reality. Glenn sat on the committee for several years. But one of his - and Nicole's - most vivid memories is screwing boards on their hands and knees for many days in a cold and dark December, as the townsfolk put their all into completing the project. Today the pathway to the span is lined with benches commemorating different members of the community. A border of colourful tiles lines both sides of the path, made by local school children, one of whom was Nicole.

"My finest moment has been serving on the Board of Directors (Glenn has been a Director since 2001) with people like Ray Gabel and Walter Hachborn who is such a visionary. It's mind-blowing because they are founding members. We've come a long way and it's been an incredible ride and we're having fun." Glenn Richards, fourth generation dealer.

The majority of the profiles in this book are stories of multi-generational families, many of which have been part of their communities for decades. Another recurring theme is the young, aggressive, MBA dealer who has carefully and strategically identified communities that offer opportunities for success and dynamic growth. These dealers typically have a master plan that includes several stores across a number of communities, often spanning more than one province.

floor, the best way to meet customers. Like so many areas in this prosperous province, their customer base is composed of a good cross section on which their business can capitalize: young people following the oil boom, a growing retirement community and large colonies of both Hutterites and Mennonites many of whom own and operate the massive farms that sprawl across the rich agricultural land of southern Saskatchewan. About 30% of their business is contractor-based.

The Evans: Parry did the leg work of finding the magic formula, and now they can concentrate on building the business.

Evans Brothers Home Hardware Building Centre
Swift Current, SK

So it was interesting to meet the Evans, Parry and his two sons Travis and Shawn (their younger son Quentin works in the lumberyard, as does their brother-in-law Brad, married to sister Mindy), who bought the HHBC in Swift Current, Saskatchewan in January 2008. I was curious to learn about the challenges facing newcomers to a small town.

Parry started pumping gas at his father's United Farmers of Alberta business in the Peace River area when he was 12 years old, so he was raised in a similar environment to that of Home Hardware. As a young man, he worked at Macleod's, learning the business. Employing a strategy of which Walter Hachborn would heartily approve, Parry grew slowly and carefully. Having owned a store within an organization whose shareholders were not the storeowners, he was attracted to the Home Hardware model and approached them about joining the family. In 1996, he purchased the HHBC in Valemount, BC. At that time, his son Shawn, who was then 21, joined the business. Travis, four years older than Shawn, was living and working in Edmonton. When they made the move to Swift Current, Travis came on board. The transition felt natural to both of them.

I wondered about the challenges of taking over an existing business in a big centre with lots of competition. Their first smart move was to rename the business Evans Brothers Home Hardware Building Centre, which has a comfortable, neighbourly ring to it. The next step was to get out onto the

The other sure fire method to get into the community spirit is to sponsor a sports organization in town. The Evans sponsor the local Triple A Minor League hockey team, the Home Hardware Legionnaires, and Swift Current's Western Hockey League team, The Broncos.

The strategy the Evans family has employed to take over and build a successful business in Swift Current is obviously working. As Parry and I walk over to the lumberyard at the end of the block, he greets customers in the car park, joshes with employees and generally seems to be having a fine time. His sons, the eponymous Evans Brothers, have grown up in the good world of Home Hardware - Parry did the leg work of finding the magic formula, and now they can concentrate on building the business. Shawn, clearly his father's right hand man, seems to be the family spokesperson, at least over the course of our interview. He sums up the Home Hardware experience, reiterating their modus operandi: "If I need an answer, I can always find it. Home Hardware is always very helpful - if someone can't help you, they will find someone that can."

ALBERTA

Terry Nordine, Vicki Stang, Rob and Angie Hauser and David Sjervan at Tabb Lane Bowling Alleys.

I first spoke to Rob Hauser, owner of Hauser Home Hardware Building Centre in Camrose, Alberta on the phone about a month before our scheduled visit to his store. Within a half hour, I had received 15 follow-up emails from him each with its own light-hearted descriptor, and more than 500 photos highlighting various events in which the store had recently been involved. Just one demonstration of the qualities that garnered Hauser Home Hardware Building Centre The Walter J. Hachborn Store of the Year Award at the 2012 Spring Market.

The organization that is closest to his heart - and Rob readily admits that he has a hard time saying "no"- is Centra Cam, a non-profit vocational training association for people with disabilities in the Camrose and surrounding area. David Sjervan is one of the program's alumnae whose fulfilling life, including a part-time job at Hauser HHBC, is thanks to Centra Cam's assessment and training programs.

Rob Hauser:

Hauser Home Hardware Building Centre

Camrose, AB

You don't win major recognition within your industry and corporation without great people. And you cannot be an active member of your community without giving back.

It's all in a day's work for a team of motivated individuals who obviously don't consider the hours they spend at the store to be a job, but rather a vocation. Rob and his wife Angie have structured a system of employee rewards and incentives that fosters a climate of commitment and participation at the heart of the business' ongoing success.

A Camrose native, Rob came to the building supply business naturally. He trained as an electrician then became a builder/contractor. By 1993, he was the manager of a local independent building supply outlet that Beaver purchased, at which point, Rob bought the business from the original owner. In 2000 Rob's was the third Beaver store to become a member of Home Hardware. From the start he recognized the opportunity the merger offered dealers: Beaver had the LBM strength and hardware distribution was Home Hardware's forte. In typical Rob Hauser fashion, not only was he busy with his newly amalgamated business, he decided it was also time to build a new store. When Camrose HHBC opened in 2006, they had grown to 30,000 square feet of retail with a 15,000 drive through warehouse and four acre yard. The staff had more than tripled from 19 (all of whom came with them to the new store) to 69 fulltime employees.

But let's go back to that astonishing demonstration of community involvement. "You can't have one without the other," Rob says. That is, you don't win major recognition within your industry and corporation without great people. And you cannot be an active member of your community without giving back. Rob's father died when he was a young boy so he relied on the community resources - sports, summer and school programs. As a result, there is a corporate emphasis on supporting community youth programs and those for the less fortunate because Rob knows first hand what a difference they can make in a young life. Giving back to the community is more than writing a cheque. The Hauser Home Hardware Building Centre looks for programs that require participation in large part because a meaningful level of involvement also contributes to their own team spirit. Time spent on any of the company's causes is considered company time and Rob pays the dues for any service club his employees choose to join.

When it comes to supporting the community in general and Centra Cam in particular, Hauser HHBC aims large. Two years ago, one of Hauser's customers built a house, with materials from Hauser HHBC sold to him at discounted rates, which raised over $100,000 for Centra Cam. Last year, the Big Valley Jamboree, a country music festival with big names like Garth Brooks and Wynona Judd, held a fundraiser, also orchestrated with Rob's creative and material input, that raised over $20,000 for the organization. Not only did Rob design the big prize, a fully furnished and completely outfitted cabin, Camrose HHBC donated the works - from building materials and furniture to pots and pans.

But the biggest Centra Cam fundraiser by far is the annual one-day bowl-a-thon held every March at Tabb Lane Bowling Alleys not far from the store. Each team has five bowlers who raise money through pledges. David, of course, is on the Hauser HHBC team. The team that raises the most money wins the cup. Competition is fierce and the excitement amongst the alumnae is palpable. Needless to say, the store is a regular winner of that grand prize. But ultimately Centra Cam is the big winner - typically another $20,000 is raised at this event every year.

Downstairs from the administrative offices an entire wall is covered with countless awards honouring Hauser Home Hardware Building Centre's contribution to the Camrose community, many of them dating back to its days as a Beaver Lumber, from 1993 to 2000. The awards include the 2005 Camrose Chamber of Commerce award for Community Service, the "Proud of My Home" award in 2007 and again in 2008, 2009 Franchise Operation of the Year from the Chamber of Commerce, the Gold "Proud of My Home" award in 2010 and 2011, with pride of place going to The Walter J. Hachborn Store of the Year Award that they were especially proud to receive from Walter himself in 2011. The following year they were recognized by industry peers and awarded the Hardware Merchandising award for Top Canadian Building Supply store over 25,000 square feet.

I was forewarned: whenever I mentioned the name "Glenn Norton", people said, "Glenn's a real character." And they were right. We arrived early for our photo session at Glenn's HHBC in Fort Saskatchewan, north of Edmonton, so we wandered around the yard. Suddenly, a solid man wearing dark glasses, red Home Hardware jacket, and black shirt and dark trousers, appeared at my shoulder. "What have you discovered in your travels so far," he growled. "That everyone is decent and hardworking, right?"

Despite his tough guy demeanour, Glenn has a big heart and over the years the business has contributed generously to the community, covering the spectrum from kids' hockey and lacrosse teams to Ducks Unlimited and CAT scan machines at the new hospital that was being built when we first spoke in the spring of 2011. He says it's a joy to make a contribution to the boys' and girls clubs, knowing that they can make an enormous difference in so many young lives. "I think whatever the community can do to help them to become contributing members of society benefits all our futures," he

Glenn Norton: *"I'd rather have a steady hand and an honest partner and that's what Home Hardware has given to all of their dealers."*

Home Hardware Building Centre Fort Saskatchewan
Fort Saskatchewan, AB

He's a man who always cuts through to the essence and while he mugged for the camera, clearly enjoying himself, he was delivering a stream of nonstop information.

A native of Winnipeg, Glenn worked in marketing and finance for the Beaver organization for over 20 years, becoming VP of Franchise Development for Eastern Canada and ultimately VP of Operations for Western Canada. When he was asked to move back east, he decided to make a change and bought the Home Hardware Building Centre in Fort Saskatchewan in 1997. Foreshadowing what happened a few years later at the corporate level, Home Hardware amalgamated the local Home Hardware and Beaver stores, maintaining the original Beaver location for the new incarnation.

His decision was an informed one, based on 23 years with Beaver Lumber. He had done his homework and felt that Home Hardware had "by far the best distribution system in North America for hardware and building supply retailers." After serving five years on the Home Hardware Board of Directors from 2007 to 2011, today he has an even greater respect for the company and says that the decision he made 16 years ago was "absolutely the right one."

Glenn and his former brother-in-law, Gord Sarvis, are partners in the business, an arrangement that allows them to share the responsibilities of a 13,000 square foot retail and 10,000 square foot warehouse and lumberyard operation on over five acres of land.

says succinctly. Glenn says the commitment to community is at the heart of Home Hardware, which understands the needs of their dealers, their families and employees and what it means to be a successful and vibrant part of the communities in which they operate. "They encourage it. They live it day to day in what they do," Glenn states flatly. "I've seen lots of companies close up and personal and I can tell you that there is no other company that I've ever worked with that kind of credibility and sincerity."

And what about his reputation as a joker? The interview for his position on the Board is a classic illustration. He had to make a presentation at the market. (He points out unnecessarily that he is almost the complete opposite of Walter Hachborn, 5 foot 10 inches and 250 pounds to Walter's diminutive size and tiny frame, dark complexioned in contrast to Walter's shock of white hair. I got the picture.) He opened his presentation by saying "A lot of people don't know that Walter is my uncle, and I appreciate this opportunity to join the family on the Board." He got a laugh, of course, but for the remaining two days of the market, people were constantly approaching him to ask if Walter really is his uncle!

He quickly became serious again when asked to sum up the Home Hardware difference: "Sometimes people say they could be a little more aggressive and they could be a little more flamboyant. Well, you can keep your flamboyance. I'd rather have a steady hand and an honest partner and that's what Home Hardware has given to all of their dealers. You'd have to go a long way to find another organization with such fine morals and standards."

Glenn may be a character, but he possesses a lot of it as well.

If you want to see the fusion of Home Hardware past, present and future at its best, visit the Rurka family's Home Hardware Building Centre in Lloydminster. Richard Rurka and his wife Donna and three of their four children run the business: their oldest, Tasha and her husband Jeff, Sarah and David, a twin. The other twin Lori, works in her husband's family business. Together, they share extraordinary enthusiasm and energy for the business.

A family business has its own challenges. Apparently brother David resigned five times. "But I never accepted his resignation," Richard is quick to point out. He would write the "I regret to inform you" letter, his parents would read it, laugh and stick it on the fridge. "Go put on your red shirt," Donna would say.

The Rurka Family: The two-acre garden centre - with its ice cream stand, goats and greenhouses - is a seasonal delight.

Home Hardware Building Centre - Lloydminster
Lloydminster, AB

Richard Rurka started in the lumber business in the early 1970s: Molson's was hiring 10 business grads to introduce the Home Centre concept to their Beaver stores and customers. After a three month training course, he landed in Edmonton as assistant manager at a local Beaver Lumber. From there, he went to head office in Calgary. He spent the next three years setting up stores and was Assistant Manager first in Red Deer and then at Market Mall in Calgary. After that, he worked for an independent lumberyard in Red Deer that joined Link along the way, thereby becoming a member of Home Hardware following the merger in 1981.

In 1999, the Rurkas pulled up their Red Deer roots and moved to Lloydminster, a mid-sized city that straddles the Alberta-Saskatchewan border. Like so many, the Rurkas sold everything to finance their decision. The store was going to be a challenge, with nowhere to go but up, Richard recalls.

When the family moved to Lloydminster, the kids were teenagers, when kids often draw away from their parents. In their case, they grew closer. The Rurka children always felt part of the Home Hardware family even though they did not work in the store when they were young. "We were forced to volunteer," Sarah jokes. They all fully intended to go to university and pursue other careers. But then something unusual happened: "We all went to university," Sarah says. "But we all came back." She credits her parents for subtly sowing the seeds: Richard and Donna always involved them in the business, "from designing the business cards to writing the business plan." Even Tasha's new husband Jeff, who had worked at the store while he was a student and graduated university as an engineer, fell in love with Home Hardware and started a fulltime career in the store.

They're a competitive bunch, but in the ten-plus years that they have been working as a unit, they have each found their niche. "We've also mastered the art of the apology," Tasha adds. They credit their mother with her insights into their respective strengths. After staying home to raise four bright over achievers, Donna is now an integral part of the unit. The family has attained a level of comfort and trust that is impossible to find anywhere else. David is in charge of technology and building supplies. Tasha manages human resources - they have a staff of 55 in the 25,000 square foot operation. Jeff is responsible for general management and inventory control. Sarah is the marketing and public relations genius, and works alongside her mom running the garden centre.

The store is remarkable. The Rurkas quickly recognized their opportunity in a small town without a lot of retail choice. Initially the business was 75% contractor, but today the contractor-retail split is pretty even. They had a goal to offer their customers everything they needed to build a house and to make that house into a home. The coffee shop is another distinctive touch. The two-acre garden centre, with its ice cream stand, goats and greenhouses, is a seasonal delight where the family's talent for special events achieves full expression.

Their work is their life and the Rurkas have earned their place in a small town where it is possible to remain a newcomer for a long time. Their decision to close on Sundays made them the talk of the town. "We got letters of support," Richard says. "People understood that it gave us, and by extension everyone in the community, a day off to spend with family."

The Ladybug Ball

You might not expect hundreds of people to show up for a ladybug release. But then you wouldn't know about the marketing genius of Sarah Rurka. The idea took flight a few years ago when Donna and Sarah, both organically minded, were looking for a natural solution to the aphid problem in their greenhouses. Tasha found a supplier on Vancouver Island who raised and sold ladybugs as natural aphid terminators. The first year they bought 10,000 and released them one night after the store had closed. Naturally, everyone took photographs and they designed a poster featuring the ladybugs in their profusion. Customers were curious and sorry to have missed something so cool. A light went on and the next year the Ladybug Ball had its formal debut. When we visited in June 2012, the Ball was in full flight. Dozens of adorable children flitted about in bug costumes. Mark Cullen made a presentation. People ate ice cream cones, and cookies, queried Mark about plant care, coaxed ladybugs to crawl up their arms. The ladybugs gathered, the kids ran around looking cute, the cash register hummed and everybody had a fabulous time.

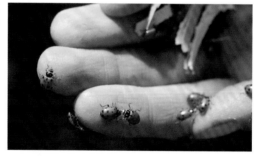

The Young Leaders of Home Hardware:

Being part of Home Hardware has always meant a lot to the Rurkas. The values espoused by the corporation are their core beliefs as well. Over the years, as Richard became, according to his children, a member of "the old boys' club", the Rurka children had the opportunity to meet a lot of people in the industry including members of Home Hardware's Board of Directors. It didn't take them long to feel "at Home." When they started to attend the Home Hardware markets, they began to build their own network of peers, people who share the same unique perspective that comes with being the next generation in a well-established industry. In true Rurka fashion, they came up with a creative idea that Home Hardware has embraced. They took the idea to Tony Krotz, who along with his team Jacqui Cressman and Sherri Amos, arranged for the inaugural meeting. And so The Young Leaders of Home Hardware was born. The group's mandate is to assist the next generation of Dealer-Owners and future Dealer-Owners in supporting each other as they grow their businesses and find their place within the company and the industry.

The Young Leaders group held its first meeting at the 2010 Spring Market. Since then Young Leaders from across the country interact regularly through on-line forums, have monthly on-line virtual meetings and get together in person at Young Leaders events at each Market and an annual retreat. During these interactions the Young Leaders share details about their stores and what they do well, and have round table discussions to learn from each other and build bonds that will hopefully last a lifetime.

Home Hardware has always actively pursued the notion of owners passing along the business within their families, which Sherri Amos, Retail Education and Communication Assistant Manager and leader of the group, points out is one of the great strengths of the Home Hardware model and is unique in today's retail environment. The Young Leaders group is making a key contribution to the process of ensuring the continued success of the Home Hardware family business.

Jim Asplund, Director of Education at Coyote Flats Pioneer Village just outside Picture Butte, cannot say enough about what Home Hardware has done for the facility. Not only did Roelof sell them the land (at a discounted price) on which the heritage buildings are situated, all the paint used in the restoration of many of the beautiful buildings came from Home (the staff worked with the volunteers to ensure that the colours were faithful to the originals). Together the buildings, assembled from different communities in the area, the tractors and engines, represent the pioneer spirit that built southern Alberta not that long ago.

I don't suspect that Roelof has held still very long throughout his life ("His middle name is Impatient," says Fern whose energy level is nothing to sneeze at). Everywhere we went we were witness to his productivity and ingenuity. The hospitality they showed us during our visit was extraordinary, even by Home Hardware Dealers' high standards. We enjoyed a delicious barbecue dinner cooked at the Heinens' impressive outdoor kitchen, one of three that Roelof has built. The second is at their incredibly beautiful and peaceful island get-away in Oldman River just 10 minutes out of town and the third is at their winter home in Maricopa, Arizona, which they bought in 2010.

There is no Butte in Picture Butte. The hardworking pioneers decided a long time ago that a butte had no business being just picturesque so they used the earth to build an artificial lake for the sugar factory that operated for more than 40 years before it too was demolished. The reclaimed bricks from the factory can be found in the house that Roelof Heinen built across the road - his company did the demolition. Several of the tidy houses in town are also faced with the same handsome material that glows in the

growth spurt in 1992 when Walter suggested that Taber, 65 kilometres east, would be another good market. Business was so good, they had to renovate several times and in 2006 built what is now their flagship operation: 25,000 square feet of retail space with a 10,000 square foot drive through lumberyard. The store's distinctive roofline at the entrance suggests a prairie grain elevator and the natural light throughout the store shows the attractive and well-merchandised floor space to great advantage.

Mark, Roelof and Fern Heinen:

Butte Home Hardware Building Centre
Picture Butte, AB

He loves doing deals and unlike most Home Hardware storeowners, has never been a hands-on Dealer

warm evening sun. Roelof's Dutch roots are relatively recent: the Heinen family emigrated from Holland in 1955 when he was just 11 years old. He met his wife Fern, originally from Saskatchewan, and brought her back to Picture Butte. Roelof is one of the town's more industrious citizens. "I'm an entrepreneur," Roelof says matter-of-factly. He loves doing deals and unlike most Home Hardware storeowners, has never been a hands-on dealer although he, his wife Fern and their son Mark now own four HHBCs in southeastern Alberta, an agriculturally rich area made possible by the miracle of modern irrigation. A large deposit of oil is also rumoured to lie underground and small derricks with lazily nodding metal heads dot the flat landscape.

In the mid 1980s, Roelof was in the demolition business, not the building business. In 1986 the manager of the local lumberyard asked if he was interested in buying the business from Revelstoke that would otherwise be shutting it down. At a meeting to discuss the potential offer with his lawyer a few months later, Roelof saw a headline in the Edmonton Journal: Home Hardware buys Revelstoke. He figured that was that. A few days later the store manager visited him again: Home Hardware had offered to let him buy the business, which he wasn't in a position to do but he thought Roelof might. He suggested that Roelof call Walter Hachborn. Fifteen minutes into that phone call, Roelof recalls, "I was the proud owner of Picture Butte's new Home-All building supply centre." The fact that Picture Butte already had a Home Hardware store across the back alley concerned Roelof. Another phone call with Walter and the issue was resolved: the Heinens became proud owners of that business as well.

"I like to make things grow," Roelof says. That's an understatement. When the Heinens bought property from CP Rail and built a 12,000 square foot building to house Picture Butte's new Home Hardware Building Centre, the original owner told Roelof that it would never work - the building was too big for the community. That was 1987. The business experienced another

Roelof has always made sure that he has the right people in place. Many of their 70 employees across the four stores (in 2002 they bought the HHBC in Nanton, a town just over 100 kilometres from Picture Butte, and in the fall of 2012 opened a new store in Coaldale, midway between Taber and Picture Butte) have worked there for years. Today son Mark, who has a degree in music and mathematics, manages the four businesses, backed by veteran 30-year employee Rick Kiers as assistant manager. Rick can usually be found on the ground at the Taber store, but Mark spends a lot of time overseeing all four locations from Picture Butte, thanks to the most up-to-date computer systems that are an essential part of their operation.

Until he retired in 1999, this hands-off management style allowed Roelof to pursue a career in municipal politics (and left Fern free to teach math at the local high school until she retired in 2001. She still does the payroll for all three stores). He served as President of the Alberta Association of Municipal Districts and Counties for many years, and was on the Board of the Federation of Canadian Municipalities.

The town has benefited from their community spirit: over the years the Heinens have donated to hospitals in the area as well as the Cancer Society in both Taber and Picture Butte. In 2008, Roelof was awarded an Honorary Doctorate from the University of Lethbridge in recognition of his years of community service. And at the Home Hardware 2012 Spring Market, he received the prestigious Golden Hammer for 50 years in the building supply business. Son Mark made all the arrangements with Dianne McTavish unbeknownst to his father who was taken completely by surprise, something that probably has not happened too often in his life.

Don't be deceived by Rob Craats' mild mannered and soft-spoken ways. Behind the façade of a gentle bear, Rob is possessed of a clear vision and strong will. Thanks to his foresight, determination and courage, the second-generation family business in Redcliff, Alberta has the proud distinction of being the first western hardware retailer to join the Home Hardware family.

Rob's "gentle bear" bared its teeth in the late 1970s. At the time, they were experiencing difficulty getting product from Link, clearly having problems of its own. In August 1979, Rob caught wind of a meeting that Home Hardware, aware of the issues affecting Link and sensing an opportunity, was hosting in Edmonton. Along with two other dealers in the area, Rob attended that meeting. It was his first encounter with Walter Hachborn.

Rob Craats: Rob was impressed by the volume and variety of product in the warehouse. "Like kids in a candy store," he remembers.

Redcliff Hardware Ltd.
Redcliff, AB

Rob and his brother Walter grew up working in the hardware store that their parents, Cornelius (Casey) and Rinske Craats had owned since 1965. The family lived upstairs in the solid brick building on 3rd Street that was a furniture store when it opened in 1915. By the time the Craats family took over, it was an independent hardware operation with the full gamut of merchandise demanded by the citizens of this busy town that fronts the South Saskatchewan River only a few miles from Medicine Hat.

Rob's dad Casey was always improving things. He joined Link Hardware Wholesale in 1969, expanding the inventory mix, building new display fixtures and updating the lighting. In 1970, he bought the building next door and knocked out the wall. In the tradition of small town families, the boys worked in the store after school, on weekends and during summer holidays. After their secondary schooling ended, arrangements were adjusted and it wasn't until 1974 that brother Walter returned to become the store's first fulltime employee, in addition to their hardworking parents. In the spring of 1976 Casey had a serious car accident that resulted in the family fast tracking the succession plans already in place: Rob immediately took a leave of absence from his job as a draftsman to help. In January 1977, the two brothers bought Redcliff Hardware from their parents. They joined Home Hardware Stores Limited in 1979, which allowed them to expand their selection even more and sharpen their pricing. As the town grew and prospered, so did Redcliff Hardware. The family added to its property holdings in 1980. Walter sold his share of the business to Rob's wife Sarah in 1992, and five years later returned to the store as a valued employee. After various incarnations, a move, and expansions, the final one in 2002, the business grew to 10,000 square feet of retail space. Today it is a prominent and popular shopping destination on Broadway Avenue East, the town's main street. Life is deservedly good for this industrious family. When the time is right, Rob and Sarah's son David and his wife Stacey will become the third generation of the Craats family to own and operate the business.

After the presentation, people went up to speak with Walter. With some trepidation - he was all of 25, Walter was in his late 50s - Rob approached the man who had created Home Hardware. Rob asked him straight out: why would you want to take on more hardware dealers in western Canada? "He was standing directly in front of me and he rolled up on the balls of his feet and said - 'I want to make Home Hardware a national hardware chain.' And he said it with such conviction."

At Walter's invitation, a week later Rob and his wife Sarah were in St. Jacobs. Rob was impressed by the volume and variety of product in the warehouse. "Like kids in a candy store," he remembers. "We could see all this product that we were not able to get - for whatever reason."

They returned home and Rob told the other two dealers: "This is the real deal." That September Rob, brother Walter and their two colleagues attended the Home Hardware Fall Market where they were accepted as dealers, with the relationship scheduled to kick into high gear the following spring. Enough time to work out logistics - this was in the days before the Wetaskiwin warehouse. When Link learned of their move, their fill rates plummeted even further. Rob knew that if they didn't get product into their stores quickly they wouldn't make it to spring. He called Walter. "If you can fill a truck between the three of you," Walter said, "we'll send it out," assuring Rob that they would try to get out two or three deliveries before Christmas. Frank Hammer arrived to help them set up the Home Hardware systems. Over a ten-week period before Christmas, Rob and his two fellow dealers accepted delivery of eight truckloads. Because it took a week or more to get there, they were reordering the next load before the previous one arrived.

In 1981, Home Hardware bought Link, but by then Redcliff Hardware store had been proudly wearing its Home Hardware signage for two years.

Perhaps the reason Bill cares so deeply about disadvantaged children is that he almost never had a childhood of his own. Bill was born in Czechoslovakia in 1935. His father had already emigrated to Canada to organize a new life for his young family. He bought land from a CPR agent just south of town. One day in 1938, the agent warned him to get his family out before it was too late. He was right: the borders closed immediately after Bill, his sister and mother left the country. They arrived in Red Deer in the middle of the night and had to wait several hours to get a ride home.

At 3 o'clock in the morning, Bill's father, who had never seen him before, arrived on a bicycle.

The family had to wait two more hours for a farmer's Model T to collect them all.

The next day, his father caught a train south to Taber to work on a sugar beet farm. That was the beginning of the Welikoklads' life in Canada.

The rest is history.

Tucked away in an industrial park on the outskirts of Red Deer, Executive Home Building Centre breaks most of the rules of retail. Its location precludes drive-by traffic. The product mix is heavily skewed. The business does not take advantage of conventional Home Hardware advertising programs. (The fleet of 15 trucks is always on the move across Red Deer. Jason calls them their mobile billboards.)

Jason and Bill Welikoklad:

Executive Home Building Centre
Red Deer, AB

Although it flies in the face of convention and normal business practice, it works for them.

Nevertheless, the parking lot is full of working vehicles and inside a crowd of mostly burly customers mills about the busy order desk. "Our customers are home builders, industrial and commercial accounts," says owner Jason Welikoklad. In fact, the business is 95% contractor-based, the only Home Hardware store across the country with that emphasis on a vertical market.

Although it flies in the face of convention and normal business practice, the strategy is deliberate. In the 1970s, Jason's father Bill was a busy Red Deer contractor. He wasn't happy with the way lumberyards treated their contractor customers - no discounts for volume purchases, no price guarantees over the life of a job. So he opened his own yard, primarily to supply himself and a few of the smaller contractors who knew him. Word got around and by 1976 Bill had stopped building houses to concentrate fulltime on building his lumberyard business. He joined Link in the late 1970s and became a Home Building Centre following the amalgamation in 1981.

Initially, Executive Home Building Centre stocked some consumer-oriented product. Jason remembers that the summer he was 15, he assembled 113 bicycles, which he thought was a lot "for a lumberyard in the boonies." But most of all he remembers the atmosphere of a bona fide lumberyard - an order desk "with a couple of guys sitting behind a desk smoking cigarettes." Working in the yard, he got to know the customers. "They're building a house today. They're building a house tomorrow," he remembers. "They always need studs, they always need plywood. "

So when he came on board fulltime after completing his schooling in the early 1990s, Jason formalized the store's focus on the contractor side of the business. He remembers one of their best customers telling him that he wasn't interested in Tupperware. "Not that's there's anything wrong with

Tupperware," Jason clarifies with a small smile. "But different owners are good at different things. You've got to do what you like." Jason has always liked dealing with contractors. He's also pretty good at it. "These guys are in here three or four times a day. So even if something doesn't go right, it's like arguing with your wife or your friend - you get over it." Home Hardware's structure and hands-off style have made it all work like a charm. "We have nothing but good things to say about Home Hardware," says Bill who is proud to have been Walter Hachborn's friend since joining Home Hardware in the early 1980s.

Bill officially retired in 2012, but Jason has owned the 28,000 square foot business since 2007. He has been going to the Home Hardware markets since he was 19 - more than 30 markets by now. Home Hardware is really a big family, he says. "I got introduced as Bill's son and 20 years later - it's still the same guys. Except that people who started out in the warehouse have ended up as department managers or VPs." And when it comes to longevity and continuity, Jason points out that over a quarter of their 40 employees have worked at the store for 10 to 36 years. As Bill says, "We like to look after our staff, and they look after us."

Jason has tailored their tool department to meet the specific needs of their customers. As a result, they "own" the contractor market in Red Deer. Their tool wall is a sea of yellow DeWalt, the only power tools they sell. "We turned job sites in Red Deer yellow," he says. In fact, Executive Home Building Centre has a bigger display of DeWalt tools than any other retailer in Canada.

There is a gleaming silver herd of large, expensive-looking barbecues on the other side of the store. "Every contractor has a cabin," Jason says. "And every cabin needs a barbecue. A big one," he adds with another ghost of a grin.

Over the years the Welikoklads have donated a significant amount of money to the local Ronald McDonald House and are particularly proud of their ongoing involvement with Red Deer College: they helped fund the construction of a new campus building (a room is named in their honour). They also sponsor two annual scholarships at the trades-oriented facility - one for carpentry, the other business. The Welikoklads also enjoy helping single mothers or anyone else in need at Christmas time, with money for food, clothing and toys.

Although this book is firmly placed in the present, many of its stories are rooted in the past. The Link-Home Hardware merger is an important part of that past in which Duncan McLeod played a central role. He is the third generation owner of McLeod Home Building Centre, the oldest business in Spruce Grove, west of Edmonton.

fallen ill for a short time and later retired at 60), with his grandfather in the role of Eminence Grise and Director of Public Relations. (Bill passed away in 1981.) Around the same time, Ollie Hansen retired. Sadly, Link's performance suffered as a result.

Duncan McLeod: Working alongside his grandfather in the lumberyard, he absorbed the business by osmosis

McLeod Home Building Centre
Spruce Grove, AB

In 1906 Duncan's grandfather moved to Edmonton from Montague, PEI and worked for Revion wholesale packing house. In 1916 he relocated to Spruce Grove, purchased his business and started McLeod Mercantile Ltd., selling primarily dry goods, hardware and groceries. When he arrived, Spruce Grove boasted all of a few blocks of homes and small businesses. Business quickly evolved as the area grew up around it. Already trading goods for cattle and grain with the farmers in the area, a common practice in those days when cash was scarce, Bill found himself in the lumber business, because, as his grandson says, "lumber camps never paid on time." By the late 40's and early 50's, McLeod's sold just about everything: they were an International Harvester dealer for a few years, they sold coal, they loaded grain cars and Bill would buy and resell the grain. During hard times, Bill also quietly gave credit to local families, or fed them when they were hungry. After serving in the Second World War, Duncan's father Harry joined the business. The town continued to grow, expanding from six blocks in the 1960s to a population of over 2,000 by 1970. By now, Bill had been in the business for over 50 years and was known as the Granddad of the Grove.

At the same time that Walter Hachborn was grappling with the survival of the independent hardware dealer on one side of the country, Duncan's father Harry and a handful of other savvy business owners were doing the same thing in western Canada. The outcome was the formation of Link Hardware, built on the same cooperative model as Home Hardware. Soon Link had grown into a centralized distribution wholesaler for dealers across Western Canada with Ollie Hansen serving as its General Manager, the equivalent of Walter Hachborn in St. Jacobs. As a founding member and director, Harry attended the Annual Meetings and Duncan grew up knowing everyone within the organization, including Ollie Hansen.

By 1966, when he was 13, Duncan had a regular summer job at the busy store. Working alongside his grandfather in the lumberyard, he absorbed the business by osmosis. Ten years later Duncan was married, already with a young family, and running the business himself (his father had

A core group of dealers started looking for a solution. One day in 1980 Ollie Hansen and Walter Hachborn walked into Duncan's store. Duncan already knew Home Hardware from attending meetings in Calgary with other concerned Link dealers. Duncan still remembers that conversation: "Ollie said, 'Duncan, Link is in some troubles right now: you really should look at these people and go.'" Because his father had played a central role in Link's history and had been a long-serving member of the Board, Duncan hesitated. Ollie said, "Your dad would want you to do this." Walter invited him to the upcoming Home Hardware spring market, telling him to buy whatever he wanted - Ollie had vouched for him. "I did go," Duncan remembers. "I was so thoroughly impressed with Home Hardware that we set it up while we were there and started purchasing right away."

Duncan was not alone - the influx of Link dealers wanting to join Home Hardware only hastened the decline. In 1980 Home Hardware initiated an amalgamation deal. Link dealers were soon getting product out of Home Hardware "quicker than we could get it from Edmonton, and with excellent fill rates" which made up for the losses of the last few difficult months. For Duncan and his fellow dealers it was the credibility of both Walter Hachborn and Ollie Hansen that cemented the deal. "It all worked out great," Duncan remembers. In fact, Duncan and Home Hardware took to each other so much that for 18 years, from 1989 to 2007, he served on its Board of Directors.

Like his father, Wilson started in the lumberyard in the summers when he was in high school. After two years of university he joined the business fulltime. The bond between Duncan and Wilson is more like brothers than father and son - Duncan was only 18 when Wilson was born. Spruce Grove has moved a lot closer to Edmonton since Bill McLeod arrived in 1916. Today Alberta's capital is just 30 minutes away. The population of Spruce Grove has also grown exponentially - from four households to a population of over 28,000. From primarily farming and logging the economy has shifted to oil patch and transportation: the town is a big trucking distribution hub and home base for a lot of people who work in the oil patch. Their location off the main street can be a challenge, although there is room to expand when the time is right. Wilson is considering switching to HHBC to offer the town's growing population expanded product selection. It seems a natural evolution that builds on an almost 100 year-old reputation. As Duncan says, people who shop around quickly discover "the expertise and the service and good quality products and way more building material products than most stores have."

BRITISH COLUMBIA

· ABBOTSFORD · ARMSTRONG · CAMPBELL RIVER · GOLDEN · INVERMERE · KAMLOOPS ·

Abe's grandfather came from Russia in the 1920s and along with other members from the old country settled in Manitoba, intending to farm. Abe's mother was widowed when he was nine years old and she moved the family to Yarrow, a small community between Abbotsford and Chilliwack. Abe's grandfather loaned money to a friend to open a lumberyard in Chilliwack. In 1956 when Abe was 20 years old, he got a job at that lumberyard working in the warehouse and driving a delivery truck. A few years later, he was transferred to a second store in Abbotsford. After he got married, he joined forces with his father-in-law, a building contractor. When his father-in-law died a few years later in a traffic accident, Abe returned to working for a building supply firm. In 1971, he and a group of partners started Blackwood Building Centre. After a number of other affiliations Blackwood Building Centre joined the Home Hardware family in 1989. Senior employee Don Peters was a big fan of everything Home Hardware was doing in other parts of the country so it was an easy decision to join Home Hardware when Frank Hammer came calling. By this time, Abe's oldest son Carey had already joined the business. Brothers Bruce and Mike came on board in 1988 and 1991 respectively. The secret to a successful family business lies in a clear delineation of responsibilities: Carey is responsible for IT and running the hardware operation, Bruce focuses on Human Resources and administration and Mike manages the lumberyard and contractor business. Their other co-owner, brother Chuck became an accountant and professor. Because our visit fell on tax filing deadline day, Chuck was not able to join us for the photo session. As for Abe, he calls himself the company ambassador, a role at which he clearly excels.

At the starting line for the 2012 "Run For Water" Marathon in Mill Lake Park, one of the flattest and fastest marathon courses in BC according to its official website. (abbotsford.runforwater.ca)

There's a little gem of a painting hanging on the wall in an office upstairs at Blackwood Home Hardware Building Centre in Abbotsford, British Columbia. It depicts a Home Hardware truck delivering a load of lumber on a small barge. The painting has a classic west coast feel to it - a bit lonely, with the water, the dark trees in the background and in the foreground a

come to the adjacent Abbotsford Regional Hospital for special treatment), and the Discovery Trail, which is part of the Trans Canada Trail (the same trail that Walter walked to represent his community when that section opened in St. Jacobs in the late 1990s). The family's personal contributions have also helped to build and fund LCC International University in Lithuania.

The Konrad Family: "We don't consider it remarkable in any way – it's just a part of the day."

Blackwood Home Hardware Building Centre,
Abbotsford, BC

small figure of a man standing in front of the barge. The painting obviously has significance to Abe Konrad, who can be found most mornings seated at the desk nearby. The story behind the picture dates to July 2006. An Abbotsford neighbour and customer ordered a load of material to be shipped to one of the tiny islands that dot the coast off Vancouver where he was building a summer home. Abe decided he wanted to make the trip to see the site for himself. After the barge had been loaded, the truck driver suggested that Abe stand in front of the barge for a quick snapshot memento of the voyage to come. Abe thought nothing of it, but a few months later, the driver brought Abe the same painting that now hangs on his office wall depicting that trip, painted by the driver's sister-in-law, Barbara Wysosky.

The Konrads - Abe and three of his four sons, Carey, Bruce and Mike, operate the business - go the extra mile for their customers. Through their business Blackwood Home Hardware Building Centre they have made significant contributions to many projects that are clearly close to their hearts even if the recipients are on the other side of the world. Abe is articulate and passionate about the impact their community can have on the lives, health and well being of thousands of people in small communities throughout Ethiopia thanks to "Run For Water", an annual marathon that raises thousands of dollars used to provide neighbourhood water wells for that country. The event started in 2007 with Blackwood an original corporate sponsor. Closer to home, there is the Zajac Ranch for Children, Matthew's House (which is today just a hole in the ground but will shortly be transformed into a respite home for children and their families who must

A commitment to community is all about the health of that community, in every sense. The Abbotsford Regional Hospital is a good example. When it was being built several years ago, Abe learned that the bricks for its façade were being sourced from an American supplier, even though there was a brick manufacturer in Abbotsford. He waded in and initiated a round of discussions and negotiations that made it feasible for the contractor to give the sizeable order to the local brick manufacturer.

Hundreds of dealers in towns in every province and territory across the country quietly and consistently contribute every day to their communities. Although Abe points out that Home Hardware Dealers are not alone - business owners of every stripe are always being asked to contribute to some worthy cause - Home Hardware Dealers are certainly front and centre in every community we have visited. Blackwood Home Hardware Building Centre has donated time, energy and dollars and cents to this pretty city situated an hour southeast of Vancouver. "We don't consider it remarkable in any way – it's just a part of the day," Abe's oldest son Carey says matter-of-factly. Abe picks up a small, handwritten thank you note from a pile of papers on his desk. "We don't get a lot of these," he says. Which is why, I am sure, that small painting means so much.

Dale and Sandy Melvin:

Shepherd's Home Hardware Building Centre
Armstrong, BC

You know you're "Home" when you drive into Armstrong, just north of Vernon - the sign at the town entrance says so. Mayor Chris Pieper says so too. And it's a good thing he does because I am not sure I would have completely understood the level of community involvement on the part of Shepherd's Home Hardware Building Centre otherwise. There is the avenue of trees leading into town, the Nor-val Centre and Arena. The Boy Scouts, Junior Lacrosse, the hockey team. The swimming pool, the memorial park, the cenotaph. Shepherd's has contributed in some meaningful way to them all.

"Yes", admits Dale Melvin (who owns the business along with his wife Sandy, their son Kyle and Jim Hudson) when we speak later in the small park, a few blocks from their store. "We'll donate materials, forklifts, free trucking, as much as we can. We just ask that it not be publicized. It's community involvement in a quiet way."

Shepherd's Home Hardware Building Centre contributes to its community in another meaningful way. A relatively small store, at 15,000 square feet, Shepherd's currently employs 75 people and has had as many as 85 on staff. "The store is busy and we have kept a level of service that our customers have come to expect," Dale says.

"Our community is really fortunate to have a business like Home Hardware here," says the mayor, who grew up in Armstrong and has been on the town council for over 20 years. "Home is always part of community action. They have a great respect for community and without them there would be a large hole in Armstrong."

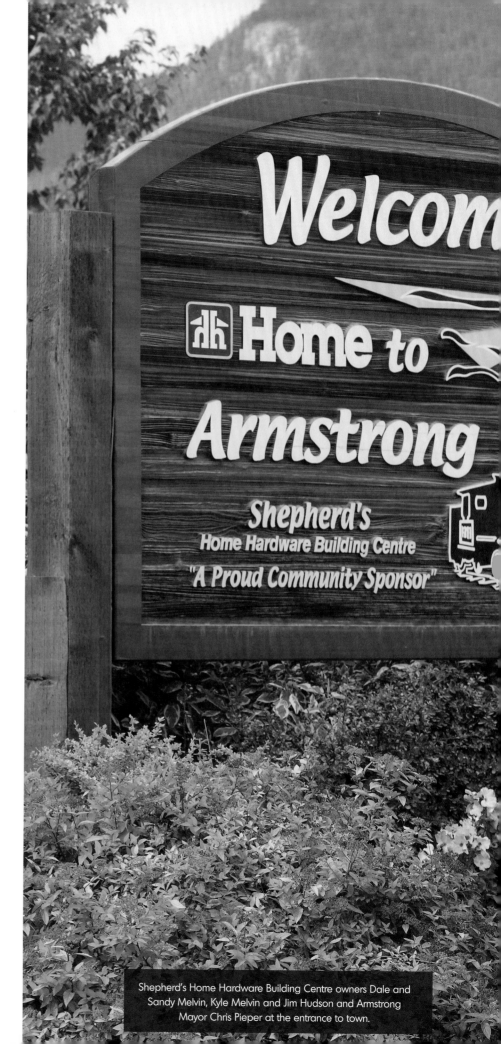

Shepherd's Home Hardware Building Centre owners Dale and Sandy Melvin, Kyle Melvin and Jim Hudson and Armstrong Mayor Chris Pieper at the entrance to town.

Dale has sat on the Home Hardware Board of Directors since 1995 (Shepherd's was originally a Link store and was one of the first to join Home Hardware in 1981 when the company started its western expansion). "We are so fortunate to have travelled Canada and to have seen it all. I feel privileged to sit on a Board of the calibre of Home Hardware's and to have had the pleasure of working with Walter Hachborn."

Maureen Brinson, her husband Harvey Hunter, a long-time Special Olympics coach, Special Olympian swimmer and Home Hardware employee Brian Jorgensen, Allison Kilby and Gary Thulin at the local golf course that hosts the annual Howie Meeker fund raiser tournament for Special Olympics.

Gary Thulin and Allison Kilby:

Pioneer Home Hardware Building Centre
Campbell River, BC

Special Olympics holds a special place in their hearts.

If you want the real story about Home Dealers in their communities, you sometimes need to be devious – these people are not known for blowing their own horns. So in Campbell River, home of Pioneer HHBC, I spoke with Maureen Brinson, long-time Special Olympics volunteer at both the local and national levels, whose day job is working for the town's Association for Community Living. She cannot say enough about owners Gary Thulin and his daughter Allison Kilby (Gary's two bothers Dean and Glen sold their shares in the business in late 2012). Pioneer Home Hardware Building Centre comes by its name honestly: the Thulin family's 100-plus-year history in town can be traced in museum exhibits, on street names and in their community involvement to this day.

The store and family have been recognized repeatedly by the Chamber of Commerce (and there are countless other awards, including Home Hardware Store of the Year for their region three years running and the National Retail Hardware Association's Retail Innovators Award in 2011, the only Canadian of three North American stores to be so honoured). "They are supportive of many, many organizations," Maureen says. "Special Olympics holds a special place in their hearts."

Their Special Olympics involvement began in 1988, the year Campbell River hosted the Provincial Games. That year established the annual Golf Tournament as the town's major fundraiser for Special Olympics. Pioneer was a $250 Hole Sponsor. Over 20 years later, Pioneer HHBC is the tournament's Gold Sponsor. In 2011, the tournament raised $30,000 for Special Olympics. And they keep it up all year: at the three-day grand opening of the new store in September 2008. Special Olympics had a booth and raised over $900 in hotdog sales. At the the store's 75th Anniversary celebrations in September 2012, Special Olympics raised over $1000 at their charity BBQ event. Maureen says, "That's exposure we can't buy."

The Association where Maureen works employs four people with developmental disabilities, including Brian Jorgensen, a Special Olympian who has a part-time job at Pioneer HHBC. Maureen spent three weeks training Brian as a greeter and she saw Pioneer's customer service and community spirit first hand. It was just before Christmas and the store was very busy. Maureen remembers in particular an elderly man who was there regularly. One of the staff would always immediately come to help him. "It could have been a roll of tape, it might have been garbage bags, but he got service like he was a $50,000 contractor."

Allison Kilby and her dad Gary Thulin are grateful for Home Hardware's Young Leaders organization started by another "next generation" Home Hardware Dealer, Sarah Rurka of Lloydminster, Alberta. Gary remembers how challenging it was for him and his two brothers when their dad, Carl Jr, affectionately known as Tubby, died shortly after Link merged with Home Hardware. "We wanted it to be different for Allison," Gary says, noting that they were able to develop and implement their succession plans effectively and smoothly thanks to help from Home. Allison says that Young Leaders continues to be a valuable, ongoing resource.

At one of the early planning meetings for this book, Walter told me, "You must visit Golden, BC. It has one of the most beautiful Home Hardware stores you'll ever see." Of course, Walter was right. In the heart of the Columbia Rockies, Golden is a small town with an industrial lumber past that continues to prosper thanks to everything it can offer outdoor enthusiasts 12 months of the year.

Golden Hardware & Building Supplies has seen many changes in its 53 years of operation, from buildings to products, name changes, and ownership within the family. But throughout, there have been two constants: community support and customer service.

Doug and Susan Birnie:

Golden Hardware & Building Supplies
Golden, BC

You know you have great staff when they can laugh at problems yet still support you 100%.

Susan Birnie, who together with her husband Doug owns Golden Hardware & Building Supplies, is a marvel of energy, efficiency and enthusiasm. She had everyone primed and ready for the photo session when we showed up on a beautiful day in early May. She and Doug would celebrate their 21st wedding anniversary the next day, Friday May 4. Doug's parents, Glenn and Joanne, (originally from Saskatchewan, who moved from Invermere to open a Link hardware store across from the town's post office in April 1960), were there, along with Susan and Doug's three children, 19 year-old Whitney and the 15 year-old twins Amelia and Leland. Even Ginny, the family Golden, was in attendance. We gathered in the office that overlooks the busy store floor, a homey, spacious area that doubles as the after-school family room for the twins. Whitney is studying engineering at the Southern Alberta Institute of Technology in Calgary, one of only five young women accepted into the class of 35 students.

In 1983, Birnie's Building Supplies joined the Home Hardware family. In 2005, Doug and Sue, who had bought out Doug's brother and sister five years earlier, opened the current 47,000 square foot HHBC in its new location with possibly the best vista in town. While it was a quantum leap, Susan says that they had to grow "with the times or risk being overlooked": the three-hour trip to Calgary is a viable alternative if stores in town don't have what you need. There doesn't seem much danger of that these days - the Golden HHBC is a showcase of product in every busy department, run by 36 "great staff".

With its imposing timber frame entrance, the store's exterior echoes the architectural flavour of the town. The view of the mountains is spectacular. Among her many other duties, Susan plans to stain the timbers later this summer. All in a day's work.

Over the years, Glenn and Doug have supported many organizations and town events. There are too many to name but the covered timber frame pedestrian bridge across the Kicking Horse River was a great accomplishment for the town. During construction of the bridge, Doug not only volunteered his labour whenever he could find a spare moment, he also volunteered his forklift, crane truck, delivery trucks, and, on occasion, the muscle power of the staff. When the truck trailer of a US volunteer was vandalized, Susan donated $500, shop space and Doug to restore it to its original state. Over the course of the six-month project, Doug and Susan made lifelong friendships with timber framers from around the world who came to help the small community create something wonderful.

When Walter Hachborn visited the original little store for the first time in the 1980s, Glenn and Joanne Birnie had him over for breakfast. To this day he still asks Susan if Mom is serving huckleberry muffins because he sure wishes he could have some. In honour of his visit, they had decorated everyone at the store with little bow ties. When we arrived, a plate of still warm huckleberry muffins prepared that morning by Joanne sat on the table in the office. We didn't merit the bowties of course, but we did enjoy a delicious muffin each after they were recorded for posterity, beautifully styled by the store's resident decorator Pam Clough.

Every year the Timber Frame Guild of North American chooses a volunteer project. In 2002 Golden was the lucky recipient of their volunteer spirit: the covered pedestrian bridge over the Kicking Horse River connects the north and south sides of the town. Doug was one of the local volunteers at the site, conveniently located a half block from the old store.

"My mom was one of the original founders of the Prince George Hospice House – in fact she died there – so it's important to me. We are a pharmacy but beyond that we try to support them in any way we can, including donating to their fundraising initiatives."

Jim Ewert and Chris Pallot:

Hart Home Hardware
Prince George, BC

Home Hardware was totally involved throughout the transition from the old to the new store.

North of downtown Prince George is an area known as "The Hart." A modern shopping centre beckons invitingly just off the highway at the top of the hill. The anchor store is Hart Home Hardware and Hart Medicine Centre, owned by Jim Ewert and Chris Pallot. What makes them an anomaly in the Home Hardware family is that they are also a full-fledged pharmacy - and a very busy one at that.

James "Corkie" Simmie was the owner of the original stores, but in an older location across the highway. His vision of the combination hardware/pharmacy came from some of the big stores he visited while travelling in the States. Corkie, a Saskatchewan native, acted as the local pharmacy, vet and hardware store. He offered charge accounts when times were tough and helped solidify a strong customer base. Jim, whose father was a surgeon and whose grandfather was one of the first doctors in Prince George, worked part time at the store, where he was bitten by the retail bug. The experience fuelled his decision to become a pharmacist rather than continue in the family tradition of medicine. When he graduated, he became Corkie's business partner, the perfect prescription for a medical man with retail aspirations.

After Corkie's passing in 2005, Jim and Chris partnered up and in January 2009, they moved the business across the highway into a brand new building, going from fifteen to twenty-three thousand square feet. Jim and Chris remember the day like it was yesterday. The mayor cut the ribbon, the parking lot was full and the cashiers were busy. Home Hardware gave them a 15% discount on some "hot" items, which was passed on to their customers. People came from across the city to see the store and to take advantage of some big savings.

"The community has just embraced it," Jim says with pride. "Home Hardware was totally involved throughout the transition from the old to the new store. They helped design the building and set up a beautiful store." It was a long road, but they've never looked back. Judging from the busy store we visited in May 2012, Hart Home Hardware and Medicine Centre is very much at the heart of the shopping community in "The Hart."

It's Friday afternoon and threatening to rain when we pull into Invermere HHBC conveniently located up the street from Kicking Horse Coffee's headquarters and café. Dealer-Owner Al Miller, quickly summoned by a member of his ever-diligent staff, walks us through the large, bright store upstairs to his office. He wears an unobtrusive headset that sees lots

With Al on board, they got into the lumber business "real quick." In 1993 Al bought out the original owners. In January 2005, the business moved from downtown into the big, bold and beautiful building - 36,000 square feet of retail space - on ten acres at the crossroads just north of town. It's impossible to miss.

Al Miller: The store has sponsored a fund-raising barbecue every Saturday morning for more than 10 years.

Invermere Home Hardware Building Centre
Invermere, BC

of action during our visit - every question is immediately answered, no problem is insurmountable following a quick query into the headset, a seamless segue from one conversation to another and, problem solved, back to the matter at hand. This is a very "can do" place.

Al Miller, the man at the helm of this busy operation, has accomplished a great deal since 1971 when Aden Shantz hired him to work part time in the Home Hardware warehouse down the road from the family farm in Elora. Al already had a connection to Home Hardware: his step-father, Charles Calvesbert, who Al's widowed mother married when Al was 16, was the local Home Hardware Dealer, and a Charter Member. Al worked from the St. Jacobs headquarters for 10 years. The first seven were spent learning the ropes in the warehouse, the last three "corporate years" as a member of the merchandising team. For the first year and a half, he travelled and worked primarily in Eastern Canada. After Home Hardware bought Link Hardware, his focus changed. Al spent the next 18 months merchandising new stores in Alberta and British Columbia as they joined the Home Hardware family. Although he was often offered a job to entice him to stay on, he turned them all down.

In the fall of 1981, fate intervened: his wife Lucy was pregnant with their first child and it was time to settle down. Al accepted a job at the HBC in Westlock, Alberta. Al knew the job gave him a tremendous opportunity to learn the other side of the business. Soon after the building supply manager left a few years later, Al was running the entire operation.

In 1988, after a few more moves, Al took a leap of faith and left his job, the first time he had been unemployed. Still very much part of the Home Hardware family, he attended the Spring Market, having told his St. Jacobs mentors, including Maynard Bauman and Frank Hammer, that he was job hunting. The owners of the Invermere store needed someone to set up and manage the building supply division of their business. Al jumped. It was a downtown store, with hardware on one side of the street and building supplies - but no lumber - on the other.

The store is actively involved with Home Hardware's corporate programs and recently worked with Tree Canada to plant 10 trees in the downtown core. The philosophy is simple and effective: "We're involved in pretty much any community event." They built a portable stage that is available around town for a variety of events. Al calls it his travelling road show that sends the double HHs all over the valley.

Closer to Home, right in the parking lot in fact, the store has sponsored a fund-raising barbecue every Saturday morning for more than 10 years. Originally, it ran for nine weeks over the summer, but has proven so successful that for the past several years there has been a Saturday fundraising event from early March to late October. Local non-profit organizations, mostly kid-oriented, line up to participate. Happily, every organization that wants a spot has been accommodated. Al's wife Lucy organizes these special events.

Although there are no succession plans in place - Al is clearly having too much fun - their oldest son Josh works in the business, as does Al's brother Don. Their 24-year old son Tim is currently working in Calgary and Sarah, their 17 year-old daughter, is into fitness in a big way. Her job is keeping Dad fit. There's no question Al Miller and Invermere are the perfect fit: Invermere with its lovely lake, golf course resorts and stunning mountain backdrop (Mount Nelson hits you in the face every time you exit the store) and Al with his love and zest for the business that he built from a conglomeration of buildings into what it is today.

Al credits his team of 65 employees for generating the ideas and enthusiasm that "make this business tick." The team spirit is in evidence when we arrive early Saturday morning to take the photograph. Nothing fazes floor manager Brian McKenzie. He quickly re-jigs the layout, setting up the barbecue tables just outside the front door to accommodate our camera rig. He has it down to a science after all these years. It may be cold and raining cats and dogs, but the energy is heart warming and the other "dogs" Al and his brother Don are cooking up are delicious.

Local partners, world class outcomes.

The southern interior of British Columbia is a popular lifestyle destination. Canada's only desert region delivers long, hot, dry summers (and relatively mild and short winters), making it the ideal location for upscale resorts and "live, work, play" developments. It is also home to many world-class wineries.

Two dealers in the BC interior have built important business relationships with local Indian Bands at the heart of two of these innovative lifestyle communities, Rick Kurzac, owner of Kamloops Home Hardware Building Centre, and Paul McCann, who owns five building centres, including Osoyoos HBC.

Russ Podgurney works in the Spirit Ridge Cultural Centre several days a week. His brilliant traditional costume combines elaborate beadwork, animal hide and crow feathers. The beadwork alone cost $17,000.

Sun Rivers Golf Resort Community lies within the boundaries of Tk'emlups Indian Band lands and offers a spectacular panorama of Kamloops, the valley and the surrounding mountains. Bighorn sheep wander the neighbourhood and lovely homes curve around the golf course. Sun Rivers is a long-term development that began in 1999 as a project with the Band to develop a higher end golf community. By 2020, there will be 2,000 housing units - condominiums, town homes and single family homes - a village centre with commercial, retail and professional offices, a resort hotel and spa, and a residence club and centre.

"When Home Hardware bought Beaver Lumber, there was uncertainty about how things were going to work. The reality is that our business probably grew 150% after we made the transition from a Beaver Lumber store, which was a traditional lumberyard that struggled with distribution, to a Home Hardware Building Centre that had a distribution system that was second to none. It actually changed our business completely. Home has given us the ability to supply more than just the sticks." Rick Kurzac

Rick Kurzac: *"It's not just about building a sub-division. It's about creating a community."*

Kamloops Home Hardware Building Centre and Sun Rivers Golf Resort Community
Kamloops, BC

Because it is on First Nation's land, infrastructure normally available in organized municipalities or regional districts did not exist. This created an opportunity for some innovative firsts: the first bundled multi-utility in Canada; dual water systems; co-funding the water treatment plant with the First Nation and providing one of the country's state-of-the-art water treatment facilities. Sun Rivers is also Canada's first geothermal community and one of 50 international finalists selected from 250 entries for the United Nations-endorsed 2011 LivCom Awards held in Korea in October.

Rick Kurzac, owner of Kamloops HHBC, has been involved in the project from the start. His store has supplied about 85% of the building materials in the entire property and he was one of the first to buy a home at Sun Rivers. Rick likes that the project demonstrates the full spectrum of Home Hardware: "Prior to the acquisition of Beaver Lumber, Home Hardware would have played a very small role in the building of houses and communities," he says. "This type of relationship and this type of development is probably one of the most unique in our company. It's not just about building a sub-division. It's about creating a community."

Rick has been in the forefront of the housing and development industry since coming to Kamloops in 1996, first as a Beaver dealer and then as an HHBC. According to Lesley Brochu, VP of Marketing and Public Relations at Sun Rivers, "Rick was one of the first community leaders to say - 'Hey this sounds like a really good thing. How can I be a part of it as a supplier, contractor and community leader.' It takes vision and some risk to see a big piece of dirt and go - oh yeah. I think that's going to turn into something really great."

DEVELOPING WORLD CONNECTIONS

Several years ago, local businessman Wayne McCrann created Developing World Connections. Rick was at a Home Builders meeting where they were asking for volunteers. Typical of Rick, he stepped up to the plate. Rick's first trip was to Sri Lanka and he took his daughter Sarah, 16 years old at the time, whose international experience to date had only been Caribbean beaches and Disney World. He was concerned that she would hate everything about it, but to his surprise and delight, the experience was transformative for her. She is now a team leader for the organization and takes student groups out to different projects every year. Rick has also become heavily involved and some local contractors and his fellow dealers have joined him on various projects including Ken O'Connor, from Gananoque and Andy McKechnie from Espanola.

Lesley Brochu, Sun Rivers' VP Marketing and Public Relations and Rick Kurzac, owner of Kamloops HHBC, at the Hoodoos Club House lounge, Sun Rivers.

Paul McCann with the general managers of three of
his stores: Mike Irvine, Kelowna HHBC, Joe Chwachka,
Penticton HHBC and Travis Loudon, Osoyoos HBC.

Spirit Ridge Resort nestles on the hillside outside of Osoyoos, the southernmost spot in British Columbia. In an area known as "Napa of the North", it offers visitors an award-winning winery, desert golf, premium accommodation and dining, a spa and cultural centre and meeting facility. The Osoyoos Indian Band has created a one-of-a-kind cultural and experiential destination through strong leadership and strategic partnerships. One of those business partners has been Osoyoos HBC, owned by Paul McCann.

travelling the country, helping dealers improve their stores. "I knew I was with the right company," he says, but something was telling him he was on the wrong side of the business. He wanted to become a Dealer-Owner, but it was a huge step. "I had some good chats with Paul Straus at the time. He was incredibly supportive. He told me that if that was my passion, I had to follow through on it." It wasn't only a business decision: he and his wife Liz, a family practice doctor and his partner in the business, chose Penticton for everything it offered them as a family as well. The first few years were

Paul McCann: The Osoyoos Indian Band has created a one-of-a-kind cultural and experiential destination through strong leadership and strategic partnerships.

Osoyoos Home Building Centre
Osoyoos, BC

Paul's HBC supplied much of the building material for the development. The architecturally arresting Cultural Centre was the first building on the site. Constructed using an ancient building technique known as "rammed earth", a labour intensive but highly durable and energy efficient building process, it was created from compacted layers of a mixture of local soil and concrete. The layers were tinted to reflect the many hues found in the surrounding landscape.

Paul has been part of the Home Hardware family from an early age. His parents owned a hardware store in a small Quebec town on the Ottawa River and joined Home in 1967. As a result, Paul formed an emotional attachment to the company that has lasted all his life. Wherever he lived, when he saw a Home Hardware store, he'd say, "Oh, I think I'll just stop in to see what it looks like." After university, jobs in Toronto and more schooling, Paul "talked himself into a job" at Home Hardware in St. Jacobs which involved

tough but Paul has never regretted the decision. He started with one store, thinking that if it did well, he would have achieved his goal. In 2001 Home Hardware bought Beaver Lumber and Paul had the opportunity to buy and amalgamate the Home Hardware Building Centre and Beaver Lumber stores in Penticton. A few years later, he bought the HHBC in Kelowna. Today he owns five stores, including one in Canmore, Alberta.

Paul has built a strong management team to run his stores. "Running one store was hard but running two was even harder. Running three was easier because I could afford to hire the resource people to take the load. That meant there were more things getting done better at the store level and in the operations of the business. I changed my focus to be more of the team leader for the company as a whole."

Peter Moyes and Fred Riley exemplify the best of small town success. Like many small towns across Canada, Merritt has experienced its share of economic challenges. In the 1980s, Merritt's major copper mine closed. Then, in the early '90s, the lumber industry went through a downturn and Merritt's major sawmill, Weyerhauser, closed. In 1993, in an effort to reinvent itself as a tourist destination, Merritt began hosting a Country Music Festival. Ten years later, Peter joined the committee to

The Moyes and Riley families came to Merritt in the early 1900s, stayed and prospered. Peter's father, a successful businessman, chose to remain in this community nestled in the Nicola Valley rather than move to the big times. His loyalty eventually passed on to his son Peter. In 1975, Peter was a building developer like his father before him, and a regular customer at Bob Magel Construction Supply Limited. Mr. Magel had died a few years earlier when his wife asked Peter if he would be interested in buying

Peter Moyes and Fred Riley:

Home Hardware Building Centre
Merritt, BC

They are involved in every aspect of their community and are respected for that.

rebrand Merritt the Country Music Capital of Canada. Over $6 million has been raised for the community, with Peter and Fred's HHBC playing a large part in the transformation. In 2005, the committee hired Canadian muralist Michelle Loughery to come to Merritt. Six years later, twenty murals adorned the walls of businesses throughout the downtown core. Thanks to the committee's ongoing fundraising acumen, Merritt can also boast the Walk of Stars, the Canadian Country Music Hall of Fame, honouring Canadian country artists including Hank Snow, Gordon Lightfoot, Anne Murray, Ian Tyson and other home-grown greats, and a beautiful performance square hosts music in the city all summer long. The Country Music Festival, which has hosted every major country music artist in North America, takes place every July. These days the town itself is truly a tribute to country music. It is also an extraordinary testament to the small town passion, commitment and hard work of visionaries, among them the folks at Merritt Home Hardware Building Centre.

Peter and Fred are very proud to be an ongoing successful business in town, providing employment, stability and acting as role models. They may not be the town's biggest employer, but they are involved in every aspect of their community and are respected for that, having received recognition from both the local Chamber of Commerce and Home Hardware (they received the Home Hardware district award for best store in 2007). Peter points out that there are a Wal-Mart and a Canadian Tire in this small town of 9,000 (trading area 13,000 population) so people have choices. "At the intersection, they can turn left to go the Power Centre or turn right to come downtown (where their store is located) and because of our reputation in the community many, many people turn right. And they do that not only because of Fred or Peter but because of the other 37 people who work here."

the business. Peter said, "I don't have any money." Mrs. Magel said, "I didn't ask you that. I asked if you would be interested." Peter said yes. He financed the purchase with his other business and Mrs. Magel continued to run the building supply store. Peter would show up every morning at 8:30 to see how things were going, then check back in at 4:30 to see how the day had gone. On June 23rd 1977, Fred Riley graduated from high school and on July 1st he had a job at the building supply store. The business was prospering and at that point, Peter, who was living and working in Kamloops, was checking in just once a week. By 1980, Fred was one of four shareholders and in 1982 he became the store manager. He was the true retailer, Peter says. By now Peter was checking in once a month to see how things were going. And they were going fine until 1992 when one of the shareholders resigned and Fred asked him to come back for a couple of weeks to help with the transition. He never left.

In 1998, they decided to buy out the other lumberyard in town, and joined Beaver to accomplish that goal. In 2000 the store became an HHBC when Home Hardware bought Beaver Lumber. Fred says of that time: "We had to make the decision if we wanted to carry on and buy Beaver Lumber's part of the business. We decided that it was a good thing to do. And it has been the best move we've made."

In front of their store mural, business partners Peter Moyes and Fred Riley show off two stars from the Country Music Hall of Fame in Merritt, BC, the Country Music Capital of Canada thanks to community leaders like them.

"The systems and services that Home Hardware has implemented and provided for dealers – no matter what size – are, bar-none, the best in Canada. The other thing is our branding. We're light-years ahead. There is no other franchise in Canada that has the abilities, the capabilities that we do. And it's because it's a Dealer-Owner franchise."

Joan Lemoine, founder of Beach Fest and Monica Mayhew, former volunteer, Bill and Carol Ormiston, owners of Parksville Home Hardware.

Some people build castles in the air, but in Parksville, British Columbia, every summer since 2000, people come from around the world to build castles in the sand. They come from around the world to see them too: in 2010, there were close to 100,000 international visitors. The event, known as The Quality Food Canadian Open Sculpting Competition, is

Home Hardware is very much a family affair: Today, Bill's wife Carol works alongside him in the store and Bill's sister and her husband, Jillian and Chris Mohr, are silent partners. They also proudly employ a number of students, including Chris and Jill's son Braeden, who will graduate from high school in 2014.

Bill and Carol Ormiston and Chris Mohr: "There is no other franchise in Canada that has the abilities, the capabilities that we do. And it's because it's a dealer-owned franchise."

Parksville Home Hardware
Parksville, BC

the brainchild of Joan LeMoine who started it to raise money for local non-profit organizations. She says that Bill and Carol Ormiston, who own Parksville Home Hardware, conveniently located just up from the beach, were behind them from the start. Among other things, the store gives the beach festival a 50% discount on the 30+ gallons of white glue they buy every year - the glue is diluted then sprayed onto the sand sculptures to harden and preserve them.

The relationship is a natural for Parksville Home Hardware. With its beautiful beaches, the town is an international tourist destination and a haven for retirees. In fact, the moderate climate and growth potential brought Bill and his parents Jim and Jean to the area over 26 years ago. His parents owned an Imperial Oil service station in Dryden, Ontario. They came to Vancouver Island for a vacation and fell in love with it. Back home in Dryden, they were friends with the local Home Hardware Dealer Howard Polk, who was on Home's Board of Directors for many years. He suggested they consider opening a Home store out on the island. Their 25 year-old son Bill came on board, moving from Calgary. They went into business at the right time: in 1985, the island's economy was turning around and Expo '86 in Vancouver delivered another huge boost to British Columbia overall. Bill's parents retired in 1995, selling the business to Bill and their son-in-law Chris Mohr.

Sixteen years later, there is still a pleasant small-town feel to this small town. Bill breaks for lunch every day at 11:30 and walks to the post office every afternoon, greeting friends, visitors and customers along the way. The store is still 7,000 square feet, "trying to be 50,000," Bill jokes. Parksville

One of their part-time employees isn't so young anymore. In fact he's in his early 80s. Frank Hammer was Home Hardware's Western District Manager from 1980 to 1995 when he retired. In 2009, he and his wife moved from Edmonton to Parksville. One day he walked into the store and asked Bill if he remembered him. Of course he did, and depending who is telling the story, either Bill asked Frank if he was thinking about part-time work, or Frank asked Bill if he needed part-time help. Whoever asked whom, for two and a half years before he retired for good, Frank could be found every Friday working at the store. Bill has always had a lot of respect for Frank and credits him with helping them build their relationships within the organization. The other individual who was instrumental in that process was Walter. Bill says that whenever he came to Vancouver Island, Walter made a point of visiting every store. "It didn't matter who you were, or what you were. There was a very nice rapport. And the island stores have a lot of pride in being part of the Home family."

A Home Hardware love story:
Bill and Carol met at the Parksville Home Hardware in 1985, the year the Ormistons bought the business. They spotted each other the very first time Carol came in. Over the course of the year, they eyed each other. But nothing happened. Until one day, after Bill had returned from a vacation on the east coast, he followed Carol out to the parking lot and invited her over for a lobster dinner. She looked at him and said, "You've had all year to ask me out. I'm moving to Vancouver tomorrow." He grabbed her shoulders and gave her a big kiss, under the amused eye of the Home Hardware truck driver. It was full steam ahead from there. Carol went to Vancouver, but a year later they were married. Two children, 26 years and 24 hours a day later, they still enjoy every day together. The store celebrated its 29th anniversary on April 1, 2014.

Ted Moffat, who owned Northern Hardware in Prince George, British Columbia, first appeared in my doorway when I started researching and interviewing for this book at the 2011 Spring Market. We sat for an hour as he regaled me with story after story. About the business, about his family, about his life in the northern BC town of Prince George where he had lived for the past 72 wonderful years. He only left because I had another interview to do. When I was making plans for our visit to Prince George in May

The store is a wonder. Its somewhat austere façade belies the treasure trove within (over 70,000 SKUs). Up the first flight of stairs to the second floor, in the back corner is the room known as "the Snake Room" because back in the day, Ted's granddad and cronies gathered there to play a card game called Solo. (According to Ted, Walter Hachborn was the only other person who knew the game.) It is a time warp, faded photos on weary walls, sagging couches and if you listen carefully, you might hear the echo

Ted Moffat: Life without laughter is really not much of a life, he told me.

Northern Hardware
Prince George, BC

2012, the flow of enthusiasm took up where it had left off - did we want to see a play the night we arrived; did we want to see Moffat House, a log house originally built in 1910 which Ted's grandfather bought a few years later. And when we arrived, after showing us around the town where his family roots run deep, Ted took us out for a delicious dinner at a wonderful restaurant one of whose owners, Grant Skelley, is also an owner of the town's Home Hardware Building Centre.

The Moffats (" With two "Fs" and one "T" - the ones with two "Ts" were sheep stealers back in northern England," Ted pointed out) are the oldest family in Prince George with a real wild west history: his great-grandfather moved from Pembroke, Ontario to Quesnel, BC in 1865, following the siren song of the Gold Rush. From there, Ted's grandfather, Alexander Moffat, moved to Prince George in 1912, when he learned that a pulp and paper mill was to be built in the town almost 100 miles away. (In fact the pulp mills did not arrive until the early 1960s.) He and a partner bought a company called Northern Mercantile for $2,000. They each had $500 in cash and approached the Royal Bank for the balance, intending to offer land they had been granted for homesteading by the government as collateral. The Royal Bank turned them down, so they crossed the street to the Bank of Montreal where the manager was more obliging. The family business has been there ever since: their account number is 5. Ted's father, Harold Alexander Moffat, affectionately known as HAM, was mayor for nine years and served on the school board for 25. But when I asked Ted if he had any interest in politics, the answer was an unequivocal: "No." ("I was approached by Bill Bennett once, whose dad and former Premier, W.A.C Bennett had a hardware store in Kelowna. The best years in BC were when we were run by a hardware owner.")

Northern Hardware opened its doors on George Street March 31, 1919. After a series of affiliations, it became part of Link and, following the merger in 1981, a member of the Home Hardware family. Ted started working at the family store when he was 12 years old - there were so many children in town that classes were taught in shifts: Ted was on the morning rotation. After graduating from high school, he studied accounting. Ironically, he struggled with the math and the penny finally dropped when he took a course in Vancouver. When the graduates' names and grades were posted in the local paper, his name was on the list, and the obituary of his original math teacher was on the same page. "He probably died of shock," Ted said. Ted started fulltime in the family business in 1960, naturally enough learning the business from the financial side out. In 1993, Ted bought out the eleven other family shareholders.

of laughter from happy days gone by. When Ted was born in 1939, Prince George was 1,500 people strong. Today it's a big small town with a small town's heart that has never lost its warmth and friendliness. Northern Hardware has survived and thrived by paying attention: to inventory control, to systems, to service, to opportunity. One year Ted challenged each staff member to identify an area of potential new growth. An employee recommended paint ball accessories, which have since proven to be a healthy sub category for the store. Not only do they "unequivocally" guarantee everything they sell for a minimum of a year, they also deliver orders over $300 free anywhere in British Columbia. Ted gave a lot of credit for the success of the business to his large, loyal and hardworking staff, the longest serving of whom is the 84 year-old CFO, Hilliard Clare, who started working on the delivery truck when he was 15. Ted's two children, Dan and Kelly, joined the business several years ago and have now become the fourth generation owners.

I asked Ted if it was hard living in a small town (population 80,000) so far from a major centre. With just the slightest undertone of indignation, Ted informed me that Prince George not only has a symphony orchestra, which recently hired a new conductor whose dad is Northern Hardware's account manager at the bank, they have a theatre company, of which he was treasurer. (Ted was also Treasurer of the Prince George branch of BC Old-time Fiddlers; although he didn't play, his oldest granddaughter is a gifted fiddler.) His father, along with then forestry minister, Ray Williston, staked out the site at the top of the hill outside of town that eventually became the campus of UNBC, University of Northern British Columbia, considered one of Canada's best small universities. Ted started and Northern Hardware continues to be involved in a major fundraising campaign for a Cancer Lodge to be affiliated with the new Cancer Treatment Centre. Ted also served on the Board of Directors of the Barkerville Heritage Society, an hour and a half from Prince George and where his great grandfather went every winter to mine for gold. When it came to community involvement, Ted took to heart his grandfather's advice: Never take more out of the bucket than you put in. Ted clearly derived enormous pleasure from life. Life without laughter is really not much of a life, he told me. And then he laughed his wonderful life-affirming laugh.

Ted lost a courageous battle to cancer on February 26, 2013.

Ted took over the business in 1993 when his father retired. He found gold nuggets in the safe, most of which he turned into rings for each of the family members. The Gold Rush is long over, but when the waters in the Fraser River are low, people still pan for gold along its bed and according to Ted, on a good day when gold is selling at $1,600 an ounce, it's still possible to make a thousand dollars a day. And, of course, you can buy all your gear at Northern Hardware.

Qualicum Beach is like a National Park, which explains why it took Bryan and Liz Virgin so long to get their new store built. The process started in 2004 but building didn't begin until 2010 and when we visited in August 2011, the new store was close to completion. The council's priority is to maintain the character of this charming town on the east coast of Vancouver Island, and the Virgins and Home Hardware worked tirelessly with them to ensure that the store, which planner Matt Richardson calls the Heidi House, satisfied both the town's aesthetic and their business needs.

Vancouver Island normally doesn't get much snow - in 2010, there was one two-inch snowfall. But when it snows, it really snows. In 2008, just before Christmas, there were three major snowstorms. Bryan remembers them all very well. On Monday, December 15, the forecast was calling for snow. Bryan was preparing his order for the week, scheduled for delivery that Wednesday. He added snow shovels, salt and ice melt to his order. Before the end-of-day deadline, he had doubled, tripled and again doubled his order.

Bryan and Liz Virgin: For Bryan and Liz, teamwork epitomizes serving their community.

Dolly's Home Hardware
Qualicum Beach, BC

The new store is around the corner from the old one and will also be called Dolly's Home Hardware, in honour of Bryan's mother. She died in a car accident in 1978 along with two of his seven sisters just months after she asked Bryan to come home because his dad Ernest had suffered a heart attack. Bryan was 20 years old. One day he was working for Woodwards in Alberta and the next day he was running his own business.

Bryan visited his father at the hospital the day he flew home. He said, "Give me the keys so I can open the store." His father said, "Well, I don't have any keys." When Bryan asked him how he opened and locked the store, his father said, "I don't lock it."

The transformation from second hand to hardware was gradual. One day, Bryan's dad, who was working with him in the store, said, "You know, we're in the wrong business - we should be in the hardware business." He also told Bryan that there was only one company to go with - Home Hardware. So one day in 1991 Bryan called to make an appointment with Paul Straus. It was 9:15 in British Columbia, lunchtime in St. Jacobs, and Paul picked up his own phone. Bryan was gob smacked that the man running the business answered his own phone (his assistant was on lunch break) and knew then and there that they were going to become a Home Hardware.

The forecasters were right and Wednesday it snowed. At about 6 PM, their Home truck driver, Mike Demone, phoned from the barge (Home trucks don't cross to the island on BC ferries because they carry propane and other items deemed dangerous goods) to ask about road conditions. The news was not good. He said he'd check back in once he got to the island. Bryan went home to clear his driveway, and got back to the store around 8:30. Mike phoned. He was in Nanaimo. It had taken him two hours to get out of the yard. He told Bryan he'd be in Qualicum Beach (50 kilometers away) at 7 the next morning. "No way," Bryan said. "You have to do your best to get here tonight." Mike explained that he was exhausted. Bryan promised they'd unload for him. They went back and forth and Bryan finally said, "Mike, nobody's on the highway, nobody's in town– it's like a desert. Tomorrow morning when this quits, it's going to be chaos. If we can have our truck unloaded and our salt and our snow shovels ready to go - it's just serving our customers." Mike showed up a few hours later. The truck couldn't get to the loading dock so everything was unloaded by hand and went through the front door. The staff went home at 3:30 the next morning. Bryan had ordered eight skids of salt and 500 snow shovels, birdseed and windshield washer. The bags of salt went onto the sidewalk because there was no room in the store. The following evening when they closed, there was no salt left to move back inside.

Bryan also took advantage of the optional delivery between Christmas and New Year, stocking up on ice melt, snow shovels and emergency supplies. The delivery arrived on the 28th. On the 29th there was another major snowstorm. Qualicum Beach Home Hardware had record day after record day, because they had the inventory and the truck made it through.

"The last thing our store does is close. It runs on generators and yes, there's a new generator-system in our new store. I was on the fire truck one miserable day in November (Bryan was on the volunteer fire department for years). One of the guys says – what a horrible day! I said, 'This is a fantastic day. It's a Duracell day.' That day, we sold about $5,000 worth of Duracell batteries."

Revelstoke seems the quintessential western town: buildings with the classic profiles familiar from old John Wayne movies line the streets. But happily there were no gunslingers to be seen the day we arrived in town. Instead, the majestic peaks of the Columbias created a breathtaking horizon: Mt MacKenzie, boasting the longest vertical descent of any ski resort in North America, Mt Revelstoke with its lyrically named Meadows in the Sky Parkway and Mount Begbie in the distance perfectly aligned between the stone grizzly bear gates that welcome visitors to town and guard the pretty band shell.

Until they sold the business to The Cubbon Group on May 31, 2013, their dad still came to the store once a day - they convinced him that he didn't need to recycle the cardboard anymore, but he still checked the mail. While the children and grandchildren of many of Peter's original customers still shop at the store, the town has enjoyed an influx of new business from Revelstoke Mountain Resort that opened a few years ago. It was good for the building supply side of the business, with skiers from all over the world building seasonal homes in the mountains outside of town.

Barry and Gerry Ozero:

Home Hardware Building Centre
Revelstoke, BC

The town is enjoying an influx of new business from Revelstoke Mountain Resort that opened a few years ago.

Until June 2013, Gerry and Barry Ozero owned Revelstoke Builders Supply just a block and a half from the original hardware store where their father Peter started working in 1961. By the late 1970s, Gerry was a banker on Vancouver Island and Barry, who had apprenticed as a carpenter, was working fulltime for the Revelstoke fire department. In 1978, the family gathered to celebrate Christmas at Gerry's home in Victoria. Peter announced that the owners of the store wanted to retire and he wanted the Ozeros to buy them out. Three months later the two generations of Ozeros were all living in Revelstoke, proud owners of Revelstoke Builders Supply. The full-time staff consisted of Peter, Anne and Gerry, Anne concentrating on the flourishing draperies business started by the wife of the previous owner. Some of that décor expertise must have rubbed off because for many years, Revelstoke Builders Supply was in the top 100 ranking for Beauti-Tone paint sales. They hired a part-time bookkeeper. Initially Barry continued to work full time at the fire hall, helping in the store whenever he could. "When I wasn't working I was working," he explained, so he soon decided to join the family business full-time. Today the store has a staff of over 30 employees.

The original Link store was an extremely compact 900 square feet of retail space out of which they sold hardware and the lumber they bought from the local mill plus windows, doors, plywood and other sheet goods. Eventually they built a warehouse for storage and kept adding onto the retail floor space until there was no room for further expansion. Not surprisingly, in addition to "doing a lot of business out of a cramped little building," the Ozeros spent a lot of time searching for more space. In 1993, they found it, a former car dealership that had started life in the 1930s as a gas station. They tripled their floor space overnight.

The Ozeros always supported their community in a variety of ways, but the annual Santa Claus Parade was very possibly their favourite event of the year. The Revelstoke Home Hardware Building Centre float would often win the big prize. They earned a reputation as the party float, but only good spirits fuelled the festivities that produced a natural Rocky Mountain high.

In June 2013, Patti Smith bought The Cubbon Group.

If you can't achieve a good life-work balance in a place as beautiful as Revelstoke, there's something wrong with you. "There's pressure because you can't schedule customers to come through the door, but we've been at it long enough that we don't let it bother us," Gerry says. After years in the business, they have each found their own way to let off steam: Gerry is the skier in the family and loves to travel. Barry's passion is Percherons. Barry's "gentle giants" Tom and Granite have been losing their winter fat and getting ready for the summer and fall fairs, with Barry in the driver's seat.

In 1912, Gerry and Barry's grandparents came from Ukraine to Canada as farmers. They crossed the Atlantic on The Temple, the ship immediately behind The Titanic. When they docked in New Brunswick they heard that homesteads were available in the fertile valley outside Revelstoke and so they kept on going, taking a train across the country to their new home. When the region was flooded in the 1960s by the Hugh Keenleyside Dam near Castlegar, the old farms disappeared under water. By then Peter had moved his family into the town of Revelstoke and was working at the building supply store that he would one day own with his two sons.

Frances has won many awards over the years - Woman of the Year, the Paul Straus PR award, among others. In 2006 Osoyoos Home Hardware was voted Best Hardware Store in Canada by Hardware Merchandise. In February 2011 Frances Sologuk received another well-deserved award for community involvement for the entire south Okanagan, nominated by a Penticton Toyota dealer. When she called to thank him, he said that he meets people everywhere who know her and what she has done for her community. He thought it was important she be recognized for that contribution. Frances says, "I'm surrounded by people who make me look good. And Home Hardware has given me the opportunity to do that. I would probably have volunteered quietly and done something even if I weren't the Home owner in town, but I can do it on a larger scale because I am."

If you ever need your faith in humanity renewed or restored, visit Osoyoos Home Hardware owned and operated by the inspirational human dynamo Frances Sologuk.

Since she and her husband Larry bought the business on the corner of a downtown street in 1985, they have been a vital part of the heart and soul of Osoyoos. For Frances, the biggest joy of owning a Home Hardware store has been the opportunity to support her community in so many ways.

1,000 people showed up to each of the two dances that summer. People plan their holidays around the event, four hours of music, prizes and good old-fashioned family fun. Larry is DJ and Frances emcees, alongside former mayor Tom Shields, another Ontario ex-pat. There is no charge to dance the night away and the event raises money for the community, and over the years has contributed to town projects including the Pioneer Walkway and gazebo on the shores of Lake Osoyoos. These days there's also a big emphasis on Special Olympics.

Frances Sologuk:

Osoyoos Home Hardware
Osoyoos, BC

I would probably have volunteered quietly and done something even if I weren't the Home owner in town, but I can do it on a larger scale because I am."

Virtually everywhere you look you see evidence of that commitment. There is Tony Batista, as of 2011 a 22-year veteran employee of Osoyoos Home Hardware who proudly wears a nametag labelling him The Boss. Frances remembers when Tony started working in the store, a timid 22 year-old with Down syndrome. "It was like he was stuck to my hip. I'd turn around and bump into him. I am in awe some days watching the progress he has made since then. When a customer, who doesn't know Tony, walks in and asks him how to fix a toilet, and Tony takes him over to the plumbing department, you know that you have broken down a barrier." Tony is also a Special Olympian and that organization has a special place in the special place that is Frances' heart.

Zecheriah Nyarza is another example. He came to Osoyoos from Sudan in 2006 through a church sponsorship. His parents had been killed. Zech had no job, younger brothers to raise and support, very little education and no English. The church asked the community for help. Many responded, but Frances' Home Hardware was the business that gave this lovely young man a start in his new country.

But the annual Street Dances are what has made Osoyoos Home Hardware famous far and wide. In 1986 Frances decided to have a sidewalk sale. Things were a bit slow, so she brought out a cassette deck and put on some music. A few moms and kids started "bopping around" so Frances grabbed some items to hand out as prizes. Twenty-five years later, in 2011, about

The store has been located on a busy downtown corner since 1942. It's what Frances calls "a retro-downtown store" and they market it that way. There are cooking classes, courses, a zigzag layout that entices you from one product-packed department to the next – hardware, housewares, seasonal, pets…The store is famous for its amazing selection. Frances remembers a customer coming in looking for an inflatable. He said, "I looked all over Vancouver, no wonder I couldn't get one – they're all here!" She says she wishes she were 30 years younger. "I'm more excited about what we have to offer now than in all my 26 years in the business."

Frances likes to quote the philosophy of Charles Schulz, creator of the immortal Peanuts comic strip. It goes something like this: Who won the Oscars in 1943?' Who won the Grammy? And you can't remember any of that. Now, name the teacher who influenced you the most; someone you would like to spend a week with; someone who has influenced your life. In answer, Frances puts Walter Hachborn right up there with her family. She says, "He influenced me in business but he influenced me more as a person and how I relate to business."

The first thing I see when I walk into John Kehler's big, bright and beautiful HBC in Vernon is a line of bras dangling above my head. That gets my attention right away - bring the fight to beat breast cancer out into the open.

John Kehler:

Home Building Centre - Vernon
Vernon, BC

"People really like shopping here and it is because we do a lot of things outside of selling hammers."

The feeling of openness is evident everywhere - from the "physical plant" to the people who work in it. And the energy goes beyond the four walls, across Vernon. The store and staff are involved in so many community causes that John has set up a system to assign SKU numbers to the different charitable entities they fundraise for throughout the year, to make everything easy to track and manage. "I sometimes wonder - how much does this cost me," John says. "I know it takes a huge amount of time with the staff but to me it's important. People really like shopping here and it is because we do a lot of things outside of selling hammers."

That's an understatement, and typical of the unassuming modesty Home Hardware Dealers display when it comes to their leadership roles in communities across the country. But Ruth Edwards, Executive Director of the North Okanagan Hospice Society's Hospice House in Vernon, is not so reticent. She says that the amount of support the society has received from John and his staff over the years is incredible: for instance, the Vernon HBC donated all the roofing materials and the sitting room fireplace. In addition to other initiatives that take place throughout the year, John's store makes an annual donation with proceeds from a Ladies-Only golf tournament, with every hole catered by suppliers and male staff. Long-time employee Daphne Coleman, inspired by the Ladies in Business group she belongs to, brought the idea to John. He was very open to the idea, on condition that she organise it. The original decision to support the hospice was a collective one, inspired by a Hospice Building Expansion Campaign and the fact that one of the HBC staff had a family member who had been a resident there. So it is all very personal. To date they have raised over $146,000.

According to Ruth, the Vernon HBC has the distinction of being one of five of the many donors to the hospice who have exceeded the $100,000 mark. "They have become part of our family," she says. "They're not just donors, and like all our donors, have become partners. They have a tremendous community spirit."

"I think ours was the last deal to be done (when Home Hardware was negotiating the Beaver Lumber buy out) and it was incredibly complicated. I was at the market and Walter was doing a book signing. He saw me and pulled me aside and whispered in my ear, 'I am sorry it's taken so long. Thanks for being patient. Everything will be just fine.' I said to him, 'The handshake is everything.' My lawyer and accountant were really worked up. This was a big dollar transaction and they had never heard of a deal where your word is your bond. I said, 'You don't understand. This is Home Hardware. This is Walter.' We only completed the deal eight or nine months after the fact. As complicated as it was, I really liked it. I liked the culture. Walter started it and it carries through. There is integrity that runs throughout the company, mutual trust and mutual respect. And it all started with Walter and a handshake." John Kehler, Vernon HBC

The Vernon HBC team:
John Kehler, Hospice director Ruth Edwards,
Daphne Coleman, Tanis Lobe and Bob
Anderson. The garden at the hospice is
tended entirely by volunteers.

Garry Wittich has had his feet to the fire more than once. Twice literally. The first time was late December 2003 when the bowling alley next door to the Westbank store he owned until May 2012 burned to the ground. The store sustained severe smoke damage and they were closed for two months. Garry cannot say enough about the help he got from PIB Insurance, the distribution centre in Wetaskiwin and his Area Manager (and good friend)

Peter Rubingh is manager of the Princeton store and his wife Cheryl worked in the Westbank location's paint department, so it is in truth an extended family business. These days, after selling the Westbank business, Garry is enjoying a well-deserved semi-retirement. But during his tenure "on the floor", Garry was never afraid to go up against the competition. His stores, regardless of location, have always offered service that the Big Boxes don't.

Garry Wittich: Garry and his family business are not afraid to go up against the competition.

Princeton Home Hardware
Princeton, BC

Terry Smith to get the store up and running again as quickly as possible. Another bright spot (and Garry always emphasises the bright side) was that after the store re-opened in March 2004, they were able to expand to 10,000 square feet when the store next door closed. Then in 2009, a major forest fire threatened the town, now formally renamed West Kelowna. The fire came so close to their plaza that the RCMP shut it down for two days. The only reason the nearby sawmill wasn't lost was that the employees held the fire at bay with water hoses. When we visited in August 2011, the ugly scars of the fire's devastation were still visible in the hills above town.

Garry has also had his feet to the fire figuratively with enormous competition from the Big Box stores which came to the community of Westbank in the past few years. While it has been challenging, he has stood up to that as well. It all comes down to family, he says. And Garry's business has always been a true family enterprise. The Westbank business started in 1987 in a 3,500 square foot store on Main Street. In those days it was Garry, his wife Gloria and Garry's sister Elva. When they sold the store, their son Aaron, two daughters Shauna and Connie and son-in-law Chris and another 20 employees all worked in the business. Over the years numerous brothers, in-laws, nieces and nephews all worked there as well. In 2007 the family bought the Home Hardware store in Princeton, about an hour and a half away. That was a good move: the copper mine in Princeton reopened in 2011 after twenty years, bringing people back to the community.

These qualities have been recognized: In 2007 the Westbank store won the Chamber of Commerce Key Business Award, which goes to the outstanding retailer in town. It also won the 2005 Hardware Merchandising Outstanding Retailer Award for best hardware store in Canada under 10,000 square feet.

Garry insisted that this story focus on his family. But it is impossible to overlook Garry's heart, which is large and generous and right there on his sleeve. He worked hard to ensure that the family business would carry on as he enjoys retirement. These days he is devoting more time to his beloved Rotarians in Westbank, where he and his wife still live. The Rotarian group to which he belongs built the West Kelowna Water Park, an entirely volunteer initiative. His fellow Rotarian, Gary Young, was the (retired) engineer in charge of the project. According to Garry, his friend donated hundreds of hours to the project. Garry doesn't say anything much about what he himself donated, but I have a pretty good idea.

I was first "introduced" to Azim and Nawaz Virani, who with their brother Firoz own Simpson Hardware in West Vancouver, when I was visiting Dan Gould in Newfoundland, as far on the other side of the country as one can possibly be. Dan told me a story that dated back over 25 years, when he was a store merchandiser and came to Vancouver for several weeks to work on the Viranis' original store that they took over from Jim Simpson in 1981, the same year that Home Hardware bought Link.

Another story needs to be told for balance: in the early morning hours of May 17, 1993, someone set fire to the Viranis' building. It took the fire department five hours to put out the blaze, by which time the store had been totally demolished. The Viranis had to shut down the business for a year - 51 weeks to be precise. (The ledger shows what that does to the bottom line all too clearly.) Then they felt the positive power of community: the business next door offered them free office space, Manuella and Jurgen,

Azim and Nawaz Virani:

Simpson Home Hardware
West Vancouver, BC

It is a testament to the Viranis that their reaction was to laud him for his courage.

Today Canada is a vibrant multi-cultural society, particularly in its urban centres. West Vancouver is no exception. But in the early 1980s, it was less so and when Dan Gould, a young man from Newfoundland, showed up at Simpson Home Hardware, he had not met any East Indians, especially not exotic, articulate and educated East Indians from Kenya, like the Viranis. Dan readily admits that he was experiencing a mild form of prejudice, which, like most forms of that unfortunate condition, is a product of ignorance. Happily, Dan's condition was cured quickly and completely by exposure to the Virani brothers and their thriving business.

Unfortunately not everyone in the community initially proved so open minded. Nawaz produced an old battered ledger almost Dickensian in its decrepitude where the story is laid out in fading pencil figures. Business dropped off quite sharply after the family took over from Jim Simpson - Azim, Nawaz and their uncle, with whom they also owned a dry cleaning business and where Nawaz first worked when he came to Canada in September 1979 bought the business together. Less than two years later, it turned around and the numbers just keep climbing from there. Nawaz, a man full of stories, has another story, a human one but in its own way equally graphic, to illustrate the challenges they faced as new business owners with faces that were a different colour than the majority of their customers (at least in those days):

A few years after they had opened, Azim remembers an elderly gentleman coming in and asking to speak with him in his office. After Azim had made him comfortable, the man told him that when Azim and Nawaz bought the store he and some of his friends decided to no longer shop there, although they had been regular customers over the 25 years that Jim Simpson had owned it. "It's just that you were different coloured people; we didn't know you," he said quietly. "But now, I've come to apologize to you." It is a testament to the Viranis that their reaction was to laud him for his courage, not deride him for his original cowardice.

owners of a local Swiss restaurant named Chesa, ran a tab for them and refused to accept cash payment when the new store opened, insisting instead that Nawaz write a credit note with which they would purchase merchandise. The business returned and grew exponentially after they reopened. (There's the ledger again to prove it!) Nawaz and Jurgen still meet for lunch regularly. But the story of their customer, Mrs. Carter, an elderly lady who lived next door to the store, can still bring tears to the brothers' eyes. One morning the day's mail included a letter from Mrs Carter saying how sorry she was about the fire. She was not very rich, she explained, but had received an unexpected refund, and wanted to share her good fortune: she enclosed a cheque for $500 that she hoped they could use. Azim returned the cheque with thanks, but she continued to keep an eye on their progress. When she read in the community paper that they were having problems with building permits, she began attending City Council meetings, warning the politicians not to "make trouble for the Boys at Home Hardware."

Some of Simpson's Home Hardware "United Nations" staff outside the store: Mac Pinney, Justin Stewart, Adrian Brahbar and Fred Kayser along with Azim and Nawaz Virani.

THE NORTH

. DAWSON CITY, YUKON . WATSON LAKE, YUKON . WHITEHORSE, YUKON . YELLOWKNIFE, NORTH WEST TERRITORIES .

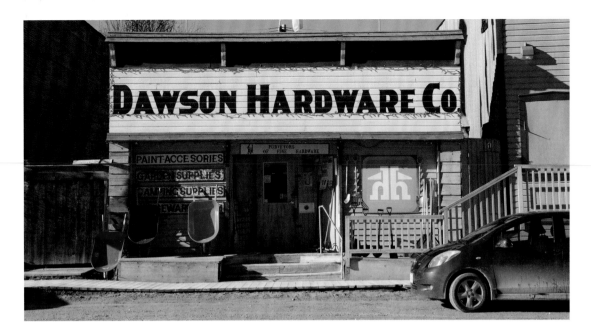

Dawson City lies six hours north of Whitehorse in the heart of the Yukon wilderness - the highway runs beside the Yukon River, the Selwyn and other Rockie-esque ranges forming gleaming ridges in the distance.

Susan Herrmann:

Dawson Home Hardware
Dawson City, YK

In remote communities, customer loyalty is guaranteed. Instead of taking it for granted, Susan, Tina and Shane see it as a responsibility: these people are neighbours as well as customers and if someone is in a tight spot, they

"A business is like a baby – you want to make sure that it can stand on its own and walk on its own and look after itself."

In 1896, gold was discovered on Rabbit Creek (renamed Bonanza Creek), by "Skookum" Jim George Carmack and Dawson Charlie. It sparked the Klondike gold rush of 1898 and Dawson City and Yukon Territory were born. Two years later the town had the third largest population west of Winnipeg, after Portland and Seattle. Today it has subsided back to a modest 1,200 souls, although thousands of tourists over the summer season can increase that number fourfold.

Dawson City looks like a film set. The building that today houses Dawson Home Hardware is the Real McCoy, dating to 1901. Recognizing a rich vein of potential, Ken Herrmann's uncle Steve bought the iconic building the instant it became available in 1979 and moved his already established hardware business into that perfect location on a busy street. Ken started working for Steve at that time.

Susan is a Dawson City native with a 24-karat Klondike lineage and a heart of gold. Her paternal grandfather arrived with the Gold Rush and she and her brother still have an active mining stake. The gold nugget on a chain around her neck is from her mine. Susan's daughter Tina Green started working in the family business several years ago. She met her fiancé Shane Biggs, a licensed plumber, a few years ago when he came to town from Whitehorse. His friends dared him to try to stump the pretty lady with all the answers at the Home Hardware store. Instead, they both found what they were looking for and today the two of them are in the process of learning the business inside out. Initially, Susan and Ken were reluctant for Tina to come on board, knowing how much the business demands of its owners. But Tina is happy with her decision, and with Shane added to the equation, succession plans are moving along.

help them out. It's that simple. And in a small town where everyone knows your name, they also know your phone number: there has been more than one midnight call from a distraught customer whose furnace has just quit.

Winter days are short so all the more reason to pack in as much fun as possible. Dawson Home Hardware supports a myriad of activities year round, from Yukon Trek, the big dog race from Fairbanks to Whitehorse, to the spring carnival. Snow sledding is another major winter draw and even Tina's twin eight year olds have their own machines. Their business style is appreciated: Dawson Home Hardware has been honoured with awards from both Dawson City Chamber of Commerce and the Territory.

Susan, Tina and Shane know everyone in the area, including some long gone. They tell wild stories about people with crazy names, like Two by Four Bob, recounted in confidential tones as if these people are their neighbours, not part of a storied past. They have their own nicknames - Susan is the White Tornado, Shane is Talks-a -Lot (I never did find out Tina's). But I guess that's what happens in a town with places called Gertie's, Miss Kittie Galore's Boutique and the Palace Grand Theatre, where a former house of "ill repute" is now a respectable restaurant and brightly coloured buildings line the streets like tall wooden Can Can girls about to fling up their skirts.

In the late 1990s, Ken and his wife Susan bought out Steve and joined Home Hardware. When her husband passed away after a brief illness in January 2012, Susan knew it was time for a change of pace. She plans to stay in the area, with extended visits to her home in Arizona, but is in the process of passing the business along to Tina and Shane. "I'll see how it goes," Susan says about full retirement.

There are more than a few characters in the Land of the Midnight Sun, a corner of the world that attracts and embraces people of all stripes. Including, in his own distinctive way, Dave Kalles, owner of the Home Building Centre in Watson Lake, six hours east of Whitehorse.

David Kalles: Dave is a unique combination of vocation and conviction.

Jarand Home Building Centre
Watson Lake, YK

Dave is a unique combination of vocation and conviction. He was born in Washington State in 1937, joined the army after high school then went to university. He and his young wife Alice moved to Canada when he enrolled at UBC for graduate studies in theology. He supported himself as a carpenter through school, which seems entirely appropriate.

After Dave graduated and was ordained as an Anglican priest, his Bishop immediately sent him to Teslin, Yukon on Mile 804 of the Alaska Highway. (He and Alice had to look it up in an atlas - it's about 100 miles east of Whitehorse.) He later discovered that two of his great grandfathers had been Gold Rush prospectors with successful claims so the call of the wild must have run in his blood.

In 1973, shortly after he arrived, Dave had a crisis of capability. "In some people, there's no pillar to build on," he offers as explanation. So Dave stepped down from the pulpit and concentrated on carpentry. But he never lost his faith and has always remained an active member of the Diocese: the difference after he stepped down, he says, is that the Bishop asks, rather than tells him, to do something.

By the mid 1970s, Dave was working in construction near Watson Lake, a community established in the 1940s around the creation of the Alaska Highway that had evolved into a "pretty decent-sized community." He opened a lumberyard because he was tired of driving 300 miles for materials. In those early days, the store fixtures were sheets of plywood perched on paint cans. The business grew and Dave joined Link Hardware. But when Home Hardware bought them in 1980, Dave became an independent once more, his business deemed too small for the new corporate structure. In 1997, Dave sold to Barry McCallan, in those days a member of Beaver Lumber, whose operation now owns the HHBC in Whitehorse. Ten years later, Dave bought the business back as Watson Home Building Centre (the store joined Home Hardware during the McCallan tenure). "I didn't have a heck of a lot of use for Home Hardware when I took the store over again but the more I see of them, the more impressed I get," Dave says. "I've been associated with about six other groups over the years, and it's by far the most dealer-oriented group and the easiest to work with."

Today his manager Norm Griffiths, who had worked for Dave 20 years before, runs the 4,500 square foot store. Dave says emphatically that he would not have bought back the business if Norm had not agreed to manage it. The arrangement allows Dave to focus on the adjacent factory he owns, manufacturing roof trusses, core boxes and pallets for several mining and exploration firms. "We make anything in wood," Dave says, all of which is bought through Home Hardware and, along with the hardware they order from the Wetaskiwin warehouse, shipped by independent trucking companies from Edmonton.

Tall and trim, Dave faces the world with a simple clarity that seems to suit both the spiritual and practical realities of his life. Ten years ago Dave started training and running competitively. When we met, he was en route to a half marathon in Victoria, only the third he has run. He finished in the top half of the final field, quite an accomplishment for a 75 year-old. He also ran away with four medals in the 2012 Canada Senior Games in Cape Breton. Alice passed away recently so he has lost the companion with whom he raised a family and built a good business. Around town he still drives a 1972 pickup truck and lives in the house he built that has grown up around the small trailer that was all he could afford when he was no longer a salary-earning minister. Despite those humble beginnings, Dave has been a successful and active member of the community, serving several terms as President of the Chamber of Commerce and one term as mayor of the town. He is also the longest licensed priest in the history of the Yukon Anglican Diocese that dates back prior to the Gold Rush of 1898.

Dave may no longer be a practicing minister, but he is clearly still very much invested in his church. The Anglican Cathedral in Whitehorse is a modest wooden building seated quietly in a grove of trees beside the original log church that is now a museum. It tells the stories of the early days of the church that was established in the region well before the Gold Rush of 1898: caribou hide robes with exquisite beadwork, altars, ceremonial objects. It seemed fitting to take Dave's photograph in this peaceful environment where he is obviously so much at home.

For more than forty years, Dave has fulfilled two seemingly disparate aspects of his character on his own terms. "I made a choice, and not necessarily voluntarily, between lifestyle and economics," Dave says. "I was a far better minister as a contractor than I ever was as a priest."

Canadian artist Ted Harrison designed the Cathedral's beautiful stained glass window. He had also been a warden at Dave's church in Carcross (abbreviated from Caribou Crossing) years ago. Harrison, a much-loved chronicler of life in the north, received the Order of Canada in 1987 and designed the Yukon Pavilion at Vancouver Expo '86.

245

Bryan Curial and Jason Delege, the two other members of the Whitehorse HHBC management team, join Rob Champagne and Amica Sturdy at the S.S. Klondike, one of the last surviving sternwheelers in the Yukon and today a Parks Canada museum. Bryan manages the LBM side of the store and is the one native of Whitehorse we met. Jason Delege, Retail Manager, spent sixteen years at the store in Houston, north of Prince George. He has been in The Yukon for a year, and although he claims to be a city boy, he and his young family have made Whitehorse home.

The multi-store business model is becoming more prevalent at Home Hardware. Despite their size and the sophistication of their systems, at the individual store level those we have encountered still retain the values espoused by Walter Hachborn and the founders of the company.

Centre. The 20-hour run up the Alaska Highway from the warehouse in Wetaskiwin near Edmonton is as easy as it gets in this part of the world. But with a robust mining industry, both the construction and retail sides of the business are booming.

The Cubbon Group: There are challenges to running a business in the north.

Home Hardware Building Centre - Whitehorse
Whitehorse, YK

The HHBC in Whitehorse, Yukon shows both sides of the equation at their working best: the 40,000 square foot store with 75 mostly fulltime employees is one of five stores owned by the Cubbon Group, a business conglomerate built by Barry and Jennifer McCallan who bought and sold stores across Canada. They eventually consolidated it into five stores in Trail and Duncan. BC, Hinton and Wetaskiwin, Alberta and Whitehorse where they lived and operated the store for almost 10 years before moving to Vancouver Island. Today company president Patti Smith, a minority partner based in Victoria, BC, manages the business. She travels to each of the stores in the group several times a year.

The Operations Manager for all five stores is a young woman whose character is aptly described by her last name. Amica Sturdy has spent her entire career in retail, in hardware and building materials for more than a decade. Like so many members of the extended Home Hardware family, Amica came up through the ranks, starting in the shipping and receiving department in Duncan HHBC. She has made her home base in Whitehorse, and travels regularly to the other four stores.

Rob Champagne is the heart of this busy behemoth with a management structure that has lost none of its humanity for all its efficiency. Although he is not a native, Rob has lived in Whitehorse long enough to have earned honorary status as a local. Born in Kelowna, BC, Rob moved here with his parents when he was 15. That was a few years ago, but Rob is still very much young at heart. His easygoing nature belies a sharp eye and innate business sense, all of which made him a natural for the position of Store Manager. In constant demand, he doesn't spend much time in his small office right on the store floor. Everyone knows where to find him and he confesses that some contractors won't bother to come into the store if they don't see his truck parked in its habitual spot on the edge of the large lot.

After a quarter of a century, Rob cannot imagine living anywhere else: when he and his wife go to Vancouver, he can't stand the crowds. He thinks nothing of hopping in his truck on Friday after work and driving a few hundred miles to his fishing boat in Haines, Alaska.

There are challenges to running a business in the north. Competition is fierce - 50% of the jobs in Yukon are with various levels of government. Shipping is expensive - they, along with all other stores in the Canadian north, are responsible for their own shipping from the nearest Distribution

The store sends building materials as far afield as Dawson City and Old Crow, a First Nations' community about 800 miles north. As much as 40% of their LBM business is with the remote northern communities scattered across this vast landscape; for the most part, the store and their far flung customers rely on year-round air transport.

It's easy to see why Yukon's provincial slogan is Larger Than Life. With just three hours of sunlight and -50 degrees in the peak of winter and 21 hours of brilliant sunlight in high summer, Yukon is made for people with the stamina to live and play hard year round. In addition to the spectacular natural wonderland on its doorstep, Whitehorse has a vibrant cultural life that really hits its stride over the long winter months. The Whitehorse HHBC is involved in virtually everything that happens in their active town, from Special Olympics, the local Food Bank and the Hospital Foundation to a donation to the Arctic Winter Games that were held in Whitehorse in March 2012. Although apparently most of the people who live in Whitehorse were not born in Whitehorse, most of them are here to stay. If you last one winter, they tell me, you'll never leave.

Miles Canyon claimed many casualties and much precious cargo during the Gold Rush when hundreds of boats loaded with supplies used the river as a highway. A wooden rail system around the canyon eventually eliminated the need to navigate the hazardous gorge and the hydroelectric dam downriver has tamed the Canyon that retains its natural beauty and grandeur. The Robert Lowe Suspension Bridge was built in 1922.

On June 30, 2013, Patii Smith bought the company from the McCallans.

Yellowknife is booming. Or rather, it is sparkling. An already healthy mining industry in the NWT moved to another level when gem quality diamonds were discovered in the late 1990s. The stigma of Blood Diamonds in other countries has made laser-engraved Canadian diamonds highly sought after. The only diamond mines in North America are currently in the NWT, one of them a joint venture between Rio Tinto and Harry Winston Diamond Corporation. There's also still gold in the hills. To top

direct competitor to Beaver Lumber. When his father asked him to help out for a few months, he answered the call and stayed nine years, well past his initial tour of duty. In 1994, Chuck had an opportunity to buy his own store in Yellowknife. Almost twenty years later, he is in the process of one last change, converting the 20,000 square foot store to an HHBC, which will expand its appeal to a larger segment of the community's population. Like all the other dealers in northern Canada, the Yellowknife store is responsible

Charles Corothers:

There are also unique challenges when your store is situated at the end of the road and the community becomes landlocked for several weeks twice a year.

Corothers Home Hardware Building Centre
Yellowknife, NWT

it off, the Northern Lights have become a major winter tourist attraction. Japanese culture believes that young couples that bask in their benevolent glow will be blessed with a child. Light pollution has dimmed the Aurora Borealis in Japan, but in northern Canada it still shines brightly. This has sparked the development of Aurora Village, a resort on the outskirts of Yellowknife, a town with a population of 19,000, almost no unemployment (approximately half the jobs are government positions) and a chronic housing shortage.

Chuck Corothers' HHBC in Yellowknife is thriving in this healthy economic environment. His business has been a major supplier to the mining industry for years, and the relationship continues to strengthen. Over his years in Yellowknife, Chuck has seen what he calls " the maturing of the community," with local businesses working hand in hand to continually improve the quality of life. One of their major initiatives is to enhance the available resources at the Stanton Regional Hospital. Their own MRI and mammography machine allow patients from all over the north to stay in the north, instead of having to leave their homes and families to receive care in Edmonton. Recently the mining operations collectively funded a new multiplex with a large double indoor soccer complex, running track, gymnasium and play centre. There is another massive multiplex arena with two rinks, one Olympic sized, the other NHL-sized. In a land where winter arrives in October, cross-country ski clubs abound. It is a good place to live and work.

Chuck's lineage is third generation lumberman. His father was a trouble shooter/problem solver for Beaver Lumber who moved from store to store, and their lives were like a military family's for several years, Chuck recalls. Eventually Chuck's dad opened a store of his own in Whitehorse, Yukon. By now, Chuck was working at a Revelstoke Building Supplies store, a

for shipping product from their closest Distribution Centre. Getting it right is a question of economics in every sense: it is costly to run trucks so maximizing loads is crucial, and the right product mix encourages people to shop local, rather than heading to Edmonton on one of the four airlines that flies into Yellowknife every day. There are also unique challenges when your store is situated at the end of the road and the community becomes landlocked for several weeks twice a year. A one-kilometer stretch of the Yellowknife Highway crosses the Mackenzie River, currently relying on a ferry service and an ice road to literally bridge the gap for most of the year. During spring breakup, that short stretch becomes impassable, hence the need for skilled advance ordering. The Deh Cho Bridge opened in early 2013, and will make these challenges things of the past.

Chuck is a true northerner now. He and his wife Jocelyn will have lived in Yellowknife for 19 years by the time their store became an HHBC in January 2013. They have six children, five of whom have worked or still work at the store. The baby of the family, Isabelle, is already helping out during special sales events.

Chuck is not alone in having fallen under the spell of the region, one of many who have come for a while and stayed forever. Mike Wilgosh, manager of Chuck's second store in Hay River, three hundred miles away on the south shore of Slave Lake, is a perfect example. When the store converted from Beaver Lumber to a Home Building Centre, expanding from 3,500 to 20,000 square feet, Chuck needed help. His Area Manager suggested Mike. Although he had worked for Beaver Lumber for years, Mike had never lived in the north. Chuck suggested a trial period. After six months, Mike was smitten. He moved to Hay River as Manager in 2002. And now he has a wife and four boys to complete the picture. Maybe there's something to be said about the effect of the Northern Lights after all.

Quebec

· ST-RAYMOND · WESTMOUNT · BAIE D'URFÉ ·

In 1965, Home Hardware Stores Limited and Quebec-based Rona, both members, along with western-based Link Hardware and Merchants Consolidated of United Hardware Wholesalers, entered into a gentlemen's agreement to not convert one another's stores. After Home Hardware bought Link Hardware stores in 1981 and Merchants Consolidated went out of business, United Hardware Wholesalers was disbanded and its two remaining members formed Alliance Rona LLC along with US-based Do It Best, a relationship that lasted almost 25 years. As a result, for many years, Home Hardware's presence in Quebec was minimal with a few notable exceptions. In September of 1965 Quincaillerie Rocheleau in Rouyn-Noranda became the first hardware store in Quebec to join the Home Hardware banner. Owner Gabriel Rocheleau worked in the store into his 90s and today his son Jacques remains a Home Hardware Dealer in the mining town that is the capital of the Abitibi-Témiscaming region that straddles the border with northern Ontario. There were also a few Home Hardware stores on the Quebec side of the Ottawa River: Jim Tremblay's in Buckingham (today the town has been renamed Gatineau) and Mickey Hodgson's in Shawville, both of whom are profiled in this book. Robin Jones and Whitman, a hardware retailer in the Gaspé region of eastern Quebec, was another early convert with the distinction of also being one of Canada's oldest retailers. (Its establishment dates to 1766, making it second in age only to The Hudson's Bay Company.) That business has since closed, but the trend of border retailers being converted by intrepid Area Managers who didn't speak a word of French continued until the early 2000s when Rona went public and the landscape changed. Since then, Home Hardware has seen major expansion in Quebec, and today there are approximately 100 HH, HBC and HHBC stores in the province, almost 50% of them operating in exclusively francophone communities. Three Area Managers and a facilitator, under the direction of Director, Retail Operations Quebec, Mario Durocher, who started his Home Hardware career in 1994 at the Burford paint plant, are responsible for the massive territory. A business development team has been established to maintain momentum in a highly competitive and distinct market that has embraced Home Hardware's also distinctive systems, service and branding.

Harold Dupuis, Wayne St Croix and
Gaetan Dupuis in the yard of LM Wind Power.

As we travelled across the country gathering background and taking photographs for this book, I learned that there are as many stories as there are stores. Each story is unique but collectively they represent the essence of what makes Home Hardware great. From one end of the country to the other, at the heart of so many of these success stories is the evolution of the small family business. Family businesses run by hardworking people doing what they did perhaps of necessity, but who were able to recognize an opportunity when it came their way. In the space of a generation, a

So when opportunity showed up again, literally on their doorstep, Egide Dupuis et fils were more than ready. In 2006, LM Wind Power, the world's largest manufacturer of wind turbine blades, opened a plant directly behind the store. Wayne St Croix, the industrial sales rep for Egide Dupuis et fils, met one of the young LM engineers socially and over the course of a few congenial conversations quickly realized what Egide Dupuis et fils could offer the new business. From first encounter to first order took about six months.

Harold and Gaetan Dupuis:

Egide Dupuis et fils
Gaspé, QC

The decision to join Home was based primarily on the better systems, range of products and support that Home Hardware offers.

surrounding number of these small family enterprises have established themselves as some of the most successful businesses in their communities. One of these is the Home Hardware store in Gaspé, Egide Dupuis et Fils.

In October 2011, Egide Dupuis passed away. He was 84 years old and was deeply mourned by his 11 children, all of whom still live in the Gaspé where Egide spent his entire life. The Home Hardware store in the town of Gaspé, named in his honour, now stands in his memory.

Egide worked hard all his life to support his family, first as a fisherman, then in the mines of Murdochville. In 1973, he moved his family to the town of Gaspé and started to work as a contractor, running the business from the house where the children clearly absorbed the tenets of entrepreneurialism. (Today, two of the sons own the hardware business they started with their father, three of the brothers are contactors like their dad - and store customers - and another one owns an auto-parts store in Ste Anne-des-Monts.) In 1982, less than 10 years on, the business had grown to such an extent that Egide had to move to a storefront – insurance companies don't like it when you store flammable materials like paint in the family home. By this time, Harold was at university in Rivière-du-Loup studying to be an accountant. He and his younger brother Gaetan decided to go into business with their father. And so Egide Dupuis et Fils was born. Their first store, all of 900 square feet, sold only paint and paint accessories. They soon added auto paint to the mix and two years later had to move again. In the new location they started selling auto parts. The business flourished and in 1992 they built their own store, doubling their size to just under 8,000 square feet. Over the years, they were affiliated with various banners, but in 2008, joined Home Hardware and in 2010 moved into their current location of 22,000 square feet. As with so many dealers across the country, the decision to join Home was based primarily on the better systems, range of products and support that Home Hardware offers: father and sons again recognized opportunity when it came their way.

The plant manufactures two sizes of blades, 37 and 42 meters (and began producing a third length in the spring of 2012). It produces one blade a day, five days a week, 24 hours a day and employs 250 people from the community. (The bases are built in Matane, about 300 kilometers away.) The finished blades are stacked in racks in the yard, and depending on the light, look either like narwhal tusks or nuclear warheads. It takes a truck with a split trailer to transport two blades at a time with two cars in front and one car in the back to handle the operation. Prior to that it also takes thousands of sheets of sandpaper to put the final touches on the fibreglass finish – not to mention hand tools, sheers, goggles, gloves, drills, grinders, and sanders.

The outcome of serendipity combined with entrepreneurial spirit is that today Egide Dupuis et fils essentially operates a store within the LM plant, with two employees restocking the facility three times a day as the shifts change. As Wayne says, it sounds so simple: every day the plant does the same thing—a mould gets sprayed with gel coat that hardens, fibreglass is applied and resin is vacuumed into the mould. The two pieces are stuck together. And at the end of the day the plant has produced another blade for another wind turbine that will get transported somewhere around the world. But the reality is much more complicated. Every day something goes wrong somewhere because there's so much equipment involved. Because he knows his client's product and needs and knows his community, whatever the problem, Wayne knows a supplier somewhere in the region he can phone to come up with a solution to the problem, which means an LM engineer does not have to do it.

With people and products, experience and expertise all in place, it's no wonder that Egide Dupuis et Fils Home Hardware has the wind at its back as it faces the future.

Jim Tremblay:

Today Jim claims to be the happiest man in the world. His wife says "I can't believe that at your age you go into work every day with a smile."

Buckingham Hardware
Gatineau, QC

If you are looking for the familiar Home Hardware store in Gatineau, formerly Buckingham, Quebec, you won't find it. Jim Tremblay's store has none of the bold signage that so quickly identifies the local Home Hardware in the small towns we have been visiting across the country. We pull into the parking lot where the original hardware store owned by his father stood, and walk into the building that again bears none of the conventional banners, posters and other Home Hardware insignia. Jim says the town by-laws can be stringent. I don't ask the reason for the absence of same inside. Nevertheless, a large display of Beauti-Tone paint stands at the front entrance and I sit on a Home Hardware pail during our interview. His employee and friend, 74 year-old Hilary Lawlis, throws in the occasional aside, as only someone who has lived in town all his life and worked at the store for the past 30 years would be in a position to do.

Despite Jim Tremblay's reputation as a strong-willed individual who walks his own path, the store has been part of the Home Hardware family since the beginning - Jim's father Horace was a Charter Member. Wes Garvin established the relationship in the days when he came calling on behalf of Walter Woods. After the "other Walter" hired him, the two of them set their sights on the Ottawa Valley, of which Gatineau (Buckingham) is an honorary geographic member. "We didn't have a clue who Walter Hachborn was," Jim states with characteristic bluntness. "Walter is not a big man and he doesn't have a big voice. My father had his doubts, but my mother said, 'If it's good enough for Wes, it's good enough for me.'"

Over the years, Jim has refined his reputation as a straight shooter. When a local reporter asked for his thoughts on the Big Box Rona being built down the road, he said, "I think it's great. It keeps the customers here." As far as he is concerned, he will win customers from them once they open. "We've got it all here," he points out, gesturing to the crowded aisles. "And people know it."

Today, Jim claims to be the happiest man in the world. He and his wife Huguette have three adult children - their older son has a successful business in Ottawa, their daughter has a Master's Degree in Psychology and an MBA and their youngest has an MBA from Queens. Jim cheered on his son-in-law, who still calls him Mr. Tremblay, when he attended Harvard Business School. To date there are four grandchildren but no succession plans in the offing.

It seems unlikely that someone as strong willed and outspoken as Jim Tremblay would be a politician. But that is precisely what he was for two years over two decades ago when he ran "on a whim" against someone who made the mistake of annoying him.

Jim lives on the west side of the Ottawa River, just a half mile from his Gatineau store on the east side. But in those days it took him 15 minutes to get to work every morning, thanks to a perpetually red stoplight. Knowing lights can be programmed, Jim paid a visit to the Mayor to make that suggestion. He was in turn directed to the Police Commissioner and a local Alderman. Less than happy with their response, he returned to the Mayor who invited him to attend the next Council meeting. Jim rattled the alderman so much he told him that if Jim didn't like the way the town was being run that he should run himself in the next election. Jim did just that, beating his nemesis handily. While that was fun, he admits that the reality of politics wasn't. The soul of discretion, although his facial expressions speak louder than words, Jim only says only: "It was a rowdy, rowdy two years."

Jim got his first taste of politics as a young man in his early twenties. After school, he elected to not join the family hardware business and spent a year in Sudbury before making his way to Quebec City. There he spent four years as a chauffeur to members of Premier Daniel Johnson's inner circle and cabinet. According to Jim, René Levesque got about two hours sleep a night. "I couldn't believe the rhythm at which he went. And I knew him well, because all these guys, especially the smartest people in politics, are all friends, no matter what party they are in." Although the temptation to pry is irresistible, all Jim will say is: "They were charismatic and intelligent. People don't understand that these guys have private lives too."

According to Jim, Walter Hachborn possesses the same charisma and vision as some of the great politicians of our time. He just chose to expend them differently. Forty years ago, when he came back home after four years in Quebec City, Jim spent a month in the St. Jacobs warehouse learning that end of the business. Walter would sometimes take him home for lunch. Years later, whenever he saw the Tremblays at the markets, Walter still remembered all their family details. "That's the kind of guy he is – we're all lucky to have had him there all the way."

Jean-Marc Perron has six kids of his own, and five grandchildren, which could be why his community involvement is so kid-centric. He bought the business in the early 1990s from the Brodeur family who owned it for three generations and more than 80 years. Jean-Marc is the first hardware owner in his family, but is looking to the future with four of his five sons already in the business. His daughter, who is a schoolteacher, works in the store on weekends. Taking the advice of friends who had already made the switch, Jean-Marc joined the Home Hardware family in 2006. In February 2011, they more than doubled their surface area to 8,000 square feet when they moved into a new store. Jean-Marc is very happy to have achieved a significant increase in his retail customer base in the short time they have been in the newly expanded store.

It's Remembrance Day, a beautiful autumn day. The sun is streaming through the windows of Assomption Primary School, in the downtown core of Granby, a small city on the south shore of the St Lawrence River not far from Montreal. I am sitting very close to the ground in a tiny colourful chair in a schoolroom that smells like an old lunch bag, waiting for the recess bell to ring. The moment it does, a loud tangle of youngsters bursts into the classroom and Greg, our photographer, discovers that the language of excited children is universal even when you speak English and they are chattering at you in French. But he knows it's the fancy camera

Jean-Marc Perron: The objective of the event was simple: to save lives by ensuring that every home is equipped with functioning smoke alarms.

Quincaillerie Nouvelle France
Granby, QC

that catches their eye and the excitement of being chosen for the photograph that has them all wound up. Jean-Marc Perron, who owns the Granby Home Hardware store, Quincaillerie Nouvelle France, Patrick Normandin, Granby's Fire Prevention officer, Claude Bissonnette, Home's local Area Manager plus a handful of teachers and the principal of Assomption Primary School, Jean Luc Petre, all provide simultaneous translation.

We are here because of an innovative project that came together quickly and opportunistically thanks to the creative thinking of Home Hardware Dealer Jean-Marc and the local Granby fire department. Jean-Marc has always been active in his community, since he bought the local hardware store from the Brodeur family in the early 1990s. So when the Granby fire department approached him in late September 2011 about sponsoring an event for Fire Prevention week, he jumped on board immediately. The objective of the event was simple: to save lives by ensuring that every home is equipped with functioning smoke alarms. A promotion of this type typically involves handing out free batteries and smoke detectors but Jean-Marc's idea went one important step further toward encouraging compliance: the kids had to get their parents to sign a contract promising to install the batteries into the smoke detectors. Each child also submitted a drawing for a contest with prizes donated by the firefighters.

Because there was not much time to put it all together this first year, Jean-Marc and the fire department decided to work with only one school. Jean-Marc also used the Fall Market in St. Jacobs to enlist the aid and clout of Home Hardware corporate. One of Home's vendors got involved, Jean-Marc contributed the rest and the promotion kicked into high gear in time for Fire Prevention Week, October 9 – 15. It was such a success that the tentative plan is to roll it out across the entire Granby school board for 2012. Which will mean 4,000 students across the city taking the program into their homes. This is an idea with "legs" and Jean-Marc believes it has potential to go far beyond his local fire department and hometown of Granby. It's not about promoting his business, Jean-Marc says, it's about saving lives.

Jean-Marc sponsored another great project for kids: in the winter of 2011, a young mother of three approached him with a great idea. The plan was to introduce 100 youngsters, aged 3 to 5 and evenly split between boys and girls, to different sports in 45-minute increments on Saturday mornings over the course of the summer. Jean-Marc liked the idea. They made an arrangement with a local school to use the gym on rainy days. The project was called The Home Hardware Rookie Camp and featured fifteen different sports. Each child received a t-shirt that they got to keep at the end of the season. The colourful shirts had the Rookie logo on the front and the Home Hardware logo with a number on the back. Each t-shirt is unique and over the years they have become the symbol of this activity. Eighty children signed up the first year, 150 signed up for the second year and more than 225 children have already signed up for next summer. Jean-Marc and the young mother, Geneviève Rheault, have signed a three-year deal.

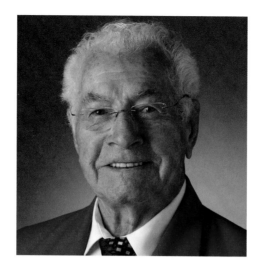

Maurice and Pierre Lane:

Les Entreprises Nova
Rawdon, QC

Maurice Lane was 79 years young in 2011. He had been in the hardware business in Rawdon, Quebec since 1956. In this small town an hour and a half northeast of Montreal, the Home Hardware Dealer is an important resource. When you are at the store seven days a week, you earn a reputation. When your family has been part of a community since the late 1700s, and you own the largest hardware store in the area, you have a responsibility. People expect you to have the answers. If they need a new faucet, they want to know which one they should buy, and if they have problems they want advice, an opinion, expertise. If they're looking for a good carpenter, they call. If they're stuck, they call you for help.

In a small building on the corner of what is today the parking lot of the Lane family's Home Hardware Building Centre, Maurice slowly and skilfully built up his business, on the ground floor manufacturing windows and doors and on the second floor, building the hardware business. For 27 of those years he and four partners operated as a Rona. Then in 2002, Maurice bought out his partners and joined forces with his son Pierre. The same year, they switched banners and opened an HHBC as a member of the Home Hardware family. It had become a true family business involving Maurice, Pierre, his wife Johanne and their son Marco who completed his Master's degree at the prestigious HEC in Montreal.

The switch to Home Hardware precipitated extensive renovations within the structure of the existing building and in 2007 major renovations were undertaken. As part of the planning process, one evening Pierre drove through town with an engineer to show him the different architectural features that he liked. The next morning, the courier delivered a proposed plan. Originally, the 19,000 square foot commercial space was divided between two floors with nine-foot ceilings. The renovations reduced the space by 5,000 square feet, but increased the height to 20 feet in one area of the store. They added a ramp that divided the building in two, 7,000 square feet upstairs and 5,000 downstairs. One of Pierre's brothers-in-law with a background in civil engineering helped them to plan and design a decent-sized parking lot, made possible by the structural changes to the building. All of these upgrades increased their business significantly.

Life was good. Business was even better. Then, one September night in 2010, they were driving back from the Fall Home Hardware Show in St.

Jacobs when they got a call. Their store had burned to the ground. You learn who your true friends are when your business goes up in flames at four in the morning. Thanks to Home Hardware and PIB, they were fully insured. Pierre's son Marco, who had gone back to school fulltime on September 15 returned to the store September 16 to help get the business back up and running as quickly as possible. It took eight months. Every employee (some have worked there 30 years) returned when the new and improved store reopened in the early summer of 2011.

Out of adversity good things often come. In the case of the Lane family, the fire allowed them to build the store of their dreams, truly the store of Pierre's dreams: "I could see it in my head. I just hadn't put it on paper." Under the direction of the experts, construction proceeded rapidly. From that point, Pierre says, everything lined up. The store has fabulous curb appeal, when come you around the corner and see it nestled in the hollow. Customers love the new and improved store, and even though it has the same amount of stock the new layout makes it seem like so much more. It's well merchandised and bright, and the walls are used to good advantage to showcase product in attractive vignettes. The aisles are wider. The drive-through lumberyard is fantastic and the shops and loading docks that link it to the main store are a hive of activity. The staffrooms and offices at the back of the store, largely designed and decorated by Johanne, are sleek, comfortable and modern. The systems are state of the art. And the well-equipped gym, designed by Marco, is a popular perk for their staff. These are the extra touches that make the difference in employee loyalty. Is it safe to say, I ask, that everything they wanted worked out perfectly? Pierre smiles. "I set the bar high," he acknowledges.

Down syndrome is the most common form of a chromosomal abnormality known as Trisomy, which has become an important cause for the Lane family. Their daughter Manu (Emmanuelle) has the condition. Every summer for over 20 years Maurice and the local division of the Quebec Police department organized a golf tournament to raise money for Trisomy research. They have also donated a significant amount of money to a special facility in a nearby town that trains young people with disabilities, allowing them to find jobs in their local communities. Manu's cousin Vincent, who also has Down syndrome, is a graduate of the school's program and works at the local grocery store.

Maurice Lane passed away October 18, 2013.

Pierre and Johanne and their two sons Marco and Benjamin (on the treadmill), and their daughter Manu (Emmanuelle) in the store's state of the art gym.

259

A Passion for Retail

Alain grew up in the business: his father had a food distribution company. And when he graduated from university, all Alain wanted was his own retail operation. His father warned him that buying a business, running it, making a living weren't necessarily going to be that simple. But Alain knew what he wanted and when a share in a small hardware store not far from their current location became available, he asked his father for help getting started. It was 1995. Back then, business wasn't exactly booming. He remembers telling his dad that they were going to go far. A year into the new business venture, his partner decided that he wanted out. Again he went to his father for help buying his shares. His dad said, "If you believe in it, I'm in." Then Alain met Renée who was working in the insurance industry, but whose family background was retail. He asked her to share his life, to go into business together. They both knew it would be hard work, but if they combined their strengths they could make something together. Renée said "yes", and here they are, with a growing and successful business. Renée remembers her family's store with great affection: "We sold everything, furniture, hardware, electronics. My father had a workshop where he could repair everything. My father was a genius, but he was not a businessman. In my case, it's probably the opposite." Renée certainly has a genius for retail. After her father passed away, Alain and Renée faced the challenge of running and building a successful business together. "Dad is looking over our shoulder, and I want to show him what we've done. We often talk about him; we think that if he were still here, he'd drop in to see what we've been up to. It's a challenge, a personal challenge to succeed. "

Alain Brochet and Renée Bellavance:

There are things you only see when you look into someone's eyes, character and kindness that people don't necessarily broadcast about themselves.

Quincallerie Home Hardware
Rimouski, QC

I left a bit of my heart in Rimouski. Many of the reasons Alain Brochet and Renée Bellavance's Quincallerie Home Hardware in Rimouski, Quebec won the Walter J. Hachborn award in 2008 are in evidence the day we arrive to take photographs and do interviews for this book. I had done my homework, read the background literature that told their histories, how and why they got into the business. I read about the dedication to their customers, employees and community, the three pillars of their business. The store is immaculate and invites you in, each department well designed, appealingly merchandised, attractive product asking to be taken home. The staff is discreet but ever present. This store obviously has all the right stuff, not only as a business but also within the community at large.

Then there are the things you only see when you look into someone's eyes, the character and kindness that people don't necessarily broadcast about themselves. But it's actually evident all around them in the way they choose to live their lives.

As we head downstairs to the meeting room, a tall young man with an open, happy face flashes us a huge smile. His name is Jean François and when we get to the boardroom, Renée tells us his story: Jean François was a "shaken baby" who came to them when he was just 12 years old. He has always lived in a foster home, not able to care for himself, and over time, his condition has deteriorated. He has become a big help around the store and like many developmentally challenged people does not like change. If he sees someone moving product on a shelf, he'll say, "I'm not sure you should be doing that - Renée may not like it! " As she says, " I protect him, he protects my property." Initially, Renée was unsure that she had the skills to manage Jean François, but his caseworker says that she has played a major role in his life. And it's easy to see that he adores and trusts her absolutely. Sometimes he has mood swings, sometimes he's impetuous and says, "I'm going to quit," but Renée always convinces him to stay. She says, "I don't want him to leave. I wouldn't want him to be exploited… As long as he's here, he's protected. He's part of the family. "

Alain and Renée are involved in a significant number of community events. But the organization closest to their hearts is the Marie Elisabeth Palliative Care Home not far from their store. A few years ago, Alain's grandmother passed away after a long and difficult illness. She died in

hospital which troubled both Alain and Renée so much that they decided to do something to ensure that other terminally ill people in their community could pass the remainder of their days in comfort and with dignity, their families by their sides. The Maison Marie Elisabeth was still very much in the planning process when they got involved and Renée was invited to sit on the organization's Board of Directors. The building was completed in 2009 and while the government provides 50% of the operating costs, the remaining 50% must be raised. That all this has come to pass and the Maison continues to thrive is in many ways thanks to the ongoing efforts of Alain and Renée, who not only oversee ongoing activities at the Maison due to Renée's position on the Board, but also make an ongoing contribution with their own active fundraising initiatives through their business.

The moment we walked into the Maison, I understood instantly what Renée meant about its pervasive peace and tranquility. As she says, it's hard to feel sad in this special place. Intellectually we all understand the inevitability of death. It takes a certain form of bravery to confront it on its terms by providing a way to help others go gently into that good night.

The seven rooms were full but the building was quiet. Peaceful in fact. Everyone smiled at everyone else. A moulding at waist level ran along the walls of the hallways of the Maison. Embedded in this moulding were plaques with the names of people who had donated to the upkeep of this tranquil hospice. I was looking at the names and thinking of my parents and despite my resolve, a little bubble of grief surfaced. On my circuit around the building, I ran into Sebastien Deland, the Quebec Area Manager who made our travels in the area so easy and productive. He has had his own brush with mortality and was also affected by the mood of the place. Almost without words, the decision was made – we wanted to be part of this place and so together, we donated a plaque, our initials and the initials of Home Hardware Stores Limited serving as a semi anonymous memento of a few hours spent here in a special place with some very special people.

Paul-Henri Aspirault and Suzette Tapp:

"I feel like I've come home with Home Hardware. I'm part of a large family, supported by a real family."

Antonin Aspirault Inc,
Rivière-au-Renard, Gaspé, QC

Very often the history of a region can be found buried in the story of a local business. The Home Hardware store in Rivière-au-Renard owned by Paul-Henri Aspirault and his wife Suzette Tapp is one such tale.

When we met on a blustery October day, I learned from Suzette and Paul Henri that the original store opened in the late 1800s. According to Suzette, it was originally a Hyman store. I had no idea what that meant, other than that " Hyman " sounded like a good Jewish name to me, and therefore a bit out of place in what I assumed was predominantly Francophone Gaspé. But when I started to dig, I quickly realized how much I didn't know about the region. In a journey eerily similar to my own forbears a century later, William Hyman's parents fled religious persecution in Russia in the early 1800s and died in Poland. Their son made it to England where he worked for a jeweler who, in 1840, sent him to New York. Three years later William was in the Gaspé working in the cod fishery, a complicated, lopsided system of credit and indenture prevalent in the Atlantic for generations. The majority of the fishermen in the region were from the Jersey Islands, which accounts for the still-remaining pockets of English in the region and the appearance of old English names, such as Tapp, in families where the language has long since disappeared. Unlike many of the Jersey-based companies that typically stationed agents in the Gaspé, William managed his business in person, eventually turning over responsibility to his son Elias and renaming the business William Hyman and Sons. William parlayed his business success into a local political career as well, becoming the first Jew in Canada to hold the position of local reeve. He also became a member of the county council, a justice of the peace and a militia captain. At the time of his death in Montreal in 1882, William left to his heirs a dock, storehouses, a warehouse, a hotel, several properties and mortgages as well as six fishing establishments, including the one in Rivière-au-Renard. The business flourished but in 1967, William's grandson Percy declared bankruptcy. The trustees bought all the stores in the Gaspésie and sold them at a reasonable price to the store managers.

By then, Paul-Henri's father Antonin was managing the Hyman store in Rivière-au-Renard, which he then bought and operated for the next 18 years. In 1986 he sold to Paul-Henri and Suzette who already worked in the store. They joined Home Hardware in 2009. "I feel like I've come home with Home Hardware. I'm part of a large family, supported by a real family," Paul-Henri says. It's a small store, with approximately 5,000 square feet of retail space and only five employees, including their son Dominic who will eventually take over the business from them as they did from Antonin. Their customer base comes from the town and surrounding area. With three hardware stores competing for the business, it is their service that makes them stand out. They are open rain or shine, even snow or fog, of which there's a lot (the night before we had flown in from Quebec City and it was touch and go whether our plane could land or would have to continue on to Ile St Madeleine). The warehouse next door and the basement are full of product that arrives every Monday afternoon on the Home Hardware truck.

The life blood of the community is still the fishery although these days it's shrimp, not cod. Rivière-au-Renard has the two largest shrimp plants in Québec. Unlike some regions, the local shrimp boats don't double as on-site processing plants but head up the estuary to the open sea then return with their catches to be processed at the plants in town. Rivière-au-Renard has the two largest shrimp plants in Quebec, each one processing 14 million pounds of shrimp annually. "We're proud of our fleet," says Paul-Henri. "They're beautiful boats."

Behind the store, hundreds of boats worth millions of dollars have been hauled up, cleaned and repainted, and have fallen into a deep winter sleep, dreaming of their return to the sea in a few short months. It's a seasonal business, a seasonal life, with unemployment a reality for some over the winter. But it's a strong and old community that has survived this way for centuries. "That's the pace here," Paul-Henri agrees. "And for sure, it's an old pace, very historic, very traditional."

Anick and Benoit Rousseau stand before the rushing waters of the Mistassibi River that roars down past the town of Dolbeau-Mistassini. A Trappist Monastery nestles into the woods on the far side of the river. At this time of the year the kayakers and rafters have all gone home but it is easy to see why the spectacular waters and savage beauty of the landscape are so popular with tourists.

There's a saying here in the town of Dolbeau-Mistassini in the heart of the Lac Saint Jean region: the town's population may be 14,000 but 15,000 people know Benoit Rousseau. Which isn't surprising. Benoit Rousseau owns the four largest building centres in the region and has clearly long been a force in the community at large. The Rousseau family started as innkeepers, and Benoit still owns the hotel in town, where we had lunch the day we visited. People dropped by to greet him and he nodded at other

Benoît and Anick Rousseau:

Rénomax
Dolbeau-Mistassini, Lac-St-Jean, QC

"If you don't develop the brand, people start leaving and you don't move forward. And if you don't move forward, you move backward."

tables nearby. Benoit is obviously a mover and shaker and has been very involved in the municipality. From the establishment of the Caisse Populaire to the building of the local arena, hospital and seniors complex, he has played a role in them all. Although he has never served as mayor, he was a town councillor in the 1990s and was especially instrumental in the 1997 voluntary amalgamation of the two cities of Mistassini and Dolbeau at the spectacular confluence of three rivers, the Mistassibi, Mistassini and Rivière aux Rats. Today Dolbeau-Mistassini is the commercial hub of Lac Saint-Jean and a popular destination for white water enthusiasts.

In 1972, Benoit opened his first hardware store in Mistassini, which underwent a major expansion to its current size in 1987. At the time it was one of the largest hardware stores in Quebec. Two years later, he bought a small hardware store in Dolbeau, which expanded in 1998 and was renamed Rénomax. In 2002 Benoit struck again, buying a third store in nearby Saint-Felicien and a fourth in Roberval the following year. Three of his five children are involved in his various businesses. His daughter Anick, and her husband, Frédéric Mas, both engineers, run the hardware and building supply division of the family enterprise, Anick as general manager, Frédéric as manager of Rénomax Roberval.

In 2005, the banner under which they had been operating was sold and the Rousseaus had to make an important decision. As Anick points out, "If you don't develop the brand, people start leaving and you don't move forward. And if you don't move forward, you move backward." So in 2008, they joined Home Hardware and during our first visit in July were celebrating their successful land purchase that will allow them to expand the Roberval store. "Backward" is clearly not a word the Rousseau family understands.

Lac Saint Jean is the blueberry capital of Quebec and with global warming, these days is even threatening Maine's "world's largest" claim. On my first visit to the region in July, I was too early for blueberries and when we returned in October, we were too late, especially for the coveted chocolate-dipped variety that are always quickly snapped up by aficionados. But we did pass many fields of vivid red slashed with horizontal lines of variegated colour, the visual extravaganza that the blueberry fields become after the fruit has been picked and the leaves are bitten by the first of the region's hard frosts.

Luc and David Grenon:

Centre de rénovation FDS
Saguenay-Jonquière, QC

Centre de rénovation FDS in the Lac St Jean region of Quebec, owned by brothers Luc and David Grenon, may be a relative newcomer to the Home Hardware family, but it has long been established in the community. Their father Yvan started the business in 1948 and the two sons bought out their father in 1982. Not fans of major change, they were with one banner for 21 years, so the decision to join Home Hardware in November 2010 was not taken lightly. During those years, the business experienced major growth and expansion and in order to continue to grow, the brothers needed to differentiate themselves from their competition. They wanted a banner that could offer them a wide range of many different products, a banner well stocked in hardware: Building materials are pretty much the same everywhere, but "Home Hardware has proven to us that it is by far the best hardware chain," David says. "I expect a banner to oversee marketing activities, produce flyers and provide national brand recognition, without me needing to do any of this locally. And that's what we got when we decided to go with Home Hardware. Home Hardware is a popular brand: everyone was familiar with the banner, even though we were the first HHBC store to open in the area."

Community involvement is part of everyday life for local businesses like Luc and David's FDS hardware store. But the Saguenay flood in July 1996, when the Lac St Jean region experienced the worst flooding in the province's history, was social commitment and involvement taken to an extreme. Scientists say such a natural disaster is likely to occur once every 10,000 years. Floodwaters swept away a shopping centre, destroyed homes and buried cars in mud. Two young boys died when a cliff gave way and landslides wreaked havoc. For David, getting to work, normally a ten-minute trip, could take over an hour due to all the blocked roads. Their store was heavily involved in the emergency relief program that helped the community get back on its feet. The iconic photograph of a house lodged in the river, symbolized the tenacity of the local residents many of whom were without water, electricity or telephone service.

There is a no-nonsense aura about David, the younger of the two Grenon brothers so I was not surprised to learn that boxing is his favourite sport. He is a trainer at the club in Chicoutimi and his son Patrick, who won the Silver Gloves in the 2011 Quebec Championship Games (he missed the Golden Gloves by one point), is one of his athletes. Their club hosted the Quebec Championship Golden Gloves competition in 2012.

Shawville is an old Irish Protestant pocket on the Quebec side of the Ottawa River. In 1857, the government handed out parcels of land to immigrants, keeping the different religions and ethnic groups separated. Over 150 years later, English and French seem to co-exist peacefully in this lovely farm region that rolls alongside the Ottawa River. Mickey (Milton) Hodgins, the current patriarch of the local Home Hardware store says, "I can count in French. I can tell the time in French. And I can sell in French."

give them a chit, which they would then exchange for flour, sugar and other goods they sold at the store. He says he wasn't very smart—and looks at me, his eyes twinkling, for a reaction - and one day his father handed him the keys to the truck and told him to deliver a one hundred pound bag of flour to Mrs. Tippins. That was the start. Mickey left school, and stayed on to look after the hardware business for his dad. He's been pretty busy ever since.

The Hodgins Family: One has the sense that the Hodgins imprint on the town that has lasted for generations will continue.

W.A. Hodgins Store
Shawville, QC

And selling is what the Hodgins family has been doing for six generations since 1857. Mickey and his daughter Anne Forbes each has their own version of the family history. Anne's is more romantic, if less accurate: Her great great grandfather Edward Hodgins left Tipperary, Ireland, landed in Canada and sailed up the Ottawa River with a load of timber that he then carted overland to Shawville to build the general store that started the business where we are standing today. Mickey thinks the business began in Ladysmith then migrated to Shawville a few years later. Whichever story is true, Edward Hodgins was never a farmer in this lovely farm country. He was always a shopkeeper. He opened his first general store, wherever it was, in 1857. His sons, grandsons and great granddaughters and grandsons and their sons have been shopkeepers ever since.

There are vestiges of the old days in the layout, look and feel of the place, the oldest building in town, although virtually all traces of the original exterior have been lost behind tin siding. Inside, however, the comfortable clutter and amazing array of goods, the easy come and easy go of customers with the light hearted badinage that speaks to years of familiarity, and the fact that the cash register is at the back of the store, all point to old time values that never disappeared. "Someone told me that a messy store does better than a neat and tidy one," Mickey says from a comfortable chair at the back of the store. He appears to have taken it to heart: the place is certainly a bit of a jumble, but Mickey brushes it off. "We don't keep our place very clean, we should renovate, but we haven't the time - we're too busy." We have arrived just hours after the weekly Home Hardware delivery and there are boxes in every aisle adding to the mayhem.

Mickey Hodgins started working part-time in the business, by then owned and operated by his father Edgar and his uncle Art, in the early 1940s while he was still a schoolboy. He'd grade the eggs brought in by farmers, and

In 1951 Mickey got married. In 1956 he became a partner. His dad died in 1964 and two years later, Mickey and his uncle joined the Home Hardware family. "It was the right thing to do," he says. Over the years, Mickey also became one of the town's major property owners and in the early 1960s developed a subdivision, selling lots and building two bungalows a year. His sister still lives in one of them. So it's easy to see why he has been "a bit too busy to do other stuff." He feels with all humility that his main contribution to the town of Shawville has been in helping to develop it.

One has the sense that the Hodgins imprint on the town that has lasted for generations will continue: Mickey and his wife Doris had four daughters and a son. A lot of them are in the business today, including his daughter Anne, who came on board right after school — "She was there when we really needed her," Mickey says gratefully — his son Ronnie who took over the business officially in 1990, and Ronnie's son Shawn who just recently came back fulltime. In addition, there are sons-in-law and other grandchildren working at the store. Around the well-maintained town, many of the beautiful old brick homes were built with materials from his mother's family's brick business. There is a mural on the wall across the road from the store, whose corporate name is W.A. Hodgins Store. The mural, painted from an old photograph of Mickey's, shows the main street of Shawville circa 1914. There's a young man on a bicycle heading up the street. It looks like a lovely, tranquil summer day, much like the one we are enjoying today. That young man is Mickey's grandfather, W.A. Hodgins.

Sophie Denis and Philippe Moisan: Sophie believes that women are good for the business.

Jean Denis Limitée
St-Raymond, QC

St-Raymond is situated in beautiful and historic countryside less than an hour northwest of Quebec City. Many people in town commute to the capital to work. Families have lived in the region for generations. The town prides itself on its heritage and architectural guidelines have restored the town's main street to the original vintage look that, like so many communities across the country, was blasted by the urban blight of the 1950s and 60s. There is an attractive quasi-Victorian feel to the façades that line rue Saint-Joseph, which includes the official "front" entrance of Jean Denis Limitée, the Home Hardware store named in honour of the current owner's great-grandfather. In 1928, he started the business on the corner just down the street and across the road. These days, of course, most customers come in through the "back" entrance of the current store that they moved into in 2005 with its spacious car park.

Today the fourth generation Denis to own the business is a vivacious, attractive, funny and articulate dynamo named Sophie Denis. She manages to be everywhere at once in this very busy store without ever messing a hair on her elegant head or flipping up a collar of her red Home Hardware jacket that she wears so stylishly. Her husband Philippe Moisan is co-owner. They officially bought out Sophie's father Jean-Guy in 2000 and over the years have divided the responsibilities of the business between them.

Sophie broke with family tradition when she joined the business in 1995. Until then, each subsequent Denis generation had produced one son who had in turn taken over the family business. But after studying management, an eight-year career in banking and a return to school to study business, it was Sophie who joined the business (Sophie's brother works for the Canadian Coast Guard). She always wanted to be a business woman but was concerned that no one would take her seriously: "If my father had owned a jewellery store it would have been easy; a hardware store was a different matter." In fact, Sophie believes that women are good for the business. For example, these days a hardware store doesn't just sell paint—it sells design, colour, fabric, wallpaper and accessories. So having more women in the business to understand a female perspective supports this trend in hardware.

Philippe came on board in 2000. Prior to that, he had been a farmer and he and Sophie and their children Augustine and Felixe-Antoine still live near the farm. That same year, the company switched banners and joined Home Hardware, a difficult decision that her father and husband immediately supported. In typical fashion, Sophie played devil's advocate, wondering who in St-Raymond would be able to pronounce " Home Hardware"? To compound the situation, one of her uncles is an ardent Quebec nationalist and she was afraid he would never darken their door again when they became a member of Canada's largest hardware retailer. But Sophie's dad took him aside : "Yvon," he said, "you've lived here all your life. Have you never gone to a Canadian Tire or McDonald's?" Yvon couldn't argue with the logic. Now, of course, Sophie and Philippe are committed, passionate members of the Home Hardware family.

After the changeover, with all the product selection that was available through Home Hardware, it became a challenge to fit everything into the original 4,000 square foot store. So after 78 years in the same location, the store was moved across the street. When we visited in the fall of 2011, it was still the same 10,000 square feet they had acquired in 2005 but there were expansion rumours in the air. One of their 18 employees has been with the company for 30 years, four for more than ten years. And while Sophie's mother Louise can occasionally still be found on the cash along with Sophie's young daughter Augustine, these days, after 53 years in the business, Jean Guy goes fishing a lot in the summer and is a currently taking saxophone lessons.

Community service is central to the values of this family business. Sophie has always done a great deal of volunteer work through the church which is an important part of her life. At the time of our visit, the store was still closed on Sundays ("All our customers are at mass," Sophie points out), but they are not sure how long that will last. Sophie is also president of the downtown commercial development association and is involved with the region of Portneuf's health services. Philippe has been a member of the Optimist Club since 1993 and is a director of the local Chamber of Commerce. All of this is on top of the 50 hour weeks they each put in at the store.

In 2011, Sophie starred in one of the commercials in Home Hardware's national television campaign. "I am proud that Home Hardware chose me, a business woman who they believe in and trust to represent the company nationally on TV. There's a very special connection between Home Hardware and us: it's as if they adopted us from the get-go. I feel a bit like the teacher's pet!"

Three generations gather atop Mont Laura for a family photograph. Jean-Guy and Louise, their daughter Sophie Denis and her husband Philippe Moisan and their two children Augustine and Felixe-Antoine. There is no pressure on the next generation to make a commitment to join the business at the appropriate time. But Felixe often says, " Do you think we'll ever walk into this store and not own it ? "

Evaline Julien-Denis

Jean Denis' son Armand took over the business in the 1940s. For years his wife Evaline Julien-Denis worked in the store and raised her family in the apartment upstairs in the original building on rue Saint-Joseph. When her husband died, Jean-Guy, her only son of four children, continued the tradition and joined her in the business. Already in her 90s by the time the store moved to its current location, Evaline was nevertheless part of the overall event and once a year, took a tour in her wheelchair. She always kept an eye on the business from the seniors' residence where she lived next door.

When we visited in November 2011, Evaline was 102 years, six months and five days old. She passed away in March 2012.

Brothers George and Alan Hogg were
photographed November 9, 2011 in
Westmount Park, another area landmark.
The beautiful 26 acre park was laid out
in 1912 in the spirit of Frederick Law
Olmsted, landscape architect for
Mont Royal Park (the mountain) and
New York City's Central Park.

George and Alan Hogg:

Quincaillerie Hogg
Westmount, QC

Westmount is one of the "grandes dames" of one of Canada's oldest and most interesting cities.

To have a proper understanding of Westmount, it helps to think of it as a metaphorical island surrounded by the City of Montreal on the island of the same name. Known as much for it mansions on the hill as for its Anglo heart, Westmount is one of the "grandes dames" of one of Canada's oldest and most interesting cities. Nevertheless, there's still a small town feel to Westmount's "downtown" that runs four short blocks along picturesque Sherbrooke Street between Grosvenor and Claremont Avenues. Since the early 1990s, Hogg Hardware has been the neighbourhood hardware store, a familiar landmark on the north side of the street. In 2010, owners and brothers George and Alan Hogg made two key decisions: to swap locations with the SAQ (liquor store) and to join Home Hardware. The move involved several months of extensive renovations that meant temporary digs several blocks further west beyond the borders of Westmount. They are now permanently ensconced as Hogg Home Hardware on the corner of Victoria and Sherbrooke, all of five doors from their original location.

The Hogg family traces its Montreal and Westmount roots to the early 1800s. In 1901, George Hogg, the great grandfather of George and Alan, bought Guaranteed Pure Milk Dairy, followed a few years later by Purity Ice Cream. George was also mayor of Westmount in the 1940s. The Hogg family sold the dairy in the late 1980s and the three brothers, George, David and Alan, went into the hardware business, opening in the location that had previously been occupied by an earlier Montreal institution, Pascal's Hardware. It was a natural decision to continue in the vein of a traditional old style hardware store, perfect for the challenges, needs and limitations of an urban location. And perfect, in fact, for the unique demographics of Westmount, the city within a city. In the early 2000s, they opened a second store on Nun's Island, another distinctive community, and an actual island at the foot of the island of Montreal. It too has a unique style and flavour, one that is diametrically opposite to Westmount. The Hogg business is a tale of two cities really - the differences instantly illustrated in what sells where. The Nun's Island store serves a semi-suburban community of new build homes, and seasonal sales of furnace filters are brisk. Not so in traditional Westmount where its older dwellings are still largely heated by hot water radiators. In the Westmount store, it's silver polish sales that shine, for all those special occasions that call for the family silver.

LA FÉDÉRATION DES COOPÉRATIVES DU NOUVEAU-QUÉBEC

The Quebec arctic is a massive expanse of land that encompasses the James Bay and Ungava Bay regions. It was there that a group of 14 remote communities, some with a mere 150 people, established a cooperative organization very similar to the one we all know and love. In this story, Peter Murdoch, who worked for the Canadian Polar Commission in the 1960s, was Walter Hachborn's equivalent. He knew the languages of water: the FCNQ's Sea Lift operation is located just two minutes up the road from the warehouse. Twice a year, mid-June and mid-September, goods are loaded into 20-foot containers (there is no infrastructure to handle standard 40 foot containers in the far north) and trucked to Baie Ste Catharine on Montreal's south shore. From there, they are loaded onto a ship that sails down the St Lawrence, into the Labrador Sea and up into the Hudson Strait,

La Fédération des Cooperatives du Nouveau-Québec:

Baie d'Urfé, QC The founding and operating philosophy and structure of the FCNQ almost directly parallel those of Home Hardware, so the relationship makes perfect sense.

the Inuit and understood their communities and their needs. A very few of these remote communities had independent general stores, and several of the Inuit and Cree elders approached Peter about establishing a collective that would allow them more control and buying power. The result was La Fédération des Cooperatives du Nouveau-Québec, a non-profit, community-owned organization founded in 1967. In 2001 the FCNQ became a Home Hardware Dealer. Although they don't "fly the banner", Home Hardware is one of the co-op's several suppliers. The founding and operating philosophy and structure of the FCNQ almost directly parallel those of Home Hardware, so the relationship makes perfect sense.

Today the FCNQ is a completely independent, self-funded operation with a Board representing the participating communities. Its warehouse is in Baie d'Urfé, on the western tip of the island of Montreal. With 150 employees, the facility offers a turnkey operation to its owner-members in the far north whose stores range in size from 5,000 to 15,000 square feet. The services cover a spectrum: bookkeeping and accounting, petroleum distribution, cable TV, banking, postal and internet services (the primary form of communication), a travel agency, hotel and hunting/fishing camp management and serving as agents for the Inuit art that is a major source of income for the communities. When a store closes for the day, all the follow up and back up systems associated with running and managing a business are performed by the FCNQ from the administrative office hundreds of miles south. The warehouse behind the office is an amazing storehouse of household items: Guy Saurette, the Cooperative's senior buyer says, "If it's in your house, we sell it."

The difference is that these houses are in communities inaccessible by road. The FCNQ uses two methods of shipping. There is year round ground transportation to the end of the road two days away in La Grande, the northernmost point in Quebec. From there, the containers are loaded onto small planes - every community has a landing strip. The vans usually head out twice a week throughout the year. The other transportation method is by

dipping into Ungava Bay and then continuing along the Quebec coast of Hudson Bay and James Bay. The boat now takes ten days to get to its first stop. When it arrives in the individual communities, a crane drops a barge into the water and the designated containers are taken to shore. When Guy started working at the FCNQ, shipping stopped for the season in September. Now it continues into late October. If necessary, emergency supplies can be sent directly from Montreal's Pierre Elliot Trudeau airport in nearby Dorval.

The return trip brings a precious cargo of Inuit art, an important source of income to the Inuit. The works include beautiful stone and bone carvings, many of them depicting powerful mythological and cultural icons and themes, as well as works on paper and fabric. The Federation, functioning as an agent for these artists, sells the art to galleries internationally. Peter Murdoch's son Rick is Director of Sales and manages an art department of four people for this side of the business.

I asked Guy if there was a particular special order that stood out in his mind. "A fish tank," he answered after some thought. It's a pleasing thought to know that despite being so far from Home, even gold fish can find a home.

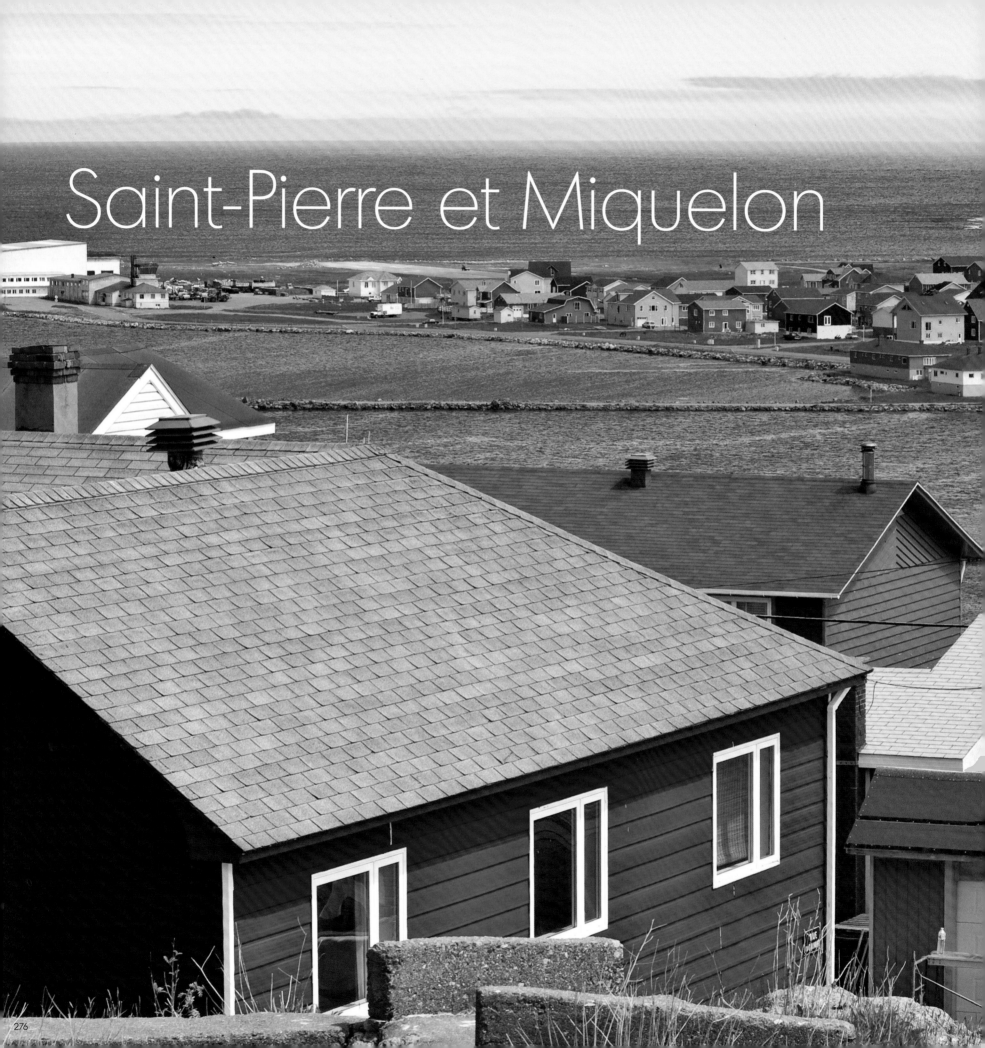

Saint-Pierre et Miquelon

Marcel Dagort has the distinction of owning, with his older brother Gustav Dagort, the one and only Home Hardware store in France. That would be France's 242 km² overseas territory a one hour ferry ride and just eight kilometers off the tip of Newfoundland's Burin Peninsula, known as Saint-Pierre et Miquelon. The sister islands of Saint-Pierre et Miquelon changed hands between the English and French 14 times before the Treaty of Paris in 1816 put an end to the tug of war and associated destruction,

1989, Marcel and his brother took over the business. Today Gustav's two daughters Delphine and Edith and Marcel's oldest daughter Emilie are also involved.

Although there are import taxes as well as freight to pay on product shipped to their store, because they are part of France, the Dagorts don't have to pay (or charge) HST or other Canadian taxes. Plus there's the

Marcel & Gustav Dagort:

Saint-Pierre et Miquelon, France

thereby rendering them the only piece of French property remaining in all of North America. In fact, eventually, the only piece of Europe on the continent.

The Dagort family has been in Saint-Pierre et Miquelon since 1792. Given the date Marcel suspects that the move from France had something to do with the revolution - 1792 was the year prior to the Reign of Terror and if you wanted to keep your head on your shoulders, it was probably a good idea to make yourself scarce from the motherland.

Although it's a pretty exotic history and an interesting geographic oddity (the islands' currency is the Euro, electricity is European voltage and you'll need your passport to set foot on land when you disembark from the ferry), the main industry on the sister islands is not tourism, it's the fishery. After the collapse of the cod fishery, the French government invested heavily in infrastructure - an airport and hospital were built and a diesel power plant is in the works. Today aqua culture, particularly scallops, is creating new jobs - think Coquille Saint Jacques: the "Royale of Miquelon."

You can take the islands out of France geographically, but you can't take France out of the islands, so Saint-Pierre et Miquelon are known for their gourmet food, typical French cuisine. In fact, the Dagort family owned a grocery store and a bakery until the late 1980s and was also involved in the shipping industry. But in 1998, they joined the Home Hardware family. From croissants to crow bars is quite a shift: the family built a commercial shopping centre in 1990 which housed the supermarket, the hardware store and boutiques until 2003 when they built a new space dedicated to a state of the art modern Home Hardware Building Centre.

Marcel loves the business and has been "behind the counter" since he was a child. It's a true family enterprise. After their father passed away in

exchange rate to consider. Island power runs on 220 volts 50 cycles, so they cannot buy any appliances or power tools from Canada. Some of Home Hardware's programs don't work for them and they have to develop their own advertising, but despite it all, the Dagorts are happy to be part of Home Hardware. "Home Hardware is a very good company," Marcel states, "and they work for the dealers, which is important." Home Hardware shipments come every week from Halifax and Marcel says that they have never missed the boat.

Tourists come mainly from Newfoundland. According to Marcel, no one else knows who, what and where they are. When he's at the market, he spends half his time trying to explain that Saint-Pierre is not in Quebec. Home to a huge colony of puffins, the islands are on the whale watching circuit as well. In addition to nature lovers, Saint-Pierre recently hosted the Canadiens old timers hockey game between former NHL players and the Saint-Pierre old-timers and senior hockey team. Mario Tremblay, Stephane Richer and Patrice Brisebois among others were on the ice. Afterwards, Tremblay, who is a commentator for the hockey broadcasts on Quebec television, gave highlights of the game and encouraged people to visit. According to Marcel, it was probably the best publicity the islands had ever received.

Something of Canada has obviously rubbed off, because Marcel complains about the weather, joking that on Saint-Pierre et Miquelon, summer starts August 1st and ends August 2nd. Winters can be tough, with lots of snow. The islands are also famous for their fog: a few years ago they broke a record for July with a grand total of 52 hours of sunshine that month. But Saint-Pierre et Miquelon are truly part of France, celebrating Bastille Day on July 14th and I am willing to bet that they have the best croissants in North America.

Corporate

STAFF AND SENIOR MANAGEMENT

Bill Tiffin: "Working with Walter was the greatest education I ever had – better than any university."

Retired: Advertising Manager
St. Jacobs, ON

Tucked comfortably into a corner of the cafeteria at the Fall 2012 Market, Bill Tiffin, Home Hardware's first Advertising Manager, settles in to tell me the story of his life. His tiny telltale giggle indicates a funny story is on its way. After more than 50 years as part of the extended Home Hardware family, Bill has more than a few of them.

In the 1950s, Bill was the south-western Ontario salesman for a Toronto housewares and giftware firm. One day he got a call from Harry May, Area Manager for Hollinger Hardware. Walter Hachborn wanted to talk to him. The following week Bill went to Chatham to meet Walter. "I was standing in the Chatham Hotel lobby looking for the President of Hollinger Hardware and he was standing there looking for the salesman and neither one of us knew what the other looked like. Finally we were the only two people standing." Although Bill wasn't in the market for another job, Walter's enthusiasm won him over. Next thing he knew, Bill was in St. Jacobs meeting Henry Sittler and Arthur Zilliax, the two other gentlemen at the heart of the concept about to become Home Hardware. Bill joined the company as a District Manager, in those days, he says, a fancy term for salesman. Four years later, Walter asked him if he'd like to get off the road and become Advertising Manager. To that point, Walter had managed the advertising himself, as he managed pretty much everything else. He worked with The Printery in St. Jacobs, to produce the small flyers that constituted their advertising campaign in those days. Shortly thereafter Bill and his family moved to St. Jacobs. "And that's how it all started," he says. One day Walter sent a gentleman named Al Fisher to Bill's office. Like all good salesmen, persistence was Al's middle name. He worked for RBW Graphics, a printing firm in Owen Sound, a few hours northeast of St. Jacobs. He had been calling on Walter for several years, looking to get the business. Al invited the new Advertising Manager to Owen Sound for a plant tour. Bill was impressed: "Their people were like our people, " he says. Bill produced Home Hardware's first catalogue by himself, cutting and pasting everything together. "I couldn't draw a tree," he snorts, "so I had a lot of help from RBW from thereon in." The first 100-page catalogue they produced as a team remains a career highlight for Bill.

Bill and Al Fisher worked together until Al retired in 1993. They still relive old times twice a year at the semi-annual Home Hardware markets, every one of which Bill has attended. When Bill retired in 1998 there were 11 people in the art department, 10 more than when he had started 38 years earlier. (And another 10 fewer than there are today. Instead of "sporadic" flyers, the art department now produces 32 National flyers for the Home Hardware banner, 14 for the LBM division, a minimum of 33 optional flyers and annual and Christmas catalogues.) John Penner, who took over the account in 1996, has handled every aspect of Home Hardware's print business and more for Transcontinental Printing, which bought RBW Graphics in April 1992. "It was a great thing dealing with them," Bill remembers. "You know, over the years I was Advertising Manager, a lot of people would say, why don't we get another printer, why do we keep using the same advertising agency? I figured maybe things would change after I retired. But, they're both still there – so I must have been right."

For the first ten years of his Home Hardware life, Bill accompanied Walter to district meetings, a central component of the company's organizational structure and expansion strategy at the time. They were all conducted outside regular working hours. "Walter would drive one way and I'd drive back," Bill remembers. "Usually at 3 o'clock in the morning."

The little laugh makes another appearance. "Now Walter does not appreciate cats," Bill says in his best raconteur's voice. "One night before a meeting, we were at the home of Area Manager Wes Cook. We were in the living room and there was the biggest cat I have ever seen sitting on a small round table. I thought, that darn cat is going to jump into Walter's lap - you could just see it in his eye. And sure enough, Walter was in mid sentence when the cat-and it was a BIG cat-landed right in his lap."

"Working with Walter was the greatest education I ever had – better than any university," Bill says. "Walter never asked anybody to do anything that he wouldn't do himself. He would always say, 'It's a great company, Bill. And you were there every step of the way.'"

Roy sums up the difference between working for
Walter and working for Paul: Walter would say,
"This is what we're doing." With Paul it was, "Let's
sit down and talk about it and come up with
ideas and then make a decision."

The Gilles family has a storied history with the local hardware store on the corner of King and Albert Streets that today is known as Home Hardware. The grandfather, Henry Gilles Sr. owned the original hardware store on that site. Gilles Hall in the Sittler Building is named in his memory. Roy Gilles, known affectionately as Gus, is a true St. Jacobite. He grew up in town and has known Ray Gabel since he was six or seven years old, which is quite some time ago now.

He would say, 'If we don't have our dealers, we don't have anything so we've got to get this stuff out.' It was nothing to work three and four weekends in a row."

Those were years of major growth. The company sent Roy across Canada to learn how other businesses were automating their systems. He would return to St. Jacobs and adapt what he had learned to meet their specific

Roy Gilles: "When an opportunity came along, no one sat down and said, do you think we can handle this? Everybody jumped in and we just did it."

Retired: Warehouse and Trucking Division Manager
St. Jacobs, ON

Although he wasn't a poor student, Roy wasn't a committed one either and couldn't wait to start working. His first job was with Ontario Hydro. A bad experience and a rumoured transfer convinced him it was time for a change. Next stop was Bell Telephone. But after he was married, Roy was no longer keen to spend months away from home. By now, his older brother Henry was working in the warehouse at Hollinger Hardware (Henry had left school at a young age to support the family, his mother having been widowed when baby Roy was only three years old). In 1958, Roy decided that perhaps Hollinger Hardware might have a job for him as well. Walter Hachborn hired him as a picker. Roy's employee number was 026. In those days, if a truck full of whatever showed up at 5 o'clock, you'd go home for dinner but come right back afterwards to unload the shipment. Dealers would often arrive for some impromptu after hours shopping. Soon the business was getting too big for such spontaneity. By the early 1960s, the warehouse was so busy that people started working in shifts and Roy was promoted to Shift Supervisor. It was in that capacity that he hired Terry Davis. "He was a hippie," Roy remembers, "but he was a good worker and always had good ideas."

Operations moved to the current location on Henry Street, and Walter Hachborn asked Roy to become Warehouse Supervisor after Simeon Martin retired. Roy was also instrumental in the building and organizing of Home Hardware's Eastern and Western warehouses in Debert, Nova Scotia and Wetaskiwin, Alberta. During his tenure, warehousing became must more sophisticated with the advent of computerized tracking systems. "The dealers always came first." Roy says. "Mr. Hachborn had high expectations.

needs. "When an opportunity came along, no one sat down and said, do you think we can handle this? Everybody jumped in and we just did it."

In addition to his role as Warehouse Supervisor, Roy was also responsible for the Home Hardware fleet. Before Roy retired in 1998, Paul Straus asked him to oversee one last project, the new addition to the Burford plant, a process that took eight months. When he retired, his dual responsibilities were split between two people, Don Kirck taking over the Warehouse and Gerry Gerber the trucking division.

Retirement suits Roy. These days he plays a lot of golf and seldom stops back into Home Hardware although he lives only minutes away. He almost never comes to the markets: he remembers what they always said when he sat on the Market Committee: the Market is for the dealers. They're not making any money if they're talking to you. But he remembers the early markets at the Waterloo Lutheran University and when they moved to the new warehouse. The building had to be emptied for the set up and then everything had to be restocked and returned to normal when the market was over.

Roy likes to think of all the people who started their careers in Home Hardware's warehouse. He rattles off a list of familiar names. "They were all kids. They'd start in June and work until September and then they'd work Saturdays and a few years later they were back getting full time jobs."

When he walks into the Graham Ferguson Hall, Bill Ferguson knows he is fortunate to work for a business that remembers and honours the people who played a role in its formation. Bill comes from a storied Home Hardware family. His father, Graham, was Home Hardware's first Chairman of the Board and in the Henry Sittler building in St. Jacobs, there's a large room named in his memory. So if anyone were to follow in his father's

take the trolley down King Street and work in the store until 6 o'clock where he started learning the retail trade. After graduating from university, he worked in the store fulltime for three years. Before Home Hardware's corporate succession program, the Fergusons had their own plan: 10% of the shares and profits were put aside annually for Bill to buy the business when the time came. But before that could happen, Bill realized that he

Bill Ferguson: "We provide the tools for entrepreneurs. It's up to them to take these tools and run their business."

Dealer Support Director
St. Jacobs, ON

footsteps, you might expect it to be Bill. And although he spent a lot of time "behind the counter", both before and over the course of his 35 years with Home Hardware, Bill chose to build his hardware career on the corporate side.

In the beginning, Graham Ferguson was a teacher whose first job was in a one-room schoolhouse in Minto Township. He spent WWII teaching servicemen in Toronto, then in 1951, purchased Imlah Brothers hardware store in Fergus which is where and how he met Walter Hachborn, whose wholesale business, Hollinger Hardware was one of Graham's key suppliers. In the late 1950s, small towns were in transition. The car was becoming king and new highways were making it easy for people to get behind the wheel and out of town. It was no coincidence that the Big Box stores, about to change the face of retail and small towns, appeared at this time. As a businessman and the altruist he would be all his life, Walter wondered what would happen to these small towns and the small businesses at their economic heart. As a result, Walter formulated an innovative idea based on models he had been researching in the States: if independent hardware retailers banded together into a buying cooperative, they would have a much better chance of controlling their own destinies, not to mention surviving. Walter recognized that he needed a group of dealers to not only buy into the concept, but to actually buy the company. A successful relationship between supplier and retailer is never strictly business: a personal connection is forged as well. Such was the case with Walter and a group of 122 independent dealers, including Graham Ferguson, who banded together in 1964 to form Home Hardware Stores Limited. A core group of 10 dealer-owners, with Graham as their designated Chairman, was appointed the first Home Hardware Board of Directors.

In 1965, Graham left retailing to return to teaching but very quickly realized that his heart was in hardware. Soon thereafter he was working with Walter to find another store. By 1966, the family had moved to Kitchener, with Graham the new owner of the Home Hardware in the Frederick Street Plaza, bought from Ernie Franks, the same dealer who had hired the budding hardware entrepreneur, 14 year-old Denny Winterburn, in the mid 1950s. Bill's mother's parental priority was access to education and so the family lived several miles away in neighbouring Waterloo, near the universities that her two younger children would soon be attending. Meanwhile, every day after school, Bill, the baby of the family and still in tenth grade, would

didn't want to wake up one day "and be someone who had only worked in his father's business." So like other "Home Hardware babies", he left, with his father's blessing. And like his father before him, went to college and became a teacher. But unlike his father, he ended up in Saskatchewan, "where the prairie meets the pine". And then one day, just into his second year of teaching, he got the call - Graham was ready to sell the business. And to the question, was Bill ready to buy it, the answer was still no. Bill already understood that the retail routine was not for him. He still wanted to experience other things. Nevertheless, like his father, Bill soon realized he didn't want to be a teacher. He waited until he had three job offers, including one from Home Hardware, before he let himself follow his heart and head back to Home. Like everyone who joins Home Hardware corporate, Bill started in the Distribution Centre, first packing, then picking.

His next job was managing Home Hardware stores in transition between owners. To Bill it sounded ideal, romantic even: he'd spend a few months in different towns, getting to know the community and when the new owners arrived, helping them to acclimatize. And before it became routine, Bill would be onto the next town, the next challenge. The reality was a bit different, the longest stint three years in Windsor, the first few months spent living luxuriously at the Y. He still reminds Paul Straus of his frugality for the company periodically. Then for three years, Bill was Area Manager for Eastern Ontario, which transitioned into Manager of Dealer Development for Central Canada with Eastern Canada added to those responsibilities a few years later.

For the past 10 years, Bill Ferguson has been Director of Dealer Support. Along the way he realized that he loved selling the concept of Home Hardware more than the products that Home Hardware sells. He has got pretty good at it over the years and usually knows whether a prospective dealer has the right stuff. He would try to emphasize that the program was not a franchise model. "I'd tell a prospect, 'This isn't like McDonald's. We don't have a binder this thick that says you put one dab of mustard on, not two. We provide the tools for entrepreneurs. It's up to them to take their entrepreneurial skills and those tools and run their business." Based on these skills and a willingness to work hard with Home's tools, a prospect could do very well. Bill wanted to ensure that every prospect fully understood the commitment, the risk and the reward.

These days, Bill sticks close to St Jacobs. But in the early days, he spent a lot of time on the road. Two road stories:

Walter always favoured comfortable cars. On one occasion, a group of them were on their way to a district meeting in Wawa. Walter had Bill driving a "talking car." It was 5 o'clock in the evening and they had spent the day on store visits, working their way towards Wawa from Hornepayne with nothing in between, just bush and rocks. Bill ignored filling up, lots of gas he thought, but thirty minutes later the car announced that the gas tank was low. Eventually, they ran out of gas and coasted onto the shoulder. Time was marching on. Bill flagged down an approaching truck. The window rolled down, and great gusts of suspicious-smelling smoke came wafting onto the evening air. Despite their reservations, Bill asked the driver if he could take Walter into Wawa so that he, at least, would get to the meeting on time. They agreed and also agreed to come back with an emergency gas ration. Bill remembers watching the truck pull away, Walter's little head in between the two bigger ones, and wondering if he'd ever see him again. Eventually the truck returned with some gas and they all made it to town a little late for the meeting. Afterwards, Walter asked Bill if he had paid the fellows for the emergency gas delivery. Yes, he replied. "That's good," Walter told him. "I paid them too."

The legendary Fabian Aylward loved to drive and he loved to talk. On road trips through Newfoundland, he insisted on doing them both simultaneously. Fabian would be in the driver's seat with someone riding shot gun - never Bill, for reasons that will become evident—and three in the back. When Fabian told a story, he had to look you in the eye. Bill remembers cowering in the back seat, afraid to look, with Fabian swivelled about to tell his tale. Bill still marvels that they all lived to tell any tales at all.

When I was a little girl one of my favourite games was to make believe I was an elevator operator at the classic Montreal department store, Ogilvy's. In my pretend white blouse, plaid skirt and de rigeur short white gloves, I'd expertly slide open a beautifully ornate but invisible metal door, and announcing a floor level, reveal the imaginary merchandise in all its ephemeral splendour. When Bruce Hammer was the same age, he had the real thing: his parents John Jacob and Dorothy Hammer had a hardware

Canadian manufacturers to close and China's arrival on the scene took care of another third. Those remaining found ways to compete. Bruce and his team of Product Managers, including Dick Trussler, Don Stirling, Jim Carruthers, Morgan McCabe and Doug Psutka, were already looking overseas for suppliers. Along with the Bay, Sears and Leon's, Home Furniture (the name changed in 1992) was in the forefront of this trend.

Bruce Hammer: Bruce's enthusiasm for furniture is in his DNA: he says his father would sell the sofa out of their own living room.

Manager, Home Furniture
Elmira, ON

store in the town of Neustadt, an hour north of St. Jacobs. On Wednesday afternoons, when hardware stores in those days were traditionally closed, five year old Bruce and his dad would "rumble down the road" to St. Jacobs, to pick out their order. "I remember pushing the cart around. My dad would just pick the merchandise off the shelf and we'd go to the back door and someone would write it up on the clip board and from there we'd go into Kitchener, make the rounds and then go back home again." One of his most vivid memories is of playing on the elevator in the retail store.

Like many enterprising small town merchants in those days, Bruce's father operated two businesses from the location on Mill Street: in addition to his hardware business, he was also the town's undertaker. Bruce remembers that when he turned 13, he and his older brother John would alternate to accompany their father on calls that invariably came in the wee hours of the morning. And no matter what time they got back to bed, they were always up in time for school the next day. The Hammers were Charter Members of Home Hardware and after their father retired, the two sons took over the business. During those years, from 1980 to 1985, Bruce served on Home's Dealer advisory group, which is no doubt where a deep-seated idea took shape in his mind: he wanted to be Home Hardware's first Area Manager for their fledgling furniture division, called Homeland in those days. By the mid 1980s, it was time for Bruce to make his move. At the spring market in 1985, he approached Walter Hachborn with the idea. Walter took it one step further and offered Bruce the position of overall Manager of Homeland. He was 32 years old when he found himself on the corporate side of Home Hardware. He remembers his first day "on the job". He was a familiar face around the St. Jacobs offices, so when Walter walked him up to his new office on the second floor, Dick Trussler asked if he was in for a meeting. Walter said, "This is your new boss. Bruce is going run the division. Find him somewhere to sit." And Walter turned around and walked back to his office.

Bruce's enthusiasm for furniture is in his DNA: he says his father would sell the sofa out of their own living room. "A customer would come into the store and there'd be a blue couch they liked. My father would say, 'We have the green one at home.' He'd bring them over to look at it and tell them, 'You can have this one for $50 less.' My mother would come home and ask, 'Where's the couch?' And dad would say 'Someone wanted to buy it!'"

When Bruce went from the family business to managing the furniture division, there were major changes on the horizon for the furniture industry. In the late 1980s, the Free Trade agreement forced about one third of

In 1985, Homeland had 121 store numbers: "They would issue a store number to any dealer who said they could put a recliner in the corner," Bruce says with a smile. As a result, he did not consider them to be true furniture stores. And neither did the industry that had them slotted into the ready-to-assemble, rec room category. That was not strictly true-Ray Gabel's father Bruce, the division's first manager, carried many of the great Canadian names in furniture. Nevertheless, when Bruce Hammer became manager, Homeland wasn't able to access the quality furniture lines he needed to recruit serious dealers for a revamped furniture division. A Catch-22. On top of that, some of the current dealers weren't happy with the change of management. Needless to say, Bruce had his hands full. In addition to recognizing and respecting the distinct personalities involved, Bruce was also learning that with furniture, Canada has many distinct regions. "I had no idea that sofa and chair combos are popular in the east, but it's sofas and love seats that sell in the west." Bruce was learning that and a lot more in his forays across the country, with the strategy of whittling down the stores to the ones with the best potential. Today Home Furniture has approximately half the stores it had when Bruce became manager 27 years ago, and an excellent reputation for quality.

One of the key roles of Divisional Managers is to expand the dealers' tool kits to allow their entrepreneurial talents to flourish. Bruce believes that the combo store concept - a Home Hardware Building Centre or Home Hardware and Home Furniture store, usually under one roof - does exactly that. Combo stores allow dealers to differentiate themselves from the Big Box competition and offer turnkey convenience to today's busy, fashion conscious and savvy consumers. Bruce says that the concept works thanks to the close relationship Home Dealers already have with their customers: "Home's Dealers offer trust and service that you just don't get anywhere else. So we have expanded the product assortment to include furnishings. What better way to build your business than to appeal to people already in your store because they are planning or building a renovation project?" Home Furniture helps them furnish their dreams.

For Bruce, being part of the Home Hardware family has been a wonderful journey. "The culture is unique," he says. "Walter set the standard high: we all work for the dealers. You just don't think any other way."

Bill Ladouceur:

Retired: Manager, Dealer Operations
Elmira, ON

Bill is excited about the combo store concept emerging as one of Home Hardware's new business models.

Bill Ladouceur came by his name naturally - an unusually sunny outlook complements his gentle manner.

Bill first got into the furniture business in 1977 when he began working with his two bothers, Bob and Dan, in the Home Hardware store in Belle River near Windsor, Ontario. They sold furniture on the second floor of the store and when Home Hardware's Board of Directors made a serious commitment to furniture and formed a separate banner in 1978, the brothers decided it was an opportunity. They opened a 3,000 square foot store next door to their existing hardware business. Bill always had an interest in the furniture side of the business and immediately moved over to managing the new division in the new location. The Home Furniture store in Belle River was the first of its kind in Canada, initially known as Homeland Furniture. They were pretty much on their own in those days and virtually all their purchases were made directly with vendors through purchase orders: there was no inventory, no warehouse and no distribution centre as there are today. And no marketing or training vehicles relevant to the furniture division either. In 1985, the Belle River furniture business was growing to the point where brother Bob bought an old Pro Hardware building that allowed them to open a new 6,000 square foot store.

After 26 years in furniture retail, in 2003 Bill decided to sell the business to his brother Dan who owned and operated the Home Hardware store in Belle River (which he sold to the Seguin brothers of LaSalle). Bill was active in his community and before he sold the store he and his wife Sandy, a registered nurse in Emergency and Trauma, decided to make a donation to decorate and furnish the entire "Quiet Room" in the Emergency Department of the Hôtel Dieu Grace Hospital in Windsor. This is a special room that allows families the privacy to grieve the loss of loved ones.

Bill was thinking of retiring, but when he told Bruce Hammer, Bruce said, not so fast. Bruce knew that Bill could put all of his firsthand experience to good use and convinced Bill to make the move over to the corporate side. In 2003, Bill began working on contract in the education department, developing and teaching Advanced Retail Skills. He travelled extensively across Canada, working with Dealer-Owners and their staff, teaching them selling skills, product knowledge and the systems and services of Home Furniture. In 2007, Bill became Manager of Dealer Operations and while he travelled extensively, he became more focused on the financial side of the business at the store level.

Despite all its challenges, Bill always retained a deep-seated love for the furniture industry and was happy to spend 36 years in the Home family, helping Home's Dealers.

Since 1991 Home Hardware has donated its private label Unival extended life anti-freeze for the Lancaster bomber at the Canadian Warplane Heritage Museum in nearby Hamilton.

Kate Ritchie and Cathy Currie:

Beauti·Tone Paint and Home Products
Burford, ON

When people talk about tanks moving in, the first image that comes to mind is typically not a pleasant one. But in the case of Home Hardware's paint plant in Burford, Ontario, the day the tanks moved in (spring of 1980) has a much different connotation. It was a highly visible commitment to Beauti-Tone, the company's private label brand of paint that today is the equal of quality brand names like Benjamin Moore, Sico and Cloverdale. Although Home Hardware registered the name "Beauti-Tone" in 1963, for the next 15 years, the paint was manufactured by Sherwin Williams. In 1978, Home Hardware decided it was time to start making its own paint and hired Eric Irving to manage the new endeavour. The question was where the plant was going to be. Several locations were put forward, and the winner was an old rope factory in Burford, a pleasant drive through rolling countryside southwest of St. Jacobs. Kate Ritchie was working in the paint department of the local Burford Home Hardware store at the time and remembers the store owner Warren Kuehl taking Walter on a "walk about" of the building. In his typical fashion, Walter saw the potential beyond the building's dilapidated condition: in particular he liked the proximity to St Jacobs, the fact that the town had a rail line and that the property gave them lots of room to grow.

The plant had its manager and its building. Next it needed a chemist. In 1979, Eric hired Cathy Currie, fresh out of university with a chemistry degree. It was her first (and only!) job to date. When she joined Home Hardware's fledgling paint division, the building was being gutted and the pipes and other equipment for an automated delivery system were being installed. Then the tanks moved in. Ten fibreglass bulk storage tanks, each with a 7,000-gallon capacity, rolled through town on individual flat bed trucks, stopping traffic as they made their slow way through the streets of the small town to the plant. From there, a wall of the plant had to be knocked down and each tank hoisted inside and positioned in place by a crane. More than 30 years and 50 million gallons of paint later, the tanks are still in place.

In 1983, the plant began manufacturing cleaning and automotive products.

Bev Bell:

Behind the façade of her tiny, elegant person, there's a great big kid, always waiting to pop out in your face.

Creative Director, Beauti-Tone Paint and Home Products
Burford, ON

When I caught up with Bev Bell, Home Hardware's Creative Director for Beauti-Tone Paint and Home Products, she had just returned from spending March Break at Disney World with her five grandchildren. She was a bit giddy, which she blamed on a week spent with five children under age 10 and five grown up kids. But in my experience, behind the façade of her tiny, elegant person, there's a great big kid, always waiting to pop out in your face.

Bev has parlayed that eternally youthful joie de vivre into a career that has allowed her irrepressible creativity to flourish. From an early age, she was making furniture and homes for her ever-expanding collection of dolls. She graduated to seeking inspiration from fashion and design magazines. "If I could see it," she says, "I could make it." After high school, she went to Design School, got married and worked for a commercial design firm for a couple of years before having her children.

Being a stay at home mom was too restrictive, and she soon started her own small home décor business. She also taught Adult Education classes in décor at the local high school. The Bells moved to Saudi Arabia for two years, where Bev's husband Tim, appropriately enough, was working for Bell. Although women were not officially supposed to work, Bev circumvented the prohibition and was soon working in the library of the International School that her two young children attended. She also created a summer camp for the children of expats on the Bell compound where they all lived.

On their return to Canada, the Bells were posted to Thunder Bay. Bev found creative outlet working at a florist and volunteering as a docent at the Art Gallery in town. Eventually she got a part-time job at St. Clair Paint where her destiny started to unfold. After the family moved to Orangeville in the early 1990s, Bev was looking for a greater challenge. When she heard of a job in the paint department at the Orangeville Home Hardware store, Bev knew that opportunity had just knocked. Over the period Bev worked at the store, paint sales accelerated. Bev was not just selling paint, she was selling inspiration in a can. After three years, Home Hardware invited her to join the corporate side, which is when we met.

Today, working with Home's agency and public relations department, Bev Bell is responsible for the division's advertising, media relations, colour cards, colour systems, dealer training and education as they pertain to colour. She is also Home's Paint and Decorating Expert for Home at Home magazine. Her irresistible seasonal creations along with her leading edge decorating and colour advice and product recommendations have been hugely popular mainstays in every issue since the magazine was launched in May 1994.

"The nicest thing about working with Home Hardware is that it's a family company," she says. "When people learn that I work at Home, they always have a story to tell about a great experience they had at their local store. I love that."

Ken Curtis: *"Here I was, an 18 year-old farm boy, being interviewed by the boss."*

Retired: Printing Manager
St. Jacobs, ON

Who doesn't remember their first job interview? Ken Curtis certainly does. But, unlike the majority of the working population today, Ken's first job was also his last. And while that is not all that unusual at Home Hardware - the average tenure of Home Hardware's corporate office staff of more than 2,000 people is 15 years; 570 have been there over 20 years and another 200 more than 30 years - it is very unusual in today's working world.

It was the summer before his last year of high school and Ken and his father made the rounds to the small towns near the farm where they lived: in the morning, they went to Elmira, stopped in at the Uniroyal plant, then in the afternoon, went to St. Jacobs and Ken made the long, terrifying trip up the stairs at Home Hardware on Main Street for an interview with Walter Hachborn. "I was petrified," Ken recalls, more than 45 years later. "Here I was, an 18 year-old farm boy, being interviewed by the boss." The only thing he remembers about the experience is his father looking out the window to the Dominion Hotel across the street and saying to Walter, "Keep him away from there."

Ken was hired as an order picker and the following year, after he graduated from high school, started working fulltime but with a different foreman. He remembers the two of them arguing over him - the fact that one of them had trained him the summer before but the other got the benefit of his experience when he came on board fulltime!

After the company moved into the new Henry Street facility in 1968, Walter asked Ken to run the special order and returns department. A few years later, he applied to a job posting in the printing department. Two people had left on the same day and Walter asked Ken if he thought he could manage both jobs. He did, and got the job, working for Neil Schmidt. He eventually became supervisor and manager of the department.

Ken has seen a lot of history at Home. He loves the fact that in the early days everyone pitched in to do whatever needed to get done, and as a result, learned the business inside out: he helped merchandise a store in Perth with Kraemer Woodcraft, and even drove a truck when they were short of drivers.

During a postal strike, the dealers had to phone in their orders, so everyone in the office - about 50 in those days - pitched in. He remembers that Walter was in every department "with his sleeves rolled up."

He remembers the sad moments too, the day of Jack Schelter's funeral being one of them. Jack was the company's first truck driver, and eventually became the dispatcher. He was also Santa Claus for years. Ken remembers Jack as a "super loveable, laughable, likeable guy." Then one day he was gone. The funeral was downtown and he was being buried in the cemetery across the street from the Home Hardware offices. It was decided that the entire staff of the building would go outside and line both sides of the street. He remembers the sombre feeling as they waited silently for the long line of cars to turn onto Henry Street and make its slow way through the quiet crowd honouring the man with whom they had worked for so many years as he made his last journey. Ken still gets emotional, thinking about being part of that moment.

The only other time he remembers the staff lining the street in the same manner was on a happier occasion, when Walter led the procession up Henry Street for the opening of the Trans Canada Trail.

Ken is a fixture at the Home Hardware markets and has often served on the Market Committee. He tells a story that he believes helps to explain Home Hardware's success: "We would always hear the same complaint after every market: 'There are so many darn kids in strollers, people can't work the booths properly. There should be a rule that nobody under 14 is allowed to attend.'" But, Ken remembers, someone else would immediately counter: "That's not the Home Hardware way." So that idea would get put to rest and then, the next market, it would come up again, get put to rest, and so on. Ken says, "Over the years that I have been at Home Hardware, I've seen so many dealers coming to the market with a kid in hand, like Chuck Hillock's dad, like Karen Maxwell's dad, and then 25 years later, you see that same kid, grown up, with his or her own store, with their own kid in hand. So, had we enforced that 'no kids under 14' rule, these things might not be happening."

I caught up with Larry Kondro by phone early one morning before he headed out from his Edmonton home to Bingo - these days, he volunteers several times a week at different charities, and gives a lot of his time to his church. "I keep busy," he says. In fact, as part of a 70-member perogi team at his church, Larry recently helped peel 600 pounds of potatoes that produced 1,500 dozen pierogies in one morning.

western warehouse opened in January 1985. By 1989, he was Area Manager for central Alberta and western Saskatchewan, working under the direction of Frank Hammer. When Frank retired, Larry became Dealer Development Manager for western Canada in 1996. Which is when he hired Gerald Stuart as Manitoba Area Manager. "I found him to be an excellent young person," Larry says. "I knew for a fact that he was always looking for a good store."

Larry Kondro: "I couldn't have worked for nicer people."

Retired: Manager, Dealer Development
Western Canada

Although he officially retired in 2003, Larry is still available for special assignments with Home Hardware. It's a mission he has always been proud and happy to accept. "I tell you, Holly," he says, "if I had to do it all over again, I would be happy." I can hear the memories and affection in his voice as clearly as if he were sitting across the table from me.

I can also understand why Gerald Stuart and Larry Kondro clicked so immediately: they are uncommonly enthusiastic go-getters. They both started their Home Hardware careers in a similar fashion although they each ended up in a different place within the organization. Born and raised just north of Edmonton, Larry initially worked on the oilrigs. By the early 1960s, he got a job at Northern Hardware, a western wholesaler. When he started working as a receiving clerk, nails came in 50-pound kegs. He quickly and steadily moved up to order filling then onto the order desk. In those days, orders were mailed in - no Purolator, he points out. From there it was a natural evolution to sales, Larry's next position for several years. Northern Hardware closed in 1966 and Larry joined Link Hardware that same year, working at their distribution centre in Edmonton. By the late 1970s, Larry sensed growing problems at Link and called Walter Hachborn, who he had met, along with Henry Sittler, at Winnipeg meetings of United Hardware, the industry organization of Canada's then-largest hardware retailers, Rona, Falcon, Link and Home Hardware. Walter assured Larry that he would try to find a place for him within Home Hardware. Two years later when Link amalgamated with Home Hardware in 1981, Larry became the Distribution Manager in Edmonton then moved to Wetaskiwin when the

Larry's voice is bright with memories and enthusiasm: "I couldn't have worked for nicer or better people," he says. He remembers the District Meetings and how much he learned from Walter Hachborn on those long road trips. Walter also brought his "no stopping for lunch" policy with him to the new Home Hardware territory of western Canada: like a few other people I have spoken with, Larry remembers eating a lot of apples. Paul Straus often joined them on the road trips. Larry remembers Paul asking him how many bushels of grain a grain elevator would hold. And when he admitted that he had no idea, Paul professed surprise: "I thought you knew your territory," he'd say. Larry quickly realized that in addition to being gently teased, Paul was distracting him as the long miles clicked along.

Larry had some sound advice for new dealers: in the beginning, pay yourself just enough to make a good living. After you've paid off your debt, Larry would add, you can pay yourself whatever you want. This is what former VP of Finance Elaine Girardi called the "wieners and beans phase" when she was guiding Home Hardware Dealers through difficult times to business success. Elaine joined Home Hardware in 1981 as an accountant and ended her career with the company in 1997. She was promoted to Corporate Controller in 1989 and appointed Vice President of Finance in 1995. Elaine was responsible for assembling and leading the team that took Home Hardware from manual to computerized accounting systems.

In 1997, Bill Simpson was working for Oshawa Foods (now Sobeys). He and Wendy, his wife then over 30 years, lived in their dream home (three acres and a short par 3) in Caledon. Their three sons were grown and had moved on to lives of their own. Life was on an agreeably steady course. Then fate intervened. A friend of Bill's was working with KPMG, Home Hardware's auditor. He told Bill that Home Hardware was looking for a VP,

"I was a newcomer, and no spring chicken, who knew nothing about the hardware and building supply business. My team and others were absolutely incredible at helping me learn and understand Home's corporate systems and services. I know firsthand how competitive employees at some companies can be, so I had a point of comparison. And there was none of that. 'How can I help you?' is the Home Hardware work ethic."

Bill Simpson: "It's a truly caring company with a unique culture."

Retired, Vice-President, Administration and CFO
St. Jacobs, ON

Finance. His interest piqued, Bill submitted his resume and was invited to a preliminary interview with Paul Straus. When he arrived, he was amazed at the scope of the operation tucked away in St. Jacobs. For the follow-up interview, Bill asked if he could bring Wendy along. On that occasion, Paul took them on a comprehensive tour of the facility, a challenge for Wendy, who had worn dressy shoes "to impress the boss."

When Bill joined Home Hardware shortly thereafter, the management group was actively pursuing an acquisition to take the company to the next level in the Canadian market. It was an interesting time. "We were looking at another company," Bill remembers, "but when the Beaver opportunity came up, we all knew that it was the right fit and would make Home a major player in the LBM game." Bill's role was the face-to-face negotiating with Molson, and working with new bankers to arrange financing for the deal. "Negotiating the deal was a fascinating challenge, a real David and Goliath scenario," he says. He believes that ultimately Home Hardware was able to purchase the business and real estate at an attractive price. "The team got it done, and it was the best thing that could have happened for both existing Home Hardware and Beaver Lumber Dealers. Plus, the people who came over from their Markham head office really enhanced our management team."

While Bill had not expected such an intense first few years with Home Hardware, his learning curve benefited from the Home Hardware culture. "Most of my colleagues had been here all their working lives," he explains.

Bill retired in January 2010 in order to spend more time with Wendy, who had health issues. Tom McCauley, who was turning 80 ("I don't think anyone retires here until they're 90," Bill says.) and was still an advisor to the Audit and Security Committee, said to Paul, "I think it's time to pass the torch. Do you know anyone who would like to take over?" Paul asked Bill, who agreed, as long as he could be of assistance. "So I really never left," he laughs. "The timing was good for Tom and I love it, because it keeps me in touch with the people and the company, and all the exciting things that happen at Home."

Bill insists that no other company has the Home Hardware model. "It's a brilliant, well thought-out design that allows both Home and their dealers to be strong and healthy. And," he adds, "it's a truly caring company with a unique culture. When I came out of university, if I'd asked myself where I would like to work, if I knew then what I know now, I'd have come looking for Home Hardware. I would have come in a heartbeat and stayed forever."

Shortly after Bill started working with Home Hardware, he and Wendy moved to the area. "I commuted from Caledon for one winter," he says, "and that was enough." Wendy "had only fourteen requirements" he remembers fondly. The home they found in Paradise Lake ("You go to St Clements and turn left.") is a little piece of heaven.

For many years Paul and his wife Jo-Anne have been avid horse people on the farm outside of St. Clements where Paul's parents originally lived and where they have lived and raised their family since 1975. It was Jo-Anne who initially got into breeding and showing quarter horses and is a champion equestrian. Paul says that mucking out stalls and meeting people from all walks of life at the shows they attend are a change of pace for him. But it sounds to me that he's simply doing more of what he has been doing all his life: rolling up his sleeves, working hard at whatever needs to be done and enjoying every minute and aspect of the ride.

This photograph is of Paul Straus and Lady, one of Paul and Jo-Anne's 17 horses.

When I started to research this book, I was forewarned that some Home Dealers might be uncomfortable talking about themselves. While I encountered endearing and genuine modesty in everyone I interviewed, undoubtedly one of the more reticent individuals was Paul Straus, one of the very people who forewarned me.

Paul was very generous with stories about his children (both of whom work within the Home Hardware universe; Brian is a Product Manager, his other son Adam works at PIB); his grandchildren; his wife Jo-Anne's accomplishments as an equestrian. He was forthcoming about his childhood: the third youngest of a large family, Paul grew up in St. Clements, a small

for candidates. That meant looking outside the company. By now Paul was Vice-President, Controller. The new position created with Walter's retirement was VP General Manager. At first Paul was unaware that a search for Walter's replacement was underway. When he did learn of it, he told me during one of our interviews, his reaction was typically humble: "If they thought I could run the place, they would have asked me, right?"

I returned to Walter for elaboration: "We were close to hiring an outside candidate," Walter confirms. "But when it came down to it, something was not right." His wife Jean clarifies: "I think it's wise to choose from people you know and who know you. When someone else comes in who doesn't

Paul Straus: There is no doubt it takes a very special individual to be CEO of a company with hundreds of bosses.

President and CEO
St. Jacobs, ON

community down the road from St Jacobs. His father was a carpenter and was widowed when Paul was only five. Everyone was expected to work hard. When Paul finished high school, the guidance counsellor suggested he apply for work at several local companies, including Hollinger Hardware. "I don't want to work in retail," Paul said. He remembers being interviewed by Walter and "grilled" by Henry Sittler. He was hired; his first job was working with Art Miller in the accounting department, along with anything else that needed to be done, multitasking that was expected of the entire workforce. As he was learning on the job, Paul was also taking courses to increase his skill set. He enrolled in the Registered Accounting Program almost immediately but switched to IT several years later, when the company computerized, and took courses in that new field. In fact, Paul wrote Home Hardware's first computer program and installed the first computer at the corporate offices in St. Jacobs.

Art Miller was getting ready to retire and Paul assumed Finance as well as IT and Human Resources. They were running accounting on bookkeeping machines and Paul had hired Elaine Girardi to look after accounting. Elaine computerized and set up the books and ran the accounting department. She also worked with dealers who had payment problems. When Elaine left, Paul hired Bill Simpson who was a tremendous support. He was instrumental in the Beaver purchase and since his retirement has been appointed Secretary of the Audit and Security Committee. Currently Grant Knowlton has assumed the Vice-President, Finance position in the Accounting Department.

Although Paul's utter devotion to Home Hardware is always evident, when it came to discussing his own accomplishments at the executive level, he clammed right up. So, I resorted to subterfuge and asked Walter Hachborn who hired Paul as an accounting clerk in June 1963. "Paul was my right hand," Walter said simply. "He was always there."

As with countless individuals who were fortunate enough to get a job with Home Hardware in St. Jacobs, Paul Straus advanced through the organization. The difference was how far he travelled.

There is no doubt it takes a very special individual to be CEO of a company with hundreds of bosses. When Walter decided to retire from the day-to-day responsibilities in 1988, the Board requested a formal search

understand the systems, that's really uprooting. Paul had come up through the ranks. He understood the philosophy of the company and the systems in place that were working." Most of all, Paul not only understood, but lived and breathed the credo established by Walter: It's not about the individual; it's about loving and working with the people. Dealers always come first.

Paul had some very big shoes to fill when he became Executive Vice-President and General Manager in 1989. In 1998, he was appointed Vice-President and CEO and in April 2010, he became President and Chief Executive Officer. Over the years and between the two of them Walter and Paul made the transition look effortless. "Walter never said, 'Why are you doing this or that?' He didn't come to the meetings, but I would always let him know ahead of time if I was going to make any changes."

In the years since he joined the company, Paul has helped Home Hardware evolve from 122 independent hardware dealers to close to 1,100 stores in communities from coast to coast to coast. At the executive level, Paul has been one of the stewards of momentous change and growth for Home Hardware. The acquisition of 55 Revelstoke stores in 1980 and Beaver Lumber in 2000 allowed the company to become a dominant force in the LBM category, which, together with the hardware and furniture banners, has made Home Hardware a strong and competitive presence across the country. But as much as he cherishes these highlights, Paul speaks with equal pride of the satisfaction he derives from seeing dealers of every size profit and grow, the pleasure in developing programs that contribute to the company's continued success and the nature of a business that - despite the lawyers' chagrin - is still often conducted with a handshake. A man who modestly maintains that he does not see himself as a leader, Paul Straus exemplifies the qualities at the heart of Home Hardware success. "I learned in the trenches," he says. "I paid attention and watched the great leaders in our organization succeed and excel. I have been lucky in my career to be guided by some of the industry icons as well as thousands of independent entrepreneurs. Perhaps most important, I have enjoyed every minute of it."

Terry Davis:
In 1970, fresh out of high school, 19 year-old Terry Davis started working as a stock picker in the Home Hardware warehouse.

Executive Vice-President and Chief Operating Officer
St. Jacobs, ON

Although Terry Davis' father was a veterinarian, hardware was in his DNA: Terry's grandfather was a senior sales executive for EMCO, a London-based hardware company. In 1970, fresh out of high school, 19 year-old Terry Davis started working as a stock picker in the Home Hardware warehouse. Forty-two years later, he is the company's Chief Operating Officer, responsible for all operational aspects of the business, from marketing, merchandising and distribution to information technology.

In fact, it was IT that launched Terry's career. In the fall of 1970, he saw an ad in the Kitchener-Waterloo Record for a computer operator at Home Hardware. Home's computer department was adding a second shift and needed another operator for the NCR equipment. Terry applied for the position, aced the aptitude test and started his new job in January 1971. "As a computer operator my main job was to get the orders ready. It took a long time to sort files," Terry remembers. To pass the time productively, he started reading the computer programming books lying around. Paul Straus saw his interest and sent him on a two-week programming course. By the fall of 1973, Terry was writing proprietary programs for Home Hardware and became Manager of the Department in 1981. He is particularly proud of the software he wrote to solve a problem in the order system: with the old system if a product was not available at the time a dealer placed an order, that request got dropped from the system and the dealer would have to re-order. The program he wrote kept unfulfilled orders active, so that when the product did arrive at the warehouse, the outstanding order was filled without the dealer having to do anything more about it.

When Paul was appointed General Manager in 1989, he started inviting Terry to attend Board meetings. Around the same time, Peter Lunt, then VP Marketing, left the company. Terry took his place running the cross-country District Meetings that were held every fall for a number of years before advances in communications technology rendered them obsolete. Terry was clearly being groomed. His responsibilities continued to expand. In April 1990 he was appointed VP, Information Services. In 1995 his title changed to VP, Marketing and Information Services; from 1997 to 2000 his title was VP, Information Services and Dealer Development; in 2000 he became Vice-President, Information Technology, in 2005, his title became Vice-President, Information Technology and Strategic Planning; in 2007, Vice-

President, Administration and Strategic Planning and in 2010 Terry Davis was appointed Executive Vice-President and Chief Operating Officer.

Looking to the future, I asked, would the changing retail reality change the Home Hardware culture? "We have some large multi-store Dealer-Owner operations," Terry said. "But I believe that at the heart of it, you're still talking to somebody who remembers and knows the value of looking after customers. These dealers aren't sitting in an office that is detached from the business because it's so big. No matter how many stores they have, the dealers are hands on with their customers. And as long as you have that relationship with your customer, I don't think you'll have the disengagement that you can get in a more corporate retail frame."

How would you define the Home Hardware difference? I asked. "Every company is set up to make money. So, you can just make money or you can make money and also look after people. Our culture is to look after our dealers. The philosophy of our operation is that everybody contributes. I couldn't have done anything without somebody else doing his or her job. It just doesn't happen."

For Terry Davis, one of the strongest symbols of Home Hardware is Walter Hachborn's office chair. "It's the world's oldest office chair," Terry says with affection. "It's picked apart and it shows that he doesn't see any reason to spend money that isn't for the betterment of the dealers. I've always thought that when we sign up new employees they should go into Walter's office to see that chair: Here's the founder of Home Hardware – he still comes in to work – this is his chair – this is his office – look at this chair."

"I'd been working here for a little bit and Del Schneider (who I was a picker with) and I passed Walter in the hallway. Del said 'Hi Walter.' I remember being astounded that he would call him Walter. In my family you always called the friends of your parents or any grown man 'Mister.'"

Eric Konecsni:

Vice-President, Operations
St. Jacobs, ON

Eric justifiably considers his major achievement to have been overseeing the transition of 138 Beaver Lumber stores during the conversion to Home Hardware in August 1999.

When I told Eric Konecsni, Home Hardware's VP, Operations, that I had never seen him smile, he smiled. The fact is, this busy man who often seems as if he has the weight of the world on his shoulders, has a lot to smile about as he looks back on more than forty-five years in the industry, 13 of them with Home Hardware.

A Westerner, Eric worked at a Beaver Lumber store in Saskatoon while going to university in the late 1960s. In 1972, after graduating with his Commerce degree, Eric transferred to a new concept Calgary Home Centre store, where he started as a Merchandising Manager and left as a Store Manager in 1978 when he became the Regional Merchandise and Marketing Manager for the Prairie Provinces. In 1986, he was transferred to Vancouver to become BC's VP, Operations. In 1990, he was transferred again, this time to Ontario as that province's VP, Operations. Two years later he assumed responsibility for all of Canada as Vice-President, Operations, and was the last General Manager of Beaver Lumber. This man was in the trenches and behind the scenes over the entire period that Beaver's parent, Molson, flirted with the Home Centre concept and later "Big Box" retailing. Eric's experiences over those years were a fascinating foray into the world of big business. When Molson sold its interest in Beaver Lumber to a deceptively mild mannered company headquartered in the tranquil Ontario countryside, it must have been an interesting transition, although Eric stresses that the sense of family within the Beaver organization itself was always very strong. Perhaps that is one reason the integration of the two organizations has been so successful.

Eric justifiably considers his major achievement to have been overseeing the transition of 138 Beaver Lumber stores during the conversion to Home Hardware in August 1999. The challenges of folding a company established in 1906 into one that came into being almost 60 years later were significant. As Eric says, "The issue for Beaver Lumber Dealers was: I've been green and gold for 100 years – how do I become red?" And the answer, involving a myriad of components, demonstrated the resolve and skill of the individuals managing the process on both sides and the good faith of the dealers involved. Ultimately, after a great deal of hard work, it came down to two distinct cultures finding common ground, created by the mingling of their respective strengths: Beaver Lumber Dealers now had access to the wonderful world of margin-rich hardlines—not to mention 100% ownership of their businesses—and Home Hardware was now in the lumber and building materials business in a serious way. Everyone involved came out a winner.

As VP, Operations for Home Hardware Stores Limited, Eric Konecsni oversees almost 1100 stores under Home's four banners. All four Directors of Retail Operations, to whom the 20 Area Managers report, along with Real Estate and Construction, Dealer Development (Banner Conversions) and Dealer Support Services, report to Eric. He offers me a raft of facts and figures - percentages, current and future expansion plans, real estate, incremental sales growth, Five-Year Plans, the mysterious minutiae of charting course and guiding a company through today's economic reality; the business and science (and art) of business.

I ask him if he had found the transition from Beaver to Home Hardware difficult. "Not difficult – just different," he says. "The cultures were day and night. Home Hardware is truly a family culture. Molson's was big business and as long as you delivered results, you were wonderful. If you didn't deliver results – you were out on your ear." But that was then and this is now and Eric has clearly taken to an environment that allows him to focus on a long-term perspective, rather than the pressure of delivering short-term results to shareholders constantly demanding them. "Home Hardware doesn't manage stores," he says. "We leave that to the experts. Home Hardware brings programs and services to dealers to help them sell more products and make more money." And then, of course, he gives me another big smile.

When I was the editor of Home at Home magazine, I always looked forward to my regular meetings with Ray Gabel. His suggestions and ideas were invariably an improvement on the original. One of his idiosyncrasies was a habit of abruptly getting up and wandering off, like an absent-minded professor, usually when we were in the throes of discussion. Abandoned in mid-thought, the first few times this happened I'd wonder

and wagons went bankrupt, Ray and then-buyer Kerry House approached the Mennonites to take over the category. Through word of mouth and the internet, this same supplier is now also making similar products for a number of North American retailers. But the relationship with Home Hardware, with a level of trust established through a shared geography and common heritage, is unique.

Ray Gabel: Ray lives the Home Hardware credo of "service, service, service."

Vice-President, Merchandising and Marketing-Hardlines
St. Jacobs, ON

if I had inadvertently offended him. I quickly understood that he had made a connection - inevitably involving a new product-that was relevant to the topic at hand.

Ray's connections are mental steppingstones to invention and innovation. With the mind of an engineer and marketing instincts that are a legend in the industry, Ray Gabel has had a long and illustrious career of successful connections that have profited Home Hardware. The company's relationship with the Mennonite manufacturers, whose sophisticated businesses are nestled innocuously in the bucolic farmland surrounding St. Jacobs, is probably the best example. And it came about because Ray Gabel made a critical connection one evening many years ago.

"I used to smoke cigars and drive around the country listening to the baseball game on the car radio," he told me in September 2011 as we headed out to Joe's Wagon, Home Hardware's first Mennonite partner. (The image was so extraordinary that I scrambled for my notebook.)

One summer evening in 1991, Ray idled his car at the end of Joe Martin's long lane. He had heard that a few Mennonites were already manufacturing on a small scale. He thought about the plastic price ticket holder - a simple thing with two prongs that slid onto pegboard—that Home Hardware was currently sourcing from a supplier for 22 cents a unit. Then he drove up the lane and that same evening, Joe and Ray put their heads together and designed a mould that cut the unit price of one small item in half. From that connection a long lasting and mutually beneficial partnership was born. Over the years Home Hardware has invested over $1.5 million in moulds with a growing roster of Mennonite manufacturers providing the man power and machine time.

More than twenty years later the number and complexity of items manufactured for Home Hardware by the Mennonites are significant. From a simple plastic mould for an item they didn't even sell, the list now includes snow shovels (over two million shipped to date), plastic lawn rakes (over one million), boot trays, plastic pails, paint trays, and many more. In fact, when Home Hardware's original supplier of wooden sleighs, toboggans

Ray's initial Mennonite connection was through his mother's Swiss forbears who moved to the area in the 1800s. Ray was born in the beautiful stone Steiner House across from The Stone Crock on St. Jacobs' main street where his grandfather had a butcher shop on the ground floor. His father, Bruce Gabel, was one of the fortunate men with a job - as a leather cutter in a shoe factory - during the depression years of Ray's childhood. By 1945 Bruce was working at Hollinger Hardware down the street and when Ray was 17, he started there too, the same year that Walter Hachborn and Henry Sittler bought the business from Gord Hollinger.

"I really loved what I did," he says. "I had a chance to do everything. I unloaded trucks; I swept the floor; put stock on the shelves; I waited on customers; I was a packer, a shipper, priced invoices and did purchasing." It was the ideal environment in which to learn the business inside out. Ray was there when the retailers closed their stores on Wednesday afternoons to come shopping themselves; he was there when they went out to the warehouse. By 1954 Ray was working closely with Henry Sittler who managed the company's purchasing department and was known within the industry for his acumen. The two of them travelled to the big shows in Chicago and Atlantic City.

Ray Gabel believes in hard work, good works and the good of the company. He truly lives the Home Hardware credo of "service, service, service."

Ray attended the meeting at The Flying Dutchman in 1964 that officially ushered Home Hardware into existence. He rattles off the names of many of the original dealers who attended that meeting, "a pretty prestigious bunch," as he recalls. Shortly thereafter, Ray Gabel officially took over the purchasing position for the new company. He was appointed Vice-President, Merchandise in 1979 and today, backed by Joel Marks who joined Home Hardware with the Beaver Lumber acquisition, is responsible for a department of 16 industrious Product Managers and their 29 assistants.

Bruce White

• Integrity can be an overused word
• but Bruce believes that it is at the heart of Home Hardware.

Vice-President, Merchandise and Marketing-Lumber and Building Materials
St. Jacobs, ON

Like every division of Home Hardware, the LBM division is there for the benefit of its dealers, 511 strong as of April 2012. And Vice-President Bruce White never misses an opportunity to tell them about all the Home Hardware tools at their disposal. "The game plan is there," he says. "And if the dealers utilize all those tools that are available, they will be very successful." The program is obviously working: in 2004, the LBM division surpassed the billion dollar sales mark, one of the highlights in Bruce's 35 year career at Home Hardware.

Bruce borrowed the LBM division's model from the OPP: "Excellence in what we do. Integrity in who we are." Integrity can be an overused word but Bruce believes that it is at the heart of Home Hardware. Part of that integrity has to do with giving back to the community at large. Several years ago the LBM division started a tradition of a volunteer work project over several days during their annual convention, usually held somewhere warm and sunny in February. The division has done five work projects in third world countries to date. They work with third party DMCs (Destination Management Companies) to identify and facilitate appropriate programs for their group's skills. HHBC dealers Rick Kurzak and Ken O'Connor have been an inspiration. The two HHBC dealers are independently involved with Developing World Connections, an organization that builds schools and other resources essential to a country's stability and future growth.

There is no shortage of organizations, communities and countries in need and it is thanks to Meridican, the Group Incentives Consultants firm with which they are currently working, that they find the groups that can best use their help within the available time and budget. Although it is impossible to bring building materials to Mexico, for example, where they recently built a school in Puerto Vallarta, dealers from different parts of the country are tasked with bringing along tools, safety glasses, ground sheets, work gloves and other items in their luggage.

The program operates under the tagline "You've made a difference". Participating LBM dealers devote two days to the projects. With four shifts of 75 people each, they can move mountains. And they do. Bruce says, "The local contractors will say 'You haven't got a hope of getting this done,' but by the end of the shift, people are saying, 'We've finished this part. What else can we do now?' Everybody gives their all to it."

There's likely one recent project Bruce wishes he hadn't put quite so much effort into, but it's hard to refuse the man who hired you all those years ago: "We spent months working to get Walter railing for his deck on his home in Abaco (in the Bahamas). I told him that a 90 year-old man should NOT be tackling that job." But, of course, Walter being Walter, he didn't pay any attention to the advice and ended up falling off the deck and landing himself in the hospital. And it was the same stubborn streak that had him up and walking at the 2012 Spring Market just a few months later.

When Bruce White joined the company in 1978, Home Hardware was essentially Ontario-based with some members in Atlantic Canada. Bruce was charged with the task of building the lumber division that had been established in 1972. The initial focus was on developing Atlantic Canada, where Bruce worked closely with Eric Caldwell, who is still the LBM Division's Atlantic Merchandise and Marketing Manager. When the company acquired Link in January 1981, it really put Home Hardware on the map in Western Canada. Bruce took advantage of the opportunity to work with Frank Hammer, the Western Area Manager, to convert new dealers out there.

As a result of their efforts and success bringing dealers into the LBM division across the country, Home Hardware was earning a reputation for being more than just a hardware company. And then came the Beaver acquisition, one of Bruce's major undertakings and an accomplishment of which he is justifiably proud. It was October 25, 1999 and Bruce arrived at the Beaver offices in Markham, Ontario to make a conference call to the dealers to announce that Home Hardware had just bought the company from Molson's. Gaining their trust was a big challenge, Bruce recalls, and despite the huge task of conversion that lay ahead, it was definitely a win-win for everyone. Eventually "they realized that what we talked we walked and that's when everything started to really come together." The Beaver acquisition meant that the LBM division was in a position to really expand. "We brought over the Home Installs program, Contractor Marketing, and Architectural Solutions from Beaver and they have allowed us to be a true player within the corporate structure of Home Hardware."

Darrin Noble is an anomaly at Home Hardware: he has only worked there since 2007. He is also the company's newest Vice-President, appointed along with John Dyksterhuis in November 2011. Between the two of them, they assumed the responsibilities of one of Home Hardware's favourite sons, Don Kirck, who passed away suddenly at the age of 55 in 2011. Working from the Beauti-Tone Paint and Home Products Division in Burford, Darrin is responsible not only for that division but for W.D. Packaging, which covers the HOME BUILDER and HOMEPAK programs which both operate out of Elmira.

like doing it and I've learned that it does not deliver results. If that's what you want me to do, I'm the wrong guy." When he had been at the company for a very short while, Walter and Paul asked him – are the people happy? "And I guess they knew something that we didn't learn at the big companies – if you look after the people, the numbers will follow."

His first step was to learn the Home Hardware culture and earn the trust and respect of the people. "My message was: I've had some success building brands and working internationally and you guys are doing a fabulous job

Darrin Noble:
"If I could sum up Home Hardware in two words it would have to be collaboration and trust."

Vice-President, Beauti-Tone Paint and Home Products
Burford, ON

Darrin is clearly someone who enjoys what he's doing and he was quick to recognize how fortunate he is to work for Home Hardware. Darrin has always been a paint person, and managed a number of well-known retail and commercial brands, in addition to working for a multi-national firm for 17 years before joining the Home Hardware family. Darrin knew Doug Thiemann, the former General Manager of the Paint Division when they both served on the Board of Directors of the Canadian Paint & Coatings Association. It was Doug who first suggested that Darrin leave corporate Toronto and join Home Hardware. Darrin admits that he had some preconceived notions about the conservative nature of the St. Jacobs company and although he had been born and raised in small town Ontario, he had lived and worked most of his adult life in Toronto and liked its excitement and fast pace. But Doug persisted and Darrin was invited for a plant tour. "I was absolutely amazed. Not just at the technology but at the competence of the people and the level of cooperation that was clearly evident. If I could sum up Home Hardware in two words it would have to be collaboration and trust." Darrin sensed those two qualities at his first meeting with Paul Straus and Don Kirck, qualities that were lacking in his career at the time.

As the introductory process continued, Darrin realized that in addition to the genuine warmth, "behind that unassuming and approachable demeanour, the wheels behind their eyes were turning fast." He remembers Don Kirck giving him a three decimal point answer to a question he had asked about production volume. "I was stunned by the level of information and knowledge he possessed." By the time he got back to his office in Toronto, he had made up his mind. "I came to Home Hardware and it was the best career decision I have ever made."

Darrin did not want to be brought into the paint division to disrupt all that had been built. He remembers telling the hiring committee: "I know how to restructure a division and how to fire staff - I've done plenty of that. I don't

building a brand that's entirely developed here in Canada. Let's put that together and build a power brand that absolutely leads this market."

Darrin knows that when Walter started the Burford plant, he wanted to produce high quality paint that offered tremendous value to dealers and customers. Twelve years ago, the plant produced two million gallons of paint. Today, with the renewed focus on enhanced systems and technologies, it makes four million with the same number of production people, a higher gallons-per-man-hour than any other plant in North America or Europe. Darrin says that his appointment to Vice-President was a proud moment. "It's one thing to be a VP in advertising or banking where everyone seems to be one, but at Home Hardware it is a huge honour because they are truly bestowing trust on you. The unfortunate thing is I lost Don Kirck along the way. He was a terrific guy and a great mentor to this plant. I learned a lot from him. But I had anticipated learning a lot more. If I could put it all back, Don would still be at my side."

"I started on a Monday and the next day, the NRHA was honouring Ray Gabel at a dinner. We arrived on two coaches and everyone was wearing their red jackets. I didn't have one at that point. I met Bill Ferguson around the table. Joe Cimicata was at the same table. Bill handed me his card and said, 'I'll set you up with the tie and red jacket you should be wearing right now.' Then Joe handed me a business card. But it wasn't his: it was my original CIL card from when I was 27 years old trying to sell him paint. And then he said, 'You know – we met before that.' And sure enough – when I first moved to Toronto – to see the bright lights and all that stuff - I moved into a house with five other guys. I went into Joe's store and bought a gallon of mis-tinted Hunter Green CIL paint to paint my basement bedroom in that house. And Joe remembered that."

One of Home Hardware's great strengths is its self-sufficiency and inner resourcefulness. Many of its systems, standards and procedures are proprietary. At the corporate level, a great deal has changed over the years. In the early days, Dianne remembers, not much was written down. There were few formal policies, no Director orientation, procedures, Conflict of Interest policy or Code of Conduct for Directors. The role, responsibilities and overall structure of the Board have become much more complex since then. Board members are dealing with greater complexities, guiding a major Canadian company so that any decisions are always in the best interests of the company and its shareholders, the Dealer-Owners. Much of this evolution was instigated, researched, developed and implemented by Dianne McTavish over the years in her position as Home Hardware's Corporate Secretary.

Regardless of its ingenuity, no company can function without outside expertise. After Mr. Zilliax, who was a lawyer and one of the three co-founders of Home Hardware, passed away, legal counsel was provided by Gordon Mackay Sr. , with a large and successful practice in his hometown of Waterloo. Home Hardware always had a special place in his heart, remembers his son Gord Mackay Jr. In fact, Gordon Sr. was Home's Assistant Corporate Secretary for many years. Gord's father had an excellent relationship with Walter Hachborn and was proud to have been part of a company that grew from relatively humble beginnings into a major player in the market. Gord Jr. articled with his father's firm and became Home Hardware's in-house counsel in 1994. Today he and Catherine Brohman, who joined the company in 2010, handle the many and varied legal responsibilities of the company. Gord's focus is primarily with the Dealer-Owners, from helping bring new members into the fold to applications from existing dealers for changes in ownership, relocations, expansions and changes in trading identities. Like so many of his Home Hardware colleagues, Gord remembers the Beaver acquisition as a career highlight, a period of extraordinary hard work rewarded by a sense of great accomplishment for everyone involved.

LeRoy Rellinger was Home Hardware's accountant from the Hollinger Hardware days (before the more recent relationship with KPMG). LeRoy would usually show up, unannounced, after lunch. "He'd have his scribbles on ledger paper," Dianne remembers, which she would then transform into a balance sheet or quarterly statement.

Dianne is one of the key "go to" people at Home Hardware. "When you don't know who to call, call Dianne," she says with a smile.

Dianne McTavish:

Vice-President and Corporate Secretary
St. Jacobs, ON

We are two seconds into our interview when Dianne McTavish demonstrates the memory for which she is famous. I ask when she started with Home Hardware. "May 26, 1976," she says. "No," she immediately corrects herself. "It was May 25, 1976."

The youngest of nine children, Dianne was raised on a farm north-west of St. Jacobs. The sudden loss of both her parents before she was 16 was life-changing for Dianne. In her words, "I grew up fast." She lived with her oldest brother and his family until she finished high school. She was all of 17.

Paul Straus, in his then-position as Controller, needed to replace his administrative assistant who was taking maternity leave. He canvassed the local high school's business department for candidates. Her grades exempted her from writing final exams so Dianne was able to start immediately. From school to a job with Home Hardware was quite a coup: Home already had a reputation as an excellent place to work. Dianne's organizational instincts kicked in: she remembers a box of dealer agreements on a shelf, no organization, no filing system. Needless to say, that state of affairs didn't last long.

Dianne acknowledges that she has a memory "like no one else." Much like Walter, she remembers peoples' names and their history. She attributes a lot of it to having "grown up in the business," in the days when there were fewer dealers. After the Link amalgamation in 1980, Revelstoke in 1987, and Beaver in 1999, suddenly Dianne had a lot more to file away in her steel trap of a mind. She has always taken pride in her attention to detail and the expanding business gave her ample opportunity to put it to excellent use. When Paul Straus took over as Executive Vice-President and General Manager in January of 1989 Dianne took on something new herself, the role of Assistant Corporate Secretary. It marked the beginning of her involvement with the Board of Directors. Dianne's predecessor, Ed Norman, passed away on March 17, 1997 and Dianne was subsequently appointed Corporate Secretary. On April 19, 2004 Dianne was appointed Vice-President and Corporate Secretary. There are three people with whom Dianne worked in the early years whose passion and knowledge continue to inspire her: Ed Norman, Gordon Mackay Sr and LeRoy Rellinger. Their dedication and commitment contributed enormously to making the business what it is today.

Dianne's husband Dave also works at Home Hardware. In fact, he has worked there longer than Dianne. Their two grown children have both recently completed university. Apart from gardening, Dianne's passion is Home Hardware. She is completely focused on the company's mission to help its dealers be successful, not only in their communities, but as family-owned businesses.

Having lived and breathed the world of hardware for 36 years, Dianne has enjoyed seeing it become more receptive to the influences of women, not only as they have assumed ownership of family businesses, but as they ascend the corporate ladder. There are three milestones that for Dianne reflect the changing role of women in a historically male-dominated industry. The first was when Marie Leger, from Moncton, New Brunswick, became the first woman to be appointed to Home Hardware's Board of Directors on April 25, 1988. The second came on April 14, 2003 when three women were appointed to serve on that same Board - Brigitte Michel-Finlay, from Sudbury, Ontario, Christine Hand, from Conception Bay South, Newfoundland, and Ada Kelly, from Dorchester, Ontario. And the third was at the Spring 2012 Market when Christine Hand was appointed Chairman of the Board. One of the good things about working in hardware is that there are people to fix the glass ceiling when it shatters. Just ask Dianne.

Grant Knowlton:

Vice-President, Finance
St. Jacobs, ON

"I already knew the culture – I knew some of the people – knew how they looked after the people and how it was a great company – one that I admired."

When Grant Knowlton was 15 years old, his uncle bought a hardware store in Coldwater, Ontario. For the next few years, working at that store was Grant's summer job. When he was 18, his father, along with the uncle who owned the store and another brother, decided to buy a grocery store in nearby Midland and convert it to a Home Hardware store. As part of the process, the Knowlton brothers paid a visit to St. Jacobs to meet Walter Hachborn. Grant went along on that trip. He was in his last year of high school. He remembers Walter asking about his plans after he graduated. Grant was already interested in business and said that he was thinking of going to Ryerson in Toronto (in those days not an accredited university), where he lived. Walter looked him square in the eye: "Why would you do that?" he asked. "You should go to university. And by the way, I am on the Board at Waterloo Lutheran University. That's where I think you should go."

Grant did exactly what Walter had told him to, after knuckling under to bring up his Grade 13 marks in order to be accepted. While he was at school, his father and uncles opened the new store in Midland and sold the Coldwater operation. After he graduated with a business degree in 1977 (WLU was Wilfred Laurier University by then) Grant joined the family business. Three years later, newly married, Grant moved to Listowel and after a couple more years working in the hardware industry, joined an accounting firm, going back to school to earn his CA designation at the same time. The hardware bug nailed him again when he saw an ad in the paper for an accounting position at Home Hardware. He applied, got the job and started working in St. Jacobs. It was 1988. He worked his way up through the department, becoming Corporate Controller in 1997. "You park your ego with this company," he says. "You have to roll up your sleeves and work hard, without expecting a lot of recognition. But it comes." In 2005, Grant Knowlton was appointed VP, Finance.

My standard question as to whether he ever wanted to own a hardware store is really moot - been there, done that. He says he felt he could do better, for Home Hardware and for himself, by taking advantage of his training as a Chartered Accountant.

Grant has experienced Home Hardware's distinctive culture from both sides: "When the family owned the store, we were down here for the markets with all the people and the exposure and you had the feeling you were part of a big company. And you had someone like Walter. For my father and uncle, Walter was God and he walked on water. So when I started working here and saw Walter every day, my father was …" Words appear to fail him, much as they must have for his father all those years ago. "To get the opportunity to come here and work on the corporate side was a bonus because I already knew the culture – I knew some of the people – I knew how they looked after the people and how it was a great company – one that I admired."

Grant and his wife still live in the house they bought in Listowel two years after they got married in 1980. Although he has no plans to retire, life has slowed down a bit for Grant these days. That is probably a good thing - at times in his career he has been accused of being a workaholic (just ask his wife, a recently-retired teacher), most memorably during the Beaver acquisition, a momentous time for everyone privileged to be a part of it. Reaching the billion dollars sales mark was another highlight, which figures, especially for someone with a head for that sort of thing.

"That chance meeting with Walter changed my direction in life," Grant says. "It helped me to build a successful career with a great company."

"I think the biggest difference at Home Hardware is how everybody cares, not only about the dealers but also about each other. Every business will tell you that people care but at Home Hardware people really care, to the degree that they don't feel right going home without knowing that things are looked after."

One of the many things I very much like about Home Hardware is its culture. Home Hardware is a people business: it cares about its customers, the dealers, its vendors and of course its employees. It has a strong history of supporting and developing people. Promotion is based on performance and values and earned on merit. One of Home Hardware's most recent appointments to the position of VP is an excellent example. There is a certain symmetry to John Dyksterhuis's career trajectory. John

Pallet program, the global leader in pallet and container pooling services. It ensured quality control throughout Home Hardware's supply chain. A few years later, in 1992, the department, under the direction of Don Kirck, introduced radio frequency technology, essentially barcode scanning. He was also there when EDI (Electronic Data Interchange) was introduced that allowed Home Hardware to communicate electronically with suppliers. "There have been a lot of key innovations," John says, "and I've been lucky:

John Dyksterhuis:

For John, the best part of the job is the people; overseeing "all the good people" who make it happen in Distribution - over 1,000 of them - gives John great pride.

Vice-President, Distribution
St. Jacobs, ON

was born and raised in Palmerston northwest of Waterloo. He started working at a small family business in the hospitality industry. After reaching the position of assistant manager by the tender age of 20, John realized that the job did not offer room for his ambitions. He looked around for a place that could and applied at Home Hardware. After a compact interview process with Roy Gilles - he started work one week after his follow-up interview - John was hired as an order processor in the St. Jacobs Distribution Centre.

It was 1986 and although John knew Home Hardware offered him "more opportunity than you could ever imagine" he didn't imagine that 25 years later he would be Vice President responsible for the very same department in which he began his Home Hardware career. His current position as Vice-President, of Distribution encompasses the operational aspects of all four Home Hardware distribution centres - St. Jacobs, Elmira, Ontario, Debert, Nova Scotia and Wetaskiwin, Alberta. His area of responsibility includes the daily production side of the business along with maintenance, credits and returns and Home Hardware's private fleet of 150 power units and more than 500 trailers. (Home Hardware has received the Large Fleet Safety Award from the Private Motor Council of Canada four times since 2005.) For John, the best part of the job is the people; overseeing "all the good people" who make it happen in Distribution - over 1,000 of them - gives John great pride.

Over the years, John acquired a comprehensive understanding of the company's operations. After nine months "picking" in the warehouse, Laverne Martin promoted him to the position of "Freight Analyst". In that role, he was responsible for analyzing freight costs and the myriad complexities that job entails. By 1990, he was Receiving Manager which coincided with one of the warehouse expansions which opened a world of opportunity: John was involved in the implementation of the CHEP

over the years, I have been involved with many of the major projects."

In 1995, John moved to Ray Gabel's Hardlines department as a Product Manager, which was when I would have met him. Those were early days for Home at Home magazine, and my role was to develop editorial content tied to product categories and specific vendors who in turn supported the magazine through advertising. The revenue generated helped to offset production costs of the high quality magazine. I could not have accomplished this four times a year without the endless support of all the Product Managers, and of Ray Gabel. In those early days I spent a lot of time canvassing the Product Managers for ideas - for stories, products and vendor support, always the critical component. John, whose categories eventually grew to encompass Building Products and Heating, was meticulous: he would have prepared detailed lists, his handwriting tight and precise, crowding a lot of information onto every page. John also crowds a lot of work into every day, usually arriving by 6:30 in the morning and leaving about 12 hours later. It's a pattern that was in evidence early in John's career at Home Hardware and is the basis for a funny story about his first encounter with the man who would eventually appoint him Vice-President. One evening, around 6 o'clock, John was in the parking lot trying to get his car started so he could go home. It was a warm spring evening and he had the hood up and was tinkering with the engine. He took off his shirt to prevent grease stains. Someone, who at the time he did not recognize, came up behind him and asked if he needed any help. John declined with thanks and after the man walked away asked someone who he was. Paul Straus, he was told.

When I ask about his passion, John doesn't mince words: "My passion is to always excel at what I do. I don't believe in doing things by halves." It is no surprise then that John has a whole world of respect and gratitude for everything Home Hardware has allowed him to achieve.

John Rogez, VP, Information Technology, has a soft voice and a lovely Cape Breton accent that means he talks very-very quickly. He has a perpetual air of quiet astonishment that is enormously endearing. John is responsible for Home Hardware's computer systems – both internally and externally in the stores across Canada. Approximately 165 people work in his department. That's a lot of IT.

After that rocky start, hilarious now but not so much then, along with the challenge of finding housing in a university town, John was astonished to realize that the sense of family he had experienced in Truro was at work in St. Jacobs. Thanks to the Home Hardware "network", they were able to find a lovely home and quickly settled in.

John Rogez:

To say that John Rogez is a Montreal Canadiens fan is an understatement. He is obsessed. He is passionate.

Vice-President, Information Technology
St. Jacobs, ON

And it represents quite the journey from Glace Bay, Cape Breton where John was raised. In 1982, John and his girlfriend Wilma had recently graduated from university. Wilma was sending out job applications for them both, including one for John to a simple PO Box in Truro, Nova Scotia. He was invited to an interview at Home Hardware's Distribution Centre in Debert for a job in the computer operations department. (He tells a funny story about borrowing his mother's car and being stopped by a policeman on the way back home because the headlights were malfunctioning so the cop figured he was signalling oncoming traffic. John thought it was a bad omen, but instead, he landed the job and started working the night shift.) John was astonished by how he and his fiancée were so quickly and naturally absorbed into the Home Hardware family: they helped the young couple find a place to live, they signed him up for the company baseball and hockey teams, they even made him MC at that year's Christmas Party! In 1985, Home Hardware switched from distributed databases to centralized data processing, and John was invited to transfer to St. Jacobs. Home Hardware brought him to St. Jacobs to look around. More astonishment: "I met Walter Hachborn and he knew my name, where I was from – and I'm thinking 'You're kidding me.' This guy met me once and he knows all about me. He's really a brilliant, brilliant man. And the Home Hardware culture keeps getting passed along, to Paul, then Terry - the values just keep going."

Ontario was a big move - their families were in Cape Breton where John had envisioned his life unfolding. John and Wilma decided to cement one big decision with another and were married on April 13, 1985. They arrived at their Waterloo hotel on April 16, tired from the long trip. Someone (who shall remain nameless) had decided to play a trick: earlier that evening, a couple purporting to be John and Wilma Rogez checked into the "Honeymoon Suite" John had booked. When the real John and Wilma showed up, they were told "they" were already here, and therefore could not be who they claimed to be!

John was appointed Vice-President in October 2007. He knew that others were being considering for the role and was honoured to be included in the preliminary process. When he was summoned to Paul's office the final time and offered the position, he was so astonished that he had to pinch himself. He had to keep it hush-hush, until Paul advised the Board and Senior Management—hard for someone whose sense of gratitude and excitement were very difficult to contain. Fortunately, Paul told him he could tell Wilma. John says that Board meetings and Strategic Planning sessions are "pretty cool", but he especially likes unveiling new technology at the Markets. "That's always a highlight," he says in his soft voice. "If we can help someone do better at their business – hey, we're doing something right."

To say that John Rogez is a Montreal Canadiens fan is an understatement. He is obsessed. He is passionate. When he was very young (about three years old) his dad would let him stay up to watch the Habs play, rinsing his face with a cool cloth and feeding him goodies to help him to stay awake. These days, with the NHL package it is possible to watch a game every night. "When Wilma asks "What's on tonight,' I say, Honey, you know what's on!" But when the kids were young - one daughter, Rebecca is a student at Dal pursuing her MBA, the other, Melissa is at Conestoga College, currently doing a work placement in Home Hardware's Marketing department - there was no hockey on Friday nights. "We'd do a family activity and then go home and have pizza and watch a movie—that one night was kind of sacred." If you know John and his complete and total mania for hockey, that truly is astonishing.

SHIPPING
AND RECEIVING

SITTLER
BUILDING
ENTRANCE

STAFF
PARKING

"You feel good about working with good people. You feel good about working with a company that has the reputation Home Hardware has. You feel proud telling people where you work. You're going to hear this from everyone: We have great people here."

Stew Gingrich:

Vice-President, Human Resources
St. Jacobs, ON

"In a world where job loyalty is virtually nonexistent, Home Hardware is an anomaly. The people who work at Home Hardware stay at Home Hardware."

In 1972 Stew Gingrich was a 19 year-old kid from Saskatchewan who followed his older brothers east after he finished high school. After six months in a small town near London, Stew moved to Kitchener-Waterloo and started looking for a job.

I am not sure whether the Vice-President, Human Resources would approve of the way Stew landed his first job at Home Hardware. A friend working there tipped him off about a job driving the furniture delivery truck at the retail store downtown. But he lost out to someone else. Shortly after that disappointment, the same friend told him to call Paul Straus at home. He spoke with Paul's wife Jo-Anne who said she was to ask if he wanted a job. Well, of course he did. That Sunday night, without benefit of an interview, he reported to the warehouse for the 11 o'clock shift and Aden Shantz put him to work. It was September 24, 1972. His successful rival on the furniture truck, Ivan Unruh, and he both started on the same date. Stew always told Ivan he (Stew) had seniority because he started on the night shift the day before. "But later, I always put Ivan's name before mine when we reported anniversaries in the Staff newsletter," Stew says with a laugh. After a year of night shift, Stew applied for a posting as Returns and Credit Manager and left the warehouse. He was about to be married, so the timing was good. In 1981, he made another move, becoming Personnel Manager. At the time, there were about 200 employees at Home Hardware. Today there are more than 2,000. Over time, the position changed to become Human Resources Manager, then Director of Human Resources and in April 2004 Stew Gingrich was appointed Vice-President, Human Resources.

Stew likes working with people; he likes the multi-generational phenomenon that happens throughout Home Hardware as well as within individual family-owned stores. He points out that husbands and wives find each other "on the job." He attributes it partially to the fact that the community itself is small and close knit even though Home Hardware is the largest employer in Woolwich Township. Families tend to remain in the area for generations. But mostly he credits Mr. Hachborn with establishing a culture that attracts and retains loyal, hardworking employees. "He is so sincere, so genuine, so real: all our staff can see that," Stew says. "And he's such a humble person – he just doesn't want to be recognized for all the things that he has done."

As VP, Human Resources, Stew knows very well the kind of individual who will succeed at Home Hardware. "The people who are successful with us don't say – that's not my job. They do whatever they need to do and then they do more because it's part of who we are."

That is why, the night before our interview, Stew was in the warehouse into the wee hours of the morning along with other members of the Senior Management team, cooking up burgers at the night shift's summer staff barbecue.

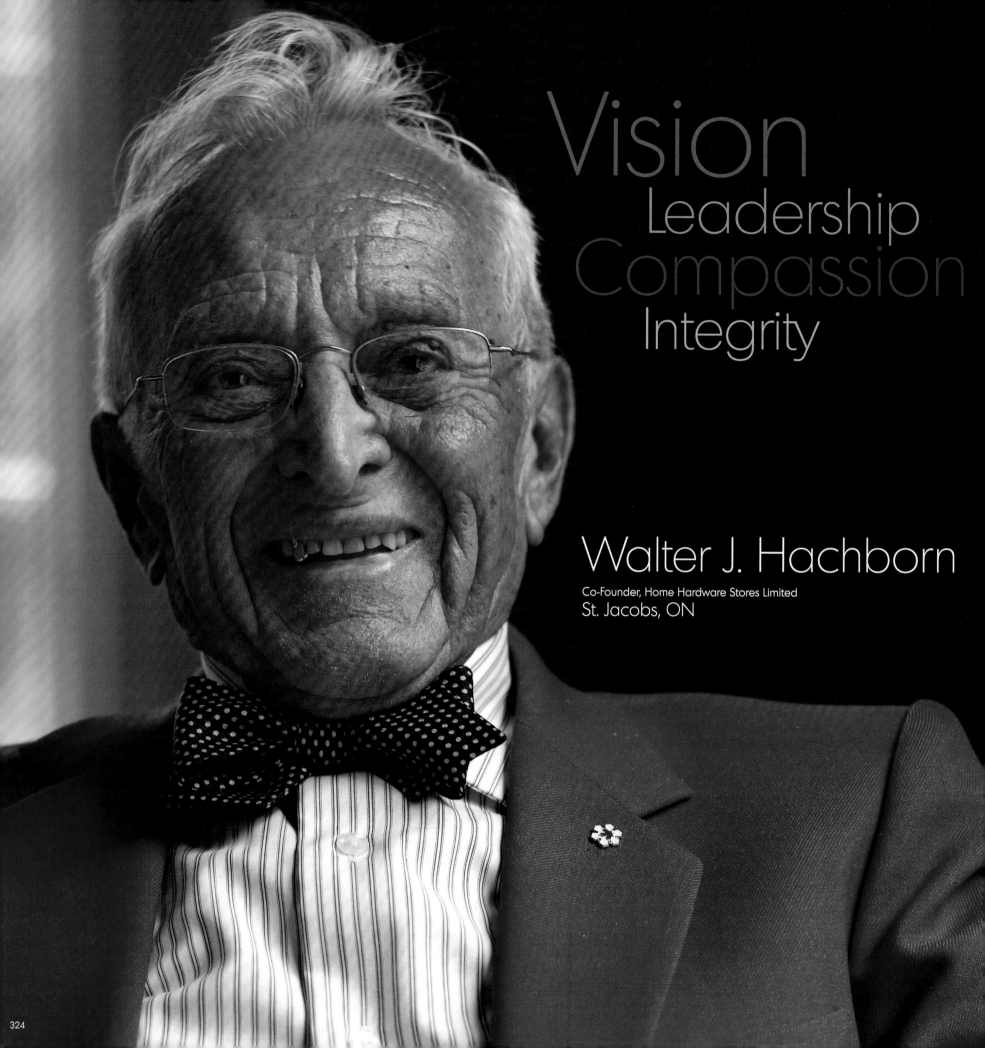

Vision
Leadership
Compassion
Integrity

Walter J. Hachborn

Co-Founder, Home Hardware Stores Limited
St. Jacobs, ON

Henry Sittler:

Co-Founder, Home Hardware Stores Limited
St. Jacobs, ON

As VP, Merchandise, at Home Hardware Stores Limited Ray Gabel heads up a team of Product Managers who are responsible for buying millions of dollars worth of products from around the world for the Home Hardware Dealer-Owners across the county. But to this day he maintains that he learned everything from the man he still calls Mr. Sittler.

Henry Sittler was born in 1904 near the small town of Wallenstein, about 12 kilometers northwest of St. Jacobs. He started his retail life in his early twenties, working as a clerk at Welker's General Store in St. Jacobs. Before he was thirty, he had been hired away by Henry Gilles who owned the hardware store down the street. He remained as a key player and General Manager throughout its transformation from Gilles Hardware to Hollinger Hardware, from retail only to the decision to move into wholesale. In 1949, Henry Sittler, Walter Hachborn and Arthur Zilliax, a lawyer, bought the business from the Hollinger estate and their successful partnership resulted in the creation of Home Hardware Stores Limited in 1964. In those early years, many major vendors refused to treat the Dealer-Owned company as a legitimate wholesaler, because they were under pressure from other wholesalers to not recognize them as such. Henry Sittler's

persistence and negotiating skills ensured the company's wholesaler status and earned him tremendous respect within the industry.

In the meantime, a young Ray Gabel, fresh out of high school, came to work at the business on King Street North where he learned the value of a dollar from his mentor Mr. Sittler. "He was very cost conscious," Ray remembers. "But he was also up on the trends from the shows he visited and the trade magazines he scoured. So he was always willing to take chances on new products."

The working relationship that Ray and Mr. Sittler forged when Ray joined the company in 1950 was invaluable to the young man who had taken so thoroughly to the hardware business. According to Ray, even after Henry Sittler officially left to become General Manager of United Hardware Wholesalers in 1967, "his heart was always with Home Hardware." It was his mentoring that gave Ray the grounding that has seen him become an industry legend in his own right. Their relationship became a template for many others within the organization and beyond. "No one was threatened by anyone else," Ray remembers. The mantra was, and remains, dedication to the cause.

Home Hardware Giving

In its own quiet way, Home Hardware has an extraordinary reputation for generosity, giving from the heart. In addition to its official corporate charities, Tree Canada, Communities in Bloom, Special Olympics and Sick Kids Foundation, Home Hardware also contributes generously and continuously to the ongoing fundraising initiatives of several organizations including the Mennonite Relief Fund and the Joy and Hope of Haiti. And on the thankfully rare occasion when disaster strikes close to home, Home Hardware is always there. One of the more remarkable illustrations of a grassroots and collective response occurred in August 2005 when a tornado ripped through the region north of St. Jacobs.

Although "Marnie and the Tornado" sounds like a sweet children's story, it was anything but. Marnie Drost has been an art director at Home Hardware for over 20 years. She and her husband live on a large working cattle farm north of St Jacobs.

Marnie Drost:

Home Hardware Staff
St. Jacobs, ON

At 2:20, she got a call. It was her husband Tom, who seldom calls her at work. She knew immediately something was wrong. "What happened?" she demanded. "We were hit by a tornado," Tom said.

It was Friday, August 19, 2005. Marnie remembers the day all too clearly: she was working in the Home Hardware studio, without benefit of windows. Suddenly the electricity went out and she could hear rain pounding against the building. She wondered idly whether it was raining at home - it had been a very dry year. At 2:20, she got a call. It was her husband Tom, who seldom calls her at work. She knew immediately something was wrong. "What happened?" she asked. "Everyone's fine, but you need to come home," Tom said. "We were hit by a tornado." As she drove north, along normally bucolic country roads, the devastation escalated - roads blocked by fallen trees and tangled wire. The police were diverting traffic. Marnie traced a circuitous route along back roads, arriving at the far end of the farm where Tom had said he would rendezvous with her by "the fallen tree" - was there only one, she wondered? Everything was down as far as she could see. She was wearing red shoes that she took off to crawl through the debris. The farm was unrecognizable. While she had been working, blissfully unaware of the carnage at the farm, 450 cattle had already been transported out of the danger zone, including a barn whose roof had totally collapsed. Only two animals had to be put down due to injury. Marnie wondered about their home, a beautiful 19th century stone original. Fortunately, it had not sustained much damage, although they had lost 20 two hundred year-old maple trees. (Their elderly neighbour across the road remembered seeing the trees slowly bending over in one direction, then straightening up and slowly bending all the way over in the other, like seniors at an exercise class.)

By end of day Saturday, the trees had been cleared. But the work had only just begun: as the saying goes, when you're 90% finished, you're halfway done. On Monday morning the phone rang. Ray Gabel and Paul Straus were on the speakerphone. What can we do, they asked. A donations jar was put in the cafeteria. Home Hardware kept them supplied with water and work gloves. And people from Home Hardware started showing up to join the work crews. The local Mennonite relief group spent several full days on the site. Marnie was astounded at how fast they worked. Feeding the crews—sometimes as many as 200 people—was a huge organizational feat, funded in large part by ongoing donations and thanks to a double fridge, all organized by Marnie's endlessly resourceful and enterprising friends and associates at Home Hardware, Jennine Camm, Jessica Passmore and Tammie Piel to name only a few. Retired Home Hardware employee, June Bauman, renowned for her Christmas food day confections while still working, "cooked up a storm", Marnie recalls. Marnie remembers meal times: the Mennonites washed up, waited for everyone quietly, then bowed their heads and prayed. The Mennonite Relief Trailer placed on site was kept stocked with tools, hardware and other work crew essentials, thanks to the generosity of Home Hardware's Product Managers and vendors and, as Marnie calls them, "the head honchos" managing the relief effort at their end. In addition to all the support for the Drosts, Home Hardware also sent over a trailer to a neighbour whose pipes burst and house flooded after the hydro was turned back on, so that she could store her furniture during the mopping up exercise.

Years later, the Drosts are still cleaning up after "Freaky Friday" as the media labeled it, although the farm long ago returned to its busy former state. When we first visited in late 2011, the last barn standing still wore its buckled-in roof like a badge of honour. By the following spring, it too had been repaired. The Drosts are eternally grateful to Home Hardware for the steady, quiet and critical support that the company provided on so many levels when it was needed most. Home truly is where the heart is.

Raymond Carrière: Communities in Bloom was the perfect fit for Home Hardware.

Communities in Bloom

From the core values at the organization's heart to the manner in which the contact was originally forged and the partnership's subsequent evolution, the story of Communities in Bloom is classic Home Hardware and illustrative of them all.

Raymond Carrière began his career in parks management with the National Capital Commission in Ottawa. By the mid 1980s, he had moved back to Quebec where he was Park Manager in Ville St Laurent, north west of Montreal and where he was introduced to In Bloom, a beautification program in which almost 500 Quebec communities participated. In Bloom was established in the UK, France and Ireland, but, Raymond was surprised to learn, did not have a presence in Canada outside of Quebec. So in the mid 1990s, a group of volunteers, along with a few sponsors, set about to remedy that. What started as a simple annual contest between Park Managers from various cities across the country bloomed into the successful national organization that is Communities in Bloom today.

Raymond laughs at their naiveté in those days: "We thought we would start this nice program and then either the government or another organization would take it on. Well, that didn't happen – and it's a good thing because it meant we had to find funding ourselves. We looked at grants, we looked at registration from the communities but we also looked at sponsorships." Some of their original sponsors came from the agriculture industry, including Green Cross and Nutrite, which were Home Hardware vendors. The introduction to Home Hardware came through Frank Zaunscherb who owns the Burlington-based marketing firm ZRB that created the Communities in Bloom logo. Another client was Green Cross whose product manager, Barry Newcombe, realized that Communities in Bloom was the perfect fit for Home Hardware.

And so the introduction was made and in 2002, Communities in Bloom became a Home Hardware corporate sponsorship partner. It didn't hurt during the wooing process that towns in the area around Kitchener-Waterloo, including Stratford and Woodstock, were already Communities in Bloom participants so the people they were meeting in St. Jacobs recognized the name from the signs they saw in and around their communities. It also didn't hurt that the Home Hardware store in Charlottetown, PEI was already an enthusiastic participant in their local Communities in Bloom as was the community of Lloydminster, Saskatchewan, home of the dynamic Home Hardware family, the Rurkas.

It's an ideal marriage not least because Communities in Bloom communities are also invariably towns where a Home Hardware is to be found and Home Hardware's structure allows Communities in Bloom to benefit from "the trickle down effect": not only does Home Hardware corporate sponsor Communities in Bloom at the national level, but many dealers now become involved at the local level: the store in Stratford hosts a barbecue every year in support of their local chapter. Canada's most loved gardener, Mark Cullen, is a Communities in Bloom ambassador as he travels across the country promoting Mark's Choice gardening tools and products. In fact, Communities in Bloom offers Mark as a prize to winning communities.

Raymond says that Home Hardware "gets" Communities in Bloom, both corporately and at the dealer level. "Yes," he acknowledges, "at the end of the day, they are involved because they want to bring people into their stores. But that's not the only reason. They really want to do something in the community. I've been pleased to see over the years that even if many dealers are not the presidents of the local business chapters, they are members. "And also avid, knowledgeable gardeners, apparently. Communities in Bloom surveys show that communities are getting good advice from the local Home Hardware Dealers.

"There's always a local garden club or horticultural society but there is also the local downtown business association. There are the social clubs like the Lions, and the Legion." So Home Hardware is "not a sell, but a fit". Like so many people who have had the good fortune to work with him Raymond cannot say enough about Mr. Gabel, as he calls him. At one of their annual meetings, Ray was leafing through the Communities in Bloom magazine remarking on the quality of the photographs. He kept murmuring, "These are nice pictures." The wheels were obviously spinning - no surprise there - because a few days later, Raymond got a call from Rob Wallace, Home Hardware's manager of Public Relations. "Mr. Gabel has suggested that you might like to work with us on our charity calendar next year." That was in 2011 and Communities in Bloom and Home Hardware communities across the country have been featured in the calendars every year since then.

Raymond pays tribute to Home Hardware and Ray Gabel: "If we're still with Home Hardware, it is because of Mr. Gabel's appreciation of Communities in Bloom. Whatever we've done, it has always been a discussion, a handshake. Yes, we sign the 15 page contract, but Mr. Gabel has always believed in building the relationship." He says that at its heart, that relationship has always been about respecting the dealers and respecting the local communities. "They give us funds. They give us resources. And then they say 'thank you' for involving them in the program. I always say that it should be the other way around. We should be thanking them."

The Joy and Hope of Haiti

Since the first school was built all those years ago, Home Hardware has been a committed supporter of The Joy and Hope of Haiti.

Haiti, still a beautiful island, was once considered the jewel of the Caribbean. Now, through years of civil strife, poverty, disease, natural disasters and neglect, the country has been reduced to a seemingly helpless state. The infant mortality rate is 80.3 per 1000 and one in three children does not live past the age of ten. Chronic malnutrition affects 23% of children under five and 65% of these same aged children suffer from anemia.

Haiti also has an 80% illiteracy rate. Typically, only one member of a family is chosen to go to school. Educational facilities are primitive. Children are packed into small, hot, dark classrooms, two to a desk. Tiny slate boards and chalk serve in place of pencils and paper. Teachers earn very little and often go unpaid. Recreational facilities are non-existent.

Despite it all, this is where you will find the hope and future of Haiti. Twenty-three years ago a small group of men, aware of the desperate state in the country, founded a volunteer organization to build schools in northern Haiti. They called themselves The Joy and Hope of Haiti and devised "Their children. Our challenge" as a mission statement, believing that the cycle of poverty and government ineptitude can only be overcome by a new generation of educated children.

Since then twenty-six schools, including a trade school, have been built by that small group of volunteers. Every year teams of volunteers have returned: men, women and youth volunteers from different professions and walks of life. The Canadian visitors work hand-in-hand with local Haitians to plan, build and operate the schools. Thousands of kids now fill the classrooms. The children also receive a nutritious meal, in most cases their only meal of the day.

Since the first school was built, Home Hardware has been a committed supporter of The Joy and Hope of Haiti. In co-operation with its suppliers, Home donates building materials, most of which are not readily available in Haiti. And each year, in the form of hundreds of donated items, Home actively supports The Joy and Hope of Haiti's annual fundraising dinner and auction where annually over $100,000 is raised for the ongoing school construction and feeding programs.

Ray Gabel, who oversees the donation process, is proud that Home Hardware has been able to contribute to the efforts of this group of dedicated volunteers. "The fact that they went to Haiti with a purpose 23 years ago and remain there today, despite all the turmoil, devastation and hardship, is why thousands of Haitian children can attend school today. We especially like the fact that because the group is entirely volunteer, every penny raised goes directly to building and maintaining the schools."

Home Hardware suppliers & vendors:

One of the many pleasures of an invitation to the semi-annual Home Hardware markets is the chance to be part of the great "vendor gathering" that plays such a role in these events. From the set up days prior to the market itself, to the pre-market seminars and the three long days of the market, there is always opportunity to catch up with people who, over the years, have become friends even if we only see each other occasionally. Most of these people have been coming to the Home Hardware market for years. The majority of them have been working for the same company for years as well. There's a continuity that is very much in keeping with Home's own culture. The relationship between a retailer and its vendors speaks volumes. So it is no surprise that, without exception, everyone I have ever spoken with at these shows has only good things to say about the company that has invited them to attend. Home Hardware has hundreds of valued vendors. Given space limitations, this book can only highlight a precious few of the stories I have heard over the years. The stories have been chosen because each, in its own way, expresses the regard and affection these individuals have for Home Hardware.

NESCO® American Harvest®

Roger Smith, partner with United Sales and Marketing, Aileen and George Bolton at the US & Marketing booth at the Home Hardware market Fall 2011, Aileen's last show. Roger and Aileen first worked together in the 1980s at Black & Decker and have been friends ever since. Roger, who lives around the corner from Aileen's son Neil in Etobicoke, organized a surprise 80th birthday party for Aileen at The Benjamin Inn in 2010, where Aileen has stayed for the duration of each market since the hotel in downtown St Jacobs opened in 1988.

Aileen Passmore: "I have done many, many trade shows, but going to the Home Hardware show is the most fun of all."

In September 2011, Aileen Passmore worked her 50th and final Home Hardware market having just celebrated her 81st birthday. She has been a fixture at these markets where she first started "demo-ing" for Black and Decker and was currently cooking up a delicious storm in Roger Smith's United Sales and Marketing booth. It's likely that everyone who has regularly attended the markets over the years knows Aileen. She's a good person to know, with her reputation for sharing whatever goodies she is currently concocting. Walter Hachborn knows her as "the cookie lady". To some, she's "the pie lady." A few years ago, Aileen was picking something up for her daughter Brenda Empringham at the Home Hardware store in Sunderland where Brenda lives. She noticed that the dealer was looking at her with a funny expression and when she got to the check out, he said, "I know you from somewhere." Aileen said, "You may very well know me, but I doubt you know my name." Suddenly his eyes lit up and he said, "Now I know who you are: you're the bread lady!"

For long time market attendees, she is like a mother, a sister, or at the very least, a long lost friend. Everyone loves Aileen, not just for her cooking, but also for her gentle, contagious enthusiasm, her deep-seated decency, work ethic and her obvious love for her "job."

True to form, when I visited Aileen at her home in Gravenhurst, one of Muskoka's venerable towns, she had prepared a spread – fresh fruit and warm muffins that we shared as she told the stories that illustrated her abiding affection for Home Hardware. She is as generous with her hospitality as she is with her cooking: Several years ago, she told me as we settled in, a Home Hardware employee was shopping around to buy a store of his own. Two of the Product Managers, Sandy Jordan and Susan Benner, went along with him one day. They called Aileen from Huntsville to let her know that they would be in Gravenhurst shortly. As their car pulled into the driveway, Aileen pulled a pan of cookies out of the oven.

Aileen and her husband Jim, who celebrated their 60th wedding anniversary in 2011, have lived in their comfortable year-round home on the shores of Gull Lake since 1989. With its lake view and lawn stretching down to the shores of the lake, it must be as beautiful throughout the quiet winter as it is now in its summer glory.

For a long time, Jim never really understood Aileen's love affair with Home Hardware. Several years ago, however, he joined her on a vacation trip bus tour to the Maritimes. As they were driving through Grand Falls, New Brunswick, Aileen asked the driver to stop so that she could go into Timmy and Carm Toner's store in town. She was greeted like a lost relative, the Toners insisting that she and her husband stay with them. Aileen gently pointed out that they were travelling with a full busload, but Aileen's husband suddenly understood what she had been talking about for all those years.

As with so many other vendors, Aileen feels like an honorary member of the Home Hardware family. And that sentiment is obviously reciprocated. In May 2011, the local Gravenhurst store, just five blocks from Aileen's house, had a grand opening to celebrate new owners Ian and Tara McNaughton (the original owners, Rob and Kaja Clark, still own Home Hardware stores in Bracebridge and Huntsville and go to "Walter's island" Abaco in the Bahamas every winter). Aileen had gone into the store to introduce herself and to welcome them (the McNaughtons, a young couple, spent five years looking to buy a business, eventually choosing Home Hardware because it matched their family and business values). The McNaughtons immediately invited Aileen to be the hostess at their grand opening. For four days, she arrived every morning with a cake that she picked up en route (no, she did not bake it herself!), made a big pot of coffee and stationed herself just beyond the front door. She wore her Walter bow tie pinned to her lapel. It was her distinct honour and pleasure to introduce the Mayor of Gravenhurst, Paisley Donaldson to Walter and Jean Hachborn when they came through the door the night of the Grand Opening. Walter and Jean have a summer home on an island in Kashe Lake, just south of town. Walter turned to Jean and said, "This lady is a real veteran. She cooks and cooks and cooks!"

Aileen is a true "show person". She says, "I have done many, many trade shows, but going to the Home Hardware show is the most fun of all." One of her favourite treats has been the opportunity to meet the families of the dealers over the years. On one occasion, Aileen could see from the dealer's yellow badge that she was from Wadena, Saskatchewan. In true hometown fashion, Aileen asked her if she knew Eva Earley, Aileen's great-aunt. The dealer gave a little gasp and said, "She's my mother's best friend!" (Cindy and Perry Banadyga have since moved to Alberta where they own the local Home Hardware store.)

Aileen had told two old friends about our pending visit and we planned to speak by phone during my visit with Aileen. George Bolton worked for Charlescraft until his retirement in March 2011, and Wally McTaggart ended his sales career with The Holmes Group in 2004. I have had the pleasure of knowing both of these fine people for many years and understand how much they value their relationship with Home Hardware. In George's case, that goes back to 1978. His first market in the fall of 1978 was the last one held at Bingemans.

Vendors often have great stories about their experiences with different Product Managers and George was no exception. Don Kenesky, who has long been a buyer with Home, is famous for his long pauses. According to George, newcomers to his office all have to go through their initiation. George remembers his baptism by silence: he waited downstairs to be called up and when he got into "DK's" office, Don was sitting there flipping through a massive stack of paper, all the Home Hardware listings. George wasn't sure whether to start talking or wait for Don to finish whatever he was doing. He quickly learned that this was Don's "method" but still laughs at the memory.

Wally McTaggart

Wally McTaggart and Aileen are in touch on a regular basis, even after he retired (for the second time) in 2008 from The Holmes Group, the company for which he had worked for eight years. I was at his official retirement party in April 2004 at the Lions Head Golf and Country Club hosted by Home Hardware with Gerry Byle as Master of Ceremonies. Ray gave a speech that night, at the end of which, Ray and Sandy Jordan presented Wally with a Home Hardware red jacket. The symbolism of this gesture was enormous and Wally was profoundly moved. Apparently special permission was received from Walter Hachborn and Paul Straus in order for this to happen – after all, as Wally points out, dealers invest huge amounts of money, talent and time for the privilege of wearing the Home Hardware red jacket. "I have always respected that coat, so I don't wear it around," Wally told me. The one occasion on which he did, there was a funny case of mistaken identity. Wally and his wife Dianne were at a special anniversary celebration at the Farringdon Church on the outskirts of Brantford, where they lived. A man came up to him and said quietly "I know who you are." And Wally said, "Well, you've got me," not recognizing the fellow at all. "Yes," the man continued, "you're that RCMP officer who's investigating the murder of that girl out in BC." Wally said, "Wow, you really put that together," not confirming or denying anything. "You understand that I can't say anything," he continued, "so I'd just like to shake your hand and wish you a pleasant day." He hasn't worn the jacket since but he still treasures it. Every year around Christmas, he and Ray, who have known one another for over 40 years, have a good long chat on the phone to catch up.

George White's parents LaVerne and Freda owned a farm in the beautiful countryside near Arthur, Ontario. In the mid 1950s they started All Treat, a package business selling dehydrated alfalfa and manure to wholesalers in the area, one of whom was Hollinger Hardware. In the early 1960s, they added birdseed to the product offering. According to George, when your family owns a business, you always work there, learning it inside out along

George White:

All Treat Farms
Arthur, ON

the way, but he did not officially join the family firm until 1973. It was the last thing he thought he would do, but almost 40 years later, George heads up a company that is proud to be one of Home Hardware's oldest suppliers.

Like other long time vendors who essentially grew up with Home Hardware, some of George's favourite moments involved bringing new products to Ray Gabel that together they would introduce to the market. Today Home Hardware remains one of All Treat's largest customers, buying from them a range of soils and mulches, much of it branded Home Hardware private label. "They are always open to new ideas," George says. "If they think it's a good idea, they'll try it and if it fails – it fails." But for the most part, they succeed, and as far as George is concerned, Home Hardware is the best company to work with in the industry. When things go wrong, as they occasionally do, "they'll work with you – they won't take all those years of past history and reliability and trust and just throw them out the door. If everyone were like that, life would be a lot easier. And nicer."

It often fell to Ray Gabel to gather vendor support in the form of advertising surcharges. One year, All Treat was having a tough time paying the required amount. Invoices kept arriving in the mail and George knew the time had come to address the issue. He sat in Ray's office attempting to explain the reason for their tardiness. Ray pulled out a pair of earmuffs and put them on his head. He grabbed a Billy stick from another drawer and started thwacking it against his hand. Finally, he waved a cheque from another small local vendor in George's face. The message was clear: no more excuses. George took a closer look at the cheque. "Well," he said, "if I didn't sign the cheque either, I could give you one too!"

George has a running joke with Walter Hachborn who is the same age as his father LaVerne (who passed away in 1994). "I always call him Mr. Hachborn – and he looks at me and says, ' George, you know my name is Walter.' I've done this my whole life because I know that's what he'll always say."

In 1969, Don Choi moved from Sweden to Canada. For one year he and his brother ran a profitable Toronto-based business importing wigs from Korea. The following year, Don used his share of the profits to buy a United Cigar store in a mall in Kitchener. As fate would have it, the plaza also housed a Home Hardware store owned by Graham Ferguson, a Charter Member and Home Hardware's first Chairman of the Board.

Don Choi:

Donald Choi Canada Ltd.
Waterloo, ON

Graham convinced Don that his future lay with Home Hardware and introduced him to Ray Gabel. Although he had no hardware experience, it was the perfect match: Don understood the import business and Ray understood people. It was also timely. Home Hardware needed to start developing private label products. Don, with his knowledge of the Far East as an emerging manufacturing resource, was an ideal partner in this new initiative. "Ray's principle was quality, quality, quality," Don says, sitting in his warehouse a few miles down the road from Home Hardware.

The first item Ray asked Don to source was a cast iron fireplace grate. It was Don's first foray into a new world of opportunity and he was nervous. " Home Hardware already knew the quality they expected, so if I chose wrong, I was finished," he remembers.

In fact, it was just the beginning. With Ray as Don's guide through the new world of hardware merchandise, and Don as Ray's guide through the new world of the Far East, the two embarked on a remarkably successful working relationship that started in Korea, moved onto Taiwan and in 1980 expanded to mainland China. Forty-two years later, while the company has other clients, mostly furniture retailers, Donald Choi Canada Ltd. has an exclusive relationship with Home Hardware in the hardware category. "We trust each other and when I have that kind of trust placed in me why would I explore other opportunities with other people?" Don asks rhetorically. The product mix is extensive, from power tools, gardening tools and plumbing to housewares and the Kuraidori family of kitchen products. "If we didn't find new items we would be stale," Don says, acknowledging that working with Ray on new product development is still one of his favourite responsibilities. In all the years they have worked together, Home Hardware has never cancelled an order. If he makes a mistake, he is given the opportunity to fix it. So it is no surprise that at 72 years old Don still has the air of someone who loves what he does. "Every day," he says, "my goal is to make Home Hardware happy."

"We were catering the Home Hardware show in St. Jacobs just after 9/11," Lawrence recalls. "Walter and I were talking about how this had affected things. Walter just said, 'Lawrny, don't worry. This won't last forever.'"

Lawrence Bingeman:

By the early 1970s, Bingemans became to the Home Hardware markets what a horse is to a buggy.

Bingemans
Kitchener, ON

Lawrence Bingeman stands in a landscaped bowl, a sprawling conference centre and sweeping parking lot to his left, another large building and outdoor pavilions behind him. He's looking at a colourful geometric tangle that is a water park and there's some major construction underway at the top of the hill that will be a Boston Pizza and Kingpin Bowlounge by next summer.

Welcome to Bingemans. What was a family hobby farm years ago is now a massive, and still growing, multipurpose amusement park and conference centre on the edge of Kitchener, only moments away from St. Jacobs. The Bingemans are rooted in this soil. Lawrence's parents, Marshall and Erma, came from long established Mennonite stock. Marshall was a local veterinarian and knew all the farmers in the area. He also knew Walter Hachborn and the two became quite friendly. Lawrence remembers that whenever they saw one another, they fell into a good half hour conversation. These occasions often took place at Hollinger Hardware, always a highlight for young Lawrence: he remembers Henry Sittler at the till and Walter gathering the order from all the gleaming wooden cabinets, drawers and neatly organized shelves.

It had always been Marshall's dream to convert the lovely rolling acres of his farm into a people place. In 1960, the project got underway with an outdoor swimming pond. Later that summer it became apparent that the facility needed a rain shelter. After many discussions, the Bingemans built the shelter and that's when the Lodge was born. In 1962 a group of young people approached Marshall and Erma. They wanted to use the Lodge (on off days) for roller-skating. After much talk and persuasion, the Bingemans agreed. Roller-skating proved to be quite lucrative and in 1964, an official outdoor roller rink was constructed. After a rainy summer, it was decided to put "a lid" on the rink. It has undergone significant changes since those early days and is now Marshall Hall.

By the early 1970s, Bingemans became to the Home Hardware markets what a horse is to a buggy. Home Hardware's markets were held in Marshall Hall every spring and fall for 14 years. Vendors set up in Marshall Hall and across the way the Embassy Room was divided to accommodate the cafeteria and provide space for additional dealer meetings. Walter parked a small trailer, known as his "closing room," between the two buildings where he held private meetings.

Lawrence says that the Home Hardware crews quickly had the massive undertaking down to a science: set up took two days and teardown lasted overnight. The next morning the place was spotless.

By the early 1980s, Home Hardware's expanded warehouse allowed them to host the markets on site - the logistics were still huge but not quite as disruptive as having to move everything down the road. Lawrence's brother Jonas worried that they had lost the business. "You can't look at it that way," Lawrence told him. "In fact, it's an opportunity. We'll continue to do the catering, and our own facility will now be available for other events." And so it has remained just as Lawrence foresaw. People who know him better can judge whether Lawrence was born with this optimism or whether it rubbed off after so many years of working alongside Walter Hachborn, a man for whom Lawrence has the highest regard. I suspect it's a bit of both.

We decided to photograph Lawrence in front of the big welcome sign at the foot of the sweeping driveway into the Park. Lawrence's son Mark who works in the family business after earning a business degree at Michigan State University, immediately suggested changing the wording on the sign to spell out Home Hardware. It's clear that, as with so many of the suppliers and vendors with whom Home Hardware has been associated since the 1960s, Bingemans would have been a success even without the long time business partnership they have enjoyed for years. Still, Lawrence pays homage to that relationship. "It means a lot to us to have a loyal customer that we have grown with and that has grown with us, " he rumbles. "And that's the case with Home Hardware."

With a twinkle in his eye, Lawrence leaves me with one final story: "My dad always told me that when Walter was a young man the local farmers were very concerned about Walter's future. They hoped he'd get a good job because he didn't have the size or the strength to be a real successful farmer."

Morris Saffer:

Saffer Advertising Group
Toronto, ON

In effect, they were trying to brand inconsistency. And that, according to Morris, is where Walter and Ray demonstrated their genius once more.

There is a saying; it takes one to know one. And in the case of Walter Hachborn and Morris Saffer, the adage is apt. Morris Saffer is known as the pioneer of retail advertising. In the 1960s, he became the advertising manager of a national chain of retail stores. Morris was introduced to a world of opportunity in which he has thrived. His timing was excellent - it was the era of the explosion of retail mass marketing. In those early days, he met Sam Walton in Wal-Mart's infancy, toured through Target, Marshalls and many more American retail chains. Back in Canada, where he was based, retail was changing too. Through a series of mergers, Morris became the advertising director of Zellers, the biggest discount store chain in Canada. He learned virtually every aspect of the retail business by rolling up his sleeves and doing it. In 1968, at the ripe old age of 28, he decided to strike out on his own. Within a year, his former employers had all become his clients. Plus many more who had heard about him and what he was doing for others in their industry.

One of those people was Walter Hachborn. Walter read an article that Morris had originally written as a treatise for a course he had taken at the Harvard School of Retail that was picked up by virtually every retail publication in Canada. In essence, it introduced the concept of retail branding. Like so many brilliant ideas, it was incredibly simple. Branding is about consistency, Morris wrote. When you understand that you are a brand and you think about yourself as a brand, every decision comes from one source. "The Store is the Brand" became his trademark philosophy. And that is where kindred spirits connected. Morris still remembers the phone call from Walter: "'Hey Saffer. Read your article – heard you're some sort of hotshot advertising guru. Can you make Home Hardware into a brand? And I said 'Yes. I can.'"

Although Morris knew nothing about Home Hardware at the time, he knew about large chain retailing. And by now Home Hardware was in that category. So Morris made the drive to St. Jacobs for the first time. In those days, he remembers, "There were a couple of fields and then there was the warehouse."

Morris met Bill Tiffin, who was Home Hardware's advertising manager at the time, and Ray Gabel, already Home's merchandising manager extraordinaire. "Bill was one of those guys who if he believed in you and knew you could help him, he helped you," Morris remembers. This partnership continued with future Advertising Managers Bruce Shuh and Jack Baillie. But it was Ray who became his champion.

It became obvious that television was the way to go. However, there was one small problem: There was no budget. So Ray brought in all the vendors, and Morris pitched them on funding the concept. Then Morris pitched the dealers on the new direction that Home Hardware needed to take with their advertising. It was accepted. "So, in the same way that Walter built the idea of Home Hardware as a buying organization, now their marketing moved to a whole other level."

By now it was the early 1970s, and together Home Hardware and Saffer pioneered the concept of 52 weeks of TV advertising, likely the first retailer anywhere in the world to make that commitment.

But the challenge was the concept of consistency at the heart of Morris' thesis. The name Home Hardware meant different things in "every single nook and cranny of the country." In effect, they were trying to brand inconsistency. And that, according to Morris, is where Walter and Ray demonstrated their genius once more: by accepting that it was the name that would be consistent. "We weren't saying, 'To be Home Hardware you must have this store.' We were saying, 'Join our family with whatever store you are.'" But every store would be branded, inside and out, with the now famous "Double H." It was a big challenge and a big gamble. Morris says that this decision, the first of many, demonstrated to him Home Hardware's key strength: to make decisions that have been in the best interests of every one, even if in some cases, it's not in any one individual's best interest.

A perfect example of this democratic decision-making process occurred following the Beaver Lumber acquisition. The original commitment had been to keep the two divisions separate but Morris felt that would create an impossible marketing communications situation. More critically, adding the bigger building centre-focused Beaver stores to Home Hardware would really strengthen the brand. Management asked the Board for approval to change the corporate structure. Paul Straus, Eric Konecsni, Bruce White, (Home Hardware's VP, Merchandising and Marketing-LBM) and Morris went on the road, to make the case for amalgamation under the Home Hardware brand to both Home Hardware and Beaver Dealers. Their acceptance of this strategy established the strong foundation that allowed Home Hardware to compete successfully in the years ahead.

In Morris' opinion, Home Hardware works because everyone comes together for the common good, even with all the disparity that exists. Another epiphany: The system works because of the integrity of the individuals and very quickly, that integrity became the branding of the company. Morris recognized that, in those days, no other retailer had individual dealers running their own stores. The dealer became the brand and the spokesperson for the company, represented by "Home of the Handyman", the commercial that to this day has the highest recall of any in Canadian history. The next evolution was "Help is Close to Home," taking the relationship between consumer and dealer one step further. When research showed that consumers didn't make the connection that all those people in red coats and red shirts were actually owners, the agency came up with the campaign "Home Owners Helping Homeowners," which reinforced that the dealer was also the owner, strengthening credibility and trust. So the owner as the brand superseded the dealer as the brand. This branding strategy has stood the test of time. Despite the enormous growth of big box home improvement stores and other competition, Home Hardware has grown stronger and stronger, building ever-increasing share of market. Today, over 99% of Canadians can correctly identify the "Double H" logo. That's at the iconic level of McDonald's Golden Arches.

Morris gives a lot of credit to Ray Gabel for the role he played in the evolution of Home Hardware's marketing program. "He is running this huge business and making massive decisions about buying massive amounts of product but there is no real authority to force these dealers to buy it. They buy it by co-operation not by coercion… and that just doesn't exist elsewhere in retail."

Morris points out that when you're the President of a thousand Presidents, as is Home Hardware's CEO Paul Straus, there is a different approval and thought process than if you were the President of a thousand stores that you owned. "It is the responsibility of Home Hardware's President to make every store profitable – or have an opportunity to be profitable. You're running a big chain, competing with big chains, yet you are also worrying about the individual stores' profitability. If that's not a balancing act of genius nothing is. With Home Hardware there's no doubt the boss is the dealers. We're not dedicated to our own success, we're dedicated to the dealers' success because we believe that will create our own."

Nour Trading Inc. is located in Waterloo, just a few kilometers down the road from Home Hardware. It is one of Home Hardware's oldest suppliers. Theirs is just one of countless stories that demonstrate the loyalty, honesty and respect at the heart of every vendor/supplier relationship Home Hardware has established over the years.

Mac Fleifel: Nour Trading Inc. adopted the Home Hardware model: slowly, methodically and carefully "working their butts off."

Nour Trading Inc.
Waterloo, ON

Company founder Mac Fleifel is an elegantly compact man who speaks with the greatest affection and respect for the company that not only gave him his first job in Canada, but also encouraged and supported him in his own successful business.

In 1974, Mac Fleifel was 19 years old, newly arrived from Beirut in search of a new life in a new country. Canada as a safe haven is easy to understand. But the choice of St. Jacobs is intriguing. In fact, it is a good demonstration of the pragmatic reality of many immigrants: he chose Canada because his aunt and uncle had emigrated here a few years earlier. By now they owned a gas station and repair shop in St. Jacobs. But Mac's first real job was not pumping gas. It was working in the Home Hardware warehouse.

Applying for your first job is hard enough. Applying for a new job in a new country where you hardly speak the language must be seriously daunting. Good omens are important. A few weeks after making a job application at the Home Hardware offices in St. Jacobs, Mac passed Mr. Hachborn, as he still calls him, on his way home one evening. The two made eye contact - Mac believes it was his brush with destiny - and the next day, Human Resources called him in. After a very short interview, "considering my English," Mac says with a smile, he got the job.

Ten years into its existence, Home Hardware was still a relatively small operation, with Mac often working alongside Walter Hachborn, Paul Straus and Ray Gabel. A year after arriving in Canada, Mac experienced his first major snowstorm. It kept much of the workforce at home that day. But Mac lived in town and could walk. Late that afternoon, he was packing orders in solitary splendour when he looked to his left and saw Mr. Hachborn at the next table doing the exact same thing. That made an indelible impression on the young man. " Mr. Hachborn became my role model," Mac says all these years later.

There were many things that Mac liked about Home Hardware. He could work as hard as he wanted (which he did) and clocked a lot of overtime: he remembers once, Paul Straus was handing out the weekly paycheques, and joked that Mac had made more money that week than he had. He liked that everyone rolled up their sleeves and tackled whatever needed to be done.

He liked the open door policy where everyone was accepted as an equal. In Lebanon, Mac's father and uncle had a small shop that manufactured paint brushes the old fashioned way - by hand. As a result, Mac knew a lot about making paint brushes. "If I were to start manufacturing paint brushes," he asked Ray Gabel one day, "how many do you think Home Hardware might buy?" "Oh, probably pretty much everything you could make," was the answer. Armed with a letter of intent from Home Hardware and a simple business plan, Mac was able to borrow the money he needed to set up shop. He was 24 years old. His first and only customer at the time was Home Hardware. Nour Trading Inc. adopted the Home Hardware model: slowly, methodically and carefully "working their butts off", recalls Director of Marketing Bob Shaw, who joined the company in 1987. "It is the integrity from the top down that manifests itself in how Home Hardware does things on a day to day basis, that really is unique," he says of the client who is still foremost in their hearts despite the company's rapid expansion since those early days.

Today Nour Trading Inc. is Canada's largest manufacturer of paint brushes, applicators and accessories and an industry leader internationally. They have manufacturing facilities in Canada, the Middle East and Asia and their products are sold around the world. Virtually everything he learned during those first years at Home Hardware Mac Fleifel has applied to his own business. The company may be lean, but the group is structured like a highly functioning family unit - albeit an international one: the VP of Production, Dung Nguyen is from Viet Nam, the Middle Eastern operations are managed by Mac's brother Hassan and the Waterloo-based Marketing Director for the entire operation, Bob Shaw, is originally from Quebec. If it were not for Home Hardware's faith and support over the years, coupled with his determination, Mac says, his chances of success would have been slim. That history has led to a highly productive and mutually beneficial relationship between the two companies. Approximately 80% of the product they sell into Home Hardware is private label and Ray and Mac often work together on new product development.

When Ray and Mac get together, Ray will often preview some of the new products that Home Hardware is developing. Mac loves that first moment when he walks into the warehouse. It is much changed over the years. But, he maintains, the smell is still the same. And the memories come flooding back. This is where a young man had his first chance in a new country; where he was treated not like an outsider but as a member of a family, where he learned to speak English, was treated with respect and given the opportunity to prove himself. This is a place Mac will always call Home.

Stan Libera:

Libera Graphics
Toronto, ON

Every Thursday at 10 AM Stan Libera arrives in St. Jacobs for his weekly meeting with Ray Gabel, Joel Marks and the Home Hardware Product Managers. For at least an hour, sometimes longer, the group goes over the latest line up of new products. It's a ritual that has lasted more than 15 years.

Libera Graphics' relationship with their largest client goes back twice that length of time, the result of an introduction from a company that manufactured paint products, at the time an emerging and expanding category for Home Hardware. Today Libera Graphics designs the packaging, logos and labels for most of Home Hardware's in-house private label products, from Benchmark, Natura, Home Gardener and Mark's Choice to Kuraidori kitchenware.

Like Home Hardware, Libera Graphics is a family business, although with a staff on a much smaller scale. Stan's daughter Belinda Libera has worked with the company for 18 years and his other daughter Elisa McLellan came on board in January 2013, alongside her husband Jeremy one of the firm's resident designers. Stan enjoys the creative process at those Thursday morning sessions, fortified by the bottle of juice Ray always has waiting for him. Stan has always been impressed by Ray's foresight in product promotion as well as his ability to pick successful products, at times even coining their brand names. For Stan and his small but flourishing business, it has been a pleasure working with the company that they have grown alongside of for 30 years. "I wish all our clients were like Home Hardware," he says simply.

Bruce sums up the relationship this way: "Insurance is as foreign to Home Hardware as hardware is to us. Home Hardware allows us to operate independently, but our success is their success." These days, when Bruce and Walter talk about the good old days, Walter refuses to take any credit for what he has accomplished. "He'll say, 'Look at the insurance thing that you've built – I mean – who would have thought?' And I say, Well Walter, you thought of it. Otherwise we wouldn't be here!"

It is not very often that your largest client becomes your business partner. However Home Hardware has always had a habit of forging new territory. Shortly after Home Hardware Stores Limited was born, Walter Hachborn went shopping for a general insurance agency to supply fire and liability insurance to the new network of dealers. He found the right fit with a London-based general insurance agency owned by a former Army associate, Herbert Farrow. By consolidating their business with Farrow Insurance, Home Hardware was able to achieve significant savings for both their corporate property and their dealers' inventories and properties.

the elevator shaft." He was confronted by his former associate, Bob Disotell. "Thanks a lot," Bob said. "Home is my only account, so now they'll fire me." "That's good," Bruce said. "You just grab that box and take it down to the van. You're now in charge of PIB's General insurance division, because my strengths are in the Group and Life Insurance end of the business." Bob Disotell worked at PIB from that point on, serving as President from 1987 until he retired in 1995, in true Home Hardware fashion going from an employee to a shareholder during that time.

Bruce and Bob Burnham:

Programmed Insurance Brokers Inc. (PIB)
Elmira, ON

Respecting the philosophy behind independent businesses and their ability to make their own purchasing decisions, Home Hardware never mandated that their dealers were obligated to buy their insurance from Farrow. The two companies were highly compatible and by the mid 1970s, Farrow Insurance expanded and hired Bruce Burnham as one of their agents to travel across the country to sell insurance to the Home Dealers, one store at a time. As Home Hardware continued to build their network, Farrow did likewise. However, in the late 1970s, Farrow sold his commercial insurance business to a large Canadian insurer, and the personal relationship was lost. The "friendly family group" dynamic was gone.

The Home Hardware management group was aware that Tru-Valu in Chicago, which had proven an inspiration in years past, had their own offshore insurance agency. Could they do something similar? They approached their key contacts at Farrow, including Bruce Burnham, and discussed the possibilities of partnering with them on a new insurance entity. Home Hardware would be their first client. (A Canadian legal requirement at the time stipulated that majority ownership of an insurance brokerage needed to remain with the insurance side.)

In September 1980, Programmed Insurance Brokers (PIB) was formed and opened for business in the Home Hardware warehouse in St. Jacobs, Ontario with three employees. They, in essence, became the insurance agency of Home Hardware's corporate properties and inventory, group benefits and retirement plans. Within a year, they were hiring and Bruce's cousin Bob Burnham joined the firm.

Bruce remembers the day in 1981 that the fledgling PIB was advised by Paul Straus and Walter Hachborn to take over the individual dealer accounts from the company that had bought Farrow Insurance. A young and very nervous Bruce Burnham arrived at the reception desk of the company with an Agent of Record letter that gave him permission to remove the files. "Everybody was in a three-piece suit and I had a van downstairs and the people to carry out all the files. I was lucky that they didn't throw me down

In 1984, PIB moved to their present location in Elmira after Home Hardware snapped up a sweet property deal: a 200,000 square foot building plus twenty acres of land at a rock bottom price. That same year, PIB and Home Hardware formed the RWAM Trust and RWAM Insurance Administrators Inc. (the Retailer, Wholesaler and Manufacturers Group Insurance program), which allowed them to expand into the business of group benefits. PIB became the marketing and sales engine and RWAM became what the industry refers to as a third party administrator (TPA). A TPA performs all of the administrative and claims functions of an insurance company, except they do not assume any risk.

In the beginning, Home Hardware represented 100% of the revenue generated by PIB. The goal was to grow the business through multiple insurance offerings to multiple clients across the country. Today, 90% of all Home stores purchase some sort of insurance product from PIB and RWAM, whether it be commercial fire insurance, group benefits, retirement savings or life insurance. However, premiums from Home Hardware now represent just 25% of PIB's overall business. It is a credit to their programs and competitive pricing that today over 75% of PIB and RWAM's revenue is generated from non-Home Hardware clientele.

The complexities of the insurance industry can tie most people up in knots in no time, but it quickly becomes apparent how fiendishly clever Home Hardware has been in structuring this arm of their business, which simultaneously provides an essential service to their dealers and at the same time contributes very handsomely to the profit sharing model. Further expansion opportunities are, of course, being explored. That quiet business savvy seems to be part of the Home Hardware DNA.

Today PIB and RWAM have over 225 employees, with branch offices in Halifax, Nova Scotia; Edmonton, Alberta and Blenheim and London, Ontario. The corporate Head Office is located in Elmira, Ontario. In the fall of 2012 they completed a 20,000 square foot addition to their office space.

Rick Kenny:

Rick has endless admiration for Home Hardware's negotiating skills, its open-door policy and total commitment to the dealers.

KS Solutions Sales & Service Inc.
Barrie, ON

At Katz's Deli in north Toronto, I met with a quintessential member of the hardware brotherhood. Rick Kenny has been a hardware man since he was 18. "I was born in Barrie and raised everywhere, like the toilet seats I used to sell," he said with the easy humour of a natural salesman. He started working at McDonald Sales, a "young gun fighter selling package plumbing repair parts." His mentor was Jim Miller, a former WW2 pilot shot down in the Battle of Britain who came to Canada and worked for D.H. Howden out of London, Ontario until he retired at 65. McDonald Sales scooped him up at that point and he in turn took young Rick under his wing. When the eager youngster told Jim he wanted to learn all the tricks of the trade, Jim countered: "I'll teach you the trade. The tricks will come naturally, if you are any good." After his first year at McDonald Sales, Rick won salesman of the year. He won it again the following year and was transferred to Winnipeg. After a few years in the prairies, he was sent to BC and in 1995, asked for a transfer back to Barrie, his hometown.

His first call to Home Hardware was not auspicious: Don Kenesky spent virtually the entire visit delivering a diatribe that made it clear his first, foremost and only priority was Home Hardware. To this day, Rick maintains that Don is one the finest buyers he knows because of his absolute and complete dedication to getting the best deal for the Home Hardware Dealer-Owners. And the logical corollary is the utmost respect Rick himself has for the company. He maintains that it is Home Hardware's common sense approach to common business practices, always geared to the Dealer-Owner, which has seen the company prosper and thrive over the years. Rick has endless admiration for Home Hardware's negotiating skills, its open-door policy and total commitment to the dealers. At the same time, he has been repeatedly moved by Home Hardware's quiet, unstinting and generally unsung generosity to people in need, from sales people in companies from which they buy product to victims of catastrophes and disasters around the world. "They don't brag and boast," he says. "They just make significant donations where and when they are needed."

As much at home with the dealers in their stores as he is at corporate office in St. Jacobs - he spends about 30% of his time at the store level - Rick obviously loves the business he is in: today, after a two year stint as MAAX's North American key accounts manager, he, and partner Paul Sutton, have their own agency, KS Solutions. Their company represents manufacturers including MAAX, Kindred and Belanger and a number of other international companies, most of them related to the plumbing/ hardware industry. He has worked with many of the major North American retailers, including Sears, Lowes, Orgill, Canadian Tire, and of course Home Hardware. "We aren't looking to do business with everyone," he points out. "We want customers with whom we share common philosophies."

Rick believes that the greatest show on earth is the semi-annual Home Hardware market that allows vendors and dealers to come together without Canada's geographic challenges. "I'll be at their one hundredth market in April 2013, and I'd love to make it to their two hundredth."

Conclusion:

In 2013, as Home Hardware prepared to celebrate its first 50 years, the company was honoured to be named one of Canada's Best Managed Companies, Canada's leading business awards program that recognizes excellence in Canadian-owned and managed companies. The awards program was established in 1993 by Deloitte, CIBC, National Post and Queen's School of Business. It recognizes Canadian companies that have implemented world-class business practices and created value in innovative ways across a broad swathe of categories, including brand management, leadership, leveraging and developing core competencies, designing information systems and hiring the right talent to facilitate growth. Over the three-year period I spent researching, writing and producing this book, I had the extraordinary opportunity to see these qualities at work in a wide array of Home Hardware stores across the country. Regardless of the location, size and complexion of the operation, at every Home Hardware, Home Building Centre, Home Hardware Building Centre and Home Furniture Store, I was met by Home Dealers, their staff and families each of whom embodied and expressed the qualities that garnered Home Hardware the recognition and honour of that award.

This was a book I had always wanted to write. My expectations as to what I would encounter and the stories I would be privileged to tell were exceeded everywhere I travelled. Canada is a vast, varied and vital country, peopled with industrious, committed and enterprising individuals, each one making a distinctive contribution to the whole that is our home. Over the past fifty years, Home Hardware has become an important part of that larger national story. As it embraces increasingly complex systems, technologies and economic realities, Home Hardware retains at its heart the original values of individualism, hard work and decency that I witnessed everywhere I visited. It is a potent combination that will continue to serve it well as Home Hardware and its thousands of Dealer-Owners, employees, suppliers and customers forge into the future.

Toronto, June 2013

Paul Straus receives the award as one of Canada's Best Managed Companies from Steve Metson, Senior VP Western Canada, CIBC Commercial Banking.

Dealer Listing:

Alberta

Fulton's Home Hardware Building Centre	Airdrie
Alix Home Hardware	Alix
Athabasca Home Hardware Building Centre	Athabasca
Standish Home Hardware	Banff
Sanderman Home Hardware	Barrhead
Barrhead Home Building Centre	Barrhead
Bashaw Home Hardware	Bashaw
Beaumont Home Hardware	Beaumont
Beiseker Home Hardware	Beiseker
Summit Home Center	Blairmore
Bonnyville Home Hardware	Bonnyville
Boyle Home Hardware	Boyle
Brooks Home Hardware	Brooks
Sunley Home Building Centre	Brooks
Hauser Home Hardware Building Centre	Camrose
Valley Home Building Centre	Canmore
Canmore Home Hardware	Canmore
Cardston Home Hardware Building Centre	Cardston
Castor Home Hardware Building Centre	Castor
Dee Jay Hardware Ltd.	Claresholm
Coaldale Home Building Centre	Coaldale
Cochrane Home Hardware Building Centre	Cochrane
Coronation Home Hardware Building Centre	Coronation
Heistad Home Furniture	Coronation
Kaplers Home Hardware	Daysland
Devon Home Hardware	Devon
Didsbury Home Hardware	Didsbury
Drayton Valley Home Hardware Building Centre	Drayton Valley
Poplar Ridge Home Building Centre	Drayton Valley
Waddell Home Hardware	Edgerton
Cold Lake Home Hardware Building Centre	Edmonton
Timberjack Home Hardware Building Centre	Edson
Woodland Home Building Centre	Fairview
Boyts Home Hardware	Fairview
Coutts Home Hardware	Forestburg
Fort McMurray Home Hardware Building Centre	Fort McMurray
Home Hardware Building Centre - Fort Saskatchewan	Fort Saskatchewan
Fox Creek Home Hardware Building Centre	Fox Creek
Grande Cache Home Building Centre	Grande Cache
Home Hardware - Grande Cache	Grande Cache
Grande Cache Home Furniture	Grande Cache
Grande Prairie Home Hardware Building Centre	Grande Prairie
Woodland Home Hardware Building Centre	Grande Prairie
Warwick's Home Hardware	Hanna
Hardisty Home Hardware	Hardisty
High Level Home Hardware	High Level
Hunter Home Building Centre	High Level
Pops Home Hardware Building Centre	High Prairie
High River Home Hardware Building Centre	High River
B & E Home Hardware	Hines Creek
Hinton Home Hardware Building Centre	Hinton
West Peace Building Supplies Ltd.	Hythe
Innisfail Home Hardware	Innisfail
Jasper Home Building Centre	Jasper
Killam Home Hardware Building Centre	Killam
Kinuso Home Hardware	Kinuso
La Crete Home Hardware Building Centre	La Crete
Venture Building Supplies	Lac La Biche
Nowco Home Hardware	Lacombe
Lamont Home Hardware	Lamont
Home Hardware Lethbridge	Lethbridge
Agrifab Home Building Centre	Linden
Home Hardware Building Centre - Lloydminster	Lloydminster
Magrath Home Hardware Building Centre	Magrath
Empire Home Building Centre	Manning
Tannas Bros. Hardware Ltd.	Marwayne
McLennan Home Hardware Building Centre	McLennan
Hill Home Hardware	Medicine Hat
Milk River Home Hardware Building Centre	Milk River
Morinville Home Hardware	Morinville
Morinville Home Furniture	Morinville
Nanton Home Building Centre	Nanton
Country Home Hardware & Clothing	Newbrook
Okotoks Home Hardware Building Centre	Okotoks
B & M Home Hardware Building Centre	Olds
Peace River Home Hardware Building Centre	Peace River
Butte Home Hardware Building Centre	Picture Butte
Sommer Home Hardware Building Centre	Ponoka
Larson's Hardware Limited	Provost
Executive Home Building Centre	Red Deer
Redcliff Hardware Ltd.	Redcliff
Rusinko Home Hardware	Redwater
Rimbey Home Hardware	Rimbey
Home Hardware Building Centre - Rocky Mountain House	Rocky Mountain House
Sherwood Park Home Hardware Building Centre	Sherwood Park
Timberland Home Hardware Building Centre	Slave Lake
Spirit River Home Hardware	Spirit River
McLeod Home Building Centre	Spruce Grove
St. Paul Home Hardware Building Centre	St. Paul
Stettler Home Hardware	Stettler
Schwartz Home Building Centre	Stettler
Strathmore Home Hardware	Strathmore
Sundre Home Hardware Building Centre	Sundre
Swan Hills Home Hardware	Swan Hills
Taber Home Hardware Building Centre	Taber
Hoffman's Hardware Ltd.	Thorsby
Three Hills Home Hardware Building Centre	Three Hills
Trochu Home Hardware Building Centre	Trochu
Valleyview Home Hardware	Valleyview
Vegreville Home Hardware	Vegreville
Viking Home Hardware Building Centre	Viking
Wolfe's Hardware Ltd.	Vulcan
Wabamun Home Hardware	Wabamun
Wabasca Home Hardware	Wabasca
Gibson's Home Hardware	Wainwright
Westlock Home Hardware	Westlock
Home Building Centre Wetaskiwin	Wetaskiwin
Whitecourt Home Hardware Building Centre	Whitecourt

British Columbia

Century Hardware Ltd.	100 Mile House
Blackwood Building Centre Ltd.	Abbotsford
Pearce Hardware (1977) Ltd.	Aldergrove
Shepherd's Home Hardware Building Centre	Armstrong
Robertson Home Hardware	Burnaby
West-Can Home Hardware	Burnaby
Burns Lake Home Hardware	Burns Lake
Pioneer Home Hardware Building Centre - Campbell River	Campbell River
West's Department Store (1979) Ltd.	Castlegar
Chase Home Hardware Building Centre	Chase
Chetwynd Home Hardware Building Centre	Chetwynd
Fortin's Home Hardware - Airport Road	Chilliwack
Fortin's Home Hardware	Chilliwack
Grand Pappy's Home Furniture	Chilliwack
Wells Gray Home Hardware	Clearwater
Central Builders - Home Hardware Building Centre	Courtenay
Home Hardware Building Centre - Cranbrook	Cranbrook
Home Hardware Building Centre Creston	Creston
Home Hardware Building Centre - Tsawwassen	Delta
Duncan Home Hardware Building Centre	Duncan
Fernie Home Hardware Building Centre	Fernie
Diemert Home Hardware	Fort Nelson

Fort St. John Home Hardware Building Centre	Fort St. John
Galiano Trading Company Ltd.	Galiano Island
Gibsons Home Hardware	Gibsons
Golden Hardware & Building Supplies	Golden
Boundary Home Building Centre	Grand Forks
Grand Forks Home Hardware	Grand Forks
Reitsma's Home Hardware	Houston
Invermere Home Hardware Building Centre	Invermere
Westsyde Home Hardware	Kamloops
Kamloops Home Hardware Building Centre	Kamloops
Kaslo Home Hardware	Kaslo
Mara Lumber Home Building Centre	Kelowna
Kelowna Home Hardware Building Centre	Kelowna
Westside Home Building Centre	Kelowna
Bavarian Home Hardware	Kimberley
City Centre Home Hardware	Kitimat
Ladysmith Home Hardware Building Centre	Ladysmith
Home Hardware - Lake Cowichan	Lake Cowichan
Langley Home Hardware	Langley
Hagen's Home Hardware	Mackenzie
Mackenzie Home Building Centre	Mackenzie
Haney Home Hardware	Maple Ridge
North Coast Supply Co. Ltd.	Masset
Mayne Island Home Hardware Building Centre	Mayne Island
Robson Valley Home Hardware	McBride
Home Hardware Building Centre - Merritt	Merritt
Nakusp Home Building Centre	Nakusp
Nakusp Home Hardware	Nakusp
Applecross Home Hardware	Nanaimo
Nanaimo Home Hardware	Nanaimo
Hipperson Hardware Company Limited	Nelson
Nelson Home Hardware Building Centre	Nelson
Slocan Lake Home Hardware	New Denver
Pearson's Home Hardware	North Vancouver
Osoyoos Home Hardware	Osoyoos
Home Building Centre - Osoyoos	Osoyoos
Parksville Home Building Centre	Parksville
Central Construction Materials Ltd.	Parksville
Parksville Home Hardware	Parksville
Pender Island Home Building Centre	Pender Island
Home Hardware Building Centre - Penticton	Penticton
Westcoast Home Hardware Building Centre	Port Alberni
Dunlop's Home Hardware Building Centre	Port Hardy
Mitchell Brothers Merchants Ltd.	Powell River
Northern Hardware & Furniture Co. Ltd.	Prince George
Hart Home Hardware	Prince George
Prince George Home Building Centre	Prince George
Prince Rupert Home Hardware Building Centre	Prince Rupert
Princeton Home Hardware	Princeton
Dolly's Home Hardware	Qualicum Beach
Willis Harper Home Hardware	Quesnel
Home Hardware Building Centre - Revelstoke	Revelstoke
Central Saanich Home Hardware	Saanichton
Home Building Centre - Salmon Arm	Salmon Arm
Mouat's Home Hardware	Salt Spring Island
Scotch Creek Home Building Centre	Scotch Creek
Trail Bay Home Hardware	Sechelt
Sunshine Coast Home Building Centre	Sechelt
Home Hardware - Sidney	Sidney
Smithers Home Hardware	Smithers
Sooke Home Hardware	Sooke
Squamish Home Hardware	Squamish
Summerland Home Hardware	Summerland
Batten Hardware Ltd.	Surrey
Home Hardware Building Centre - Trail	Trail
Valemount Home Hardware	Valemount
Gandy's Home Hardware	Vancouver

Magnet Hardware (1991) Ltd.	Vancouver
MacPhail Home Hardware	Vancouver
Blight's Home Hardware	Vancouver
Hewer Home Hardware	Vancouver
Taylor Bros. Hardware (1974) Ltd.	Vanderhoof
Fishers Hardware (1976) Ltd.	Vernon
Home Building Centre - Vernon	Vernon
Burnside Home Hardware	Victoria
Oak Bay Home Hardware	Victoria
Ross Bay Home Hardware	Victoria
Home Hardware West Kelowna	West Kelowna
Simpson Home Hardware	West Vancouver
Whistler Home Hardware	Whistler
Home Hardware Building Centre - Williams Lake	Williams Lake

Manitoba

Arborg Home Hardware Building Centre	Arborg
Ashern Home Hardware	Ashern
Beausejour Home Hardware	Beausejour
Brandon Home Hardware Building Centre	Brandon
Reilly's Home Hardware	Carberry
Carman Home Hardware	Carman
Churchill Home Building Centre	Churchill
Dauphin Home Hardware	Dauphin
Countryside Home Building Centre - Fisher Branch	Fisher Branch
Flin Flon Home Hardware Building Centre	Flin Flon
Gimli Home Hardware Building Centre	Gimli
Grandview Home Hardware	Grandview
Rawlings Home Hardware	Hamiota
Hamiota Home Hardware	Hamiota
Peguis Home Hardware	Hodgson
Holland Home Hardware	Holland
Killarney Home Hardware	Killarney
Lac Du Bonnet Home Hardware Building Centre	Lac Du Bonnet
Molgat Shopping Centre Ltd.	Laurier
Lundar Home Hardware	Lundar
Minitonas Home Hardware	Minitonas
Minnedosa Home Hardware	Minnedosa
Morden Home Hardware	Morden
Morris Home Hardware	Morris
Neepawa Home Hardware	Neepawa
B & D Home Hardware	Onanole
Rivers Home Hardware	Rivers
Roblin Home Hardware	Roblin
Rossburn Home Hardware	Rossburn
Russell Home Hardware	Russell
Selkirk Home Hardware Building Centre	Selkirk
Shoal Lake Home Hardware	Shoal Lake
Snow Lake Home Building Centre	Snow Lake
Souris Home Hardware	Souris
St. Laurent Home Hardware Building Centre	St. Laurent
Stonewall Home Hardware	Stonewall
Swan River Home Hardware	Swan River
The Pas Home Hardware Building Centre	The Pas
The Pas Home Furniture	The Pas
Thompson Home Building Centre	Thompson
Virden Home Hardware Building Centre	Virden
Whitemouth Home Hardware	Whitemouth
Parkside Home Building Centre	Winkler
Home Furniture and Appliances - Winkler	Winkler

New Brunswick

Blanchard Home Hardware Building Centre	Allardville
Baie Ste Anne Home Building Centre	Baie-Sainte-Anne
Bathurst Centre de Rénovation Home Hardware	Bathurst
Blackville Home Building Centre	Blackville
Campbellton Home Hardware	Campbellton

Tediche Home Hardware Building Centre . . . . Cap-Pelé
Caraquet Home Hardware Building Centre . . . . .Caraquet
Wiebe's Home Building Centre . . . . Centreville
Chipman Home Hardware Building Centre . . . . Chipman
Clair Home Hardware . . . . .Clair
Dalhousie Home Hardware . . . . .Dalhousie
Dieppe Home Hardware Building Centre . . . . Dieppe
Betts Home Building Centre . . . . Doaktown
Brennan Home Hardware Building Centre . . . . .Florenceville-Bristol
Simms Home Hardware Building Centre . . . . Fredericton
Fredericton Home Hardware. . . . . Fredericton
Wilkins Home Building Centre . . . . Fredericton
Grand Bay Home Hardware Building Centre . . . . Grand Bay-Westfield
Toner Home Hardware. . . . . .Grand Falls
Island Home Hardware Building Centre . . . . Grand Manan
Island Home Furniture. . . . . Grand Manan
Hampton Home Hardware Building Centre . . . . Hampton
Watson's Home Building Centre. . . . . Harvey-York Co.
F. J. Brideau Centre de Renovation Home. . . . . .Haut-Shippagan
Brideau Centre de Renovation Home Hardware . . . . Lameque
Dupuis Home Hardware Building Centre . . . . Memramcook
DiCarlo's Home Hardware Building Centre. . . . . Minto
LeGresley Home Building Centre . . . . .Miramichi
Newcastle Home Hardware. .Miramichi
Elmwood Home Hardware Building Centre . . . . Moncton
Cook's Home Hardware Building Centre . . . . Moncton
Magnetic Hill Home Hardware Building Centre . . . . Moncton
Nackawic Home Hardware Building Centre . . . . Nackawic
Neguac Home Hardware Building Centre . . . . Neguac
Roblynn Home Hardware Building Centre . . . . Oromocto
Riverside Home Hardware Building Centre . . . . .Plaster Rock
KV Home Hardware Building Centre . . . . .Quispamsis
Le Villageois Centre de Renovation Home Hardware . . . .Rang-Saint-Georges
Richibucto Home Hardware Building Centre . . . . Richibucto
Downey Home Hardware Building Centre . . . . Riverview
Caissie Building Supplies . . . . Rogersville
Payzant Home Hardware Building Centre . . . . Sackville
Loch Lomond Home Hardware Building Centre . . . . Saint John
Hatfield Home Hardware Building Centre . . . . Saint John
Saint-Antoine Home Hardware Building Centre . . . . .Saint-Antoine
La Coopérative de St-Quentin Centre de Renovation Home Hardware . . . .
. . . . Saint-Quentin
Salisbury Home Hardware Building Centre. . . . . Salisbury
Shediac Home Hardware . . . . .Shediac
St. Andrews Home Hardware . . . . .St. Andrews
Boyd Bros. Home Hardware Building Centre. . . . . St. George
St. Louis Home Building Centre. . . . . St. Louis-de-Kent
Sussex Home Hardware Building Centre . . . . Sussex
Tracadie Home Hardware. . . . . Tracadie-Sheila
Stewart's Home Hardware .Woodstock

Newfoundland and Labrador

Newhook's Home Hardware Building Centre . . . . Arnolds Cove
White Bay Home Hardware Building Centre . . . . Baie Verte
White Bay Home Furniture . . . . Baie Verte
R. Churchill Home Building Centre . . . . Bay Roberts
Clarke & Clarke Home Hardware Building Centre. . . . . Bell Island
Durdle's Home Hardware Building Centre . . . . .Bonavista
Botwood Home Hardware Building Centre . . . . Botwood
Buchans Home Hardware Building Centre . . . . Buchans
Dalton's Home Hardware Building Centre . . . . Cape Broyle
Carbonear Home Hardware Building Centre . . . . Carbonear
W. G. Garland Limited .Carbonear
Tulk's Home Hardware Building Centre . . . . Carmanville
I. J. Smith Home Building Centre . . . . Chapel Arm
Clarenville Home Hardware Building Centre . . . . Clarenville
Handyman Home Hardware . . . . Conception Bay South

Corner Brook Home Hardware . . . . .Corner Brook
Avalon Home Building Centre . . . . Cupids
Deer Lake Home Hardware .Deer Lake
Larick Home Hardware Building Centre. . . . . Doyles
Fogo Island Home Hardware Building Centre . . . . Fogo
Aylwards Home Hardware Building Centre. . . . . .Gander
Glovertown Home Hardware Building Centre . . . . .Glovertown
McDonald's Home Hardware . . . . Goulds
Aylwards Home Centre. Grand Bank
Grande-Digue Home Building Centre . . . . Grande-Digue
Exploits Home Hardware Building Centre. . . . . .Grand Falls - Windsor
E. J. Cram Home Hardware Building Centre . . . . .Greens Harbour
Goose Sales Home Hardware Building Centre . . . .Happy Valley-Goose Bay
Home Furniture - Goose Bay. . . . . .Happy Valley-Goose Bay
Jackman's Home Hardware Building Centre . . . . Harbour Breton
Arch Collins Home Hardware Building Centre . . . . Hare Bay
Hulan's Home Hardware Building Centre. . . . . .Heatherton
Labrador West Home Hardware Building Centre . . . . .Labrador City
Turnbull's Home Hardware Building Centre. . . . . L'Anse au Clair
Greenwood Home Hardware Building Centre. . . . . Lethbridge
Lewisporte Home Hardware . . . . Lewisporte
Aylwards Home Centre. . . . . Marystown
W.W. Young Home Hardware Building Centre . . . . .Musgravetown
Peter's River Home Hardware Building Centre . . . . .Peter's River
Aylwards Home Centre. . . . . Placentia
Young's Home Hardware Building Centre . . . . .Plum Point
Abbott and Haliburton Home Building Centre . . . . .Port au Port
Sheaves Home Hardware . . . . Port-aux-Basques
Rocky Harbour Home Hardware Building Centre . . . . .Rocky Harbour
Roddickton Home Hardware Building Centre . . . . .Roddickton
Springdale Home Hardware Building Centre . . . . Springdale
Rumbolt's Home Hardware . . . . St. Anthony
Smith's Home Hardware . . . . St. John's
Aylwards Home Centre. . . . . St. Lawrence
Roberts Home Hardware. Stephenville
Farr's Home Hardware Building Centre . . . . Summerford
Trepassey Home Hardware Building Centre . . . . .Trepassey
Triton Home Hardware Building Centre. . . . . Triton
Thomas Winsor & Sons Limited . . . . Wesleyville
Hindy's Home Hardware Building Centre. . . . . .Winterton
Witless Bay Home Hardware Building Centre . . . . Witless Bay

Northwest Territories

Evans Electric Ltd. . . . . Fort Smith
Hay River Home Hardware. Hay River
Hay River Home Building Centre. . . . . Hay River
Home Hardware Building Centre Inuvik. . . . . Inuvik
Corothers Home Hardware Building Centre . . . . Yellowknife

Nova Scotia

Harrison's Home Hardware Building Centre . . . . .Amherst
Amherst Home Hardware .Amherst
Annapolis Home Hardware Building Centre . . . . Annapolis Royal
Highland Home Building Centre. . . . . Antigonish
Baddeck Home Hardware. Baddeck
Wilson's Home Hardware Building Centre . . . . Barrington Passage
Berwick Home Hardware Building Centre . . . . Berwick
Bridgetown Home Hardware Building Centre . . . . .Bridgetown
Gow's Home Hardware . . . . Bridgewater
Buck's Home Building Centre. . . . . Bridgewater
Gow's Frig-Air Ltd. . . . . Bridgewater
Mary Lake Home Hardware Building Centre . . . . . Caledonia (Queens Co.)
Maple Leaf Home Hardware Building Centre . . . . Canning
Chester Home Hardware . . . . Chester
Cheticamp Co-op Home Hardware Building Centre . . . . .Cheticamp
Payzant Home Building Centre - Dartmouth . . . . Dartmouth
Wilson's Home Hardware Building Centre . . . . Digby

Enfield Home Hardware Building Centre . . . . .Enfield
Harbax Home Hardware Building Centre . . . . Glace Bay
Greenwood Home Hardware. . . . . Greenwood
Chedabucto Home Hardware . . . . Guysborough
Hantsport Home Hardware Building Centre . . . . .Hantsport
Jeddore Home Hardware Building Centre . . . . Head of Jeddore
Hubbards Home Hardware . . . . Hubbards
Ingonish Home Hardware Building Centre . . . . Ingonish Beach
Kennetcook Home Hardware . . . . Kennetcook, Hants Co.
Rockwell Home Hardware . . . . .Kentville
Brady Home Building Centre. . . . . Liverpool
Liverpool Home Hardware. Liverpool
Lockeport Home Hardware .Lockeport
Landry Brothers Home Hardware . . . . Louisdale
Payzant Home Hardware Building Centre . . . . .Lower Sackville
Meteghan Home Hardware Building Centre. . . . . Meteghan
Middleton Home Hardware . . . . Middleton
Allen's Home Building Centre . . . . Middleton
New Ross Home Hardware Building Centre . . . . .New Ross
Waterford Home Hardware . . . . New Waterford
Brooklyn Home Hardware Building Centre . . . . Newport
MacRae Home Hardware . . . . North Sydney
Oxford Home Hardware Building Centre. . . . . Oxford
Harrison's Home Hardware Building Centre . . . . .Parrsboro
Proudfoots Home Hardware Building Centre - Pictou . . . . Pictou
Home Hardware Building Centre - Port Hawkesbury . . . . . .Port Hawkesbury
North End Home Hardware Building Centre . . . . Port Hood
Cameron Home Hardware Building Centre . . . . .Porters Lake
Harrison's Home Building Centre . . . . Pugwash
Pugwash Home Hardware. Pugwash
Gammon Home Hardware Building Centre . . . . .Sheet Harbour
Woodworkers Home Hardware Building Centre. . . . . Shelburne
Woodworkers Home Furniture . . . . Shelburne
Ettinger's Home Hardware Building Centre. . . . . .Shubenacadie
D & J Home Hardware Building Centre. . . . . Springhill
St. Peter's Home Hardware Building Centre. . . . . St. Peters
Proudfoots Home Hardware Building Centre . . . . Stellarton
Stewiacke Home Hardware Building Centre . . . . Stewiacke
Wilson's Home Hardware . . . . Sydney
Gillis Home Building Centre . . . . Sydney River
Tatamagouche Home Hardware Building Centre . . . . .Tatamagouche
Harris Home Hardware Building Centre . . . . .Truro
Truro Home Hardware . . . . .Truro
Home Hardware Building Centre - Willow Street . . . . .Truro
Redmond's Home Hardware . . . . Upper Tantallon
Charman's Home Hardware Building Centre. . . . . Wallace
Del's Home Building Centre . . . . West Pubnico
Sissiboo Home Hardware Building Centre . . . . Weymouth
Whycocomagh Home Building Centre . . . . Whycocomagh
Windsor Home Hardware . . . . Windsor
Swinamer's Home Building Centre. . . . . Windsor
Rafuse Home Hardware Building Centre . . . . .Wolfville
Home Hardware Building Centre - Yarmouth. . . . . Yarmouth

Nunavut
West Baffin Eskimo Co-Operative Limited. . . . . .Cape Dorset

Ontario
Acton Home Hardware . . . . Acton
Ailsa Craig Home Hardware. . . . . Ailsa Craig
Ajax Home Hardware . . . . .Ajax
Alexandria Home Hardware Building Centre. . . . . Alexandria
Aiken Bros. Home Hardware. . . . . Allenford
Alliston Home Hardware Building Centre . . . . Alliston
Levi Home Hardware Building Centre . . . . Almonte
Almonte Home Furniture . . . . Almonte
Wigle Home Hardware Building Centre . . . . Amherstburg

Angus Home Hardware . . . . .Angus
Apsley Home Hardware Building Centre . . . . Apsley
Arkona Home Hardware. . . . . Arkona
Arnprior Home Hardware .Arnprior
Arthur Home Hardware Building Centre . . . . Arthur
Atikokan Home Hardware . . . . Atikokan
Aurora Home Hardware Building Centre . . . . Aurora
Aylmer Home Hardware . . . . Aylmer
Secord Home Building Centre. . . . . Aylmer
Ayr Home Hardware . . . . Ayr
Bancroft Home Hardware .Bancroft
Allandale Home Hardware Building Centre . . . . Barrie
United Lumber Home Hardware - Barrie North . . . . Barrie
Robinson Home Hardware - Barrie . . . . Barrie
Barry's Bay Home Hardware Building Centre. . . . . .Barry's Bay
Yakabuski's Home Hardware. . . . . .Barry's Bay
Beamsville Home Centre . . . . Beamsville
Beaverton Home Building Centre . . . . Beaverton
Belle River Home Hardware . . . . .Belle River
Home Hardware Building Centre - Quinte West. . . . . Belleville
Waller Hardware Ltd.. . . . . Belleville
Belleville Home Building Centre . . . . Belleville
O'Neil's Home Hardware . . . . Binbrook
Town and Country Lumber . . . . Blenheim
Blind River Home Hardware Building Centre . . . . .Blind River
Bobcaygeon Home Hardware . . . . .Bobcaygeon
United Lumber Home Hardware - Bolton. . . . . .Bolton
Lalonde Home Hardware .Bourget
Bowmanville Home Building Centre. . . . . Bowmanville
Bracebridge Home Hardware. . . . . Bracebridge
Bradford Home Hardware . . . . Bradford
Brampton Home Hardware . . . . .Brampton
West Brantford Home Hardware . . . . Brantford
Brantford Home Hardware. . . . . Brantford
J & K Home Building Centre . . . . Brantford
Bridgenorth Home Hardware . . . . .Bridgenorth
Pare's Home Hardware. . . . . .Brighton
DeSena's Home Hardware . . . . Bright's Grove
Billings Home Hardware . . . . Brockville
Brockville Home Hardware Building Centre. . . . . Brockville
Reliable Home Furniture . . . . Brockville
Brooklin Home Hardware .Brooklin
Heritage Home Hardware Building Centre - Bruce Mines. . . Bruce Mines
McDonald Home Hardware Building Centre. . . . . Brussels
Buckhorn Home Hardware. . . . . Buckhorn
Warren's Home Centre Limited . . . . Burford
Burks Falls Home Hardware . . . . .Burks Falls
Home Building Centre - Burks Falls. . . . . .Burks Falls
Appleby Home Hardware .Burlington
Aldershot Home Hardware . . . . .Burlington
Calabogie Home Hardware. . . . . Calabogie
Grand River Home Hardware . . . . Caledonia
South Cambridge Home Hardware Building Centre . . . . . . .Cambridge
Preston Towne Home Hardware. . . . . .Cambridge
Westgate Village Home Hardware . . . . .Cambridge
Campbellford Home Hardware Building Centre. . . . . Campbellford
Judd's Home Hardware . . . . Cannington
Burchell's Home Hardware. . . . . Cardinal
Carleton Place Home Hardware . . . . .Carleton Place
Deka Home Building Centre . . . . Carp
Haldimand Building Centre . . . . .Cayuga
Collins Home Hardware Building Centre . . . . Chapleau
B & D Home Hardware. . . . . Chatham
Chatham-Kent Home Hardware Building Centre. . . . . Chatham
Hatten Hardware Ltd.. . . . . .Chatsworth
North West Lumber Co. Limited . . . . .Chelmsford
Hatten Home Hardware Building Centre . . . . .Chesley

Kraemer Woodcraft . . . . St. Jacobs
Fairway Lumber Company . . . . St. Jacobs
Home Hardware - St. Jacobs . . . . St. Jacobs
Home Hardware - Retail Store, Furniture Division . . . . St. Jacobs
Sam's Home Hardware . . . . St. Marys
St. Marys Home Building Centre . . . . St. Marys
Geerlinks Home Hardware Building Centre . . . . St. Thomas
Stayner Home Hardware . . . . Stayner
R & S Home Hardware . . . . Stirling
Meuble Home Furniture . . . . St-Isidore
Hodgkinson Home Hardware . . . . Stoney Creek
Schell Lumber Home Building Centre - Stouffville . . . . . . Stouffville
Stratford Home Hardware Building Centre . . . . Stratford
Stratford Home Furniture . . . . Stratford
Strathroy Home Hardware Building Centre . . . . Strathroy
Streetsville Home Hardware . . . . Streetsville
Sturgeon Builders' Supplies . . . . Sturgeon Falls
Skakoon Home Hardware . . . . Sudbury
A & J Home Hardware . . . . Sudbury
2nd Avenue Home Hardware . . . . Sudbury
Evans Home Building Centre . . . . Sudbury
Pilgrim's Home Hardware . . . . Sunderland
Sunderland Home Furniture . . . . Sunderland
Kidd's Home Hardware Building Centre . . . . Sundridge
Sutton Home Hardware . . . . Sutton West
Schell Lumber Home Building Centre - Sutton . . . . . . Sutton West
Trousdale's Home Hardware Building Centre . . . . Sydenham
Mills Home Hardware . . . . Tara
Zehr Home Hardware . . . . Tavistock
Tecumseh Home Hardware Building Centre . . . . Tecumseh
Grant Home Hardware Building Centre . . . . Temagami
Terrace Bay Home Hardware Building Centre . . . . Terrace Bay
Thamesville Home Hardware . . . . Thamesville
Thessalon Home Hardware . . . . Thessalon
Thornbury Home Hardware Building Centre . . . . Thornbury
Central Home Hardware . . . . Thorold
Memorial Home Hardware Building Centre . . . . Thunder Bay
Tilbury Home Hardware . . . . Tilbury
Home Building Centre - Tilbury . . . . Tilbury
Crompton Home Hardware Building Centre - Tillsonburg . . . . . Tillsonburg
Timmins Home Hardware Building Centre . . . . Timmins
Danforth Lumber . . . . Toronto
Dickson Home Hardware . . . . Toronto
Sunnybrook Home Hardware . . . . Toronto
Wiener's Home Hardware . . . . Toronto
Royal Home Hardware . . . . Toronto
Pape-Danforth Home Inc. . . . . Toronto
S. Jose Hardware Limited . . . . Toronto
Downtown Lumber . . . . Toronto
Deer Park Home Hardware . . . . Toronto
Parkdale Home Hardware . . . . Toronto
College Home Hardware . . . . Toronto
Bastone Home Hardware . . . . Toronto
Imperial Home Hardware . . . . Toronto
Pollocks Home Hardware . . . . Toronto
New Canadian Lumber . . . . Toronto
Pat's Home Hardware . . . . Toronto
Hillcrest Home Hardware . . . . Toronto
Toronto East Home Hardware . . . . Toronto
Toronto Beaches Home Hardware . . . . Toronto
Imperial Home Furniture . . . . Toronto
Tottenham Home Hardware . . . . Tottenham
Trenton Home Hardware Building Centre . . . . Trenton
Rashotte Home Building Centre . . . . Tweed
Tweed Home Hardware . . . . Tweed
Uxbridge Home Centre Limited . . . . Uxbridge
Val Caron Home Building Centre . . . . Val Caron

Vankleek Hill Home Hardware . . . . Vankleek Hill
Home Furniture - Verner . . . . Verner
Vineland Home Hardware . . . . Vineland
Penner Home Hardware Building Centre . . . . Virgil
Walkerton Home Hardware . . . . Walkerton
Wallaceburg Home Hardware . . . . Wallaceburg
Beach Builders Supplies . . . . Wasaga Beach
Washago Home Hardware . . . . Washago
Weeks Home Hardware . . . . Waterdown
Glenbriar Home Hardware . . . . Waterloo
Ontario Seed Co. Limited . . . . Waterloo
Watford Home Hardware Building Centre . . . . Watford
Wawa Electric & Hardware Limited . . . . Wawa
Home Building Centre - Wawa . . . . Wawa
Cox Home Hardware Building Centre . . . . Welland
Cox Home Hardware . . . . Welland
Wellandport Home Hardware . . . . Wellandport
Wellesley Home Centre . . . . Wellesley
Wellington Home Hardware . . . . Wellington
Knight's Home Hardware . . . . West Lorne
Westport Home Hardware . . . . Westport
Herlehy Home Building Centre . . . . Westport
Wheatley Home Building Centre . . . . Wheatley
Spadoni's Home Hardware Building Centre . . . . White River
Wiarton Home Building Centre . . . . Wiarton
Sadler's Home Hardware . . . . Wiarton
Lannin Home Building Centre . . . . Winchester
Yorktown Home Hardware . . . . Windsor
Riverside Home Hardware . . . . Windsor
Seguin Home Hardware . . . . Windsor
Countryside Home Hardware . . . . Windsor
Seminole Home Hardware . . . . Windsor
Gray Home Hardware Building Centre . . . . Windsor
Stainton Hardware (Wingham) Limited . . . . Wingham
Woodbridge Home Hardware . . . . Woodbridge
Deka Home Building Centre - Woodlawn . . . . Woodlawn
Home Hardware Building Centre - Woodstock . . . . Woodstock
Wyoming Home Hardware . . . . Wyoming

Prince Edward Island
Alberton Home Hardware Building Centre . . . . Alberton
Home Hardware - Charlottetown . . . . Charlottetown
Stewart and Beck Home Hardware . . . . Montague
Stewart & Beck Home Building Centre . . . . Montague
Beck's Home Furniture, Gifts and Interiors . . . . Montague
North Rustico Home Hardware Building Centre . . . . . North Rustico
O'Leary Home Hardware . . . . O'Leary
Main Street Home Hardware Building Centre . . . . Souris
Home Hardware Building Centre - Stratford . . . . Stratford
Callbecks Home Hardware Building Centre . . . . Summerside
Summerside Home Furniture . . . . Summerside

Quebec
Quincaillerie Centrale Acton Vale (1987) Enr. . . . . Acton Vale
Materiaux Dallaire Enr. . . . . Alma
Les Materiaux 3 + 2 Ltee . . . . Amos
La Federation des Cooperatives du Nouveau-Quebec . . . . Baie-D'Urfé
Quincaillerie Beauceville Inc. . . . . Beauceville
L'Acadien Bricoleur Inc. . . . . Bécancour
Centre de Rénovation Pine-Hill Inc. . . . . Brownsburg-Chatham
Matériaux Lavergne Inc. - Charette . . . . Charette
Materiaux Charlesbourg Inc. . . . . Charlesbourg
Jacques & Frere (1985) Inc. . . . . Charny
Centre 2 M.R.C. Inc. . . . . Chibougamau
Domaine du Rénovateur de Coaticook . . . . Coaticook
Bouchard Materiaux Inc. . . . . Cookshire-Eaton
Centre de Renovation Daveluyville Inc. . . . . Daveluyville

Rénomax Dolbeau . . . . Dolbeau-Mistassini
Rénomax Mistassini . . . . Dolbeau-Mistassini
Centre de Renovation Germain Inc.. . . . . Donnacona
Quincaillerie Eastman . . . . Eastman
Surplus Malouin - Farnham . . . . Farnham
Quincaillerie J.M. Rioux Inc.. Forestville
Égide Dupuis et Fils Inc.. . . . . Gaspé
Antonin Aspirault Inc.. . . . . Gaspé (Rivière-au-Renard)
Buckingham Hardware Inc.. . . . . Gatineau (Buckingham)
Quincaillerie Nouvelle - France . . . . Granby
Surplus Malouin - Granby . . . . Granby
Entreprises M. Lapierre Inc. . . . . .Havre-Aubert
Barnes Magasin Général . . . . Knowlton
Quincaillerie Home Hardware - La Pocatière. . . . . La Pocatière
Centre de Renovation Home Hardware de L'Anse. . . . . . .L'Anse-Saint-Jean
Centre de Renovation Gervais Roch . . . . .L'Epiphanie
Matériaux St-Etienne . . . . .Lévis (Saint-Etienne)
Quincaillerie G. C.. . . . . .Malartic
La Cour a Bois #148 . . . . Mansfield-et-Pontefract (Fort Coulonge)
Centre de Rénovation Home Hardware Marieville . . . . . . .Marieville
Centre de Renovation Home Hardware de Matane . . . . . .Matane
Home Hardware Mont-Laurier. . . . . Mont-Laurier
Nadeau Matériaux De Construction Inc. . . . . Newport
Quincaillerie Hogg Inc. - Nun's Island . . . . Nun's Island
Dale's Home Building Centre . . . . Otter Lake
Quincaillerie Papineau . . . . .Papineauville
Nadeau Matériaux De Construction Inc. . . . . Percé
J. B. McClelland & Sons. . . . . Poltimore (Val-des-Monts)
Société coopérative agricole de Princeville . . . . .Princeville
Les Entreprises Nova Inc. . . . . Rawdon
Quincaillerie Home Hardware - Rigaud . . . . Rigaud
Quincaillerie Home Hardware - Rimouski. . . . . Rimouski
Quincaillerie Chartier Enr.. . . . . .Rivière-du-Loup
Rénomax Roberval . . . . Roberval
Breton & Thibault Ltee. Rouyn-Noranda
Quincaillerie Rocheleau S.E.N.C. . . . . Rouyn-Noranda
Pièces D'Autos Deschênes Enr. . . . . .Sacré-Coeur-Saguenay
Centre de Rénovation FDS Inc.. . . . . Saguenay (Jonquière)
Rénomax St-Félicien . . . . Saint -Félicien
Magasin Marcel Thériault Inc. . . . . .Saint-Alexandre-de-Kamouraska
Materiaux Goudreau et Fils . . . . Saint-Alexis-des-Monts
Quincaillerie Saint-Ambroise Enr.. . . . . .Saint-Ambroise
Q.S.B. Inc.. . . . . Saint-Bernard
Canexport Construction Inc. . . . . .Saint-Bruno
Magasin Pierre Machabée . . . . .Saint-Chrysostome
Centre de Matériaux St-Donat. . . . . Saint-Donat
Quincaillerie Théorêt Home Hardware . . . . Sainte-Adele
Maurice Laganiere Inc.. . . . . Sainte-Anne-de-la-Perade
Morel et Fils Sainte-Anne-des-Plaines . . . . Sainte-Anne-des-Plaines
Tho-Val-Trem Inc.. . . . . Sainte-Brigitte-de-Laval
Quincaillerie Côté & Castonguay Inc.. . . . . . Saint-Édouard-de-Lotbinière
Matériaux Lavergne Inc. - Saint-Étienne-des-Grès . . . . Saint-Étienne-des-Grès
Roger P. Ross & Fils Inc. . . . . Saint-Eugene-de-Grantham
Quincaillerie Alphide Tremblay & Fils Inc. . . . . .Saint-Hilarion
Ferronnerie Désilets . . . . .Saint-Hugues
Pièces et Accessoires St-Jean Inc. . . . . .Saint-Jean-Port-Joli
Quincaillerie St-Lazare . . . . Saint-Lazare
Morel et Fils . . . . .Saint-Lin-Laurentides
Quincaillerie Fleury . . . . Saint-Paul-de-l'Ile-aux-Noix
Quincaillerie du Massif Inc. . . . . .Saint-Philémon
Quincaillerie Gaetan Caron et Fils Inc. . . . . . Saint-Prosper-de-Dorchester
nis, Limitee . . . . .Saint-Raymond
Renovation Home Hardware - Valleyfield . .Salaberry-de-Valleyfield
Inc. . . . . Sayabec
radis et Fils Inc. . . . . Senneterre
Store . . . . Shawville
ent Enr.. . . . . .Sherbrooke

363

Quincaillerie J. Fortier . . . . .Sherbrooke
Quincaillerie 4 Saisons Enr.. .Sherbrooke
Georges Laflamme Inc.. . . . . St-Charles
Georges Laflamme Inc.. . . . . .Ste-Claire
Roger P. Ross & Fils Inc. - St. Germain . . . . St-Germain-de-Grantham
Volumat Inc.. . . . . Sullivan (Val D'Or)
Quincaillerie Home Hardware - Sutton . . . . .Sutton
Ross Electric Home Hardware . . . . Temiscaming
Centre de Rénovation FLD Inc.. . . . . Témiscaming
J.A. St-Pierre & Fils Inc.. . . . . Temiscouata-sur-le-Lac
Quincaillerie Prince Rupert . . . . Terrebonne
Reno L'Abri - Trois Pistoles . . . . Trois Pistoles
Quincaillerie M. Plante Inc. Trois-Rivières
Quincaillerie Côté Inc. . . . . Val-Bélair
Quincaillerie Choquette Scott . . . . .Valcourt
Materiaux J. Lajeunesse Inc. . . . . Val-des-Bois
Rene Thomas & Fils Inc.. . . . . Varennes
Ville-Marie Home Hardware . . . . Ville-Marie
Materiaux Beausoleil Centre de Renovation Home . . . . Wakefield
Surplus Malouin Inc.. . . . . .Waterloo
N.S. Girard Inc. . . . . Weedon
Quincaillerie Hogg Inc. - Westmount . . . . .Westmount

Saskatchewan

Harvey's Home Centre . . . . Assiniboia
Home Hardware Building Centre - Battleford . . . . .Battleford
Petit's Lumber & Hardware Ltd.. . . . . Buffalo Narrows
Candle Lake Home Building Centre. . . . . Candle Lake
Home Hardware (Canora) . . . . Canora
Carlyle Home Hardware . . . . Carlyle
Davidson Home Hardware .Davidson
Demers Home Hardware . . . . Debden
Baxter Home Hardware . . . . .Esterhazy
Schilling Home Hardware Building Centre . . . . Estevan
Foam Lake Home Hardware. Foam Lake
Hanson Home Hardware Building Centre . . . . Fort Qu'Appelle
Gravelbourg Home Building Centre. . . . . .Gravelbourg
Zak's Home Building Centre . . . . Hague
Craig Home Hardware Building Centre. . . . . Hudson Bay
Humboldt Home Hardware Building Centre . . . . .Humboldt
Kamsack Home Hardware. . . . . Kamsack
Kindersley Home Hardware Building Centre . . . . .Kindersley
Kipling Home Hardware . . . . Kipling
La Ronge Home Hardware . . . . La Ronge
Langenburg Home Hardware . . . . Langenburg
McHanson Hardware & Electric . . . . Leask
Thomas Home Furnishings & Hardware . . . . .Macklin
Hodson Home Hardware . . . . .Maple Creek
Meadow Lake Home Hardware Building Centre . . . . Meadow Lake
George Home Hardware . . . . Melfort
Melville Home Hardware. . . . . Melville
Allied Lumberland Ltd. (Moose Jaw) . . . . .Moose Jaw
Richardson's Home Hardware . . . . Nipawin
Home Hardware Building Centre - North Battleford . . . . . . .North Battleford
Richards Home Hardware . . . . .Outlook
Preeceville Home Hardware . . . . Preeceville
Home Building Centre - Prince Albert . . . . .Prince Albert
Regina Home Hardware . . . . Regina
Allied Lumberland Ltd. . . . . Regina
Muir Barber Limited . . . . Regina Beach
Rosetown Home Hardware .Rosetown
Valley Sports & Hardware (1995) . . . . Rosthern
Thorsness Hardware Ltd. . . . . Saltcoats
Reid's Home Hardware. . . . . Saskatoon
Home Building Centre - Saskatoon . . . . Saskatoon
B.W. Baerg Truss Manufacturing Ltd.. . . . . Saskatoon
Shellbrook Home Hardware . . . . Shellbrook

Spiritwood Home Building Centre. . . . . Spiritwood
St. Walburg Building Supplies Ltd. . . . . .St. Walburg
Evans Brothers Home Hardware Building Centre. . . . . Swift Current
Watrous Home Hardware Building Centre . . . . Watrous
Weyburn Home Hardware. . . . . Weyburn
Hilderman Home Building Centre . . . . Wolseley
Lamb & Hunter Home Hardware . . . . Wynyard
Wynyard Home Building Centre. Wynyard
A. Myrowich Home Hardware Building Centre. . . . . Yorkton

Yukon
Dawson Home Hardware . . . . Dawson City
Jarand Home Building Centre . . . . Watson Lake
Home Hardware Building Centre - Whitehorse . . . . .Whitehorse

France
Marcel Dagort S.A. . . . . 97500 Saint-Pierre et Miquelon